Diamonds

Diamonds

myth, magic, and reality

Crown Publishers, Inc., New York

Editor-in-Chief	**Robert Maillard**
Scientific Consultants	Hugh E. K. Allen; Richard T. Liddicoat, Jr.
Editors	Ronne Peltzman; Neil Grant
Art Director	Marcel Pijpers
Associate Art Director	Liney Li
Artwork and Maps	Sue Casebourne

Library of Congress Cataloging in Publication Data

Legrand, Jacques
    Diamonds myth, magic, and reality.

    Bibliography: p.
    Includes index.
    1. Diamonds. I. Title.
TS753.L43   553'.82   79-19036
ISBN 0-517-53981-0

Printed in the Netherlands by Smeets Offset, Weert.

This work was conceived and produced with the collaboration of

Hugh E. K. Allen

Lecturer, Royal School of Mines, Department of Industrial Mining, University of London

Louis Asscher

President, The Asscher Company, Amsterdam

Philippe Chevalier

Director, Sibeka, Brussels

Raoul Delveaux

General Director, Hoge Raad voor Diamant (HRD), Antwerp

René Delville

Civil Engineer, U.I.L.V.; Société Diamang, Brussels

Maurice E. Giard

Honorary President, Chambre syndicale française de la Bijouterie, Joaillerie, Orfèvrerie, Paris

Eduard Gübelin

Gemologist, CG, FGA, Lucerne; Honorary Professor, University of Stellenbosch

Jona S. Hatsor

MJur; Director, I. Hennig & Company Ltd., Tel Aviv

George Kaplan

Vice-President, Lazare Kaplan & Sons, Inc., New York

Godehard Lenzen

DGemG, FGA, GG; Director, National Center of Gemology, Idar-Oberstein

Richard T. Liddicoat, Jr.

President, Gemological Institute of America, New York and Los Angeles

Bruno Morelli

Director, MIBA, Zaïre

Guy van der Schrick

General Manager, Diamant Boart, Brussels

Henri-Jean Schubnel

Curator, Laboratory of Mineralogy, Muséum national d'Histoire naturelle, Paris; President, French Gemological Association

Jean-Claude Serre

Head, Department of Geological Mining, Bureau de Recherches géologiques et minières de France (BRGM), Orléans

Norman R. Smith

Director, International Department, Unicorn Industries DPD Ltd., Great Britain

Hans Stern

Jeweler, Rio de Janeiro

Herbert Tillander

Diamond historian; Founder and President, Finnish Gemological Association, Helsinki

Under the direction of Jacques Legrand

Acknowledgments

The production of this work would not have been
possible without the generous assistance of the public
relations departments of   De Beers and
                            The Diamond Trading
                            Company, London
who not only provided guidance, but also introduced us
to most of the authors who contributed to this book.

Our debt is equally great to a number of individuals,
eminent members of the profession, whose skilled advice
and indulgence in answering our many questions
provided us with inestimable help.

Thanks, too, for their close and active cooperation, to: the
Anglo-American Company, Johannesburg; B. Arunkumar
& Company, Bombay; the Banque Diamantaire
Anversoise, Antwerp; Bharat Diamond Industries,
Bombay; British Zaïre Diamond Distributors, Kinshasa;
the Centre français des Pierres précieuses, Paris; the
Centre d'Information du Diamant, Paris; Consolidated
Diamond Mines, Oranjemund and Kleinzee; the
Coopérative "Le Diamant," Saint-Claude; the Diamant
Boart, Brussels; the Diamond Corporation of West
Africa, Freetown; the Diamond Information Center, New
York; Drukker N.V., Amsterdam; the Établissements
GayFrères, Annemasse; the Établissements Ramet,
Schamisso, Antwerp; the Établissements Paillette,
Vassort, Paris; Fink et Spitzer, Antwerp; the Gemological
Institute of America, New York and Los Angeles;
I. Hennig & Company Ltd., Tel Aviv and London; the
Israel Diamond Institute, Tel Aviv; J. Walter Thompson,
Paris; the London Star Diamond Company, Bombay; the
Ministerio de Energia y Minas, Ciudad Bolívar; Scierie
Janssens, Antwerp; M. Schnitzer & Ch. Gruenstein, Tel
Aviv; the Selection Trust, London; Sibeka, Brussels; the
Société minière de Bakwanga (MIBA), Mbuji-Mayi; the
Société minière de Tejucana, Belo Horizonte; the
Sindicato nacional do Comercio Atacadista de Pedras
Preciosas, Rio de Janeiro.

Finally, we wish to express our gratitude to the curators
of the Smithsonian Institution, Washington, D.C.; the
Residenz Schatzkammer, Munich; the Grünes Gewölbe,
Dresden; and especially to the Direction générale des
Musées de France. In authorizing us to photograph the
treasures in their collections, they have given this book a
special radiance.

Jacques Legrand

Contents

I   **From Myth to Reality**

12   **The History of Diamonds**
12   The Diamond in the Bible
13   India: The First Producer/Adamas: The Ancient Criteria of Value
16   Legend, Myth, and the Study of Nature
22   The Ancient Trade Routes
26   Production Methods in India   *G. Lenzen*
28   The Diamond Trade in Europe from the 13th to the 18th Century   *G. Lenzen & R. Delveaux*

39   **Famous Diamonds of India**
39   Beliefs and Superstitions   *R. Maillard*
43   The Koh-i-Noor
46   The Orlov
48   The Regent
51   The Hope (The Great Blue Diamond)   *M. E. Giard*

54   **The Brazilian Era: 1730–1780**
54   The Principal Diamond Fields
56   Working Methods
59   Masters and Slaves
60   Facts and Figures
61   The Portuguese Diamond Policy
63   Brazil and the Diamond Trade   *G. Lenzen*

66   **Southern Africa and the Birth of a Great Industry**
68   The Discovery of Diamonds
69   The First Diamond Rush
73   The Fabulous Kimberley Era
74   The Beginning of Organized Production
75   Cecil John Rhodes
77   Barney Barnato
80   De Beers Consolidated
82   The Control of Output
83   Ernest Oppenheimer
84   The Basis of the Modern Market   *G. Lenzen*

II   **The Rough Diamond and Its Origins**

88   **Geology of the Diamond**
88   Geology
92   Prospecting   *J.-C. Serre*

99   **Southern Africa**
100   Production/Recent Discoveries
102   Development of New Mines
106   Open-pit Mining
108   Underground Mining
113   Mining on the Atlantic Coast
117   Treatment and Recovery
123   Security
124   Craftsmen in a Communal Enterprise   *H. Allen*

125   Tanzania
125   The Williamson Mine   *H. Allen*

127   Zaïre
127   The Creation of La Forminière
129   A Clue Not Followed
130   A Missing Label and a Wooden Box   *R. Maillard*
131   The Deposits of the Tshikapa Region
132   The Mbuji-Mayi Deposits
136   The Future   *J. Legrand*

137   Angola
137   A High Yield of Gemstones
138   The Hunt for Kimberlites
139   The Lucapa Theory   *R. Delville*

142   Sierra Leone
142   Discovery
143   The Nature of the Deposits
144   Early Developments
145   Clandestine Digging and Illegal Trade/New Legislation
146   Dealers and Traffickers
148   The Monrovia Market
150   The Creation of Buying Offices
154   Industrial Production
155   Production by Local Diggers   *J. Legrand*

159   Venezuela
160   Miners in the Jungle
161   Guaniamo and Diamond Fever
169   A Solitary Dredge on the Paragua   *J.-C. Serre*

172   Brazil
172   The Origin of Brazilian Diamonds
173   Geology and Psychology: The Brazilian Diamond Seeker
174   The Deposits of Mato Grosso
176   The "Mining Triangle" of Minas Gerais
177   Diamantina
178   The Tejucana Mine   *J. Legrand*

180   Other Producers
180   India
182   Borneo
184   The Soviet Union
186   Other Countries   *H.-J. Schubnel*

187   World Production

188   The Central Selling Organization   *J. Legrand*

III   From Rough Stone to Polished Gem

192   Mineralogy and Crystallography
192   Pure Carbon
193   Cubic Structure/Hardness
194   Density/Conductivity/Crystalline Shapes/Cleavage/Macles/Optical
        Properties
195   Color/Absorption Spectra
196   Inclusions and Flaws/Crystallization and Synthesis of Diamonds
197   Diamond Simulants in Jewelry   *H.-J. Schubnel*

198   History and Evolution of Diamond Cutting
198   Cleaving/Sawing
199   Rubbing/Grinding
200   Polishing

201 Cut/Make/Fire and Brilliance/Foiling and Tinting
202 The History of Diamond Cuts
203 Refinement of Natural Forms
205 Fancy Cuts
206 The Thick Table Cut
207 The Mirror Cut
209 The Tablet Cut and Lasque Cut/The Rose Cut
210 The Brilliant Cut   *H. Tillander*

214 The Modern Brilliant Cut
216 Modern Fashioning Techniques
219 Faceting/Drilling and Sawing by Laser
220 Standards of Appreciation   *G. Kaplan*

221 Clarity and Color
221 Clarity and Inclusions
222 The Gemologist's View of Inclusions
226 The Jeweler's View of Inclusions/Colors of the Diamond
228 The Origin of Diamond Colors
230 Artificial Colors   *E. Gübelin*

232 Exchanges and Cutting Centers
232 Antwerp   *R. Delveaux*
236 Amsterdam   *L. Asscher*
239 Israel   *J. S. Hatsor*
242 Bombay and Surat
245 Other Exchanges and Cutting Centers   *J. Legrand*

247 Investment in Diamonds and Diamond Certificates
248 The Birth of Certificates/Action by the CIBJO
249 Choosing a Jeweler   *R. T. Liddicoat, Jr.*

IV   From Jewelry to Industry

252 The Diamond in Jewelry
252 A Passion Shared: The Mughal Emperor and the Sun King
253 Vestments to Adorn the Sun
255 Agnès Sorel: Women Adopt the Diamond
256 The Treasure of Charles the Bold/Artists and Goldsmiths in the
    Renaissance
259 Renaissance Jewelry
262 The Seventeenth Century: Pomp and Puritanism/The "Brilliant Century"
264 The Nineteenth Century   *M. E. Giard*

268 Modern Jewelry
270 Some Aspects of Modern Jewelry
271 Gold or Platinum?
273 The Birth of a Piece of Jewelry
274 Paris, the Jewelry Capital   *H. Stern*

276 Synthetic and Industrial Diamonds
276 Synthetic Diamonds   *G. van der Schrick*
278 Industrial Diamonds and Their Uses
279 From Inner Earth to Outer Space   *N. R. Smith*

281 Appendix

284 Index

287 Bibliography

I

From Myth
to Reality

The History of Diamonds

The story of the diamond begins in a remote era of the world's history, lost in the mists of time. For untold ages the diamond lay hidden and unregarded within the earth, until man at last recognized it as the most precious of all nature's creations and began to use it for his own delight and benefit. We will probably never know exactly when the first diamonds were discovered. But we do know that from ancient times until the eighteenth century, India was the world's sole supplier.

The Diamond in the Bible

Although it is impossible to locate the first discovery, there are very early documents that mention the diamond and perhaps explain why man showed such special interest in it. Many histories maintain that the diamond has been known since ancient times, citing a biblical reference, Exodus 28:18, in which the famous "breastplate of judgment" worn by the high priest of the Hebrews is described as being adorned with twelve precious stones, including a diamond. This interpretation, however, is based on versions of the Bible that translate the Hebrew word *yahalom* as "diamond," assuming that it bore the same meaning in biblical times as it did many centuries later. So far as we know, this breastplate was derived from the rites of the Egyptian pharaohs. Modern reconstructions based on data furnished by an-

cient documents show that each of the stones that decorated it was set in a rectangle of about 2.5 by 1.5 inches (6 × 4 cm). If one of these had been a diamond, it would have been several times larger than the famous Koh-i-Noor! Moreover, the fact that these twelve stones were engraved with the names of the twelve tribes of Israel makes it even less likely that any of the stones was a diamond. Nor is the reference in Jeremiah 17:1 to "a steel graver" and "a diamond point" inscribing the sins of Judah's men "on the tablets of their heart, and on the horns of their altar" very helpful. In India, the diamond was used as an engraving instrument in the second century B.C. at the very earliest, but there is nothing to indicate that artists engraved *on* the stone itself at that time. Such a technique was not used until considerably later.

Besides Exodus 28:18 and Ezekiel 28:13, where the word *yahalom* appears to describe one of several precious stones, there are two other passages in the Old Testament where the word refers in a metaphorical, poetical sense to the idea of "hammering" or "beating" (*halom* in Hebrew). In Zechariah 7:12 we are told, "Yea, they made their hearts as an adamant stone [diamond]," and in Ezekiel 3:9, "As an adamant harder than flint have I made thy forehead." Here the word *yahalom* means a stone that is harder than all others and can "hammer" them. This corresponds to what we know today about the diamond, which is classified with a coefficient of 10 on the Mohs scale as the hardest of all known minerals. But can we make any meaningful deductions from this? The criterion of hardness has only a relative significance and does not refer to a precise scale of values. The very lack of precision in the Old Testament references makes any attempt to extract firm facts from them difficult at best.

In Greek literature from a very early date the word *adamas* (which eventually gave its name, via the Latin *adamus, adamantinus*, to the diamond) is often used in a sense very close to that of *yahalom*, being similarly associated with the idea of invincibility. The first known use of the word occurs in the works of the poet Hesiod, who lived in the eighth century B.C. But nowhere in Hesiod, or in any other writing

The twelve precious stones that supposedly adorned the breastplate of Aaron, high priest of the Hebrews, and the positions they occupied. Minature from the *Lapidaire* of Jean de Mandeville (1300–72). French manuscript, 15th century. There is no mention of the diamond at this time. Bibliothèque Nationale, Paris. *Photo Bibliothèque Nationale.*

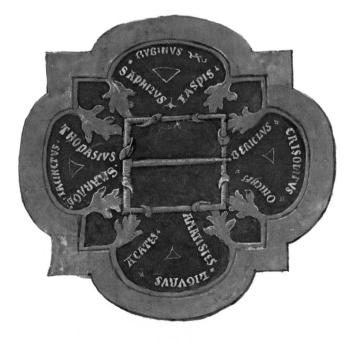

of that period, is the term applied to a diamond or any other precious stone. For some eight centuries the word *adamas* was applied exclusively to iron, to describe its unbreakable quality. Not until the first century A.D. was the word used as a noun, by that time, no doubt, designating a diamond. It appears as such in the celebrated Roman encyclopedia, the *Natural History* of Pliny the Elder.

India: The First Producer

It is curious that in all the numerous, lengthy arguments among historians over the origin of diamonds, discussion nearly always centers on the countries that acquired the gems and never on the country that produced them. From ancient times until Brazil entered the picture in the eighteenth century, India was the only significant diamond-producing country. Until the twentieth century, sources for the study of diamonds in India were largely un-

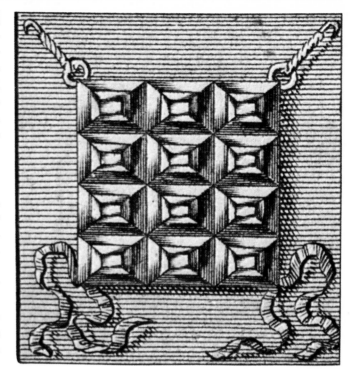

Title page from the book by Johannes Braun on the priestly vestments of the Hebrews. Amsterdam, 1698. The high priest (left) is shown wearing the "breastplate of judgment," a detail of which is shown opposite. Bibliothèque Nationale, Paris. *Photo Hubert Josse, Paris.*

available. In 1905, however, an ancient Sanskrit manuscript was discovered, the *Artha-Sastra* of Kautilya, which may be translated as "The Lesson of Profit." This remarkable work is a basic text providing invaluable details of the economic and legal history of India in the fourth century B.C. Kautilya was the minister of King Chandragupta Maurya and had helped put him on the throne of the kingdom of Magadha. King Chandragupta, who ruled from about 320 to 298 B.C., was the founder of the Maurya dynasty and may be called the first emperor of India. We know of him also through the Greek Megasthenes, who lived at his court. Until the discovery of the *Artha-Sastra*, in fact, Megasthenes was our sole source of information on this period. A careful reading of Kautilya's treatise reveals unquestionably that not only were diamonds known in the fourth century B.C., but they were commodities in a very active trade, were subject to regular taxation and customs duties, and were one of the sources of the royal revenue.

Adamas: The Ancient Criteria of Value

Why was it that people ascribed such value to the diamond before any technique had been invented to cut this "king of precious stones"? In the rough, most diamonds appear comparatively dull and unattractive. (One English connoisseur, in fact, remarked that in its rough state the diamond was no more attractive than a piece of caustic soda.) To find the answer to this question it is necessary to turn again to India, in the years between the beginning of the Maurya period in the fourth century B.C. and the end of the Gupta period in the sixth century A.D. The *Artha-Sastra* refers to a body of rules and standards of practice developed by specialists to regularize taxes and other charges applied to diamonds and other precious stones. Considering the early date, these texts, known as *Ratnapariska* (which can be translated as "The Estimation and Valuation of Precious Stones"), reveal an extensive knowledge of the subject. Within the course of about a thousand years, this body of knowledge evolved into the *Ratna-Sastra*, genuine technical manuals that were used by poets, noblemen, officials, merchants, and others. In medieval Europe such works were called lapidaries. Of those that have come down to us, two are of special interest: the *Ratnapariska* of Buddhabhatta, from before the sixth century A.D., and the *Brihat-samhita* of Varahamihira, which dates from the sixth century.

In both of these texts, the diamond is cited as the jewel *par excellence*. The reasons given for its value, however, are purely mythical; the actual nature of the diamond is never defined. Rather, the texts include a detailed list of features to be considered in assessing the worth of an individual stone. The first of these is the form of the stone, the octahedron being regarded as the ideal—"six sharp points, eight very flat and similar sides, twelve straight and sharp edges." This description is followed by a list of optical qualities: clarity, transparency, color, fire, and iridescence. Emphasis is placed on the extreme rarity of a diamond that meets all these standards. Such a stone, the text says, "would illuminate space with all the fire of the rainbow."

The octahedral form was important for several reasons. Probably the major one is the fact that the form is rare in nature. In addition, in the context of Hindu thought the octahedron symbolized the very essence of the diamond. Finally, it was only in the perfect octahedron that Indian lapidaries found the highest optical qualities, notably the highest power of light dispersion. Indeed, only a true octahedron, with its regular sides, possesses in the rough state that dazzling division of colors known as brilliance that is displayed by cut diamonds.

Considering the Hindus' emphatic insistence that the diamond's optical qualities were the effect of a mystical force, it is reasonable to conclude that these optical qualities accounted for the special status of the diamond. And its hardness? This quality too was familiar to the lapidaries of ancient India. But though they did not fail to point out the diamond's exceptional cutting power, they did not attribute any magical or religious significance to this quality. They regarded hardness merely as an additional feature augmenting the diamond's "mystical radiance."

Somewhat surprisingly, the diamond was apparently almost unknown in ancient Greece before the first century B.C., yet it enjoyed an extraordinary reputation among the Romans. Pliny wrote that of all the goods of the earth, "and not only of precious stones, it is to the diamond that we attribute the highest value." How did the diamond achieve this reputation? Here it is important to avoid the snares of hypothesis and stick rigorously to the facts we know. Starting with the principle that in its rough state a diamond is generally dull and that only by cutting does it acquire its maximum brilliance (and thus its value), certain nineteenth-century authors, despite the absence of evidence, were led into the supposition that the ancients knew how to cut the diamond, if only imperfectly; otherwise, they argued, it could never have attained its exceptional place in the hierarchy of worldly possessions. For good measure they added that since diamonds were certainly very rare in antiquity, there was little opportunity for diamond cutters to lay their hands on them. Thus they helped to spread the belief that the best diamonds from the East were not cut, but were actually found in a perfect state in nature. This kind of argument places nineteenth-century rationalism in a context foreign to it and ignores the known sources. In addition, it takes as its point of departure the very assumption that remains to be proved—that it was the diamond's optical qualitites that caused it to be highly valued by the ancients. As it happens, there is no document of Greek or Roman origin that mentions, even indirectly, the brilliance, fire, or play of colors of the diamond.

The Roman poet Manilius, a contemporary of Pliny the Elder and one of the few authors who had actually seen a diamond, offered important evidence in his *Astronomica* when he described it wonderingly as the "point of a stone more precious gold." Only a "point," yet more precious than gold! The same sense of awe was expressed centuries later, in the notable treatise on precious stones by Anselmus de Boot (Boetius), published in 1609.

The Romans gave preeminence to the dia-

Part of the *Ratnapariska* of Buddhabhatta, in Sanskrit. Mid-5th-century manuscript. "A diamond weighing 20 tandula is worth 200,000 rupakas. . . . If a diamond possessing all these qualities floats on water, that is the stone to be desired above all other jewels." Bibliothèque Nationale, Paris. *Photo Bibliothèque Nationale.*

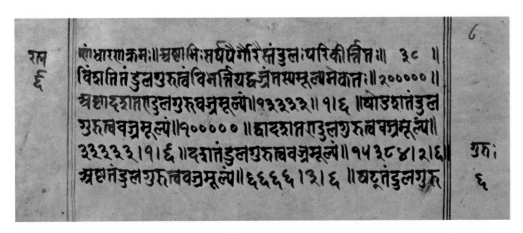

A jeweler at work. Indian
miniature, 18th century.
Bibliothèque Nationale, Paris.
Photo Hubert Josse, Paris.

cal properties. This is sufficiently proven by
the wealth of myths relating to the origins and
alleged marvelous powers of the gem. Moreover, only some very powerful motive, something transcending reason, would have im-
pelled Indian merchants, as early as the third
century B.C., to "risk their lives at sea for their
greatest profit" and make this "point of a stone"
without outstanding beauty an article of trade
beyond their own country.

When offering the Romans a product that,
being small and insignificant, fell far short of
the requirements normally demanded of a precious stone, the eastern merchants must have
speculated on the value their own society put
upon it, especially since Indian law required
that the most valuable crystals were to be delivered to the royal treasury and not exported.
The Roman interest in the diamond was not at
first sparked by the stone's intrinsic beauty,
although its rarity and hardness did make it a
curiosity. But rarity and hardness alone would
not be sufficient reasons for Pliny to speak of
the diamond as the most precious of all worldly
goods. Long before Pliny's time, the word
adamas had acquired a magico-religious
meaning, creating a deep respect comparable
to that which the Indians themselves felt for
the diamond.

We know that the white octahedron was con-
secrated to the god Indra, the incarnation of
storms, thunder, and lightning. Black diamonds, especially those in the form of twin
crystals that suggested the head of a serpent,
were dedicated to Yama, the god of death.
Vishnu, the god of the heavens, governed all
crystals, whatever their form, of so-called *ka-
dali* color, the nature of which is now uncertain. A rich field opened up for magical and
religious beliefs. In Buddhabhatta's treatise,
for example, it is said that "he who wears a
diamond will see dangers recede from him
whether he be threatened by serpents, fire,
poison, sickness, thieves, flood, or evil spirits."
It was from such beliefs, with their emphasis
on the notion of invincibility, that the Indian
merchants no doubt drew the arguments that
persuaded the Romans to buy a stone that, because of both its physical hardness and its associated magic powers, could be regarded as
the supreme earthly, concrete expression of
the quality of *adamas*. Promoted thus to the
status of talisman, the diamond acquired a
value far beyond what it would have attained
if judged by the purely esthetic criteria applied to other gemstones.

Indirect proof of the exceptional status the
diamond enjoyed among the Romans is provided by the fact that with the expansion of
Christianity the stone soon lost practically all
its value. The beliefs on which its value was

mond not because of the stone's optical qualities nor even because of its extreme hardness.
As noted earlier, the adjective *adamas*, which
gave the diamond its name, predates knowledge of the stone itself, and like the Hebrew
word *yahalom* it implies something more than
purely physical characteristics. In the realm of
simple facts nothing, not even the diamond's
great hardness, explains why such a dull, un-
polished substance should acquire the supreme value attributed to it. It follows that the
Romans, like many others, attributed to the
diamond a metaphysical significance or magi-

based collapsed and became nothing more than degraded pagan superstition. Although many medieval lapidaries continued faithfully to repeat Pliny's statements on the nature of the diamond and its magical properties, they nevertheless downgraded it to the seventeenth rank among precious stones. Even in the sixteenth century the famous Renaissance goldsmith Benvenuto Cellini (1500–71) placed the ruby and the emerald higher than the diamond. After a trip to India in 1565 the Portuguese physician and naturalist Garcia ab Horto wrote, "Here the diamond is regarded as the king of precious stones. Yet if we apply the criteria of value and beauty it is certain that, for us, it is the emerald that holds first rank, followed by the ruby." Thus the diamond lost its preeminence in Europe when the metaphysical conceptions associated with it ceased to be recognized. It regained its position only when the development of cutting techniques made it once more the most precious of precious stones.

Legend, Myth, and the Study of Nature

In the history of India, the campaign of Alexander the Great is the earliest event that can be dated with certainty. In 327 B.C. Alexander set out from Bactria and Sogdiana with 100,000 men. He followed the Valley of Kabul,

Alexander the Great arrives at the River Oxus during his expedition to India. Miniature from a German manuscript, about 1430. Bibliothèque Royale Albert I, Brussels. *Photo Bibliothèque Royale.*

fought the courageous mountain tribes that guarded the Khyber Pass, and, in the spring of the following year, he reached the banks of the Indus, the border of the country of five sacred rivers. The campaign, though short, exhausted the army, and Alexander was soon forced to withdraw to Persepolis. He died not long afterward at Babylon, in 323 B.C. The violent incursion of the Macedonian conqueror provoked a spirit of resistance to foreigners in India, which eventually led to the founding of the powerful kingdom of Magadha under the leadership of Chandragupta Maurya.

There is no evidence to suggest that during their Indian foray the Greek soldiers acquired any diamonds. Their passage through the country was too rapid. Not until several centuries later did a train of legends, mingled with dreams and fantasies involving the history of India, accumulate around the personality of Alexander the Great. Only then did diamonds enter the story.

The Valley of Diamonds. The elements that constitute the well-known legend of the "Valley of Diamonds" are first mentioned by Epiphanius (ca. 315–403), bishop of Salamis and metropolitan of Cyprus, and an ardent advocate of the faith of Nicaea. But as Epiphanius tells it, the legend concerns not the diamond but the jacinth, one of the precious stones found on the breastplate of the high priest mentioned in the Old Testament. "In the Scythian desert," he wrote, "there is a deep valley surrounded by high and rocky mountains. From the summit one cannot see the bottom of the valley, which is lost in the fog as though in impenetrable depths. The kings of the surrounding countries send their people into the mountains bordering the said valley to extract the treasures of precious stones heaped in the farthest depths. But to accomplish this task they must resort to trickery. They kill and flay sheep, then cast quarters of raw flesh into the depths where the incalculable treasures lie. Soon eagles appear from their aeries; they swoop down through the fog, seize upon the flesh, and carry it back to their nests. The precious stones adhere to this flesh, and the king's people have only to rob the eagles' nests to gather them."

Obviously, this legend cannot be ascribed to a contemporary source in India, where at this time there was a well-organized market in precious stones characterized by a highly complex price system. The distribution of the legend is therefore all the more remarkable. It reappears, for example, around 500 in the memoirs of Chinese princes of the Liang dynasty, as well as in the oldest Arab treatise on mineralogy (ca. 750), traditionally ascribed to the

The Valley of Diamonds, guarded by serpents with a lethal gaze. Overhead, birds of prey carry lumps of meat to which diamonds adhere. Miniature from a Turkish manuscript, 1582. Bibliothèque Nationale, Paris. *Photo Bibliothèque Nationale.*

writer known as the pseudo-Aristotle. It is here that the figure of Alexander the Great appears for the first time. There are other new elements as well, including the presence of serpents with a literally murderous gaze. But the most significant refinement is surely that the treatise no longer speaks of a mass of undefined gems, but of a deposit exclusively of diamonds. To quote the ancient Arab writer, "Other than my pupil Alexander, no one has ever reached the valley where the diamonds are found. It lies in the East, along the great border of Khurasan, and it is so deep that a human eye cannot see to the bottom. When Alexander reached the valley, a multitude of serpents prevented him going farther, for their glance proved mortal to men. So he resorted to the use of mirrors; the serpents were caught by the reflection of their own eyes and so perished. Alexander then adopted another ruse. Sheep were slaughtered, then flayed, and their flesh cast into the depths. Birds of prey from the neighboring mountains swooped down and carried off in their claws the flesh, to which countless diamonds adhered. Alexander's warriors hunted the birds, which dropped their booty, and the men merely had to gather it where it fell."

With variations of one kind or another, it was in this form that the legend of the Valley of Diamonds spread throughout the Middle Ages. It appears in the *Thousand and One Nights,* where it forms the basis of one of the most memorable episodes in the third voyage of Sinbad the Sailor (*Nights* CCXVII–CCXVIII). Faced with death after being cast by the giant bird Roc into an inaccessible valley that is lined with diamonds but also inhabited by serpents, Sinbad sees merchants throwing down joints of meat in order to attract vultures. Seizing one of these pieces, he ties it securely to his belt. This strategy saves him, for the meat attracts a huge bird of prey, which snatches him in its beak, carries him off, and drops him in its nest high in the mountains. Delighted to be alive, Sinbad offers the proprietor of the nest (for each merchant had his own) a splendid diamond.

Three centuries later, in his *Book of Marvels* (published in 1298), the Venetian Marco Polo, who was the first cultured European to travel across Asia and to give a detailed account of his observations, also told of the legend and located its origin in India. It has now been established, however, that the story originated in the Hellenistic East in the first century B.C.— precisely the time when the diamond trade was beginning. The legend reached China and was transmitted to the Arabs and the Persians before spreading to India and finally making its appearance in Europe.

Opposite: The Valley of Diamonds. Miniature from a Catalan atlas, 1375. The inscription on the right says, "These men went to look for diamonds; but as they are not able to descend the mountains to where the diamonds lie, they deftly throw down pieces of meat. The stones attached to the meat are eventually dropped by the birds and may thus be retrieved." Bibliothèque Nationale, Paris. *Photo Bibliothèque Nationale.*

Below: The Valley of Diamonds. Miniature from the *Book of Marvels* by Marco Polo. French manuscript, 14th century. Bibliothèque Nationale, Paris. *Photo Bibliothèque Nationale.*

The Diamond and the Blood of the He-goat. It is possible to go back even further in time, to myths that existed before the legend of the Valley of Diamonds. One of the most intriguing is the myth that links the diamond to the blood of a he-goat in a kind of parable about the laws of "sympathy" and "antipathy" governing the world of natural forces. The earliest reference to this undoubtedly ancient notion occurs in Pliny, who refers to it twice in his *Natural History.* In Book 20, discussing war and peace and the sympathy and antipathy that reign among inanimate things, Pliny mentions, after fire and water and the magnet and iron, the example of the diamond and the he-goat's blood: "The diamond, this rare joy of opulence, invincible and resistant to any other form of violence, can be broken by the action of a he-goat's blood." In Book 37, after recalling the fact that *adamas* is synonymous with "invincible force," he cites the diamond as the example that best enables us to grasp the laws of discordance and harmony (or, in the language of the Greeks themselves, of antipathy and sympathy) that govern the universe. "This invincible force," he says, "which despises the two most powerful natural elements, iron and fire, is broken by the he-goat's blood, but only when the diamond has been dipped in the fresh, warm blood of the animal and struck with many blows; for even then it breaks everything except the most solid anvils and iron hammers."

This symbolical interpretation of the universe, which originated well before Pliny's time, was perpetuated by medieval theologians and subsequently picked up by the eighteenth-century naturalists. The goat, as the symbol of base action and evil, and the diamond, as the incarnation of indomitable force, provided a fruitful source of symbolism in the Christian context. The purest and most indomitable heart (diamond) could be vanquished by the lusts of the flesh (goat's blood). Christ himself, the "pure diamond," is shaken by the cup of suffering, but Christ's blood has the power to soften the most hardened sinners. Like the myths of the ancients, Christian symbolism was based on keen observation of natural phenomena—like the unsurpassed hardness of the diamond—and thus can be explained in natural terms.

The Diamond's Power over Magnets. Not all myths, however, lend themselves so easily to rational explanation. It is difficult to understand what lay behind the belief, repeated by Pliny, that a diamond will remove the power of attraction from a magnet. This seems a very unusual quality, and it would be tempting to dismiss the belief as merely the moral of some relatively insignificant fable. But the belief is constantly repeated over the centuries by authors who must be taken seriously. One of the most unlikely places in which it crops up is in *Gargantua and Pantagruel* by François Rabelais (ca. 1494–1553), who, besides being a writer of fiction, was also a well-known physician and scientist and the editor of several medical works.

Having reached the farthest point of their voyage to the Land of Lanterns, Pantagruel and his companions come to the kingdom of the "Dive Bouteille" and are invited to enter the underground temple of Bacchus. The doors of the temple are opened and closed automatically by an invisible force, controlled by a complicated device containing plates of polished steel, magnets, and an "Indic diamond as thick as an Egyptian bean." Rabelais explains that the system functions according to a natural law, "occult and splendid," based on the attraction of iron to a magnet. He adds that the mechanism operates only when the diamond is removed, for the action of the diamond frees the steel from its natural obedience to the magnet, and the stone must be removed if the magnet is to operate efficiently. (For a more thorough understanding of this passage, one should refer to the study by K. H. Francis, "The Mechanism of the Magnetic Doors in Rabelais," in *French Studies* 13, Oxford, 1959.)

Criteria of Value and Specific Weight. Although this surprising belief in the diamond's power to neutralize magnetic force existed in the Roman Empire, it is once again necessary to go back to a distant period in the history of India in order to locate its probable roots. In making this trip to the past we should not forget the remarkable knowledge and accuracy that the Indians brought to their observations

of nature, evident in the criteria for the evaluation of diamonds contained in the fifth- and sixth-century treatises of Buddhabhatta and Varahamihira.

Among these criteria there is one that has not yet been mentioned, that of *laghu*. This is a somewhat difficult concept to grasp. Scholars have usually translated *laghu* as "specific lightness." In order to be perfect, a diamond should not only have the form of a pure and transparent octahedron, it should also be *laghu*, that is, of a low specific weight. According to the Indian texts, the diamonds of greatest value were those that "floated on water." Since diamonds are very heavy, this notion has always puzzled scholars and translators. Here again, it is important to keep in mind the historical context, and to remember that the Indian masters were famous for the subtlety of their observations. They were also remarkable theorists, skilled in the art of idealizing and systematizing their knowledge in great religious syntheses. Their attitude toward nature was far from purely rational, and striking expressions were often used in order to create vivid images rather than to convey facts. Each system, moreover, had its own dynamic, and as the aim was to establish a hierarchy of values, the predominant concern was to develop the system as far as possible, projecting it into the realm of abstraction and leaving the rational world far behind. Nevertheless, the notion of *laghu* was not just an abstract concept. It was a practical consideration, and although it is nowhere explained, it must have been founded on an observable fact of nature.

Leaving aside this difficulty for the moment, it is instructive to turn to another treatise on precious stones, the *Agastimata*, written by an unknown author sometime after the sixth century. In this work the valuation of diamonds is systematically based on their specific gravity. The ideal ratio given for a colorless and perfectly transparent octahedron is a density of three pinda for a volume of three yava and a weight of three tandula. A stone of three yava in volume and only two tandula in weight would have a lesser density, and, inversely, one of three yava and four or more tandula would have a greater density; these would be less valuable. The *Agastimata* is especially informative regarding diamonds with a density greater than the ideal ratio of three pinda. If, for example, a diamond's specific gravity exceeds the ideal proportion by one-quarter, its price, as established by the authorities, falls by half. If its specific weight exceeds the ideal ratio by half, its worth is only one-quarter that of a perfect diamond.

From this system it is evident that stones of a high specific gravity were not valued as greatly as those with less density. Since the diamond's specific gravity is remarkably constant, it is impossible to imagine variations of as much as one-quarter or one-half. Such variations can be found only when the diamond's specific gravity is compared with that of other stones, such as quartz. Apparently, then, the system of valuation used by Indian lapidaries was based on just such comparisons. Since an octahedral crystal was considered the ideal form of the diamond, all stones having that form must have been classified as "diamonds."

Diamonds and the Caste System. If this hypothesis is accepted, then two other traditions associated with diamonds become explicable. We know that the color of diamonds was once related to the caste system in India. Only Brahmins, members of the priestly caste, could possess white, or colorless, diamonds. Yellow diamonds were reserved for Vaisyas, or landowners, who supplied the populace with food, and red diamonds for the Kshatriyas, the caste of knights and warriors. Finally, dark gray diamonds, whose metallic appearance was compared to the "dark tone of a sword," were reserved for the Sudras, laborers and artisans. This division of stones among different castes according to color is also found in other civilizations and can be easily understood. If we take into account the relative rarity of the various stones, the system implies that red and gray diamonds were much more numerous than white and yellow ones, since there were many more Kshatriyas and Sudras than Brahmins and Vaisyas. As we know that a perfectly formed 1-carat octahedron was valued at 200 rupakas, and that a Sudra's wages amounted to only 1.25 rupakas a month, we may wonder how many people were actually able to buy diamonds, even allowing for the fact that the price of a gray stone was only one-quarter that of a white one. For warriors, this problem probably never arose: their loyalty had to be ensured at all costs, which meant that their wages were paramount. They were even paid in kind—directly in red diamonds. But they were not the only people to covet red diamonds. In the Kathiawar peninsula there was a rich community of Persian origin well known for its relentless pursuit of diamonds of this color. Known as Parsees, they worshiped fire, and to them red was a sacred color. We are told that the Parsees possessed unimaginable quantities of red diamonds. Given the rarity of such stones in nature, how were they able to collect so many of them?

Whatever the richness of the diamond deposits in India, it is quite certain that they were never so plentiful that everyone could buy a diamond, even one of mediocre quality.

A pagoda, a coin "current in the lands of the King of Golconda. . . . It is the best money that one can take to the diamond mines." From Tavernier's *Six Voyages. . . .* Bibliothèque Nationale, Paris. *Photo Hubert Josse, Paris.*

Detail of an Indian gold
enameled ankle ring (see
frontispiece) showing rubies,
emeralds, and diamonds,
some simply cleaved and
polished, some in the shape of
a flat rose—the "Mughal" cut.
School of Jaipur, early 19th
century. Collection M. G.
Mehta, Bombay. *Photo Guy
Philippart de Foy, Brussels.*

A Brahmin goldsmith and a Vaisya (merchant). Below: A Parsee on a journey. Indian watercolors illustrating the caste system, 1831. Bibliothèque Nationale, Paris. *Photo Bibliothèque Nationale.*

Moreover, the distribution of stones according to castes, besides reflecting a coherent theoretical system, also confirmed in a specific, practical way the strict hierarchical organization that regulated life in India at that time. When all these factors are taken into account, they confirm the hypothesis that all stones of similar appearance, even if they did not possess all the physical properties of the diamond, were judged on the same comparative scale as diamonds.

If the stones the Indians classified as diamonds were not all diamonds, what were they? The "dark gray diamond" may well have been magnetite. Magnetite, a natural, magnetic iron oxide, has an octahedral form and a specific gravity of 5.18, about one and a half times that of the diamond. Its gray color is similar to that of a sword. Magnetite is found abundantly in India, a country particularly rich in iron-ore deposits. Another iron ore, siderite, was very likely the "black diamond" mentioned by Pliny and described as being relatively heavy and soft—soft enough to be drilled. This explanation enables us to understand, without resorting to symbolic interpretations, why magnetic power was attributed to the diamond in antiquity. (It also helps to explain why, in medieval Italy, the diamond was regarded as the "stone of reconciliation" that would unite a husband and wife who had quarreled.) Because magnetite was for hundreds of years considered to

be equivalent to the diamond, its properties, quite naturally, were attributed to the diamond as well.

The "red diamonds," too, can be easily identified. Among precious stones, there is only one that is of this color and typically possesses the form of an octahedron. This is the red spinel, whose specific weight (3.6) is very close to that of the diamond (3.52). As such, it corresponds perfectly to the ideal unit of the pinda. It now becomes obvious that these were the stones reserved for the most important caste after the Brahmins, and that they were the stones that the Parsees went to such trouble to acquire to meet their religious needs. There is no doubt that, for the Indians, the similarity of form between red spinels and diamonds was a decisive factor in determining the value of the red stones.

The Ancient Trade Routes

There is very little information about the diamond trade in antiquity. The sources are few, and there are long periods for which no records exist at all. A reading of Indian lapidaries reveals that the regions of the Gulf of Cambay in northern India, the Kalinga coast in the southeast, and the Ganges plain were privileged places for trade and exchange. Kalinga and the Ganges plain were important because they were fairly close to the deposits. The Gulf of Cambay, though far from any mining area,

was nonetheless the most important export center in antiquity. Research done in such cities as Somnath, Suppara, and Barundsch confirms the role diamonds played in trade with the West during the Hellenistic period. The *Ratnapariska*, which is the oldest surviving source, mentions export of diamonds before the sixth century and even states that the stones came from the Ganges plain. From this information, some historians sought to infer that the trade had probably taken the ancient "natural route" of the Punjab, which, once the passes of the Hindu Kush were crossed, led to the famous Bamian Valley in northeastern Afghanistan. But this is only a supposition based on evidence that is far from conclusive. The point remains open to argument.

In the absence of documentary evidence, some authors have advanced the hypothesis that all diamonds found in India would have remained there until the tenth century and would not have begun to appear in the West until after the Muslim invasion of 1000, when Mahmud of Ghazni (998–1030) pillaged the upper valley of the Ganges no less than seventeen times and invaded the peninsula of Kathiawar, where he destroyed, among other things, the rich temple of Somnath. Although the destruction wrought by the Muslims was certainly considerable, the frontiers of the kingdom founded by Mahmud never exceeded the limits of the western Punjab, and it is dif-

ficult to establish that the invasion modified the trade of the period in any significant way. The empire founded by Mahmud and ruled by his successors, the Ghaznevid dynasty, never extended as far as the deposits of the high plateau of the Deccan. It was only in the twelfth century that the Ghor, or Ghuri, sovereigns reached Delhi, conquered Bihar and upper Bengal, and, after seizing Gwalior, occupied the Kathiawar peninsula. As a result of their conquests, around the beginning of the thirteenth century they acquired possession of the diamond warehouses of Bandelkhand. No evidence, however, confirms the supposition that Muhammad Ghori, who died in 1206, relentlessly dispersed and sold the contents of the Indian treasuries. According to one story of the period, he left some 400 pounds (180 kg) of diamonds when he died, but these were certainly not solely the fruits of pillage. A good part of the treasure must have come from the mines of the Panna district, which are still active today.

All things considered, there is no reason to suppose that the Indian export of diamonds developed at a comparatively late date and was founded on the treasures collected during the centuries before the Muslim epoch. On the contrary, the texts of the old Indian lapidaries, with their rates and price lists, and the descriptions given by the first Europeans to visit India, lead us to believe that since the most an-

Mahmud of Ghazni carrying away a Hindu idol. From a Hindu manuscript, 18th century. Bibliothèque Nationale, Paris. *Photo Bibliothèque Nationale.*

A caravan. Miniature by al-Wasiti from the *Maqamat* ("Conclaves") of al-Hariri, Baghdad, 1237. Bibliothèque Nationale, Paris. *Photo Bibliothèque Nationale.*

the first century A.D. Discussing the northern part of the Indian Ocean, the author specifically mentions the harbors of India then known for their diamond trade: present-day Nileshwar and a certain Bacare, which has since disappeared but was probably situated at the mouth of the Kandragiri River. This is the very first mention of diamonds on the maritime route through the northern Indian Ocean that linked the Persian Gulf with the Malabar coast—one of the principal trade routes of the pre-Roman period.

One of the most notable features of the trade relations between eastern Asia and Europe from the time of the Roman Empire to the arrival of Europeans in India in the early sixteenth century is their remarkable consistency over such a long period. A slight decline only occurred at the fall of the Roman Empire; very soon thereafter the gap was filled by the small coastal states of Italy, which soon renewed active relations with the chief Mediterranean ports—Alexandria, Tyre, Antioch, and Byzantium—where all eastern goods arrived after crossing the Red Sea or the Persian Gulf. This situation remained basically unchanged until the end of the fifteenth century, when the Portuguese explorer Vasco da Gama opened a direct sea route from Europe to the Indian subcontinent.

Though political instability had disrupted India since the seventh century and divided the country into a number of rival kingdoms, India's diamond exports had remained stable. It would therefore be natural to assume that the energetic development of trade with Europe in the Middle Ages would have increased diamond exports. But this was not so. During the Middle Ages, as in the period of the Roman Empire, only a small part of the Indian production reached Europe. Before the discovery of the direct sea route to India, Persians and Arabs held a monopoly on caravan transport, and along the entire route to the ports they gave various local sovereigns first choice of all the precious stones being shipped. Fer-

cient times, and at the specific demand of various sovereigns, there was a continuous production of diamonds destined for commercial exchange. Evidence to support this contention is furnished by the *Periplus of the Erythrean Sea*, a kind of pilot's guide to the navigation of the Red Sea and the Indian Ocean, written by an anonymous Greek author, which appeared around the time of Pliny,

vent admirers of earthly treasure and always anxious to enhance the dazzling effect of their thrones with rich jewels, the princes never failed to select the finest stones for themselves, beginning with diamonds. Pliny had said that the diamond was a thing known only to kings, and to very few kings at that. The situation had hardly changed by the seventh century, when Isidore of Seville (ca. 560–630) found no more to say about diamonds in his great encyclopedia than to describe them as "small and dull."

Besides being valued as a talisman, the diamond was used for another purpose by the Romans. As Pliny relates, it was mounted on an iron support and used as an engraving instrument, gradually replacing corundum for that purpose. This was not by any means a degrading function for the diamond, since glyptic art—carving on gems—was held in very high esteem by the Romans. The diamond made stonecutting easier and, by permitting greater precision, raised the prestige of the art, which was indeed a very ancient one, dating from the

second century B.C. There is a Chinese manuscript from that period called *Lie Tseu*, or "The Book of Master Lie," which mentions an instrument called a *kun-wu*. This was quite simply a chisel equipped with a diamond tip. The Chinese text merely mentions the instrument and its source—Fu-lin, or Rome. It says nothing about the diamond itself except that it comes from the West. Much later, in the fifth century A.D., several Chinese manuscripts specifically state that these gems come from Ta Ts'in, the Eastern or Byzantine Empire. Although it is rather surprising to find the diamond taking this route, the Chinese sources at least confirm that India was exporting her most precious stones centuries before the Muslim invasion of 1000. Moreover, it is certain that direct contact was established between the Chinese and the Indians no later than the third century A.D. and that diamonds were among the goods traded at that time. In his *Nan Chou i Wu ki*, "Inventory of Curiosities of the Southern Provinces," written in 270, Wang Chen noted that the diamond was a stone vaguely

Trade routes from the 1st century to the 3rd century B.C. *Burns Graphics, London.*

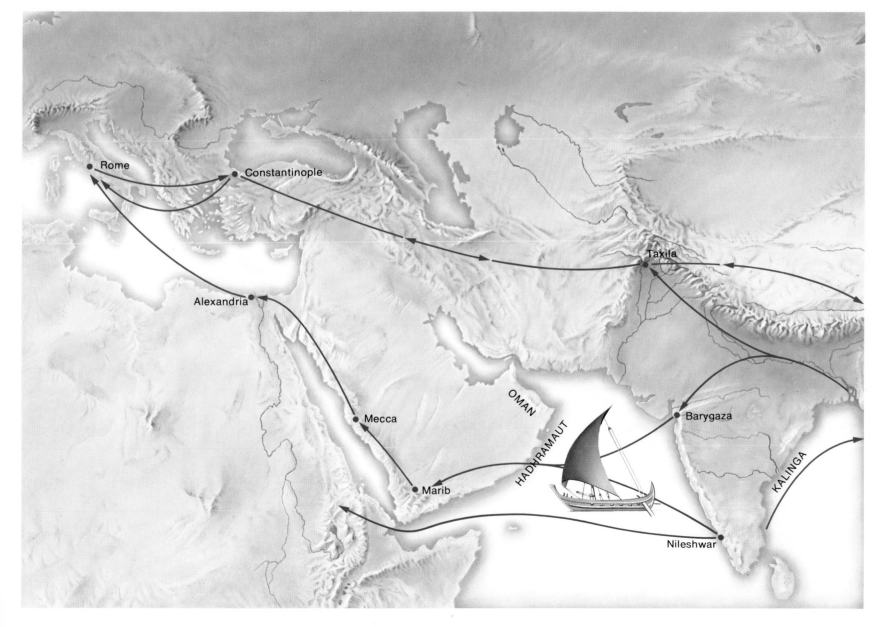

resembling a pearl, which is a fair description of a rough diamond that has been rounded off. He also mentioned the exceptional hardness of the diamond and added that "foreigners" (that is, non-Chinese) had a rather irrational use for them—setting them in rings that they wore as amulets to protect themselves against supernatural forces or to render themselves immune to poison. The remark conveys a wealth of information, and since the supernatural signs and symbols of the Chinese were entirely different from those of the Indians or of the Europeans, the writer's skepticism at the use of such a dull stone as a talisman is quite understandable.

Production Methods in India

Available historical sources provide practically no information about the production of

diamonds in India from ancient times until the mid-nineteenth century. A figure of 30 million carats has been suggested for total production over this period, but this is only a guess. No solid evidence has even been supplied to support that or any other estimate. It is to Jean-Baptiste Tavernier (1605–89) that we are indebted for the first description, reliable or not, of Indian mines.

Encouraged by Cardinal Mazarin and later by Louis XIV, Tavernier, a merchant in precious stones, made several voyages to India and left an account rich in valuable information. But he was able to visit only three of India's many mines: Raolconda (Raulconda), Gani Coulour (now Kollur), and Soumelpour. He described each of them briefly—too briefly, in fact, to give even a general idea of either the methods of operation used in the mines or of the importance of diamond production in the seventeenth century.

Paradoxically, we are almost better informed on the production methods of a slightly earlier period, thanks to the writings of Garcia ab Horto. Physician to the Portuguese viceroy in Goa, he made some notes on diamond production in 1565 following a trip to the high plateau of the Deccan. Of all his remarks, the most interesting concerns the then widespread belief that new diamonds were constantly being formed in rocks that had already been worked. Anselmus de Boot, physician to the Habsburg emperor Rudolph II, took up this idea in his treatise of 1609, and Ioannis de Laet of Antwerp discussed it in 1647. Garcia ab Horto wrote: "When the galleries, which are made as high as a man can work, appear used up, they are abandoned, but they are reopened thirty or forty years later, for in that interval new diamonds are formed." This is not simply baseless fable or legend; it is an essentially accurate description of a particular method of operation. Although it is unlikely that anyone was aware of how it worked, this process exploited the effects of natural erosion, or the weathering of the rock on the site. In river or alluvial deposits the gravel or soil merely has to be washed in a sieve or a trough, but primary ore has to be crushed. When processing methods were primitive, as they were everywhere until the middle of the nineteenth century, they were profitable only when a large mass of the ore was attacked. This inevitably meant large losses, as all the diamonds in the rock could not be recovered at the first attempt. Consequently, the work site was abandoned for a time. The "rest period" allowed natural erosion to do its work and complete the breaking down of the ore—as was done in the early days in the South African diamond fields. When the debris was washed away some years

The chief diamond mines and trading centers in India. *Burns Graphics, London.*

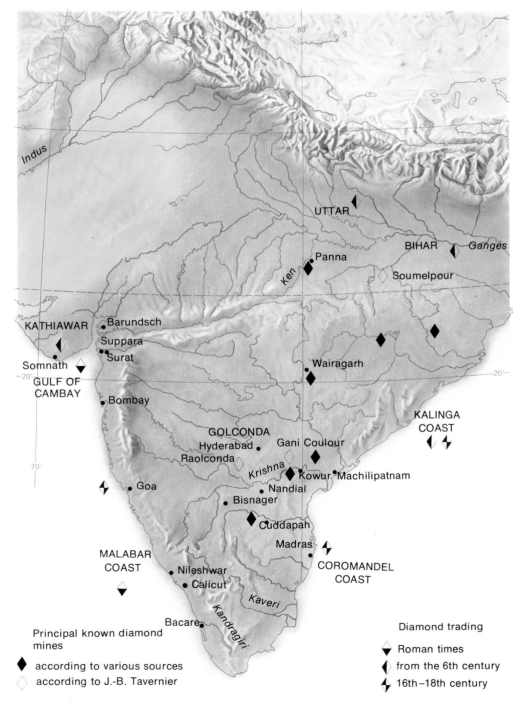

Principal known diamond mines

◆ according to various sources
◇ according to J.-B. Tavernier

Diamond trading

▽ Roman times
◁ from the 6th century
⚡ 16th–18th century

Mining alluvial deposits beside a river in India, a country where "there be mighty great abundance of precious stones." Miniature from a French manuscript, *Les secrets de l'histoire naturelle*, about 1480. Bibliothèque Nationale, Paris. *Photo Bibliothèque Nationale.*

later, more diamonds were recovered. This operation could be repeated successfully several times after varying intervals until the mine was completely empty. Before the natural process was understood, it was easy to assume that new diamonds were formed within the rock.

Garcia ab Horto's information reveals that as early as the sixteenth century, diamond extraction in India was not limited to the relatively simple work on the alluvial deposits but was also concentrated on the bedrock, not only on the surface but underground as well. Hence the necessity of digging pits or galleries. Garcia ab Horto's reference to galleries "as high as a man can work" throws new light on a remark by the Greek sailor Eudoxus of Cyzicus, who visited India about 120 B.C. and related, without elaborating, that alongside alluvial sites there was also "digging of deep galleries." The fact that these descriptions, separated by many centuries, are so similar allows us to conclude with some confidence that the gallery method of mining was already in use, not only before

the beginning of the Christian era, but probably at some very early time. In the eighteenth century, when India lost her long-held monopoly on production, diamond mining was done solely on surface sites. This in no way proves, however, that other mining techniques were not used before that.

To judge from accounts given by travelers, the methods of working river deposits apparently did not differ very much from those still in use today on small work sites in Africa. The mining work itself was obviously determined by the rudimentary means available. According to the most likely hypothesis, work began by opening quarries and then digging pits, which sometimes went as deep as 115 feet (35 m). However, it appears that in most cases workers were satisfied to dig pits only a few yards in diameter and no more than 15 or 20 feet (5–6 m) deep. When the diamond-yielding layer was reached, short lateral galleries were made, provided the surrounding rocks were sufficiently solid. Tavernier related that men

The Piazza San Marco, Venice. Miniature from a French manuscript, *Description de la Seigneurie de Venise*, late 15th century. Musée Condé, Chantilly. *Photo Giraudon, Paris.*

no less than sixty thousand persons were employed there. At the Soumelpour mine in northeastern India, which was part of the less extensive group of Sambalpur, he estimated that there were eight thousand workers. Although this evidence is decidedly fragmentary, the various estimates give some grounds for believing that diamond activity must have been rapidly intensified during the seventeenth century and that it reached its height at that time. Less than a hundred years later, after the mines of Brazil were discovered, Indian production declined sharply and finally lost all importance.

The Diamond Trade in Europe from the Thirteenth to the Eighteenth Century

Between the fifth- and sixth-century lapidaries of Buddhabhatta and Varahamihira and the first records of Arab control of the diamond supply in the thirteenth century, not a single original document survives concerning the trade in precious stones. The books that discuss gems merely repeat ancient descriptions, and even these often incorporate considerable distortions. For instance, the legendary mountain of al-Rahun, where the Valley of Diamonds was said to be found, was transferred from India to the island of Ceylon (Serendib), now Sri Lanka. This island may well have been an entrepôt for trade between India and China, but it certainly never had any diamond deposits of its own. Arab writers and geographers of the eighth century mention the diamond only in connection with the great trade routes that linked India and the Mediterranean. The oldest of these has already been mentioned—the maritime route that, starting from the Gulf of Cambay or from the forts on the Malabar coast, reached Aden, crossed the Red Sea to Ethiopia, and from there went to Cairo and finally to Alexandria. Though Pliny in his *Natural History* stated that Ethiopia was the country where the diamond originated, and though the "Ethiopian diamond" of the Romans is undoubtedly the one that interests us, there is no reason to believe that any diamond, at least any diamond in the form of a gem, ever reached Europe via this route.

Venice. For trade with Europe, the northern route seems to have been preferred. Marco Polo, in the thirteenth century, was the first traveler to mention the Persian city of Hormuz as the most important market for precious stones, notably diamonds, coming from India. From there the stones were shipped through Persia to Armenia and Turkey, or to Aleppo, in Arab territory. Aleppo was a strategic point in the last lap of the journey to Constantinople and Venice. The importance of the city is sug-

did the heavy work, while women and often children collected the stones.

Although there are no existing figures for production, the description given by Ioannis de Laet of the deposits of the Ellore (Elluru) group along the River Krishna reveals that this type of work was conducted on an "industrial" scale, at least at the beginning of the seventeenth century, for some thirty thousand men were occupied in reducing the rock and gathering the diamonds. About twenty years later, Tavernier, visiting the deposits of Gani Coulour, which were then regarded as the most important of the Ellore group, estimated that

gested by a treaty made in 969–70 between the Byzantine emperor and the Muslim rulers of Aleppo, which makes special mention of customs duties. Venice, profiting from the exclusive relationship she eventually established with Aleppo, had become the most important mercantile republic in the western world by the beginning of the thirteenth century, when the Fourth Crusade was coming to an end. As the primary link between Europe and the East, she controlled the main supply of Indian products entering Europe, and enjoyed a monopoly of the diamond trade. Venice retained this commercial dominance for more than two centuries, until the voyage of Vasco da Gama in 1498 opened a direct maritime route to India, and the market shifted to Lisbon.

Bruges. The earliest information on the nascent diamond industry in Europe comes from southern Germany, where the principal cities had maintained a continuous trade with Venice since at least the beginning of the fourteenth century. Apprenticeship in the diamond trade in these cities seems to have been subject to certain rules—one could enter the trade only by passing an examination. It is reasonable to conclude that the art of diamond cutting was fully developed by then, and that great progress had been made in a comparatively short time. All the available evidence indicates that Venice played a guiding role in this field.

The southern German cities, however, were not the only ones where the diamond business flourished. The prosperity enjoyed by the city of Bruges in the fourteenth century included a thriving diamond-cutting business. Maintaining close relations with Venice, Bruges, with Damme as its port, was one of the chief places of commercial exchange between northern and southern Europe. The diamond trade seems to have been practiced in the city early in the fourteenth century, although, surprisingly, no diamond cutter is mentioned in the city archives before 1465. In all likelihood, this odd omission can be explained by the comparatively small number of jewelers in the city. Until advancing knowledge and experience led to specialization in diamonds by certain craftsmen, diamond cutting was done by goldsmiths.

Bruges lay at the far end of a route that began at the Venetian lagoons and passed by way of Milan over the Alps and up the Rhine valley to the Low Countries. It is not only because of her canals that Bruges is called the "Venice of the North." In the fourteenth century the city contained an important colony of Italian merchants who imported, in addition to silks, diamonds from Venice for cutting. Because of the great distance separating the two cities, there was no sharp economic competition between Venice and Bruges. Moreover, since the northern trade route was, like all others, somewhat dangerous, it was certainly less risky to

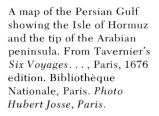

A map of the Persian Gulf showing the Isle of Hormuz and the tip of the Arabian peninsula. From Tavernier's *Six Voyages. . .* , Paris, 1676 edition. Bibliothèque Nationale, Paris. *Photo Hubert Josse, Paris.*

transport rough stones than cut diamonds. It was quite natural, therefore, for Bruges, at the end of the trade route, to become a great diamond-cutting center.

Some evidence for the status of Bruges is provided by the legend of Lodewijk van Berckem (Louis de Berquen), once credited with devising a method in which a diamond was used as the tool for cutting other diamonds. Following this invention, it is said, Lodewijk was commissioned by Charles the Bold, duke of Burgundy, to work on three stones "in order to polish them to his capacity." Some authors maintain that the largest of these stones was the famous Florentine diamond worn by the duke at the Battle of Nancy (1477), in which he lost his life. The second was a diamond destined for Pope Sixtus IV, and the third, a triangular stone mounted in a ring with two small clamps, was offered by the duke to Louis XI as a symbol of reconciliation. For his work Lodewijk received 3,000 ducats, a small fortune at that time.

Although this legend has survived for six centuries, its basis in fact is rather slight. In 1661 a Parisian jeweler of Flemish background named Robert de Berquen published a treatise on precious stones and pearls called *The Marvels of Western and Eastern India,* in which he stated that diamond cutting was invented

in Bruges in 1476 by his ancestor Lodewijk van Berckem. It would not be unduly cynical to wonder if this might not have been merely a clever piece of advertising on the author's part in order to associate his own name with so important an invention. Mountains of archives have been searched from top to bottom, not only in Bruges but also in Brussels and Lille, and all the contracts made by Philip the Fair and Charles the Bold with their suppliers have been carefully studied, but not a single document mentions the name of Lodewijk van Berckem. Nor has his name been discovered in any of the documents of the period from 1476 to 1661. All that can really be learned from the legend is that the passionate interest in jewels, especially diamonds, shown by the dukes of Burgundy inspired them to encourage and promote the jeweler's craft in their possessions in northern Europe.

Although Bruges held a preeminent position at the close of the fourteenth century, within fifty years it began to decline because of the silting up of the Zwin. Like many other economic activities, the diamond trade gradually shifted to the city of Antwerp, which had better facilities for communications and exchange. An ordinance of the city authorities in 1447 indirectly reveals this situation, and indicates that the trade in precious stones was by then in full swing and in need of proper protection. It warns citizens against the risks of dealing in false gems: "No one can buy, sell, pledge, or part with a false stone, whether an imitation diamond, ruby, emerald, or sapphire, without incurring a penalty of 25 ducats, one-third of it for the sovereign, one-third for the city, and one-third for the informer." (This interesting detail is mentioned by Jan Walgrave in *The History of Diamonds in Antwerp.*)

The Lisbon-Antwerp Axis. The transfer of activities from one city to another, already in progress in the mid-fifteenth century, was accelerated after 1498, when Vasco da Gama's voyage led to the opening of a direct route from Lisbon to the Indies. Thereafter the route linking Lisbon with Antwerp became far more important than the Venice-Bruges link. Once a year a convoy of vessels from India arrived at the Portuguese capital, and from there diamonds were distributed not only to Antwerp but also to London, Amsterdam, and Venice. As Antwerp became the chief center of distribution for the Indian products imported to Lisbon, it began to siphon off the trade in rough diamonds and cut stones, which until then had been the monopoly of Venice. The change was not sudden, however, and the Venetian republic continued to play an active role until the Portuguese, through their control of the Indian

some of their banks and merchant houses had taken in financing the Portuguese expedition to the Indies. Albrecht Dürer was commissioned by his patron and benefactor, Willibald Pirkheimer of Nuremberg, to buy diamonds when he traveled to Venice in 1505–06. In 1505 the Fuggers of Augsburg sold to the emperor Maximilian I, on credit, two diamonds for the sum of 10,000 florins. The same great banking house played a decisive role when it bought and then sold the famous diamonds that Charles the Bold had lost during the battles of Grandson and Nancy. This involvement of the most eminent financiers in the jewelry trade, and the feeling for the diamond as a uniquely valuable personal possession, are

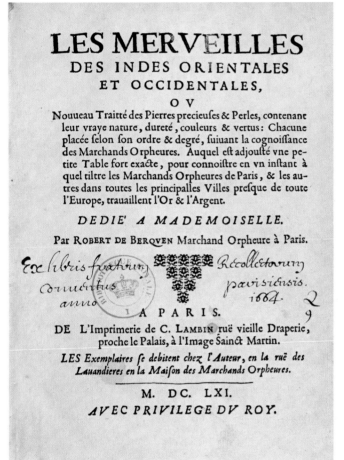

Ocean ports, eventually cut off the supplies that Venice received from Alexandria and other places. The declining maritime republic was then forced to turn to Lisbon for its rough diamonds and to Antwerp for its cut diamonds. Antwerp continued to import large quantities until the eighteenth century and, with its many fine jewelry workshops, earned a well-deserved reputation as a great diamond center.

The diamond trade has always been dependent on the existence of a flourishing money market. Before Antwerp took the world lead, the cities of southern Germany had acquired a dominant position thanks to the active part

more characteristic of the close of the Middle Ages than the beginning of the modern period. Only a few years later, in 1528, when the Welsers of Augsburg became, along with the Fuggers, the chief creditors of Emperor Charles V, the organization of the diamond trade changed significantly. Diamonds became current merchandise, and interest no longer centered on large or unique stones but on relatively small table- or point-cut stones mounted in rings or other pieces of jewelry.

The event that brought about this change was the conquest of Goa by Alfonso de Albuquerque in 1510, which enabled the Portu-

A Portuguese *não*, a seagoing merchant vessel, at about the end of the 15th century. Maritime Museum, Lisbon. *Photo Giraudon, Paris.*

Nau redonda - 1498.

guese to export huge quantities of rough diamonds to Lisbon. From the port of Goa the Portuguese gradually extended their influence over all the Indian kingdoms of the Deccan. These included some of the most important diamond-yielding deposits, especially those of Cuddapah, Nandial, and Ellore, the famous market of Bisnager, and the legendary city of Golconda, near Hyderabad. Goa thus became the port of export for Indian diamonds and remained so for some two hundred years. Jan Huyghen van Linschoten, who was in Goa in 1595, observed that rough diamonds were brought from all parts of India to be sold to the Portuguese. The only exceptions were stones weighing more than 25 mangelins (48.6 carats), which were reserved for local sovereigns.

Antwerp in the Sixteenth and Seventeenth Centuries. The monetary crisis of 1540–45, which particularly affected commercial and banking activities in southern Germany, led to a recession in the diamond trade in Augsburg and Nuremberg. Antwerp took advantage of this situation. The city was then expanding to its greatest extent and housed many foreign merchants whose wealth and power contributed to its prosperity and influence. These included an Italian family, the Affaitatis, one of the richest in Europe. Among other notable investments, the Affaitatis had financed Vasco da Gama's second voyage to the Indies, via the Cape of Good Hope, in 1502 and Magellan's voyage around the world in 1519–22. The head of the family, Juan Carlos, resided in the Château de Selsaeten at Wommelgem, on the outskirts of Antwerp. He was a major creditor of Emperor Charles V and of Edward VI of England. There were few spheres of economic activity in which he was not engaged, and quite naturally he was interested in precious stones. Still more powerful was the group of Portuguese families whose activities were confined exclusively to diamonds—the Ximeneses, the Teixeras de Sampaio, and the Duartes. The most famous of these Portuguese diamond dealers was Baron Rodriguez d'Evora, whose princely establishment on the "Meir," a street that housed many diamond merchants, earned him the nickname "the little king."

There is no contemporary work that describes in detail the role played by Antwerp in the development of diamond-working tech-

The imposing ruins of the fortress of Golconda, near Hyderabad. The old "diamond city," famous for the treasures collected by the nizams of Hyderabad, Golconda was pillaged and destroyed by Aurangzeb in 1688. *Photo Guy Philippart de Foy, Brussels.*

European knowledge of Arabia and India in 1519, at the time of Vasco da Gama's voyage, as displayed by a Portuguese maritime atlas attributed to Lopo Homem. Bibliothèque Nationale, Paris. *Photo Bibliothèque Nationale.*

niques. However, it would not be unreasonable to assume that advances in diamond working in that city were on a par with the outstanding developments in the jewelry trade as a whole at that time. It is significant, for example, that François I ignored the diamond cutters of Paris, whose existence as early as 1407 is revealed by Guillebert of Metz in his *Description of Paris,* and instead employed the craftsmen of Antwerp. There is also a very illuminating report on the Antwerp diamond trade by Ludovico Guicciardini in his *Descrittione di tutti i Paesi Bassi* ("Description of All the Low Countries"), published in 1567. "Here we see cutters and polishers of diamonds and of other precious stones who truly achieve some beautiful things," Guicciardini wrote. "Their trade in expensive jewelry is prosperous. They are more numerous here than in any other province."

Antwerp was the commercial heart of Europe: approximately 40 percent of world trade passed through its port in the sixteenth century. Naturally the diamond occupied a favored place. But the northern Netherlands'

struggle for independence from 1568 to 1648 undermined Antwerp's position, and as the city lost its dominant role, a growing proportion of its business was acquired by Amsterdam. Antwerp's decline did not occur overnight, and despite internal struggles like the conflict between the new Guild of Diamond Cutters (founded on October 25, 1582) and the rich merchants, the city's prestige apparently remained intact until the middle of the seventeenth century. Nonetheless, the capture and pillage of the city in 1585 by the troops of Alexander Farnese, acting as governor of the Low Countries for Philip II of Spain, was the first important step on the downward path. Spanish rule, along with the religious intolerance it entailed, caused a number of active and intelligent people, chiefly Protestants, to leave the country and settle either in Frankfurt or Amsterdam. Among those responsible for bringing the diamond industry to Amsterdam were Willem Vermaet, who emigrated in 1586, and Peter Goes, a native of Antwerp who settled in the Seedijk quarter of Amsterdam and married there in 1589. The exodus was not ig-

Detail of a map of Antwerp, 1565. Woodcut by Virgilius Boloniensis, hand-colored. Musée Plantin-Moretus, Antwerp. *Photo Éditions Mercator—Cliché de Schutter, Antwerp.*

1. The "Meir," where numerous diamond merchants and dealers lived, including Rodriguez d'Evora and the Wallis, Du Jon, and Fourchoudt families.
2. The *Eiermarkt* ("egg market"), where the Guild of Diamond Cutters met from 1642 to 1663.
3. Korte Klarenstraat, where the Guild (later the Fraternity) of Diamond Cutters met from 1663 until its dissolution in 1894.
4. Dominicanessenstraat, where the trade in diamonds and precious stones was carried on in the first half of the 16th century.
5. Koraalberg, where the diamond business moved in the second half of the 16th century.
6. The church of the Sisters of Notre-Dame du Mont-Carmel, where the diamond cutters prayed to the patron saints of their guild, Peter and Paul.
7. Keiserstraat, where Balthazar de Groote lived.
8. The church of St. Augustine, where the Guild (and Fraternity) of Diamond Cutters celebrated its religious festivals in the 18th and 19th centuries.

In 1787 some of the diamonds of the French crown were recut in a former Carthusian monastery in the southern part of the town. "A task has just been completed in this town," reported the *Gazette d'Anvers,* which has excited the interest of all connoisseurs and lovers of diamonds. . . . Monsieur Thierry of Ville-d'Avray, *commissaire-général* of the property of the French crown, received an order from King Louis XVI for the Oriental-cut diamonds to be refashioned. As the work could not be done in Paris, where knowledge of the art is limited, he chose Antwerp, famous for its ancient guild of gem cutters, in preference to all other places." Twenty-three grinding wheels were necessary, and the work lasted nine months.

Anna Lopez Ximenes, wife of Baron Simon Rodriguez d'Evora, one of the principal Antwerp diamond merchants of the second half of the 16th century. Anna, herself a member of an illustrious merchant family, is wearing a diamond pendant. Detail of a painting attributed to Otto van Veen. Maagdenhuis Museum, Antwerp. *Photo De Schutter, Antwerp.*

nored by the Guild of Diamond Cutters, which, armed with the thirty-nine articles of its charter, raised every conceivable obstacle against those members whom it regarded as disloyal. The result was that these men, exasperated by so much civic hostility, also chose to exercise their talents elsewhere.

The reason that Frankfurt-on-Main was the chosen place of settlement for so many of the emigrants can be easily explained. Famous for its great annual fair, the city was then enjoying a period of remarkable prosperity: after about 1570 the money market was particularly easy, contributing to Frankfurt's reputation as the most important European market for jewelry, a reputation it retained for some sixty years. Yet even in this crucial period Antwerp remained important. The diamond dealers and diamond cutters of Frankfurt continued to get their supplies from Antwerp, which still received diamonds from Lisbon, and a great many diamond cutters still resided there. In 1631 Frankfurt had only 51 diamond cutters. In Antwerp there were 164, and that does not include the considerable number who, in order to avoid the tiresome restrictions imposed

by the guild, had settled in Brussels, Malines, and Lier. This figure may seem rather less impressive when compared with the 166 diamond cutters who were still active in Venice in 1636. But the city of Titian and Tintoretto was in rapid decline, and only two years later, following the check in the supply of rough diamonds, only 22 diamond cutters remained. Despite competition from Frankfurt, the trade in diamonds also continued to flourish in Antwerp. Of course it was now somewhat smaller, and tended to be concentrated in the hands of a few families—the Fourchoudts, the Wallises, the Du Jons, the De Grootes, the Prets, the Hendrickxes, the Van Coolens, and the Clarisses, who still organized important maritime expeditions. Their most valued customers were in France, Portugal, and Spain, and in all the other territories controlled by the Habsburgs. In order to maintain or extend their influence, many had branches in various European cities. There were representatives of the Fourchoudt family in Cadiz and Vienna; Paul du Jon was in Lisbon. They had their agents too in London, Hamburg, Cologne, and Amsterdam. Peter Paul Rubens, the greatest Flemish artist of the period, was the friend of one of these merchants, Gisbero van Coolen, and through his second wife, Helen Fourment, whom he depicted in a number of paintings covered with splendid jewels, he was linked to the Balthazar de Groote family.

Nothing better illustrates the power the diamond world represented in the city's economic life than an episode that occurred in 1618 and greatly disturbed the entire corporation of Antwerp. The silk workers, whose business was suffering because of competition from various French products, had persuaded Archduke Albert and his wife Isabelle to ban the imported goods. The French government retaliated by forbidding the import of polished diamonds into French territory other than for the great annual fair at Paris. This decision, which was of course greeted with delight by the diamond workers of Paris, created a veritable tempest among their counterparts in Antwerp, for whom Paris was one of the chief outlets. The archduke and archduchess, invited by the members of the diamond cutters' guild to weigh the pros and cons of the situation, yielded to pressure. Imported French silks were again permitted, and the export of diamonds resumed.

Amsterdam and the Dutch East India Company. Frankfurt's period of eminence was soon ended by the outbreak of the Thirty Years' War (1618–48). It was during this time that Amsterdam came to the fore. A privileged city offering religious and civil liberty to anyone who wished to settle there, Amsterdam

came to exercise a near monopoly not only on
the diamond industry but also on the trade in
diamonds, and it retained its supremacy into
the eighteenth century. In addition to the Protestant émigrés from Antwerp, Amsterdam received a number of Portuguese Jews, experienced in high financial transactions, who were
forced to emigrate to escape the persecution of
the Inquisition when Portugal was annexed to

Spain in 1580. They were soon joined by Jews
from Antwerp, who also sought to escape
Spanish domination.

Clearly the liberal, republican, Protestant
Dutch were anxious to place as little dependence as possible on Lisbon and Antwerp,
which, as the receivers of rough diamonds
from India, had hitherto been Amsterdam's
sole source of supply. Their first attempt to
assert their independence dates from 1608,
when the representatives of the Dutch East
India Company at Boucadana, on the island of
Borneo, sought to draw up a contract to purchase diamonds from the king of Banjermasin.
This effort was unsuccessful, for the Chinese,
who offered the king a higher price, cut them
out. Seven years later the Dutch turned to the
Coromandel coast on the southwestern tip of
India, where they of course encountered the
Portuguese. Having been established there for
some time, the Portuguese were in a position
to offer diamonds at good prices, whereas the
young Dutch company was forced to offset its
high investment costs by seeking high profit
margins. During the entire first half of the seventeenth century, the Portuguese and the
Dutch engaged in relentless competition,
which had considerable impact on prices in
the Indian market.

In 1650 the situation changed: the Portuguese demand for diamonds declined sharply.
The reasons seem to lie in the events that were
to modify the political map of northern Europe. In 1648 the United Provinces, led by
Holland, had seized the mouth of the Schelde
River and thus gained control of access to the

Trademark of the Dutch East India Company, which appeared on the silver coins used by the Dutch in the East. Bibliothèque Nationale, Paris. *Photo Hubert Josse, Paris.*

Frontispiece from an inventory of the Dutch East India Company, 1646. Engraving by J. van Meurs. Fondation Atlas van Stolk, Rotterdam. *Photo Fondation Atlas van Stolk.*

port of Antwerp. To defend themselves against threatened strangulation, the Antwerp Guild of Diamond Cutters was forced to limit the number of its master craftsmen and to increase the dues payable by its members. These measures speak eloquently of the damage caused by the interruption of the diamond supply from Portugal. Indeed, it was now Amsterdam that supplied Antwerp with diamonds. Since the Dutch city naturally reserved the first choice for its own diamond cutters, Antwerp was compelled to make do with diamonds of inferior quality. It was during these very difficult years that real marvels of craftsmanship were performed in transforming small and mediocre stones into finely worked gems. It was not enough to preserve the weight; attempts were made to improve the quality of the cut. The Antwerp craftsmen, already well known for their skill, in these years revealed an expertise that put them in the first rank of their craft.

During the troubled period of the late seventeenth century, therefore, there remained only two important centers of diamond cutting and diamond trade in Europe—Amsterdam and

Antwerp. But the maritime hegemony secured by the United Provinces was rather short-lived. The new century had hardly begun when the star of a third city arose and grew steadily brighter. London now entered the universe of diamonds. These three cities—Antwerp, Amsterdam, and London—became the constellation of European diamond markets.

From ancient descriptions of the Golconda mines in the Ellore group, it is evident that the English became interested in India's diamond production at an early date. It appears, in fact, that certain working methods used in India were developed by a man called Wilhelmus Metholdus Anglus (Anglus meaning "the Englishman"). The correspondence of the Dutch East India Company, in explaining why the company's agents reduced their purchases as early as 1660, provides further evidence of English intervention. The correspondence indicates that since the English merchants had increased the demand, the price of rough diamonds had risen so high that the Dutch preferred to abstain from trade.

It seems that some of the company's purchases proved particularly unfortunate. Profits were so low, in fact, that they seemed unacceptable to the directors of the company, and about 1668 they decided to reduce the diamond trade to very small quantities. Whereas the merchants of Antwerp had calculated—quite correctly, as it turned out—that the demand for cut diamonds would increase, the Dutch were not of the same opinion and had wagered to the contrary. Their pessimism was surprising, for the time had long since passed when diamonds were sold exclusively to royal courts and noblemen. During the increasingly mercantile seventeenth century, the middle class was the real agent of economic development. But there was a fear of commercial setbacks, and no one was prepared to abandon the principle of a maximum profit together with a quick recovery of the capital invested. Consequently, the Indian diamond market was yielded without much of a struggle to the English, who appeared to be somewhat more willing to take risks.

But there was one factor no one had considered. During the twenty years following 1650, the diamond-cutting enterprises of Amsterdam and Antwerp still depended chiefly on imports made by the Dutch company. Here was a ready-made trade monopoly, but the company let the opportunity slip. Sixty years later, when the horizon expanded with the discovery of the Brazilian diamond deposits, the Dutch invested huge amounts of capital to secure the rich Brazilian production. Meanwhile, however, the English had taken over the supply of Indian rough diamonds.

Famous Diamonds of India

From a close reading of medieval lapidaries, it is apparent that the only definite information available about diamonds in the Middle Ages could be expressed in a few words: they came from India, they were rare, and they were of unequaled hardness. Around these basic, empirical facts a collection of diverse beliefs grew up, all having their roots in the mysterious and inaccessible Orient. The knowledge that was handed down from century to century and transmitted from one continent to another had one common source: the work of Pliny. The medieval lapidaries extracted the basic facts from Pliny's writings and attempted to amplify them by making revisions or adding new interpretations. Far from clearing up the mysteries, these additional explanations only brought more confusion and added more incredible and extraordinary tales to the lore of the diamond. On the whole, there was far less incoherence in the writings of the ancients than in the innumerable bizarre legends and superstitions that surrounded the diamond from the Middle Ages until the dawn of modern times.

Beliefs and Superstitions

Although the western world may have learned something about the mentality and the customs of the Orient as a result of the Crusades, the East remained largely a closed book. The stories of the adventures of Marco Polo, who in the late thirteenth century traveled from Venice to the kingdom of Kublai Khan and visited India and Persia, are almost the only factual accounts available about the East in the Middle Ages. Marco Polo's *Book of Marvels*, a collection of personal observations and true stories, is one of the most compelling descriptions ever published about the strange lands from which diamonds come.

Because of its supreme hardness, among other qualities, the diamond was regarded in India as a talisman capable of keeping away bad luck and danger. The notion of invincibility, which evolved from belief in its protective abilities, caused it to be highly valued in the West as a symbol of power, an ornament suitable for military leaders. Since the diamond was a symbol of courage and virility, wearing it was the exclusive privilege of men. There is no record of a woman wearing a diamond before the fifteenth century. Agnès Sorel (ca. 1422–50), mistress of Charles VII, was the first woman to depart from this tradition.

Though very few pieces of jewelry from the Middle Ages have been preserved, it is certain that diamonds were a rarity for a very long

Livre des symples medichines, a book about medicinal plants containing a section on stones and their properties: the *pierre de lin,* the Armenian stone, the devil stone, etc. French manuscript, 15th century. Bibliothèque Nationale, Paris. *Photo Bibliothèque Nationale.*

A ship bearing goods from India arriving at Hormuz. Miniature from Marco Polo's *Book of Marvels.* French manuscript, 14th century. Bibliothèque Nationale, Paris. *Photo Bibliothèque Nationale.*

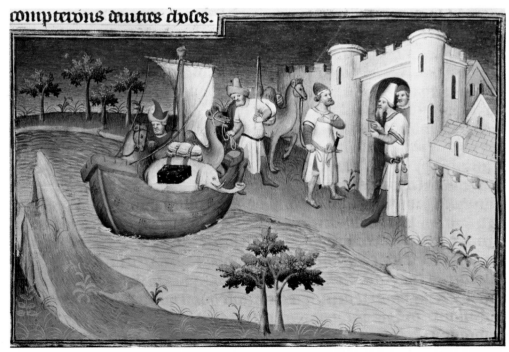

Henry IV of England.
Anonymous painting, about
1400. National Portrait
Gallery, London. *Photo
National Portrait Gallery.*

Catherine de' Medici with
the astrologer Nostradamus.
Lavis, 16th century.
Bibliothèque Nationale,
Paris. *Photo Lauros-
Giraudon, Paris.*

Henry IV of England done around 1400 and now in the National Portrait Gallery in London. The king's sleeves are adorned with two splendid octahedrons of a beautiful blue color. However, the artist almost certainly let his imagination run away with him—it is unlikely that the actual stones were as large as the diamonds he painted.

In the second half of the fifteenth century the situation began to change. Largely under the impetus of the house of the dukes of Burgundy, diamonds became more common among royalty. From then on, without completely eclipsing the other precious stones, diamonds became the most cherished items in the royal treasuries. François I (1494–1547) enjoyed wearing lavish ornaments, with the rarest gems always given the most prominent position. One of his most prized possessions was a necklace of eleven large table- or point-cut diamonds.

As more and more princes and nobles began to acquire diamonds, advancing them to the rank of the most precious stones, they gradually gave up the ancient magical beliefs connected with diamonds. Curiously, however, at other levels of society these beliefs not only persisted but generated extraordinary speculations. It was almost as if, because they could not possess this rare stone, people conferred on it supernatural abilities.

It is not surprising, then, that in the Middle Ages astrologers, who served the same function as the oracles and sibyls of ancient times, considered the protective and magical abilities of the diamond when they made their calculations. The diamond's influence was no longer limited to the battlefields and to the princes who fought on those fields. It was also something that helped protect people against sinister forces and events, something that could defeat specters and demons.

As almost no one possessed one, it was easy to credit the diamond with the most astonishing powers. It was believed capable of curing madness, of preventing natural disasters from affecting crops, of protecting homes from lightning and thunder. What simple peasant or farmer could have tested these powers? Other stories, equally incredible, have been found in the pharmacopoeia of the Middle Ages. The ancients had used precious stones in their formulas, including of course the diamond. In keeping with this tradition, medieval authors took some rather extravagant flights of fancy. St. Hildegarde (1098–1179), in her work *The Garden of Health,* advised that to stimulate the curative properties of the diamond one should hold it firmly in one hand while making the sign of the cross with the other hand. A variation of this technique consisted in holding the diamond pressed firmly against one's body in

time, and that only kings possessed them. Indeed, even very few kings were able to acquire them. The first documented evidence in Europe is found in an inventory of Charles V's furnishings, which dates from about 1379 and lists, among many other stones, *one* diamond. The first painting of a king in which it is possible to identify a diamond is a portrait of

order to warm it with the body's heat and thereby release its healing powers. But we should not be too quick to laugh at such prescriptions. A hundred years ago things were not much better. Jacobs and Chatrian reported in their book about diamonds published in 1880 that such beliefs were still alive less than half a century earlier. It was not uncommon for people to borrow from rich families precious stones mounted in rings in order to "apply them to afflicted parts of the body."

It was also thought at one time that diamond powder, taken orally, possessed curative abilities. Doctors in the Middle Ages debated this subject at great length and were of divided opinions. The proponents of such treatment, however, met with many notable failures. In the Renaissance, it was felt that diamond powder had pernicious properties, for by then it was known that it rarely cured and in fact often killed. Catherine de' Medici (1519–89) used it reportedly to eliminate certain people who were acting against her. Her enemies called the mixture she prepared "the powder of succession." Benvenuto Cellini related in his memoirs that his enemy, the powerful Pierluigi Farnese, son of Pope Paul III, tried to poison him by serving him a salad spiked with diamond-powder dressing. The strategy failed

because the man assigned to pulverize the diamond cleverly used simple powdered glass instead. (The famous goldsmith did not report how he was able to eat such a salad.)

Not until the second half of the seventeenth century was accurate information about the source of diamonds available in Europe. The information came from Jean-Baptiste Tavernier, who made six long voyages to Persia and India between 1631 and 1668, and whose reports about mining methods in India have already been mentioned.

Son of a map dealer in Antwerp, Tavernier had traveled through Europe and was able to speak almost every European language by the time he left for the Orient. A man of keen intelligence known for his precise observations, and an expert in precious stones, he was accustomed to negotiating with kings and princes and had a great reputation for honesty. Oriental rulers opened their doors to him, doors that had been closed to every other westerner. He brought back many stones from India, including twenty diamonds of 20–30 carats each. These stones fascinated the Sun King, Louis XIV. The Versailles court, for all its magnificence, had never seen such gems. Some of the diamonds Tavernier brought from India later became famous, such as the Great Blue dia-

Engravings from J.-B. Tavernier's *Six Voyages. . . .*, Paris, 1679 edition. Left: A portrait of Tavernier himself. Right: Some of the diamonds he saw in India. At the top right (no. 1) is the Great Mughal, which has never been seen since; below it (no. 3) is the Great Table, from which, according to some writers, the Darya-i-Nur, or Sea of Light, and the Nur-ul-Ain, or Light of the Eye, two of the most famous jewels of the Iranian treasury, were cut. Bibliothèque Nationale, Paris. *Photo Bibliothèque Nationale.*

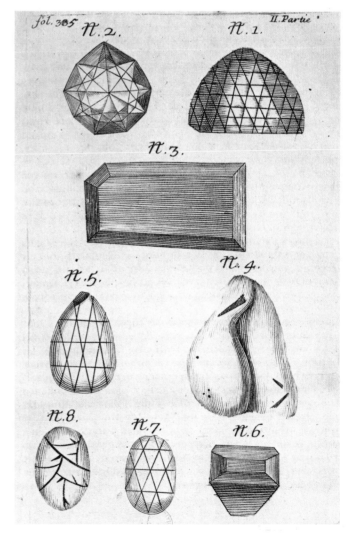

Map of the Kollur region in southeastern India, made about 1676–79 and based on Tavernier's data. The dotted line indicates the route followed by the famous French merchant, with Coulour on the Krishna River. Bibliothèque Nationale, Paris. *Photo Bibliothèque Nationale.*

mond, which he sold to Louis XIV.

Here we leave the realm of superstition and belief and enter that of history. Reality is sufficiently rich that it is unnecessary to modify it. The most renowned and precious stones in the world have been passionately desired by people for centuries. The wish to possess them has led to many adventures, some of them bloody, and changed the lives and fortunes of numerous individuals. If they still fascinate us today, it is largely because of their colorful and romantic past. Even the most beautiful and perfect gems will never equal in prestige stones like the Regent, the Orlov, the Hope, and the Koh-i-Noor.

The Koh-i-Noor

Of all the diamonds described by Tavernier, this is the most famous. Its name, which means "Mountain of Light," is itself enough to conjure up fantasies. According to legend, its origin is a fabulous one, dating from the times when the gods mingled with men.

One morning when the daughter of a poor elephant keeper was playing on the banks of the Yamuna, one of the seven sacred rivers of India, she discovered among the reeds a child clothed in golden armor. On his forehead he bore a dazzling "stone of light." The child, called Karna, was the son of Surya, the sun god, and of a princess of the reigning Kauravas family. When his identity was revealed, Karna was admitted to court and raised with the king's son. A dynastic conflict soon brought the

legitimate heirs to the throne into conflict with their cousins, the Pandavas, and the quarrel degenerated into a long and murderous war. Convinced that the diamond that adorned his forehead made him invincible, the young and fearless Karna challenged Arjuna, the most valiant of all the Pandavas, in face-to-face combat. Unfortunately, he failed to allow for the intervention of the gods, who took part in human quarrels. Divine influence in the person of Krishna himself tipped the scales of destiny in favor of the Pandavas. Karna was slain, and the "stone of light" rolled into the dust.

Soon afterward, a young woman discovered the stone by chance and brought it to Thanesar, the nearest village, where there was a temple to the god Siva. A Brahmin affixed the stone to the statue of the god, placing it in the middle of the forehead, in Siva's "third eye," the eye of illumination.

For centuries the "Mountain of Light" illuminated the temple and was jealously guarded by its priests. According to a story handed down through generations, a sacrilegious person once hid in the temple in order to try to steal the stone. He was discovered dead the next morning when the temple doors were opened. The Brahmins said, "He who possesses this diamond will possess the world. But he will also experience the worst misfortunes, for only a god or a woman can wear it with impunity." Such was Siva's decree and the origin of the evil power believed to be associated with the Koh-i-Noor. And it is quite

Muhammad Shah, dressed in a white *jama,* being received by Nadir Shah. He had hidden the Koh-i-Noor in his headdress, but the ruse was discovered, and during the course of the feast Nadir Shah obliged his adversary to exchange headgear. Thus he gained possession of the "Mountain of Light." About 1740. Musée Guimet, Paris. *Photo Hubert Josse, Paris.*

Opposite: Shah Jahan on
the Peacock Throne. Victoria
and Albert Museum, London.
*Photo Michael
Holford, London.*

Below left: The crown
of the queen mother of
England, with the Koh-i-Noor
at the center, preserved in
the Tower of London.
*By permission of
HMSO, London.*

Below right: The Koh-i-Noor
in its old form, in the Indian
style, and in its present form,
after recutting.
De Beers Archives.

true that, among those who attempted to possess it, a good number met with a tragic fate. Only when it came into the possession of a queen did the Koh-i-Noor lose its fearful power.

Historically, the Koh-i-Noor is mentioned for the first time in a chronicle of 1304 that lists it as the property of the rajah of Malwa. It was said to have come from the Visapour mines and reportedly weighed more than 600 carats when it was found. This is quite plausible, but we have no definite information on the subject and do not even know when or under what conditions the stone was cut for the first time. For two hundred years no further mention was made of it, until Babur, a descendant of Tamerlane who reigned over what is now Pakistan, invaded the Punjab, seized Lahore, and in 1526 founded the great Mughal dynasty on the ruins of the Delhi sultanate. As a sign of submission, the widow of Ibrahim Lodi, the sovereign vanquished and slain by Babur, offered the new ruler a number of gifts. One of these was the "Mountain of Light," whose price was estimated at "one day of the whole world's expenditure."

For two centuries, the fabulous stone remained in the possession of the Mughal emperors along with many other jewels, such as those that enhanced the splendor of court ceremonies during the reign of Shah Jahan (1628–58). But the power of Tamerlane's descendants at last declined. In 1738 the reigning emperor, Muhammad Shah, saw his country invaded by a general of Turkish origin, Nadir Shah, who had recently seized the Persian throne. On February 13, 1739, Muhammad Shah was defeated and Delhi was occupied. The loot was enormous and included the famous Peacock Throne of enameled gold adorned with several thousand precious stones, which the conqueror shipped to Isfahan, his capital. This throne is still part of the Iranian state treasure.

According to history, Nadir Shah did not find the Koh-i-Noor when he made his first search of the imperial treasures. He obtained it through the complicity of Udham Bai, Muhammad Shah's neglected first wife, who revealed to him that the emperor had carefully hidden the diamond in his turban. The crafty Nadir Shah devised a ruse that took advantage of the ancient custom of exchanging turbans as a sign of mutual respect. At a feast, he invited the defeated emperor to perform this ritual. Thus the splendid stone passed into the hands of Nadir Shah, who brought it back to Persia.

A tyrannical and ferocious ruler, Nadir Shah was assassinated in 1747 by four of his officers. Four kings succeeded to the throne in as many years. The fourth one, Seyd Muhammad, had his predecessor, Shah Rukh Mirza, blinded and tortured in order to gain possession of the Koh-i-Noor, but his victim resisted even the most excruciating punishments. In 1751 Ahmed Shah Durani, who had seized the throne of nearby Afghanistan, decided to intervene in Persian affairs to restore order. He released Shah Rukh, who presented him with the splendid jewel as a token of thanks. In 1793 the stone fell into the hands of Zaman Shah,

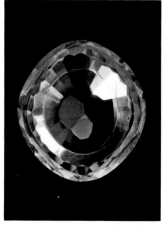

Ahmed Durani's grandson. Dethroned by his brother, the cruel Shuja-el-Mulk, and then cast into prison, Zaman refused to reveal what he had done with the Koh-i-Noor and pressed it into the mud wall of his prison cell, where it was discovered by chance some years later. Shuja wore it only a short time. Dethroned by his nephew Mahmud, he was sent into exile and found refuge with the Sikh ruler Ranjit Singh, the "Lion of the Punjab." Shuja had somehow managed to keep the Koh-i-Noor, but he was obliged by his host to "sell" it to him. When Ranjit Singh asked him the price of the stone, Shuja haughtily replied, "Take five strong men. Let the first throw a stone northward, the second eastward, the third southward, the fourth westward, and the fifth upward, into the air. Fill all the space thus outlined with gold and you will still not have achieved the value of the Mountain of Light."

Ranjit Singh had the stone mounted with two others in a bracelet of enameled gold, which is now in the Tower of London. Cut in the old Indian manner, the Koh-i-Noor weighed 186 carats. It remained in the Lahore treasury until 1849. In that year, following the defeat of the Sikhs in the Second Sikh War, the Punjab was annexed by Britain, at that time still represented by the powerful East India Company. When the treasury of Lahore was seized

The Great Exhibition in the Crystal Palace, London, in 1851, where the Koh-i-Noor was on public display. Bibliothèque Nationale, Paris. *Photo Hubert Josse, Paris.*

in lieu of the government's outstanding debts to the company, the Koh-i-Noor was presented to Queen Victoria (1837–1901). The "Mountain of Light" left Asia in 1850 and has never returned. In 1851 it was displayed in the Crystal Palace during the Great Exhibition in London, but many visitors found it disappointing. Its Indian cut did not do it justice, and it hardly deserved its name. So the queen decided to

have it recut, and a famous diamond cutter named Voorsanger, of the Coster Company, was summoned from Amsterdam. Prince Albert himself placed the gem on the 4-horsepower steam engine installed for this special purpose. In gaining the benefit of the brilliant oval cut it now has, the Koh-i-Noor was reduced from 186 to 108.93 carats.

The queen was superstitious and took seriously the old Indian legend that said that the Koh-i-Noor would bring misfortune to men who possessed it, though not to women. Consequently, she specified in her will that when the diamond was inherited by a male sovereign, it should be worn only by his wife. Her request has always been scrupulously respected. In 1937 the stone was placed in the crown of Queen Elizabeth, wife of George VI. Since then the queen mother alone has worn it on occasions of high ceremony.

Of all the precious stones among the British crown jewels in the Tower of London, the Koh-i-Noor is not the most exceptional—the Cullinan is much larger—but it is certainly the most famous, and the one with the longest history.

The Orlov

A very different story, one that borders on romance, is that of the ill fortune connected with the Orlov diamond before it reached the Russian court. The Orlov's history began in India in the mid-eighteenth century, during the Carnatic War. A French soldier who had deserted from Dupleix's army came to Srirangam in the state of Madras. He learned that a temple in the city housed a statue of the god Sri Ranga, whose eyes were made of diamonds. One "eye" was especially remarkable. Of very pure water and with a slightly blue-green tone that gained it the name "Sun of the Sea," it was cut in Indian rose fashion. Its form and dimensions were almost those of half a hen's egg, and it weighed 194.75 carats.

A mad but wonderful plan soon took shape in the fertile and unscrupulous mind of the French soldier. After a number of patient attempts, he finally succeeded in being accepted by the Brahmins as an adept in the temple's service. Alone one evening in the sanctuary, he easily removed the stone and at once set out for Madras, where he sold it for £2,000 (about £40,000 in today's currency) to an English sea captain. He in turn sold it to a Jew a few months later in London for £12,000, according to the statement of the next buyer, a Persian named Khojeh. (Khojeh never revealed how much he himself had paid for the stone.) Actually, Khojeh was a merchant, and his sole purpose was to resell the stone for the highest possible price. After trying unsuccessfully to

The Orlov, mounted on
the imperial scepter of Russia.
Diamond Collection of
the Soviet Union, Moscow.
*Photo Diamond Collection
of the Soviet Union.*

1773, chance brought him into contact with Count Grigori Grigorievich Orlov, the former favorite of Catherine the Great.

An impenitent old trooper, Orlov was not really in disgrace. But though the empress had always treated him with consideration, he had been replaced in her affections by Vassilichikov, who in turn was succeeded by Grigori Aleksandrovich Potemkin. Disappointed both in love and in ambition, Orlov had gone off like a sulky child, nursing the secret hope that the empress would change her mind and once again look upon him with favor. To rid himself of his melancholia, he left Russia and traveled through Europe, amazing everyone with his ostentatious way of life.

It was during this trip that Orlov met Khojeh in Amsterdam. When the prince discovered the existence of the splendid diamond, he had only one thought—to present it to the empress. A clever judge of human nature, Khojeh sensed in Orlov the ideal customer. His aim was to squeeze the Russian count for the highest price, and in this game of wits the Persian proved the stronger. He was gifted with almost infinite patience, and he finally succeeded in persuading Orlov to pay the astronomical price of 400,000 rubles for the "Sun of the Sea."

Orlov was now eager to return to Russia and place the splendid jewel at the feet of the em-

sell it in London, he left for Amsterdam, then an important diamond-cutting center.

He was equally unsuccessful with the rich foreigners passing through the Dutch city. Only the royal or imperial courts of Europe would be interested in such a diamond, and Khojeh failed to gain an introduction to such high circles. Desperate, he began to lose all hope of selling his diamond. Then, toward the end of

Count Grigori
Grigorievich Orlov. Once the
favorite of Catherine II, he
died in disgrace.

Ekaterina (Catherine)
Alexeievna leaving
the Peterhof on her way to
St. Petersburg, where she
was to be acknowledged as
empress, 1762. Painting by
J. C. Kestner, Peterhof.
Photo Hubert Josse, Paris.

press on St. Catherine's Day. But Orlov had not calculated well. Catherine accepted the diamond without batting an eye. The empress never wore the stone. Instead, she had it mounted in the imperial scepter. It is still there today and can be admired among the treasures in the Kremlin. As consolation for the dismissed lover, Orlov's name was bestowed on the stone. When he saw that Potemkin had definitely usurped his place in the affections of the empress, he became increasingly despondent and finally went mad. He was committed to an asylum, where he died in 1783.

The Regent

The Regent, the finest diamond in the French crown, is also the subject of legend. Found in 1698 in the Partial mine on the River Krishna, it was one of the last stones of great size discovered in India. According to Saint-Simon, a slave employed in the mines of the Great Mughal appropriated the diamond by concealing it in his private parts. A more commonly accepted, though hardly more credible, story was told by the London jeweler Edwin W. Streeter, who, in his book *Precious Stones and Gems* (1884), related the discovery of the future Regent and its purchase by Thomas Pitt, later known as "Diamond Pitt," governor of Fort St. George and Fort St. David in Madras. According to Streeter, the stone was found by a slave, who, in order to make off with it,

wounded himself in the ankle and concealed the stone beneath a bandage. He then offered the stone to the captain of an English vessel in exchange for his freedom. The captain took him on board, seized the diamond, and threw the slave into the sea. He sold the stone for £1,000 to Pitt, promptly spent the money in excesses of every kind, and, after committing murder, killed himself.

Pitt's version of how he acquired the stone—and we have no reason to disbelieve it—was rather different. He said that he bought the diamond from a merchant named Jaurchund for the sum of 48,000 pagodas (equivalent to about £19,200 in the Indian currency of the period). But this does not explain how such an important stone could have eluded the nizam of Hyderabad, the owner of the mines. If the stone was stolen, how was it missed in the very thorough search of the miners made every night? Was it the nizam himself who sold it, with Jaurchund acting as an intermediary? The mystery has never been solved.

In 1702 Thomas Pitt commissioned his son Robert to bring the diamond to Europe to have it cut. The cutting, which took almost two years, was entrusted to a London jeweler named Harris, and the result was a splendid stone weighing 140.5 carats. When Pitt himself returned to England, he was surprised to find extremely unfavorable rumors circulating about him. He was suspected of having gained possession of the diamond by rather questionable means. To prove his innocence, Pitt published a complete account of the transactions. Nevertheless, possession of the stone poisoned his life. It is said that he was constantly haunted by fear of losing it or of its being stolen. He would not show it even to his closest friends. He never slept two consecutive nights under the same roof, frequently assumed disguises, and told no one of his whereabouts. The stone, then known as the "Great Pitt" or the "Pitt diamond," was offered to every European sovereign, including Louis XIV. All declined because the asking price was too high.

In 1717 a buyer was found in the person of Philippe d'Orléans, regent of France. Pressed by John Law, the Scottish financier, and Saint-Simon, he decided after much hesitation to buy it for the crown for £135,000, the highest sum ever paid for a jewel up to that time. Including the interest charges that accumulated until the debt was finally paid off, the Regent—as it was now known—cost the royal treasury about £170,000. The duke of Orléans, whether he knew it or not, had nevertheless made an excellent business deal. In 1774, the diamond was valued at more than twice what had been paid for it, and by 1791, during the French Revolution, its value had doubled

again. As for Pitt, the profit he made from the transaction was about £100,000, which vastly augmented the fortune of a family that was to give the United Kingdom two of its greatest prime ministers (William Pitt the Elder, earl of Chatham, was "Diamond" Pitt's grandson).

When Louis XV was crowned at Reims in 1722, the young sovereign wore the finest

Napoleon Bonaparte as first consul. Painting by Jean-Antoine Gros. Detail: The Regent mounted on the consular sword. Musée de la Légion d'Honneur, Paris. *Photo Bulloz, Paris.*

Made in 1722 by Duflos and Rondé, the crown for the coronation of Louis XV bore two famous diamonds, the Sancy (at the top) and the Regent (above the band), both now replaced by imitations. The original stones and the crown itself are kept in the Apollo Gallery in the Louvre. *Photo Musées Nationaux, Paris.*

crown ever made. Covered with pearls, diamonds, and other precious stones, it was fashioned in the workshop of the crown jeweler, Rondé. The Sancy diamond surmounted the fleur-de-lis at the top, while the huge Regent was set above the frontal band. Since the jewels were to be used for other ceremonial occasions, when the coronation was over they were removed and glass copies were put in their place on the crown. The crown is now on exhibit in the Apollo Gallery in the Louvre. The Regent was subsequently incorporated in a variety of headdresses worn in turn by Louis XV and Queen Maria Leszczynska, and Louis XVI and Queen Marie Antoinette.

In 1791 the Regent, along with the other French crown jewels, left Versailles for Paris. A few months later, in September, 1792, soon after the monarchy was overthrown, all the crown jewels, including of course the Regent, disappeared when the Garde-Meuble National (the national furniture repository) was robbed. On the 20th of Frimaire of the year II of the Republic (December 10, 1793), the Convention was informed that the Regent had been found in the attic of a house in the allée des Veuves (now the avenue Montaigne) in Paris, hidden in a section of the timber framework.

The revolution proved expensive, and the republican government was compelled to borrow money. On the 25th of Thermidor of the year V (August 12, 1797), the Directory used the Regent and other diamonds as security to guarantee a loan of 4 million francs from the Berlin banker Treskow. A year later, when that sum had been repaid, the Regent was again used as a guarantee for a loan, this time from the Dutch banker Vanlerberghem. This unusually cautious man later related that his wife always kept the precious stone on her person, beneath her blouse; the stone displayed in his window was nothing more than a copy made of rock crystal. The two loans that the Regent made possible gave the revolutionary armies their large and well-equipped cavalry, whose exploits on the battlefield were to ensure Napoleon's victories. Napoleon, who regarded the stone as a talisman, reclaimed it in 1800 and had it inserted in the guard of his consular sword. When he was crowned emperor of the French in 1804, it was set in the pommel of his court sword. Eight years later, he had it mounted in the imperial sword.

In 1814, after Napoleon's abdication, the empress Marie-Louise took the Regent with her to Austria along with the other crown jewels. Her father, the emperor of Austria, forced her to return them to Louis XVIII, who kept them during the Hundred Days and brought them back to Paris in 1815 at the Second Restoration, following the final defeat of Napoleon at

The Hope, which was probably the "Great Blue" diamond of the French crown. In November, 1975, the Hope was removed from its setting and weighed. To everyone's surprise, it was found to weigh 45.52 carats and not 44.50, its assumed weight since 1830. Smithsonian Institution, Washington, D.C. *Photo Smithsonian Institution.*

Waterloo. The Regent was next found on the splendid crown that Charles X had made for his coronation in 1824. Under Napoleon III it appeared in a diadem, then in a Greek-style coronet for the empress Eugénie. Finally it was remounted as a pin so that the empress could wear it in her hair.

In 1887 the Third Republic decided to auction the French crown jewels, but the Regent was one of the few precious stones not affected by this foolish and disastrous decision. The regime doubtless believed that its true value was too high to find a buyer, and feared that it would discredit itself by selling the diamond at too low a price. It has since been placed in the Louvre, in the Apollo Gallery, where it is perhaps the most marvelous object among many historic treasures.

The Hope (The Great Blue Diamond)

If any stone deserves to be called "fascinating," it is surely the "Great Blue diamond," which today is more commonly known as the Hope diamond. Its subtle and changing color seems to hold memories of the most ancient past. Many writers have dwelt imaginatively on its legendary attributes, for in the realm of malediction the Hope diamond—in the minds of the credulous or of those with a taste for the sensational—outranks the tomb of Tutankhamen. How did this stone, known as the "cursed diamond," earn its reputation?

It is said that during one of his voyages to India, Tavernier tore a stone from a statue of the god Rama Sita. The theft, however, did not prove profitable for very long. Soon after selling the gem to Louis XIV, Tavernier was ruined and had to sail again for India, where he supposedly met an atrocious death. Some say he was devoured by dogs, others say by a tiger. The train of ill fortune continued. Louis XIV supposedly wore the diamond only once and died shortly afterward. According to another story, the stone belonged at one time to the finance minister Nicolas Fouquet, who was removed from office and imprisoned for life. Louis XIV offered the diamond to the marquise de Montespan, who subsequently fell out of favor with the king. Louis XV, who did not wear the gem, lent it to one of his mistresses, the countess du Barry, who was executed in 1793. Louis XVI did wear it, and then entrusted it to Marie Antoinette, who lent it to her friend, the princess de Lamballe. All of these unfortunates suffered the same fate during the revolution: the princess de Lamballe was guillotined during the September Massacre of 1792, and the king and queen went to the scaffold the following year.

Since the Hope diamond is probably part of the Great Blue diamond of the French crown, which was the stone brought back from India by Tavernier, it is not surprising that the Hope also has a bad reputation. However, the stories attached to the Great Blue diamond bear little relation to reality. The diamond was not stolen by Tavernier; it was discovered in a tributary of the Coleroon. Tavernier did not die in India

Below: Mademoiselle Ladrue, the Folies-Bergère dancer supposedly shot by her lover, a Russian prince said to have owned the Hope. Right: Sultan Abdul Hamid II, who owned the Hope from 1908 to 1911. The stone subsequently passed into the possession of Mrs. McLean (far right). *Photos Radio Times Hulton Picture Library, London.*

but in Moscow, after a common cold, at the advanced age of eighty-four. When he sold the Great Blue diamond to Louis XIV in 1669, Fouquet had already been in prison for seven years. As for the Sun King himself, although he was very generous to his mistresses and often allowed them to wear some of his personal jewels, he certainly had too great a regard for royal majesty to allow them to wear the crown jewels. Nor can the Great Blue diamond be connected by any stretch of the imagination with the death of Louis XIV. That durable monarch lived forty-six years after adding the Great Blue diamond to the royal treasury; his reign was one of the longest in history.

In 1672 the Great Blue diamond was entrusted to a man named Pitau, *diamantier du roi*, who cut it in the shape of a heart. He reduced it from 112 carats to 67.5 carats in the old measure (68.7 metric carats). As such, it was worn on several occasions by Louis XIV and Louis XV, set in a simple bezel. In 1749 it was placed with the ruby known as the Coast of Brittany in the pendant of the Order of the Golden Fleece. It remained there, untouched, until the revolution, when it was stolen, with the rest of the crown jewels, in 1792. Like all the orders of knighthood, that of the Golden Fleece could be worn only by men; no woman, not even the queen herself, was allowed to wear it. The Great Blue diamond can therefore be acquitted of the charge of causing the death of Marie Antoinette.

What then does explain the persistent legend of the maleficent diamond? Perhaps some confusion arose from the fact that Marie Antoinette did own a blue diamond, though it had neither the weight (it was only 5.45 carats) nor the color (it was light blue) of the stone of the French crown. Moreover, this stone was the queen's personal property, a family heirloom. In September, 1792, the Great Blue diamond was stolen from the Garde-Meuble National, and along with the Coast of Brittany ruby it fell into the hands of a certain Cadet-Guillot, who fled to London with his booty. The diamond was then recut and it is probable that the Hope, weighing 44.5 carats, came from it. It is sometimes said, though it has never been proven, that after the Great Blue diamond was recut it came into the possession of the queen of Spain, Maria Luisa. Others claim that it found its way into the duke of Brunswick's collection. Such claims show much imagination.

The fact remains that in 1830, a splendid blue diamond weighing 44.5 carats—with no indication of origin—was put up for auction in London. It was purchased for £18,000 by the banker Henry Philip Hope, for whom it is now named. Some time afterward all sorts of dire stories began to circulate: the Hopes died in

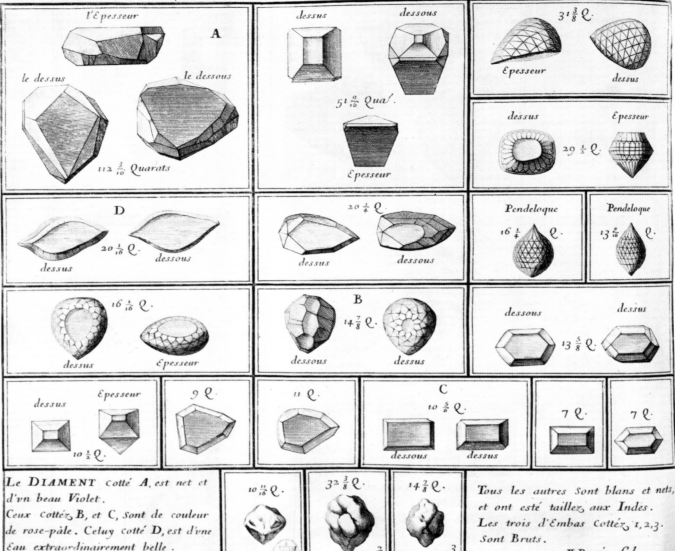

REPRESENTATION de Vingt des plus beaux DIAMENS choisis entre tous ceux que le Sᵗ. I.B. Tauernier a Vendus au ROY, a Son dernier retour des Indes, qui a esté le 6ᵉ. Decembre 1668. ou il a fait six Voyages par terre, Et en cette consideration, et des Seruices que ledit Tauernier a rendus a l'Estat, Sa Majesté la honnoré de la Qualité de Noble.

A plate from the *Six Voyages . . .* of J.-B. Tavernier, showing the twenty diamonds the author sold to Louis XIV in 1669, after his last journey to India. Paris, 1676 edition. Bibliothèque Nationale, Paris. *Photo Hubert Josse, Paris.*

poverty; a Russian prince acquired the stone and that same evening shot his mistress, Mademoiselle Ladrue, a dancer at the Folies-Bergère. The diamond was then acquired by the sultan Abdul Hamid II; he offered it to his favorite, Zobeida, and later killed her. The American millionaire Edward B. McLean bought it and disappeared with the *Titanic*. His granddaughter committed suicide after wearing the diamond, and his wife, after losing her fortune, also took her own life. Any disaster that occurred to anyone even remotely connected with the Hope was immediately blamed on the famous stone.

In reality, the diamond remained in the possession of the Hope family until 1908. In order to clear his considerable debts, Lord Hope (as he had become) sold it to the "Red Sultan," who was not the kind of man to assassinate his favorite. He was deposed in 1909 and in 1911 sold the diamond to the famous Parisian jeweler Pierre Cartier. Soon afterward, the American press magnate Edward B. McLean, who

owned the Washington *Post*, bought the stone and gave it to his wife. Mrs. McLean, far from being anxious about owning the diamond, exclaimed on receiving the gift, "It's a good-luck charm because of the word 'Hope.'" She wore it until her death in 1947. Two years later the gem was purchased for $179,920 by the well-known American jeweler and diamond dealer Harry Winston. He kept it for ten years, then decided to present it to the Smithsonian Institution in Washington, D.C., which still owns it today. This royal gift was made without a stir. On November 8, 1958, the Smithsonian received by parcel post a small package bearing $2.44 in postage stamps and insured for the modest sum of $151. It contained the Hope. Rather more rigorous precautions are taken with it today. It has been placed in a special display case made of bulletproof glass, where it has been admired by hundreds of thousands of visitors. It has killed no one. The "cursed stone of the kings of France" will henceforth have great difficulty in claiming new "victims."

The Brazilian Era: 1730–1870

In the eighteenth century a new era began for the diamond. Despite various manipulations of production by the Indian princes, the flow of the most precious stones on the European market continued uninterrupted. Supply was so well adapted to demand that an attempt was even made to set the price of diamonds by a slide rule. But then the trade began to decline—not because the Indian sources of supply were being depleted, but because of an unexpected event that permanently changed the course of history: the chance discovery of diamond deposits in Brazil.

It is impossible to verify the legends surrounding the discovery of the first Brazilian diamonds. Brazil and India, though thousands of miles apart, had one thing in common—the presence of the Portuguese. It seems that a certain Sebastino Leme do Prado, who had previously lived in India, was the first to discover—or, more precisely, to identify—the famous stones in Brazil. This occurred in 1725, not far from the Rio dos Marinhos, in the present province of Minas Gerais. The crystalline stones were being used as chips in card games by gold prospectors; apparently the prospectors had found many others, but they kept only the most brilliant. Leme do Prado immediately recognized the "chips" as diamonds.

Brought to Lisbon two years later by Bernardino da Fonseca Lobo, who was later rewarded with the post of captain general of Villa do Principe, the stones were at once shipped to Amsterdam to be appraised. The discovery was made public by the royal house of Portugal in 1729 on the basis of a circumstantiated report by the viceroy Loreço d'Almeida. By a decree of February 8, 1730, the diamond-yielding terrains were declared crown property. A special district was immediately created, the Serro do Frio ("Cold Mountain"), and troops were sent to guard it. That same year "diamond washers" founded the colony of Tejuco, which a century later became Diamantina.

The Principal Diamond Fields

When the wealth of the Tejuco deposits was realized, random searching began over the whole area. At that time the Minas Gerais was for the most part unexplored, and there were practically no means of communication. During the dry season from May to September, however, prospectors were able to go up the riverbed to begin searching, and they soon realized that the deposits extended well beyond the Serro do Frio.

It is not possible to establish a tidy chronological record of early events, which occurred rather rapidly. A few random incidents must suffice to indicate general trends. The field of Abaete, east of Minas Gerais and some 125 miles (200 km) from Tejuco, is mentioned as early as the mid-eighteenth century as the most productive. The site soon became famous and witnessed feverish days. It was here, in 1764 (or possibly 1797), that a group of outlaws who had been transported to a penal colony discovered a 1,680-carat stone subsequently known as the Braganza and long considered the largest diamond ever found. Even after cutting, it would have been twice the size of the Grand Mughal, then the largest stone known. Contrary to long-accepted stories, the Braganza never belonged to the Portuguese crown. For lack of irrefutable proof, it seems safest to conclude that this stone was not a diamond, but probably a topaz or a sapphire. Still in the Minas Gerais, but in the extreme northeast, the deposits of Grão Moghol in the Ita-

A slave dealer's premises in the Rua do Val Longo, Rio de Janeiro. Engraving by J.-B. Debret, a French artist who lived in Brazil from 1816 to 1831. Bibliothèque Nationale, Paris. *Photo Hubert Josse, Paris.*

Map of the diamondiferous region of the Jequitinhonha River and its tributaries. 1776. *Army Archives, Rio de Janeiro.*

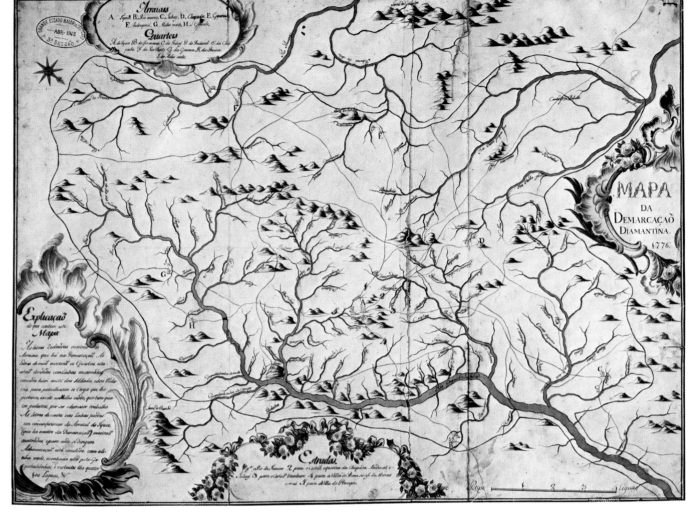

The estate of Baron de Serro during the colonial period, in the Diamantina region, Minas Gerais. *Photo Claudio Larangeira, Rio de Janeiro.*

cambirucu Valley were opened between 1771 and 1781. Despite their impressive name, they could not rival those of "Giquitigrogna" (Jequitinhonha), far more interesting according to a 1792 account by Andrada.

In the nineteenth century, the "Chapada Diamantina" deposits in the Bahia region, east of the deep valley of the Rio São Francisco, were worked between 1830 and 1840. Their importance was due chiefly to the large deposits of carbonados found there. The name "carbonado" is used to describe a thick, porous aggregate of very small gray or black diamonds. They look rather like coke and are as hard as pure diamonds. The weight of these stones, which are generally rounded in form, ranges between 30 and 40 carats, but some have been found weighing more than 1,000 carats, and one discovered in 1895 weighed 3,078 carats. They have a purely industrial use today, and are the toughest form of industrial diamonds; they were in great demand in the period immediately after the First World War, when their price rose very high.

The discovery in the Minas Gerais, west of Coromandel, of the diamond fields of the Rio Bagagem, a tributary of the Paranaiba, also dates from the mid-nineteenth century. Here a black slave earned not only his freedom but

a pension for life after finding, in 1853, the first large Brazilian diamond whose history has been fully authenticated. Called the Estrela do Sul ("Star of the South"), it weighed in its rough state 261.88 carats. A superb, pellucid stone with bluish reflections, it was cut by Coster of Amsterdam into an oval diamond of 128.8 carats, then sold to an Indian maharajah after being shown at the London Exhibition of 1862. In 1857 an even purer stone was extracted from the same region, its rough weight 119.5 carats. It is known as the Dresden, after the London merchant who bought it and had it cut in Amsterdam into a pear-shaped diamond weighing 76.5 carats. Minas Gerais was not the only part of Brazil to be worked as early as the colonial period. Areas as difficult to reach as those of Mato Grosso were also searched, and as early as the close of the eighteenth century, mining sites such as those northeast of Cuiabà were mentioned.

The importance of the Brazilian discoveries is reflected in the fact that within five years, from 1730 to 1735, the world diamond market exploded. Prices dropped by three-quarters. This dramatic fall can be partly explained by the sudden abundance of diamonds reaching Europe, but an even more important factor was the belief that a source of almost unlimited wealth had been discovered in South America and that it could be easily exploited.

Working Methods

As in India, the diamond deposits in Brazil are of secondary origin. Particularly in Minas Gerais, they can be divided into three types: high-level (plateau) deposits, low-level (terrace) deposits, and fluvial (river) deposits. Situated on the high plateaus, from 4,000 to 5,000 feet (1,200–1,500 m) above sea level, the high-level deposits were formed during a relatively recent geological period. These deposits are the result of the erosion of primary sources of diamondiferous kimberlite, the existence of which, though long suspected, was discovered by a team of French and Brazilian geologists only in 1968. Through the forces of erosion, these high-level sources eventually generated the two other types of deposit. The low-level or terraced deposits mark the ancient river courses, before they had cut a deep passage through the rock. The various reshaping processes that all these sedimentary formations have undergone explains not only their dispersion over vast areas but also the relatively low concentration of diamonds: most of the mines had a fairly brief existence, and the area was quickly worked out.

Brazilian miners soon realized that a certain type of gravel is associated with each type of deposit. *Gorgulho,* or eluvial plateau gravel, overlies conglomerates, and *cascalho,* or alluvial gravel, occurs both on the terraces (*gupiaras*) and on the present riverbeds. Working methods were rather primitive and essentially much the same as those used in India. Once the gravel was reached, it was washed in a large wooden receptacle known as a *batea* until nothing remained in the bottom except a concentrate of the heaviest minerals. The final separation of the diamonds was of course done by hand. The slaves who labored in the *lavras* (work sites) of the Brazilian fields sometimes found gold as well as diamonds.

Contemporary engravings show that by the end of the eighteenth century river courses were already being diverted in order to leave the beds dry and allow easier extraction of the *cascalho.* Because the terrain was generally uneven, it was often impossible to dig a canal to divert the river, so other methods had to be employed. A common practice was to build a stone dam in the riverbed. A temporary passage was created for the water to flow through until a wooden conduit supported by planks and bracing struts had been constructed on the banks. When the water level was sufficiently high, the overflow was diverted into the conduit. From then on the men had to work quickly. Using caissons or pumps driven by a water wheel, they drained the river and collected as much *cascalho* as possible. This was transported to a safe place, away from the rising river water, where it could be washed. The gravel was shifted by thousands of black slaves, who loaded it into large wooden containers that they carried on their heads. During the dry season the water was comparatively easy to control, but a storm could sweep away in an instant all the ingenious constructions. In their book *Le Diamant* (1880), Henri Jacobs and Nicolas Chatrian reproduced a picture of one of these works of art blocking the flow of the Ribeirão do Inferno. Their description agrees in every detail with one given by John Mawe seventy years earlier, in his *Travels in the Interior of Brazil* (1809–10), of a similar installation on the Jequitinhonha. According to the early accounts, on one or two occasions dam, conduit, and tackle were engulfed by floods.

It is quite easy to imagine the discouragement and despair felt by the diggers when the gravel collected after two or three months proved sterile. The greatest luck a miner could have was to find one of the pot-shaped cavities called *caldeirões,* which the swirling water and the wearing action of stones had hewn into the rock. Some, as large as caves, were real diamond traps. The *caldeirões* of the Ribeirão do Inferno and of the Jequitinhonha were particularly famous in the mid-nineteenth century, and fantastic stories were told about them.

Above: Slave irons. Museum of Diamantina. *Photo Jacques Legrand.*

Right: Slaves breaking up *cascalho,* guarded by overseers armed with whips. Watercolor from an anonymous manuscript, late 18th century. National Library, Rio de Janeiro. *Photo Marcel Gautherot, Rio de Janeiro.*

Washing gravel under the close supervision of the administration's inspectors. The day's finds were placed in the two baskets hanging from the crossbeams. Watercolor from an anonymous manuscript, late 18th century. National Library, Rio de Janeiro. *Photo Marcel Gautherot, Rio de Janeiro.*

Diverting the waters of the Jequitinhonha into a canal in order to recover *cascalho* from the drained section of the river. Watercolor by John Mawe, from his *Travels in the Interior of Brazil*, London, 1816. Bibliothèque Nationale, Paris. *Photo Hubert Josse, Paris.*

A box of weights used in 19th-century Brazil for weighing diamonds and other precious stones. Museum of Diamantina. *Photo Guy Philippart de Foy, Brussels.*

M. Gorceix, who at the close of the nineteenth century was director of the Mining School in Brazil, related that one of these pots in the Ribeirão do Inferno near Itaipaba had furnished more than 8,000 carats. Although such good fortune has become increasingly rare, stories of these early finds are still told today and are largely responsible for creating and per-petuating the myth of the overnight fortune that inspires every Brazilian *garimpeiro* (independent prospector).

Riverbeds were not the only sites where diamonds were found. Avidity eventually led the miners to search the high plateaus as well as the deep mountain passes, and in 1824, in a deserted region north of Diamantina, "a deposit was discovered where all a miner had to do was to tear up the grass to find diamonds." In the second edition of their book (1883), Jacobs and Chatrian state that a similar phenomenon had occurred the previous year in the Salobro Forest, two days' journey from Canavieiras and not far from the banks of the Rio Pardo, where alluvial terrain less than 20 inches (50 cm) deep proved extraordinarily rich. The rush began immediately, and in less than a year four thousand miners arrived from every diamond district in Brazil, planted their huts in the heart of the coconut forest, and, ignoring the unhealthy climate, began to search the soil with feverish zeal.

But these are rare examples. In most cases the task of extraction is not at all easy. Mountains of earth have to be overturned before the promising *gorgulho* is reached. In the early days the chief problem was the water supply, which was often far from the work site. When there was no water available at all, the only thing the miners could do was stack the soil that had been searched on sloping ground and wait for the rain to wash it. A stepped channel like a staircase prevented the precious material from being carried off by the water and lost. Although less rich than river *cascalho*, the alluvial gravel eventually required the mobilization of large numbers of workers. However, until 1888 slavery was common in Brazil, so labor posed no real problem. One matter that did cause concern was theft, never very difficult in the prevailing circumstances, especially when the ground was washed.

Masters and Slaves

Mawe relates how, for example, washing was done at Mandanga. Here an open-sided, rectangular building about 130 feet long and 45 feet wide (40 × 14 m) was specially constructed. Water ran along a plank-lined channel through the middle of the building. The building was divided into twenty compartments, each of which was linked to the central watercourse and controlled by a slave who washed the gravel with a short-handled rake. Opposite each compartment stood a stool for an administrative inspection officer. The seats were deliberately made without arms or backs to keep the surveillance officer alert. If a man found a diamond he clapped his hands and,

Rotating cylinder for washing *cascalho*. From John Mawe, *Travels in the Interior of Brazil*, London, 1816.

Bottom: Barrage on the Ribeirão do Inferno in the Diamantina region. From Jacobs and Chatrian, *Le Diamant*, Paris, 1880.

holding the stone between his thumb and index finger, gave it to the inspector, who placed it in a pan half full of water suspended in the center of the building. All diamonds found during the day were collected in this container, which was brought each evening to the principal officer commissioned to count the diamonds and keep a register. When a man was fortunate enough to find an "octavo," a diamond weighing 17.5 carats, a garland of flowers was placed on his head and he was led in procession to the administrators, who gave him his freedom, new clothes, and granted him the right to continue working for a salary. Anyone who discovered a stone weighing from 8 to 10 carats received a suit, two shirts, a hat, and a fine knife. No doubt there were commensurate (though unrecorded) rewards for finding stones between 10 and 17.5 carats.

If rewards were rare, punishment was more frequent, and rather less original. It ranged from the traditional bastinado in public to imprisonment, the yoke, and branding with a red-hot iron. The Diamantina Museum contains a horrifying assortment of instruments of torture, leaving not the slightest doubt of the authorities' malevolent imagination during this period. Yet neither fear of punishment nor the church's threat of eternal damnation was able to prevent miners from stealing: slaves and unscrupulous miners used every means available to hide their loot from the eyes of the authorities. In doing so, they only imitated their masters or copied the example of those who had been granted concessions to "farm" the mining areas. One of these, Francisco Fernandès de Olivieira, was ordered in the late 1760's to restore an enormous sum to the royal Portuguese treasury. But this amount represented only 5 percent of his profits.

All this of course took place long ago, but small towns like Serro (formerly Villa do Principe) and Diamantina are still feeling the effects, and their lively past is still discernible under their present torpor. Indifferent to the outside world, patrician families guard their secrets behind shuttered balconies.

Among the countless legends associated with these sites, the most famous is that of Chica da Silva, a mulatto woman who bewitched the young and wealthy João Fernandès da Oliveira. As royal administrator for the entire mining region, answerable directly to the king, Oliveira was a leading member of the local Portuguese society. Francisca da Silva, known as Chica, was the daughter of a Portuguese father, Antonio Caetano da Sá, and an African mother named Maria da Costa. A former slave of Francisco da Silva Oliveira, she had been freed by her master and was already the mother of two children when she met her future lover.

The streets of Diamantina are still paved with their original cobbles, while in the old houses of patrician families, people dream of times gone by, safe from prying eyes in the semidarkness of a *moucharaby* (screened balcony). *Photos Guy Philippart de Foy, Brussels.*

hooped dresses, embarking in brilliantly illuminated gondolas that followed gently in the wake of the regal vessel sailing on the calm waters of the lake. As one might guess, such extravagance scarcely pleased the local nobility, though they never hesitated to participate in the festivities. Covered with gold and diamonds, Chica behaved like a royal tyrant, occupying the place of honor in a society that was not accustomed to assigning such a position to a half-caste. These Brazilian "Thousand and One Nights" occurred between about 1761 and 1771, until João Fernandès was suddenly recalled to Lisbon to explain his actions to the king. His excesses were forgiven, but he was not allowed to return to Tejuco.

Nothing remains of Chica's ship nor of her gorgeous palace except one object: her four-poster bed is now on display in the Diamantina Museum, a building that itself was once the residence of João Fernandès.

Facts and Figures

Alongside legal production under Portuguese license, clandestine or illegal production soon developed. It is difficult to know the exact extent of such activity, but contemporary

She has been described as having had thick lips, a pug nose, and a hugely fat body. Supposedly she was dull-witted to boot. This portrait is far too gross to be credible, and João Fernandès's reputation as an honest and noble lord has been so well established that it seems impossible to credit him with so little judgment, no matter how blinded he may have been by passion. However, everyone agrees that João was utterly dominated by Chica and submitted to every one of her whims.

And what whims they were! He built for her a vast and splendid dwelling in the heart of the country, surrounded by orchards, fountains, and waterfalls. The interior was furnished in a manner worthy of the most aristocratic residence and included a chapel and a theater— the only one of its kind authorized—where fashionable plays were performed. Such an enterprise would have ruined most men, but not João Fernandès—after all, was he not the administrator of gold and diamond mining?

Yet all this was not enough to satisfy Chica. Though she had been born far from the sea, she had inherited the blood of Portuguese sailors and dreamed of sailing across the water. Her mere wish was enough. Her slave—for their roles were now reversed—had an artificial lake made in the park and installed in it a vessel large enough to hold eight people; it was a copy of a genuine seagoing ship. On certain evenings Chica held sumptuous receptions, with the guests, in powdered wigs and

A black "queen" and her attendants: a legendary representation of Chica da Silva? Watercolor, late 18th century. National Library, Rio de Janeiro. *Photo Marcel Gautherot, Rio de Janeiro.*

evidence and cross-checking of various sources gives reason to believe that it was considerable. In a country as huge as Brazil, what army could have prevented unauthorized access to the diamond fields? These areas, scattered and hard to locate, attracted outlaws and adventurers from every corner of the country. The result was a proliferation of an individual, clandestine type of miner, who was constantly prepared to disappear into the landscape: this was the *garimpeiro*, he who flees at the approach of soldiers and seeks shelter in the mountains. The word remains, though today, of course, the situation is different.

Despite the difficulties imposed by unofficial production, this is nevertheless the first period in the history of the diamond for which we possess production figures, thanks to the records kept by the Portuguese government until 1822. Although the value of these records is limited because of illegal exports, we can deduce that production was uninterrupted from 1730 onward and that it quadrupled the diamond supply in the European markets. The figures below are the average *annual* production for the periods indicated.

1730–1740:	20,000 carats
1741–1772:	52,000 carats
1773–1806:	27,000 carats
1807–1822:	12,000 carats

In 1844, after the discovery of the Cincorá deposits in the state of Bahia, there was a sharp increase in production. In 1850, and again in 1851, as many as 300,000 carats were mined, but in 1852 the figure fell to 130,000. From then until 1861 annual production remained relatively stable at about 190,000 carats. Producing such quantities, Brazil imposed new criteria on the world diamond market.

The Portuguese Diamond Policy

When in 1493 Pope Alexander VI settled the rivalry between Spain and Portugal in the recently discovered New World by dividing the world into spheres of interest for each of the two great Christian nations, his decree automatically made the Portuguese crown the future proprietor of diamond mines in Brazil. The purpose of royal power was primarily to assure its own sources of income; maintaining price stability was at best a secondary consideration. But when it proclaimed that diamond working should be entirely unrestricted, the government apparently underestimated the importance of the deposits. In order to rectify this error of judgment, a registration fee was introduced, along with a tax for each slave or laborer employed. The tax, first set at 5,000 reis, was soon reduced to 4,000 reis. Moreover, the crown reserved for itself the monopoly on transport; consequently, diamonds could be exported to Europe only in royal vessels, and the shipping charge was fixed at 1 percent of the value of the stones being transported. These measures might have worked well enough in

A detachment of soldiers led by an officer accompanying a convoy from Minas Gerais. J.-B. Debret, *Croquis du Brésil*, 1816–31. Bibliothèque Nationale, Paris.
Photo Hubert Josse, Paris.

a country where good communications would have made it possible to exercise a fair degree of control. But in Brazil, where communications were practically nonexistent, the laws were in large part responsible for clandestine mining and for the illegal trade in diamonds, which the government was unable to prevent. There was never really any question of setting up a rational and systematic method of processing the diamond resources, so any attempt to organize the trade and to control fluctuations was inevitably bound to fail. In the long run, it was the desire to ensure a satisfactory level of government revenue that prevailed.

From Individual Work to State Enterprise. In time, however, revenue proved unsatisfactory compared with the quantity of diamonds produced, and the prices in the markets in Lisbon, Antwerp, Amsterdam, and London fell by three-quarters from their previous level. In 1775 a decision was made to forbid individual working in favor of farming out the business to large enterprises. In exchange for an annual rent of 138 contos reis, a company was granted the right to work all the diamond deposits in a given area. The first crown partners were probably the firm of the Bretschneider brothers of Amsterdam and the bank of Hope and Company, which specialized in large state loans.

These rent contracts can be regarded as one of the first European attempts to restrict production in order to maintain a stable market and prices. The farmers agreed not to employ more than six hundred slaves. Actually, this restriction failed to achieve the desired aim. Because the rent was extremely high, the enterprises launched themselves into intensive production, which made it impossible to harmonize supply and demand in the market. Not until 1830, following a rise in demand, did the rough diamond again attain the price it had

reached in 1700. Under such conditions, it was of little importance that during the thirty-six years of rent collection (1735–71) more than 50,000 carats per year were produced.

According to the Portuguese crown, the rent of 138 contos should have corresponded to the sale price of rough diamonds, less operating expenses. Certain farmers who gained tremendous fortunes through fraudulent means were brought to court and forced to restore at least part of their profits. Francisco Fernandès de Oliviera, mentioned earlier, was one of these. Others, while showing more respect for the rules, nevertheless succeeded in managing very fruitful operations. The Bretschneider brothers, for example, managed to achieve annual earnings of more than 2 million gold francs. On the advice of his chief minister, the marquis de Pombal, the king refused to renew these rent contracts in 1772, and a state enterprise was created to take over the working of all gold and diamond mines. This system was still functioning in 1822, when Brazil gained its independence from Portugal.

There had always been some doubt as to how profitable the new system would be, and it appears that the results were rather disappointing. The officials in charge lacked experience, and honest bureaucrats were at a disadvantage when faced with skillful and accomplished scoundrels. Despite the strict measures taken by the government, trade by *garimpeiros* and later by *feitores* (illegal diamond dealers) reached considerable proportions. Unencumbered by expensive overhead and administrative costs, they were always in a position to do the best business.

From State Enterprise to Liberalism. It is generally believed that official production under the system of state enterprise never brought in more than 50,000 gold francs per year, which was considered a disastrously low return when compared with the profits formerly made from Indian diamonds. State monopoly was fought not only in the name of efficiency but also as a matter of political principle. Times had changed: the Brazilian bourgeoisie had political ambitions and, proud of their recently acquired independence, wanted to see liberalism prevail in every field. In 1830, under pressure from the National Assembly, King Pedro I opened the mines to private enterprise and allowed the diamond lands to be bought at public auctions. A law determined the size of the plots to be granted: they were not to be less than 345 square feet (32 sq m) nor more than 2,154 square feet (200 sq m) in area, and tax was payable according to the size of the plot. But the new regulations did not lead to the anticipated advantages and were no more successful than the previous system in ending illegal trade. Eighteen years later, a new law required that miners have a regular license valid for only four years: the fee was considerably reduced, but another imposition was introduced in the form of an export tax equivalent to .5 percent of the value of the stones. The results, however, were scarcely more encouraging. Part of the trouble lay in the poor state of communications, which had not improved very much since the early eighteenth century: there was no railway linking Diamantina with the rest of the country until 1909. Despite the considerable improvements in communications since then, the situation has not really changed. Illegal trade still seems to

have a profitable future. It is estimated that Brazil today produces more than 300,000 carats per year, but that less than one-third of that quantity is officially declared.

Brazil and the Diamond Trade

In the history of the diamond, the Brazilian episode offers a good example of what happens when a product is discussed too much as soon as it hits the market. The inevitable result is that the product's value drops. At the beginning, there were some influential rumors that the new diamonds were false—imitations only. This malicious propaganda spread rapidly throughout Europe. Did it originate in Amsterdam or in London? That question can be discussed interminably. The probability is that the rumors originated in the country that controlled the international diamond trade around 1730. In that case the accusing finger points to London.

While the blame cannot be assigned with certainty, what is certain is the extraordinary effect of this propaganda. As stated above, the price of rough diamonds virtually collapsed within ten years. To combat this development, the Portuguese conceived the idea of shipping a large quantity of Brazilian diamonds to India, where they could be sold from Portuguese Goa, thus leading people to believe they had originated in India. It appears that the Portuguese were guilty of another piece of dishonesty: a certain number of rough diamonds destined to be sold in Lisbon were first shipped

The coronation of Pedro I, emperor of Brazil, in Rio de Janeiro, December 1, 1822. Engraving by J.-B. Debret. Bibliothèque Nationale, Paris. *Photo Hubert Josse, Paris.*

to Venice for preliminary cutting, as had happened in earlier times with Indian diamonds. This subterfuge could not work for long, and when rough diamonds were finally put up for sale in Lisbon, everyone was aware that they came from Brazil. Then another rumor spread: it was said that these stones were the fruit of trade, not of mines. Even an expert as distinguished as David Jeffries, the author of a respected *Treatise on Diamonds and Pearls* published in 1756, could not make up his mind on the subject. "The commander of the fort of St. George told me," he wrote, "that, for a long time, the Brazilians had been secretly carrying on a diamond trade with the Indians of Goa; he knew they had many, but that they were not handsome and that they bought them for a low price."

The appearance of unusual quantities of diamonds on the Lisbon market could not fail to create genuine uneasiness. As a result of this insecurity, buyers abstained from trade. Furthermore, because Portuguese interests had been closely linked with England since the middle of the eighteenth century, there was equal reticence on the London market. According to David Jeffries, there were many, even among the most important London merchants, who believed that before long diamonds would become as common as glass beads. So convinced were they on this point that most of them refused to buy, no matter what the price was. Thus in Lisbon, then in London, the price of rough diamonds fell by 75 percent in a short time. Yet this situation had no influence on the price of cut diamonds.

The "Democratization" of Luxury. Since 1670 the market in cut diamonds had been stable. The average price of a fine 1-carat diamond ranged from 200 to 225 gold francs, and this price remained unchanged until about 1830. Even the revolutionary events of 1789–92 had no effect on prices. Around 1860, the price rose to between 300 and 320 gold francs, and in 1867 the price was 529 gold francs. This price rise is all the more remarkable since in 1844–45 rich deposits were discovered in the province of Bahia, which yielded an average production of more than 250,000 carats a year, increasing the supply by a factor of 22. Although all available production was immediately marketed in Europe, this new supply had only a very slight effect on the price of rough diamonds, and cut diamonds were affected even less. The dramatic expansion in the demand for cut diamonds was largely a consequence of social developments, the rise of modern capitalism, and, especially in France and England, the emergence of a prosperous middle class with new assets and responsibilities: manufacturers and small industrialists, administrators and engineers, merchants and civil servants were now acquiring a certain amount of wealth. This was the age of the democratization of luxury, when the popularity of diamond jewelry began.

The Creation of Factories. In its early days diamond working was a handicraft industry, often practiced in the workers' homes. In the nineteenth century, with the arrival of the factory era, the industry changed. In the past, women had always worked the steel grinding wheels for the stones. They were replaced in this hard and thankless task in 1822, when horse power was introduced in Amsterdam, and new workshops were set up in which diamond cutters shared their quarters with the animals. At least four such "factories" were built before 1832, though workers and animals were soon separated. In 1840 steam power was first used for diamond cutting. In the handicraft stage of the industry only a very small number of grinding wheels were used in each workshop, but the new factories had hundreds,

Diamond cutting in the late 17th century, a family industry. Engraving by J. Luyken, 1694.

Model of a steam-powered diamond-cutting factory, soon after 1840. Musée du Diamant, Antwerp. *Photo Michel Plassart, Paris.*

Jewel design by Pouget *fils*, Paris, 1762. Bibliothèque Nationale, Paris. *Photo Hubert Josse, Paris.*

all of them powered by a central steam engine. The year 1845 saw the foundation of the famous Diamantslijperij Maatschappij, which, because of its technical capacity and its financial resources, secured control in less than five years of virtually all the Amsterdam diamond-cutting establishments and owned 520 of the 560 grinding wheels in the city. Not all the workshops, however, were operated by the Diamantslijperij Maatschappij; some were leased. Thus a new type of organization was developed, the *Molenhuur,* or "wheel rental." When business flourished the shops were controlled by the Maatschappij; when there was a slump, the rental system was preferred. Actually, this type of factory was viable only after 1844, when diamonds began to arrive in more massive quantities from Bahia. The Diamantslijperij Maatschappij succeeded in maintaining its position, which amounted to a virtual monopoly, until 1870.

An Irremediable Decline? As things turned out, the prosperity of the Amsterdam diamond-cutting shops lasted for only a short period. After the sudden spurt provided by the Bahia deposits, Brazilian production declined steadily. From 200,000 carats annually between 1851 and 1856, it dropped to 180,000 during the following six years, and continued to fall thereafter. The reason was not that the Brazilian deposits had been totally used up but that only the upper layers were being worked. Extensive mining at deeper levels would have required investment on a scale that the small

private enterprises working in Brazil could never have afforded. But while production was thinning out, the demand for cut diamonds grew. Obviously, this led to higher prices. The value of a 1-carat diamond rose by about 18 percent between 1867 and 1869. The scarcity of raw materials brought the fear of unemployment to the diamond shops, and a good number of diamond workers turned to other crafts. Thanks to these reductions, things were just beginning to improve when the Franco-Prussian War of 1870 brought on a disastrous setback: every diamond workshop in Amsterdam closed down.

The effects were the same in Antwerp. Since 1850, the Antwerp diamond cutters had experienced difficulties on more than one occasion, and there too the cessation of work was complete. In addition to the slump caused directly by the war, other factors contributed to this unprecedented decline. Paris, which for two centuries had been a fruitful market for cut diamonds, and where the old goldsmiths and lapidaries had brought the jeweler's art to a degree of perfection unknown elsewhere, was feeling not only the effect of foreign wars but was also slowly recovering from the tragic events associated with the suppression of the Commune.

But at the very moment when the diamond shops were dying, an event unparalleled in world economic history occurred, creating the greatest concentration of commercial enterprises ever known. Diamond deposits were discovered in South Africa.

Southern Africa and the Birth of a Great Industry

Although diamonds were first discovered in South Africa only a little more than a century ago, some of the elements that play a part in the story of the discovery must be traced back to a much earlier time.

The wealth of India had attracted European merchants, and explorers began searching for new trade routes. By the close of the fifteenth century the Portuguese had found a direct maritime link with India by sailing around Africa. Bartholomeu Diaz and his crew traveled south along the African coast until they were able to turn east. They named the piece of land at Africa's southern tip the Cape of Good Hope, for it represented their "good hope" of finding a route to the East, which Vasco da Gama indeed did in 1498.

For more than 150 years the Cape remained an important point of navigation. In the mid-

seventeenth century, when trade with the East increased, the Dutch East India Company set up a relay station at the Cape, where, after their voyages of several months, European ships were in need of fresh supplies. On April 6, 1652, Jan van Riebeeck, with about ninety other people, landed at Table Bay and founded the Cape Colony. Thus the Dutch were the first Europeans to settle in South Africa, where they began farms to stock the Dutch East India Company's ships with supplies. The small colony soon attracted other Europeans as well. In 1668 some two hundred Huguenots, fleeing religious persecution in France, arrived to settle in South Africa.

Though thinly populated, the vast South African territory was not empty before the arrival of the Europeans. The native population consisted of Bushmen, Hottentots, and various Bantu peoples who had gradually been driven south from the overpopulated regions of central Africa. As the nomadic Bushmen moved across the country they came into conflict with the Hottentots, a more culturally advanced people who lived in permanent settlements and raised crops and livestock—the latter often the targets of Bushmen hunters. Fresh discord broke out in the sixteenth century with the arrival of the Bantu. The Bushmen were forced to retreat west, where some thirty thousand of their descendants still inhabit the Kalahari Desert. The Hottentots moved south and were thus the first Africans to come into contact with the European colonists. The contact had some dire results: many Hottentots perished from diseases introduced by European sailors, and others were enslaved to supply the labor required on the farms of the Dutch colonists, who became known as Boers (Dutch for "farmers").

European colonization progressed slowly. At the close of the eighteenth century the population was still concentrated in the immediate vicinity of the Cape, where trade and certain handicrafts were flourishing. Events in Europe, however, soon brought change. The British, at war with Napoleonic France and determined to retain their supremacy at sea, were aware of the strategic and commercial importance of the Cape, where ships of all nationalities were accustomed to call. On January 6,

The "Big Hole" at Kimberley, the largest excavated crater in the world—1,528 feet wide, 3,620 feet deep (463 × 1,097 m). It was worked until 1914. *De Beers Archives.*

A team of diggers
with their black laborers.
De Beers Archives.

Cape Town at the end
of the nineteenth century.
Anonymous woodcut.

1806, after a short battle, they seized possession of the colony.

Relations between the colonists and their new rulers were anything but good. Unaccustomed to outside constraints, the Boers had acquired a spirit of independence and were unwilling to obey English laws. The abolition of slavery in 1835 was a particular cause of complaint, for it deprived the farmers of their work force, and the compensation they were promised was never fully paid.

Bitter and disillusioned, a great many Boers decided to take their cattle and leave the region altogether to make their way north and east, where they would be free of British jurisdiction. Their journey was known as the Great Trek. Among the trekkers were men destined to become famous, such as Andries Pretorius and Piet Retief, who invaded Zulu territory in 1838. At the Battle of Blood River, in which three thousand Zulu were slain by a handful of Boers, Pretorius and Retief helped secure an area for their people's settlement.

In 1839 the Boers established the Republic of Natal, but three years later they were driven out by the British and had to head north again, across the River Vaal. In 1852 Pretorius and his companions obtained British recognition of an independent territory popularly known as the Transvaal. A second state, known as the Orange Free State, was founded two years later between the Orange and Vaal rivers. At peace with the British for the time being, the Boers still had to remain constantly on guard

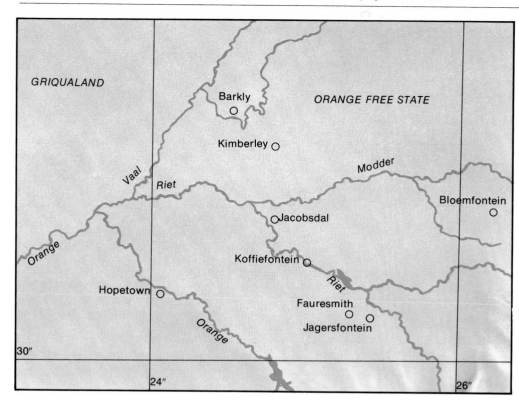

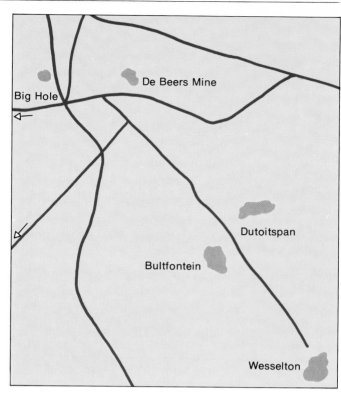

The diamondiferous region between the Vaal and Orange rivers, and (right) the principal pipes of Kimberley (scale approximately ¾ in:1 mile). *Burns Graphics, London.*

against the attacks of the Zulu and other African peoples. Their farms were built like fortresses, with defensive walls and watchtowers, each one within sight of the next so that in the event of an attack help could be quickly summoned from neighbors.

Situated at the heart of southern Africa, the huge territory occupied by the independent Boers consisted of a great plateau between 4,000 and 5,000 feet (1,200–1,500 m) above sea level. Vegetation was sparse, and except in certain depressions known as "pans," where water accumulated (and in time evaporated), water was in short supply almost everywhere. At the feet of steep hills of volcanic rock, separated by great distances, there were a few springs, which enabled the wandering Bushmen to live in the land they appropriately called the *karoo,* or desert. Close to these springs, the Boers built their dwellings.

The Discovery of Diamonds
The honor of discovering the first diamond in South Africa fell to the fifteen-year-old son of one of these farmers. The year was 1866. Young Erasmus Jacobs lived with his family on the De Kalk farm on the southern bank of the Orange River, about 30 miles (50 km) northeast of Hopetown. Searching for a stick to clear a drain one day, he picked up a stone that was sparkling in the sunlight on the riverbank and gave it to his sister. Shortly afterward, Schalk van Niekerk, a friend of the family who sold supplies to farmers in the neighborhood, visited the Jacobses. Passing the children at play, he noticed the shiny stone, so different from the others. Although he had never seen a dia-

mond, he was very fond of the colorful stones found in the region. Noticing his interest, Mrs. Jacobs decided to give him the stone.

A few months later, Van Niekerk showed the strange white crystal to a hunter, John O'Reilly, who offered to take it to the civil commissioner, Lorenzo Boyes, at Colesberg. Boyes in turn sent the stone by mail to W. Guybon Atherstone, a doctor and amateur mineralogist in Grahamstown. Careful examination convinced Atherstone that this was a diamond of 21.25 carats, worth about £500. He summarized his conclusions in a letter that reached Lorenzo Boyes at Colesberg on April 9, 1867.

The news was announced the next day in the Colesberg *Advertiser,* and Atherstone's analysis was confirmed by experts from the Cape. Bought for £500 by Sir Philip Wodehouse, governor of Cape Colony, the stone was shipped to London to be displayed at the Paris Universal Exposition of 1867–68. Named "Eureka," it was subsequently cut in London into a diamond weighing 10.73 carats and sold to a man named Peter Locan. Schalk van Niekerk received £350 and offered half to Daniel Jacobs, Erasmus's father, but Jacobs refused, claiming that his family wanted no money for an old stone. In 1966, one hundred years after the discovery of the diamond, Harry Oppenheimer, chairman of De Beers, persuaded its owner to part with the stone, and thus the first South African diamond returned to Cape Town. It is now on display there in the Houses of Parliament.

For two years no more unusual stones were found, and the discovery made by Jacobs passed into the realm of fable. The matter was reopened purely by chance. In March, 1869, a Griqua shepherd named Booi was driving his flock in the Hopetown district. On a piece of land on the Zandfontein farm, near the Orange River, he picked up a stone that shone in an unusual manner. That evening his path led him to the Paardekloof farm, where he asked for shelter from the farmer, a man named Duvenhage, who refused.

"Sir, I'll give you this fine stone if you let me stay the night," he offered. Duvenhage was not interested. "Go to Schalk van Niekerk," he said. "He likes stones. I don't."

Van Niekerk lived nearby, so Booi went

Itinerant African workers.
De Beers Archives.

there and offered the stone to the man who had first shown interest in the Eureka diamond. Van Niekerk was more experienced now and had no doubts. This was a diamond four times larger than the one Jacobs had found. When he asked the price, Booi replied simply, "Sir, whatever you wish." Without hesitation, Van Niekerk offered him all he possessed: five hundred sheep, ten oxen, and his horse. Booi left the next morning with his new possessions, unable to understand his benefactor's generosity. A few days later at Hopetown, the diamond proved to weigh 83.5 carats; Van Niekerk recieved £11,300 for it. It was then acquired by the cutter Louis Hond, who gave it its final pear-shaped form, reducing its weight to 47.75 carats. It was subsequently owned for many years by the earl of Dudley, who bought it for $125,000. On May 2, 1974, the stone, known as the "Dudley diamond" or the "Star of South Africa," was auctioned at Christie's in Geneva for $552,000.

The First Diamond Rush

Although the discovery of the Eureka passed almost unnoticed, the Star of South Africa caused quite a stir, and Schalk van Niekerk's good fortune was soon known to everyone in the country. In the following months a crowd of prospectors headed for the banks of the Vaal and Orange rivers. Pniel, the first camp, was a chaotic sprawl of tents, huts, wooden shops, and ox-drawn wagons that had been converted into homes and even stores.

The farmer Johannes Nicholas de Beer, whose name became famous as that of the largest diamond enterprise in the world. *De Beers Archives.*

Later arrivals with greater means, disgusted at the sight of what looked like a scruffy village fair, began to build a small town on a nearby hill overlooking the diggings, which resembled a huge molehill. This was Klip Drift, later known as Barkly.

We are now in the early months of 1870 and the period of river diggings. Each claim was a square measuring 30 Dutch feet (fractionally larger than English feet) along each side. The diggers began by clearing the stones covering the surface; then they dug pits, the depth depending on how close they were to the river. The gravel thus recovered was washed and transported to sorting tables, which were generally set up in the shade of canopies made of branches. Sorting was done by hand, and each stone was carefully inspected. The atmosphere was feverish, each man's ardor inflamed by his awareness that others working close by had made valuable finds.

Indeed, many finds were made, and news of the diggers' successes spread far and wide. Sailors abandoned their ships to join the dig-

A mining company's headquarters and a lawyer's office on Main Street, Kimberley, before 1800. *De Beers Archives.*

gings, and adventurers all over the world dreamed of reaching the Vaal and Orange rivers. Whole columns of people headed for the new Eldorado. The distance from Cape Town was more than 600 miles (1,000 km). The journey took about forty days by oxcart and considerably longer if made on foot, as it often was. When the diggers arrived, they settled anywhere they could find a space, giving little thought to who owned the land.

In this motley gathering, a few strong personalities stood out. Stafford Parker, an Englishman who had been a sailor and a gold

miner in California, grouped a number of men around him and proclaimed a "Diggers' Republic," which succeeded for a while. A Diggers' Committee was established to distribute claims and settle arguments. Thieves were tried in public according to laws inspired by the British navy and customs familiar in the American West.

The alluvial deposits that these first diggers were working were secondary deposits—that is, they derived from a primary source some distance away—but that, of course, was not known at the time. As it happened, the primary deposits were relatively close by. In less than two years, the main ones were discovered.

In July, 1870, a cart driver named Bam picked up an unfamiliar-looking stone on the Koffiefontein farm, near the Riet River, northwest of Fauresmith in the Orange Free State. He continued on his way until he came upon the diamond diggers on the Vaal River, who confirmed that his stone was a diamond. But when Bam described where he had found it, these "experts" were skeptical: the place was too far from the river to be of interest. Bam gathered a few friends and returned to dig where he had found the stone. They were discreet, and as the site was about 60 miles (100 km) away from the Vaal diggings, they were able to work undisturbed. Without knowing it, they had found the first primary deposit.

These events did not pass unnoticed on the nearby Jagersfontein farm. The farm manager, De Klerk, decided to follow Bam's example and search the land, especially the riverbed, which remained dry most of the year. His tools were rudimentary, and he washed the gravel in a homemade trough. In August, he found a 50-carat stone. The discovery brought other diamond seekers hurrying to the spot, but the owner of the farm, a widow named Visser, discouraged most of them by demanding a monthly fee of £2 per claim for digging rights. For several years no one realized that Jagersfontein was a primary diamond source. As it was so far from the river, and the majority of diggers still believed that only the rivers carried diamonds, it was protected from a large-scale rush. Eventually, the Jagersfontein mine was to be worked for nearly a century.

Among the diggers along the Vaal was a man named William Alderson, who had come to Africa as a gold prospector on behalf of a British firm but subsequently decided to dig for diamonds instead. His prospector's instinct soon inspired him to abandon the crowded riverbanks and head elsewhere. One day he arrived at the Dorstfontein farm, which was occupied by the Van Wyck family. He noticed a diamond embedded in the clay walls of the house. On inquiry, he was told that the clay

Shops and offices in Kimberley in the era of easy fortunes. *De Beers Archives.*

came from a "pan" just a few yards away. The farmer was not easily persuaded, but eventually he allowed Alderson to search the area. In a few days several diamonds were found. Alderson was soon joined by hundreds of diggers—for this time the site was not far from the Vaal River—who staked their claims as close as possible to the place of the original discoveries. This mine, called Dutoitspan, after Dutoit, a former owner of the farm, became one of the most famous mines in South Africa.

Early in 1871 Alderson moved on to Bultfontein, a neighboring farm whose owner, Cornelius Duplooy, gave him permission to dig. In a few weeks, on a kopje, or small hill, he discovered another deposit. That, too, was inevitably invaded by a horde of diggers, who tended to feel that a new site was better than an old one.

The idea that diamonds could be found in places other than the immediate vicinity of riv-

A Kimberley bar in the "good old days." Reconstruction at the Kimberley Museum. *Photo Jacques Legrand.*

ers was accepted at last, and the area began to be systematically searched. In May, 1871, a man named Richard Jackson arrived at the Vooruitzicht farm. There he found a digger, Corneilsa or Cornelis (like other characters who appear briefly in the early history of South African diamonds, his full name is not known), digging at the foot of a small kopje. The farm owners, the brothers D. A. and J. N. de Beer, had given him permission to dig in exchange for one-quarter of his findings. He had already recovered several diamonds, which he showed to Jackson. Excited, Jackson returned to camp to pack up, but his haste betrayed him. By the time he returned to the De Beers' farm he was only a little ahead of the cloud of dust created by those following him. In a matter of hours, the farm where Corneilsa had been working in peaceful seclusion was invaded by a horde of diggers. Like their neighbors, the De Beer brothers could do nothing to keep these rough newcomers from fighting over their land, and five months later they accepted an offer of £6,300 for their property, which they had acquired eleven years earlier for £50. Van Wyck had already been forced to sell out for £2,000, and Duplooy had accepted £2,600 for his Bultfontein property. Prices would have been considerably higher in a few months.

The De Beer family departed for more peaceful places, but their name was given to what was to become the greatest diamond company in the world. As for Jackson and Corneilsa, both were unlucky. Corneilsa sold his claim for £110, and Jackson, though he had had first choice, had selected his claim badly: it proved to be beyond the limits of the crater, and he dug up tons of earth for nothing.

Among the diggers who came from Colesberg and settled on the De Beer farm was Fleetwood Rawsthorne. One evening he was being pestered by a drunken servant, and to

Furniture and other objects in the Kimberley Museum that recall everyday life at the time of the diamond rush. *De Beers Archives.*

The "Big Hole"— the Kimberley mine— at the beginning of the twentieth century. *De Beers Archives.*

get rid of him Rawsthorne sent him off to a field a few hundred yards away. Next day the man returned with his hands filled with diamonds that he had collected near a small hill. Rawsthorne went there immediately with some friends and found what would become one of the most famous deposits. At first it was known as the De Beers "New Rush" or the "Colesberg Kopje." In fact, Rawsthorne's servant had discovered the Kimberley mine.

The four deposits mentioned above—Dutoitspan, Bultfontein, De Beers, and Kimberley—all lay within a 2.5-mile (4-km) radius. This area of unparalleled wealth contained five deposits in all, but the fifth was not discovered until nineteen years later, in September, 1890. Only 2 miles (3 km) east of Dutoitspan, it was situated on the property of the Benaauwdheidsfontein farm, which belonged to Petrus Wessel. It was first called the Premier mine, in honor of Prime Minister Cecil Rhodes, but in 1902, when another mine was discovered northeast of Pretoria and given the same name, the name of the first was changed to the Wesselton mine, in memory of the original owner of the property. Many stones of especially fine quality have been found there, and the term "Wesselton" is still often used by jewelers to designate a special category of stone.

The discovery of the primary deposits, then known as "dry diggings," increased the flow of prospectors. The camps grew and eventually merged to form a town, called Kimberley after the British colonial secretary.

At the start of the rush the British authorities asserted control and imposed their laws on the diggers. English law treated blacks and whites equally, and native Africans had the right to prospect the ground and sell what they found. In reality, however, the only effective law was the law of the jungle. Theft increased, and receivers of stolen goods were sometimes able to buy from Africans stones worth several hundred pounds for the price of a bottle of whiskey. There were all sorts of unsavory characters about, and the trade in stolen diamonds was no doubt considerable. Matters went so far that the miners, seeing that the British laws were completely ineffectual, formed a secret association to enforce laws of their own. The chief method of punishment was lynching. It was decided that any white man who bought diamonds from an African worker would be subject to the following penalties: his possessions would be destroyed, his ears would be cut off, and he would be tarred and feathered and then pilloried in the market square. All this took place in 1871, when the diamond frenzy in Kimberley was such that it was agreed that the first comer might occupy a concession

The market square in Kimberley, about 1880. From a contemporary photograph. *De Beers Archives.*

the moment its proprietor had ceased working it for eight consecutive days.

The Fabulous Kimberley Era

Immediately after the "Digger Rush" came the "Canteen Rush." In an area where wealth abounded but few facilities existed, many wandering tradesmen settled: itinerant banks, saloons, gambling houses, and shops of all kinds were set up in Kimberley. Legitimate diamond buyers, confidence men, and crooks mingled in a colorful throng. But as time passed life became more organized. Tents were gradually replaced by buildings of wood or sheet metal, which was imported at a cost of several thousand pounds. The better buildings were made of brick, which offered some protection from intense heat and cold. Curiously, the most popular article of furniture in Kimberley was the piano. The men were mad about music, as though they sought some auditory compensation for the visual dreariness of the desolate

and monotonous landscape that surrounded them. Churches and temples sprang up, and men who had never before crossed the threshold of a church attended the services of the different sects indiscriminately. Supplies could be bought daily in the market square, where every morning a host of wagons arrived, hauled by six or eight oxen and carrying the produce of all the neighboring farms. Besides the necessities of life, goods of a distinctly superfluous nature could be bought in the market. Laid out alongside wood, coal, corn, flour, vegetables, meat and poultry, household utensils, and clothing were antelope hides, rhinoceros horns, and elephant tusks. Everything was sold by auctioneers who displayed an energy and eloquence rarely seen before, even in Africa. Moreover, prices were five or even ten times higher here than they were at the Cape.

The more respectable quarters were to be found in the east. The western part of the town was occupied by the camps of African tribesmen attracted to Kimberley by the money and alcohol available there. This part of town was little more than a collection of miserable tents made of odd pieces of canvas hung between poles. The occupants slept on the bare earth. Thousands of men were gathered in this makeshift camp, providing the basic labor force for the industrial operations of the future. In general, the Africans worked in the mines just long enough to earn sufficient money to marry. Anyone who possessed a gun, powder, and oxen was in a position to choose a suitable wife, and a herd of twenty-five oxen was enough to help a suitor drive a hard bargain with a prospective father-in-law.

The Beginning of Organized Production

When the diggers arrived at the new diamond fields, they thought they were dealing with deposits like those they had left along the rivers. They saw rather larger holes, similar to the *caldeirões* in Brazil, and they were all convinced that they would soon reach bottom. Consequently, they set to work in the same way as before. Each man chose a site, laid out his claim, and started digging and shoveling with no thought for his neighbor. Because of the lack of water there was no washing: the diamond ore was crushed by hand, and the diamonds were sorted from the residue—hence the expression "dry diggings."

It is easy to imagine the congestion and the conflicts that resulted from these primitive working methods. Passages had to be reserved to give access to claims in the middle of the mine; for that purpose, some ground had to be left temporarily unworked, with the understanding that the claim holders could resume

A diamond mine as envisioned by Maso da San Friano (1536–71). From a painting in the Palazzo Vecchio, Florence. The artist's conception was remarkably close to reality: the Kimberley "Big Hole" looked not unlike this about 1880. *Photo Scala, Florence.*

work when the bottom of the mine was reached. But as excavation went deeper, no sign of the bottom appeared. The walkways were soon precariously balanced on high, crumbling walls. Certain rules made by the Diggers' Committee, forbidding combined working and restricting the number of claims that one man could hold, had to be abandoned. In 1874 the Kimberley mine contained 430 claims, divided among some 1,600 enterprises operating on the basis of common shares or subcontracting. As the crater was dug, the softer rocks on the edge of the volcanic pipe crumbled and covered the bottom. Rain mingled with excavated earth, and in the absence of adequate pumps it became dangerous, if not impossible, to continue working. This situation led to the creation of the Board for the Protection of Mining Interests, which collected contributions from claim owners to make improvements that would prevent flooding and collapsing walls.

When the walkways that divided the 430 concessions collapsed, other arrangements had to be considered, and the miners began to see the advantages of forming a group that would be able to employ more effective methods. The huge crater was covered with a veritable spider web of cables from three-tier winches arranged around the mine to service the various claims. The winches not only brought up the diamondiferous ore from the bottom, but also conveyed the miners themselves to and from the deepening site of operations.

Even before the ban on grouping claims together was revoked, some cooperation was arranged in different workings in order to meet the increasing technical difficulties. It was soon apparent that work could continue only if important investments were made—and that required firms with substantial capital. When work began, it was a simple matter to free the diamonds from the yellow ground—relatively light rock—in which they were embedded; the simplest tools were sufficient. But at greater depths the yellow ground gave way to a blue mother rock, which was much harder and denser. This rock, first called "blue ground" and later "kimberlite," was transported from the edge of the pipe to "floors," or storage areas. There it weathered and with time became more friable; it could then be processed by hand like yellow ground. But as work developed on an ever-increasing scale, such methods became impractical. It was scarcely profitable to transport the kimberlite over long distances and then wait while the huge mass went through a slow weathering process. The rock had to be attacked directly. But this was not possible without the installation of heavy equipment—crushers, agitators, and so on—

Top: Horse-powered winches bringing up the ore from the bottom of the "Big Hole." Bottom: The cables that transported men and materials to and from the mine formed a giant spider web. *De Beers Archives.*

same time, the first rough diamonds reached the market from South Africa, but their arrival had no appreciable effect on the price of cut diamonds. However, the economic crisis of 1873 and the exceptional duration of the depression that followed it did cause an important drop in prices. By 1878 the price of a 1-carat diamond was about 60 percent less than it had been in 1867.

Nevertheless, the fall in prices could have been checked to some extent if some means had existed to control South African production. During the years of economic stagnation in Europe, thousands of diggers continued to work feverishly, producing ever greater quantities of diamonds. But at the time when the fall in prices was accelerating, the diggers ran up against the insurmountable technical problems described above. Events seemed to have reached an impasse, and a relaxation of mining laws to grant concession owners the right to acquire up to thirty claims was a half-measure that failed to remedy the situation. Disillusionment prevailed, and claims were declared to be worthless. The diggers began to sell out, and prices naturally fell sharply. These developments prompted further changes in mining legislation in 1877, which finally swept away all restrictions on rights of ownership and opened the door for talented entrepreneurs like Cecil Rhodes and Barney Barnato.

Cecil John Rhodes

Rhodes was born in Bishop's Stortford in Hertfordshire, England, in 1853, one of five children of an Anglican minister. Though tall, he was in rather poor health, and he suffered a pulmonary infection in his adolescence. At the age of seventeen he decided to make a trip to South Africa, where his older brother Herbert had settled some time earlier.

On September 1, 1870, Rhodes landed at Durban, but there was no one to greet him. His brother, like many others, had gone off to the diamond fields in hopes of making his fortune. Rhodes remained in Natal for a year, until finally the news he received from his brother convinced him that he should follow in his footsteps. In October, 1871, he arrived at Colesberg Kopje, where he rented a quarter of a claim in the De Beers mine and began slaving away at it with the aid of a few Zulu. He became friendly with Charles Dunell Rudd, an Englishman about ten years older than himself, who, like Rhodes, had come to South Africa for the sake of his health. After a few months Rhodes suffered a slight heart attack and, leaving Rudd in charge, traveled north with his brother across the Transvaal. It was probably in the immense territories of the north, uninhabited by Europeans, that Rhodes

which required substantial capital resources. Gradually, therefore, the mines passed into the hands of a few major concerns, particularly companies financed by share capital.

Diamond Prices and the Crisis of 1873. It has often been said that the arrival of African rough diamonds on the market caused a drop in the price of cut diamonds, and such an assumption seems logical enough. The facts, however, are somewhat more complex. Between 1872 and 1874, more than a million carats were produced in South Africa; ten years later production had doubled, and by 1888 annual production reached 4 million carats. Despite these huge quantities, the price of rough diamonds remained stable until 1873, and its fall after that date was relatively gradual. The effect on the market for cut diamonds was different. When Brazilian rough diamonds virtually ceased to flow, the diminishing supply was reflected in an increase in prices. At the

Cross section of the
"Big Hole" at about the
time mining ceased
in August, 1914.
Burns Graphics, London.

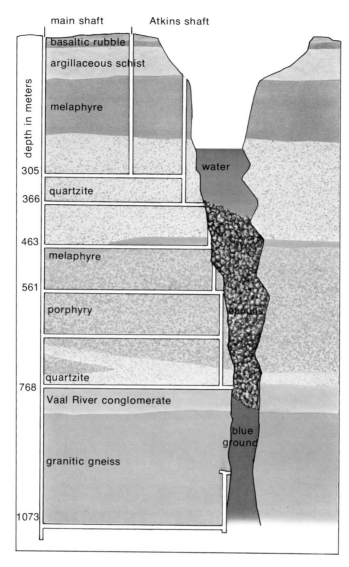

main shaft   Atkins shaft

basaltic rubble

argillaceous schist

melaphyre

depth in meters

305   water

quartzite

366

463

melaphyre

561

porphyry

quartzite

768

Vaal River conglomerate

blue
ground

granitic gneiss

1073

A trolley running on
cables took the men down the
Kimberley mine in 1903.
De Beers Archives.

first conceived his political ambitions, dreaming even then of an all-powerful British Empire that would govern this part of the world.

On his return to Kimberley, he and Rudd bought a pump that they rented to miners whose claims were flooded. Business prospered, but motivated by the desire to learn rather than to get rich, Rhodes again entrusted his business affairs to a friend and returned to England to study classics at Oxford. He graduated in 1881. Even while he was at university, Rhodes's mind was filled with thoughts of the possibilities opening up in the new world of the South African diamond. He remained in contact with Rudd and the others in Kimberley and spent some of his vacations there.

When the price of rough diamonds began to drop and the growing technical difficulties forced many miners to abandon work, Rhodes reinvested his profits to buy more claims. He was well aware of the need to amalgamate mining enterprises in order to be able to acquire better equipment, and he succeeded in convincing other major owners of the De Beers mines of this necessity. In 1881, with a capital of £200,000, he founded the De Beers Mining Company.

What Rhodes had also realized during the previous ten years was that only by concentrating all units of production in one company would it be possible to adapt the supply of rough diamonds to the fluctuations of demand on the world market. Inevitably, as experience increased and techniques improved, ever greater quantities of diamonds would be produced, but there could be no guarantee that demand would increase proportionately; local recessions and world crises would always have to be taken into account. Rhodes was no mere adventurer. He judiciously looked to the future and planned accordingly.

Rhodes proved himself a master at creating large capitalist enterprises. It is true that he found a particularly receptive audience for his proposals. In the face of increasing working difficulties, many miners were convinced that they could make more money by selling their claims than by clinging to their dreams of individual profit. The technical means employed by large companies put the small-scale workers increasingly at a disadvantage, and more and more miners were willing to exchange their claims for shares in the larger organizations. By doing just that, Rhodes managed to increase his company's capital to £2.5 million in five years.

But South African diamond production could not be controlled through the ownership of the De Beers mine alone. Others had to be brought into the organization, especially the important

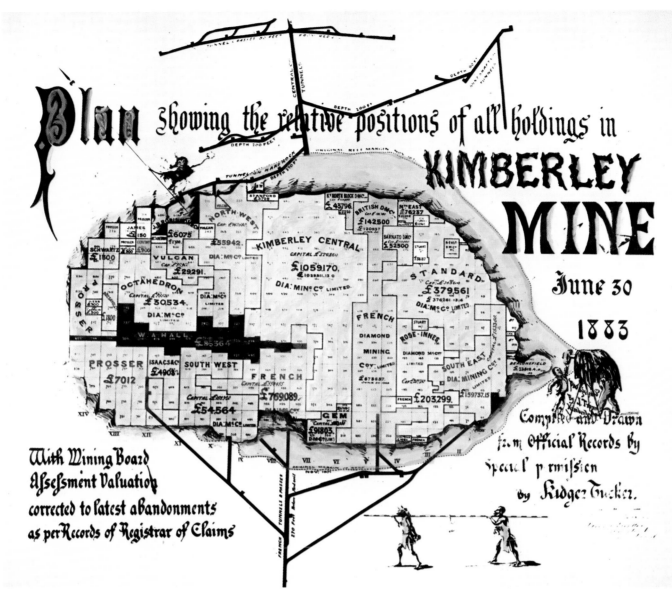

Plan of the different
concessions in the
"Big Hole," June 30, 1883.
De Beers Archives.

Following pages: The "Big
Hole" in 1879. The various
levels correspond to claims
under different ownership.
De Beers Archives.

Kimberley mine, where another masterful financier, Barney Barnato, was playing much the same game as Rhodes.

Barney Barnato

Born into a Jewish family in the East End of London, Barnett Isaacs (Barnato's real name) was familiar with poverty from birth. His parents were secondhand-clothes dealers, and he was sent off to work at the age of thirteen. During the next seven years he led a lively, precocious existence on the fringes of the entertainment world, doing a little boxing and performing with his brother in a variety act. The story goes that his brother, taking a solo bow after the act, was greeted with cries of "Barney, too!" from the audience, and from this Barnett Isaacs took the name "Barnato," by which he was known for the rest of his life. In 1873, when he was only twenty, he made the long voyage to South Africa—his mother's savings paid the fare—to join his elder brother Harry and his cousin David Harris (later Sir David) in Kimberley.

He arrived at the diamond capital with no money, and for the first few months he helped farmers sell their products in the market and performed odd jobs for miners, which gave him the opportunity to have a close look at diamonds. His early efforts as a diamond buyer were frustrated by lack of funds, but David Harris hired him as a buyer in his business. Barnato's talent soon became evident, and in 1875 he and his brother established the firm of Barnato Brothers with capital of £200.

In that same year, the miners in Kimberley reached the blue ground. Many of them believed it was diamond-sterile, while others were defeated by the difficulties of working it. Barnato, however, like Rhodes and some others, put his trust in the theories of geologists who saw in the blue ground the true mother rock of the diamond. He lost no time in buying, at the low prices prevailing, all the claims available in the Kimberley mine, especially those located near the center. He began by working the concessions himself, and in a very short time his faith was amply confirmed. Four claims that he had bought for a total of £3,000 yielded diamonds worth that amount in just

one week. It is said that in one year Barnato made about £100,000. He used his profits either to buy more claims when they became available or to acquire shares in the other companies active in the Kimberley mine, which was proving far richer even than nearby De Beers. In 1881 Barnato founded his own company, the Barnato Diamond Mining Company. The shares were sold out within a few hours of their appearance on the market, and with these new resources, Barnato went on buying. He soon gained effective control of the Kimberley Central Mining Company, the largest company then active.

De Beers Consolidated

It is difficult to imagine two men more different than these two masters of Kimberley.

The check for £5,338,650 with which Cecil Rhodes acquired the shares in Kimberley Central. *De Beers Archives.*

Bottom: Bishop's Stortford, birthplace of Cecil Rhodes.

Elegant, cultured, and refined, Cecil Rhodes even at Kimberley manifested the traits of an English gentleman. Barney Barnato retained his simple, rough ways. Unlike the moody Rhodes, he was a cheerful fellow, a down-to-earth character motivated by the simple desire for profit. Rhodes, on the other hand, nourished a grandiose vision in which diamonds were merely the means to obtain capital to fulfill his imperial ambitions.

In order to control the Kimberley mine, it was necessary to buy out Barnato's empire, and thus a personal confrontation between the two men was inevitable. In 1887 the Kimberley mine belonged chiefly to two firms—the Kimberley Central, ruled by Barnato, and the Compagnie Française des Mines de Diamants du Cap, whose concessions enclosed those of the Kimberley Central.

Backed by the Rothschilds, Rhodes offered to buy the Compagnie Française for £1.5 million. Barnato immediately topped his offer by £350,000. The competitiveness of the bidding prompted the shareholders of the French company to hold on, in the hope that an even greater sum might be forthcoming. Events came to a head in 1888. Rhodes met Barnato several times and finally persuaded him to stand aside and allow the purchase of the French company for the sum first offered. It was agreed that the French company should then be sold back to Barnato's Kimberley Central in exchange for one-fifth of the Kimberley Central's shares plus £300,000 in cash.

Barnato soon realized that he had made a mistake: Rhodes had gained a valuable foothold in the Kimberley mine, and his one idea now was to consolidate his position by acquiring as many shares of the Kimberley Central as he could get. A terrific financial battle ensued between the two men, as each bought heavily. The price of rough diamonds fell as a result of the wildly increased production in which each company attempted to prove itself a more valuable property than the other. The drop in prices was not enough to offset the effects of the spiraling contest for control, and Kimberley Central shares continued to rise despite the poor diamond market. Rhodes and Barnato, with their respective advisers, each used every possible means to convince the shareholders that they should sell to him rather than to his rival.

Barnato, whose capital resources were more restricted, began to lose ground. In March, 1888, the two men met again, and after two hours of negotiations, Rhodes obtained from Barnato an agreement in principle that merged the two companies into one. Thus, on March 13, 1888, the now-famous De Beers Consolidated Mines Ltd. was created, combining the

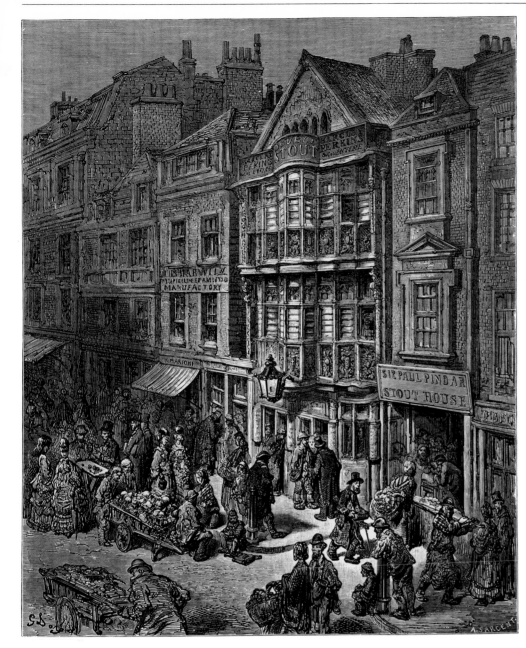

Kimberley, this was certainly the largest check ever issued at that time.

As chief shareholder, Barnato received a good part of this sum, and he was thus able to continue developing various profitable affairs in gold mining and diamond dealing. He remained an active figure in the diamond world until 1896, when, presumably because of a sudden mental disturbance, he committed suicide by leaping from a transatlantic liner on the way to England. He was barely forty-four years old.

For Rhodes, the association of the two richest mines was only a stepping stone; the next move was to join all diamond production units under one management, and he was not long in accomplishing this. When the Wesselton mine was discovered in 1890, he managed to gain a controlling interest, and in the same year he acquired an important share of stock in the Jagersfontein mine. Finally, in 1899, he gained control of the Dutoitspan and Bultfontein mines. Since De Beers also possessed most of the shares in the Griqualand West

Bishopsgate Street, in the East End of London, when Barney Barnato was a boy. Engraving by Gustave Doré.

Barney Barnato and (far right) Cecil Rhodes.

old De Beers Mining Company and the powerful Kimberley Central.

Some Kimberley Central shareholders reacted adversely, claiming in court that the merger was invalid since the two companies were involved in different activities. What particularly angered them was the budget allocated by Rhodes's De Beers Mining Company to various enterprises quite unconnected with diamonds but devoted instead to colonizing the distant territories in the north. They protested that some of their money was being used to maintain what was in effect an army, the purpose of which was certainly not to guard the mines.

They won their case, but their victory was short-lived, for Rhodes retaliated with devastating effect. In July, 1889, the firm of Kimberley Central was simply liquidated by purchase of all the outstanding shares: on July 28 Rhodes authorized a check for the sum of £5,338,650 to accomplish this purpose. Drawn on the Cape of Good Hope Bank in

Company, which specialized in alluvial deposits, the company at the end of the nineteenth century controlled 90 percent of world production in rough diamonds—for all practical purposes, a monopoly.

The Boer War and the Siege of Kimberley. It would be difficult to separate Rhodes's activities in creating the modern diamond industry from his better-known political schemes. When he became the Cape's prime minister in 1890, he felt that the moment had come to extend British control over all South Africa and to bring the Boers under the British crown. However, Paul Kruger, president of the Transvaal, refused to consider the projected federation, and Rhodes attempted to force the issue by approving the Jameson Raid. This attempt to overthrow Kruger was a catastrophic failure that ultimately forced Rhodes to resign from his post as prime minister.

This is not the place to relate the story of the South African War (or the Boer War, as it is popularly called), nor to attempt to unravel the intricacies of international imperial ambitions, in which South Africa was an important pawn. However, the fate of Kimberley itself is of direct interest.

When the war began, in October, 1899, Kimberley was in a vulnerable position close to the two Boer republics, and it was attacked almost immediately. De Beers had in fact taken some preliminary precautions: weapons had been purchased and a survey of the town had been made, with its defense in mind. Rhodes hurried to Kimberley when war broke out and took personal command during the siege by Boer forces, which lasted about four months. Thanks partly to his energy and organizational abilities, the mines were not destroyed (though diamond production ceased); indeed, the beleaguered citizens sheltered in them from the Boers' bombardments. During the siege a company engineer named George Labram (later killed by enemy artillery) made, in the company workshops, the famous 28-pound gun known, in tribute to Rhodes, as "Long Cecil"; it is now on display in Kimberley. Though seriously threatened, the town held out until finally relieved by Sir John French. Cecil Rhodes did not live to see the end of the war. He died on March 26, 1902, on his Muizenbergstrand estate, several miles south of Cape Town.

The Control of Output
When production returned to its normal level at the end of the Boer War in 1902, only two things could threaten De Beers' predominant position: the discovery of new mines operating outside De Beers control, or a crisis causing a serious drop in demand. At this time, the production of the different mines was con-

centrated at Kimberley and sold on a quota system to various international dealers who supplied the markets from their London offices. Amsterdam was one of the principal buying centers. The market there was dominated by a few large firms such as Breitmeyer and Dunkelsbuhler, as well as by Barney Barnato and Company, which remained very active under the management of Barnato's successors. As early as 1893, these buyers had formed a syndicate following a brief scare that convinced them of the wisdom of combining forces rather than remaining in vigorous competition with each other.

The two events feared by De Beers occurred almost simultaneously. The first was the discovery, in 1902, of the Premier mine, 25 miles (40 km) from Pretoria. Within five years, this mine alone succeeded in equaling the entire annual production of De Beers (about 2 million carats). It was this mine that, on January 26, 1905, produced the famous Cullinan (named after the mine's discoverer), at 3,106 carats the largest rough diamond ever found. The production of the Premier mine was sold independently, outside the diamond buyers' syndicate. But matters did not end there. In 1908 extremely rich alluvial deposits were discovered in German South-West Africa: 500,000 carats were extracted during the first year and put up for sale by a firm sponsored by the German government. This company, known as the Diamanten-Regie, collected 5 percent of the proceeds. Meanwhile, a financial slump occurred in Europe. The effects of the slump were felt so suddenly that, in order to avoid bankruptcy, dealers were compelled to liquidate their stocks at very low prices. Cecil Rhodes's work appeared to be irretrievably ruined.

By 1914 De Beers controlled only 40 percent of diamond production, and at the company's request the Union of South Africa (created in 1910) sponsored a meeting of all diamond producers, who, by common agreement, set limits for production in the following year and established quotas to avoid overproduction in the future. The quotas for 1915 were:

De Beers	48.5 percent
Diamanten-Regie	21 percent
Premier mine	19.5 percent
Jagersfontein	11 percent

The First World War broke out shortly afterward, and the agreement was temporarily suspended. A common sales office in London, known as the Diamond Syndicate, had been formed by Rhodes more than twenty years earlier. For the diamond world to be truly organized, reformed, and centralized, however, a man of great capacity—another Rhodes, per-

Sorting diamonds in Kimberley, about 1900. *De Beers Archives.*

portant American contacts during visits to London, among them Herbert Hoover, the future president. These contacts led to Oppenheimer's creation, in 1917, of the Anglo-American Corporation of South Africa. The company was active chiefly in gold mines, which brought substantial American capital to South Africa for the first time.

In 1919, after the First World War, the German colony of South-West Africa was placed under the mandate of the Union of South Africa. The prospecting rights of former owners were canceled, and Oppenheimer, after skillful negotiations, succeeded in acquiring exclusive rights for the Anglo-American Corporation. He founded the Consolidated Diamond Mines of South-West Africa Ltd. (CDM) to exploit them, and within a short time CDM was producing 20 percent of South African rough diamonds. Oppenheimer was in a position to exercise an important—and constructive—influence on the diamond trade. In 1920 he attended a meeting of diamond producers and joined with them in agreeing to sell the production of CDM through the Diamond Syndicate in London.

Despite a slight depression in trade during the early 1920's, everything went well under this arrangement until 1926, when important alluvial deposits were discovered at Lichtenburg, 120 miles (200 km) east of Johannesburg. These new discoveries triggered an incredible diamond rush. According to mining legislation of 1922, anyone could demand the right to prospect, but discoveries had to be declared within thirty days to the authorities, who, by public proclamation, awarded applicants a claim of fixed dimensions. The distribution of claims was determined by a race. On the agreed day, August 20, 1926, all the miners were lined up for a running start. As many as ten thousand people took part, including several women and a man on crutches. The official proclamation was read, a flag was dropped, and everyone rushed forward about 660 feet (200 m) to plant his peg, marking his claim in the alluvial area. At a similar rush at Grasfontein several months later, twenty thousand people competed for claims. There was a false start, so all the pegs had to be removed by the police and the race rerun a week later.

Legislation reserved 60 percent of the diamonds produced for the Union of South Africa. Despite such restrictions, the state was able to exercise hardly any influence on the production of diamonds, and even less on the trade. In a few months, several thousand miners were busy at work, and in three years they produced 4.5 million carats, worth more than £10 million. And of course the miners sold their shares of diamonds freely, with no thought for

The head office of De Beers Consolidated Mines on Stockdale Street, Kimberley. *De Beers Archives.*

haps—was required. That man was at hand. His name was Ernest Oppenheimer.

Ernest Oppenheimer

The fifth son and eighth child of Eduard and Nanny Oppenheimer, Ernest Oppenheimer was born in Frieberg, Germany, on May 22, 1880. He came to London at sixteen to work for A. Dunkelsbuhler and Company, a well-known diamond firm where two of his brothers were already employed. He soon became expert at sorting diamonds. In 1902 Dunkelsbuhler sent him to South Africa, and for fifteen years he selected diamonds at Kimberley. He also had an active social and political life and served as mayor of Kimberley from 1912 to 1915. Diamonds were not his only interest—in 1917 he joined an American engineering company involved in the operation of gold mines. He had previously made some im-

Top: The first diggers
in South-West Africa, about
1908–10. *De Beers Archives.*

Sir Ernest Oppenheimer,
the "Diamond King."
De Beers Archives.

the disturbance they were creating on the diamond market.

Meanwhile, a still more dramatic discovery was made in November, 1926, in Namaqualand. A German geologist, Dr. Hans Merensky, identified alluvial deposits on the marine terraces of the Atlantic coast at Alexander Bay, south of the mouth of the Orange River. In six weeks he collected 12,500 carats from his concession, and at the end of the following year he had extracted 1.2 million carats. Elsewhere, other countries such as the Belgian Congo (now Zaïre) and Angola were producing and selling even larger quantities. The situation had become critical: what passed through the hands of the Diamond Syndicate now represented only a small part of world production, and in order to keep prices stable, the Syndicate was forced to make purchases that stretched its financial resources to the limit. Reorganization of the diamond business was urgently required in order to preserve the livelihood of all involved in it. This was the task that Ernest Oppenheimer performed.

The Basis of the Modern Market

Oppenheimer had been invited to join the board of De Beers in 1926, and he was elected chairman in 1930. He soon revealed the full measure of his extraordinary capacities as a businessman. One of his first actions was decisive. It was no longer sufficient, he suggested, for the members of the Diamond Syndicate to be content with occasionally absorbing the awkward production of third parties in order to preserve world prices; what was required to solve the perennial threat of over-

production was a consistent policy of buying all, or as much as possible, of the diamonds produced from every other source—Lichtenburg, Namaqualand, the Belgian Congo, Angola, and other sources as yet undiscovered. In order to implement such a program, large financial reserves would obviously have to be made available. For this purpose the Diamond Corporation was created in 1930, with half of its capital provided by the chief South African producers. This was the foundation of the modern marketing system.

In 1933 the Diamond Producers Association (DPA) was formed, comprising the big South African producers, the South African government, and the Diamond Corporation. The latter had a kind of dual role: according to the agreement of 1930 it took over the business of the Diamond Syndicate and purchased diamonds produced outside the group; within the DPA it was treated as another producer, receiving a quota for its accumulated stock of diamonds, just as the producers had their quotas for the diamonds they mined.

The next step was the creation of the Diamond Trading Company. The purpose of this company was to buy and sort all the rough diamonds produced by the DPA (including, of course, the stocks of the Diamond Corporation as a member of the DPA). Finally, all the rough stones from the Diamond Trading Company were marketed through a single sales outlet, the Central Selling Organization (CSO).

Henceforth, production and sales control were essentially united within one firm—De Beers—and could be adjusted to the state of the market. It was this system that enabled the diamond industry to survive the economic depression of the 1930's. The diamonds produced in those years were stored away, not sold for what would have been abysmal prices. When the market recovered, the accumulated stocks were gradually released at great profit. The profits were used to create a security fund for future emergencies.

It is necessary only to look at the stable condition of the diamond market today to see how successful the bold changes of the 1930's have been. When Sir Ernest Oppenheimer died in 1957, the wisdom of the decisions he had made over the preceding decades had been fully confirmed. He was succeeded by his son Harry, who continued his work and increased the area of influence of the many businesses he controlled.

The system created by Sir Ernest Oppenheimer remains basically unchanged today. After the Second World War, Industrial Distributors Ltd. was created, as a member of the DPA, for the marketing of industrial diamonds, which have become increasingly important in the modern world.

Subsequent developments in southern Africa have not changed the situation in essence. In Tanzania, the origin of alluvial deposits known since the early twentieth century was tracked down by Dr. John Williamson in 1940, when he located the largest kimberlite pipe yet discovered—eight times larger than the Premier mine—at Mwadui. The Finsch mine, about 105 miles (170 km) northeast of Kimberley, was discovered in 1958, and proved to be a particularly large pipe, though not nearly as sizable as Mwadui. It was eventually bought by De Beers. The Orapa mine, second only to Mwadui, was discovered in Botswana in 1967. Orapa's production, together with that of the Letlhakane mine, which began production in 1976, comes to more than 4 million carats annually, making Botswana one of the largest African producers.

The rush near Lichtenburg in 1926: staking claims by a foot race. *De Beers Archives.*

II

The Rough Diamond
and Its Origins

The Geology of the Diamond

Formation and drift of the continents in the Cretaceous period. The protocontinent of Gondwanaland becomes divided, giving birth to the future South America and Africa. The black diamonds indicate diamondiferous regions. *Burns Graphics, London.*

Of all precious stones, the diamond is certainly the one that is geologically most familiar. Studying it has allowed us to glimpse the very innards of our planet, for the diamond is one of the few substances to reach the earth's surface from its remote depths. This unusual traveler and its companions—the minerals associated with it in the kimberlite—have been exhaustively investigated by mineralogists, physicists, and others in search of precious information about the environment in which they were created. Interest in the diamond is not purely scientific. Because of the stone's considerable economic value, it has been the subject of important research conducted for practical purposes, as well. Studies have focused on two major areas: the production of synthetic diamonds, and the improvement of prospecting methods. Scientists have examined the diamond much as a hunter studies the habits of his prey in order to track it down more efficiently. The information acquired over the years in laboratories and at mining sites enables us today to trace with some precision the major steps in the history of the diamond as seen through geological events.

Geology

We now know that diamonds crystallized under very high pressures and temperatures, which probably reached 70,000 kg/cm² and 3,630° F (2,000° C) respectively. Such condi-

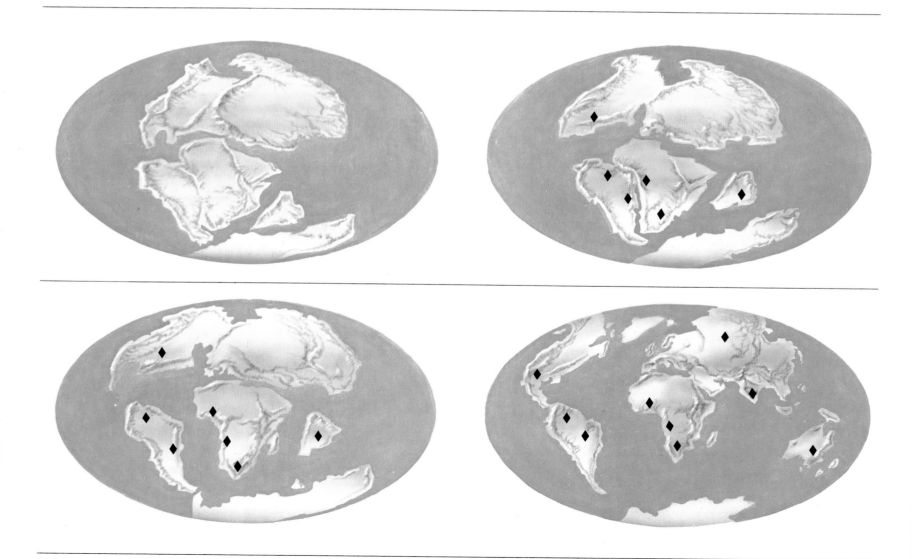

A volcano erupting.
Photo Picture-Point, London.

tions exist in nature only at a depth of about 120 miles (200 km) in the earth, or, briefly, when heavy meteorites strike the planet. The latter occurrence, however, is clearly exceptional. Although diamonds are in fact found in certain aerolites, almost all of those discovered on earth were created in the planet's depths.

This deep-seated zone, in which the growth conditions for the formation of the diamond are met, belongs to the upper mantle, which is thought to consist of ultramafic rocks with focal areas of magma. That the diamond originates from this region of the upper mantle as one of its crystal formations may be deduced from the fact that it occurs in ultramafic mother rocks and that its mineral inclusions correspond with their mineral components. The far-reaching distribution of diamond deposits from Australia via Africa to the Americas and even to Siberia and the Ural Mountains offers evidence that the magma must be widely spread and homogeneously large, although individual sectors may be quite heterogeneous. In the course of gigantic tectonic events, a differentiation of the deep-seated magma took place, leading to an alteration of the original and uniformly composed magmatic rocks and resulting in new metamorphic rocks (so-called deep-seated xenoliths, such as eclogite). Simultaneously, new rock-forming and accessory minerals, including diamond, were also formed. Consequently the diamond is a typical concomitant product of a colossal alteration of rocks.

We also know that diamonds arrived at the surface borne by a volcanic rock known as kimberlite, named after the South African city of Kimberley, where it was first found and described. The kimberlite eruptions occurred in small volcanoes, the remains of which are well known thanks to observations made at considerable depths in the mines. Some of these volcanoes escaped erosion and, since their craters were filled by lakes, still retain their sedi-

ments. When, after natural erosion or mining, a deeper level of an ancient volcano is revealed, it resembles a pipe in the form of an upside-down cone, tapering toward the bottom. The cone or pipe is generally filled with breccia, the composition of which gives some indication of the violence of the volcanic explosion. Breccia consists of fragments of many different sizes torn from the surrounding rock and fused together in the kimberlite lava. The pipes are rather small for volcanic structures, their diameters ranging from about 6.5 feet (2 m) to a few hundred yards. As it descends, the pipe narrows and is generally marked by fissures corresponding to ancient, open fractures of the earth's crust, which were filled by kimberlite after serving as paths for the magma, or molten rock, released by the volcano.

Kimberlite occurs in a great variety of forms. Some types, such as the yellow ground familiar to South African diggers, have been significantly changed by the effects of weather. The blue ground, found at a much greater depth, is of the same material, but it has not been so greatly affected by surface conditions. Blue ground is often found in the form of a very hard, dark gray rock with bluish reflections, although it may vary from this pattern.

Though we are generally familiar with the morphology of kimberlite intrusions, many points are still unclear regarding the way in which they were created. What immense force drove them along a 90- to 120-mile (150–200-km) passage to the surface? Extremely high pressures and temperatures were necessary to prevent the diamonds from changing into graphite during this passage—how were these conditions maintained? Did diamonds crystallize in the very heart of the kimberlite, which would make it the genuine mother rock, or were they torn away in passing from certain deep layers—from eclogites (garnet rock), for example, whose fragments found in certain pipes often contain diamonds? Many theories

Left to right: Kimberlite breaking through the earth's crust and forming a pipe or chimney and volcanic cone; erosion of the cone; open-cast mining, in benches; underground mining.
Burns Graphics, London.

have been developed, but none has yet provided any definite answers.

From the moment the diamond reaches the earth's surface, its history presents practically no mystery at all. The kimberlite is subjected to the action of atmospheric agents and, in time, change and erosion free the crystals from their matrix. Running water then carries them to streams and rivers and finally to the open sea, where they are lost in the enormous masses of sediment unless the combined action of coastal currents and the surf casts them ashore. Conglomerates, sea terraces, dunes, and other such formations are all secondary sources of diamonds as compared with the kimberlite pipes. Occasionally glaciers play a role in wearing down the kimberlite and transporting the diamonds to their terminal moraines, but these are merely chance occurrences in the great journey that finally leads to the sea.

One might suppose that the characteristics of the diamond in the alluvial deposits are similar to those of any other mineral. But this is not so; here again the diamond proves its uniqueness. Because it is the hardest of all minerals, it is practically insensitive to friction, and because it is immutable, it is able to withstand many geological events without being damaged. However, the diamond is not entirely indestructible: it is sensitive to violent shocks, and although the best-formed crystals, because of their rounded form and smooth surface, can resist the buffeting of natural transportation, flat diamonds, which are poorly crystallized or contain impurities, are more fragile. Thus long-distance transportation in alluvial deposits has created, through natural selection, the most perfect stones. That is why there is a higher proportion of fine stones in the marine terraces of southwestern Africa than in kimberlite pipes, where they have received less rough treatment over the ages.

In general, this is all the definite knowledge we have of the geology of the diamond. Beyond this point theories take over—some of them based, however tenuously, on proven facts, others little more than guesswork; some dependent on a respectable scientific approach, others resembling the most incredible fantasies of science fiction. The following are some of the major theories.

Most of the known kimberlite pipes of Africa and South America were created during the Cretaceous period, between 70 million and 150 million years ago. Their creation therefore coincided with the beginning of the continental drift, the great dislocation that separated South America and Africa and created the Atlantic Ocean. It has been observed that the kimberlites occur in specific areas, and that those close to the rim of the great fracture are extremely poor in diamonds, whereas those relatively far from it, in continents where the continental crust is thicker, are sufficiently rich to be worked. Radioactive dating reveals that the rocks that constitute the "heart" of these continents are among the most ancient, some at least 2.5 billion years old.

Diamonds are freed from the kimberlite by erosion and are carried toward the rivers by rain water. *Burns Graphics, London.*

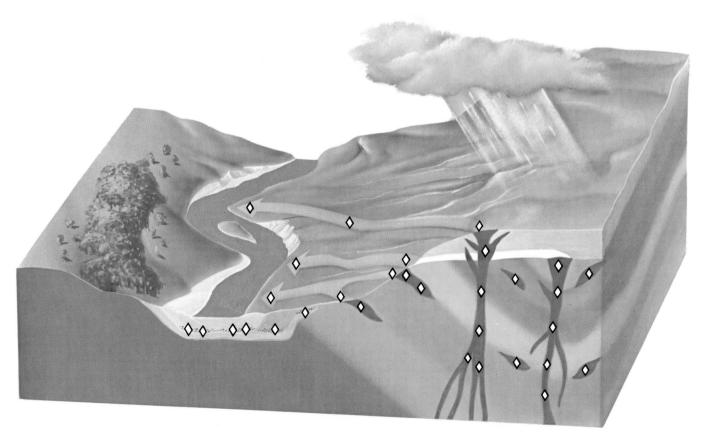

A rough diamond in a fragment of kimberlite. Muséum national d'Histoire naturelle, Paris. *Photo Guy Philippart de Foy, Brussels.*

Though it is impossible to prove that these facts are significantly connected, observations over so broad an area, encompassing several thousand kimberlites (only a few dozen of which are actually workable) provide weighty evidence that it was the opening of the Atlantic Ocean that permitted the violent volcanic activity that led to the formation of the kimberlite. Only the most ancient sections of the continents were thick enough to fall to the lowest depths of the earth's mantle and thereby enable the diamonds to rise to the surface. This is only a theory, but it is essentially based on firm data, and it gives us at least a solid working base.

It is also possible for quite different theories to be developed from the same empirical observations. Many diamonds were discovered, often purely by chance, in the region of the Great Lakes in the United States, in gravel and clay deposits left by glaciers after the ice age. The path of these glaciers can be re-created with some precision by studying the striae left on the lower parts of the rocks, and there is strong evidence that the diamonds may have

been borne by ice from Hudson's Bay in northern Canada. Some writers have suggested that Hudson's Bay itself is nothing less than the scar left by the impact of a giant meteorite. This theory may seem rather implausible, but there are arguments in its favor. On this already largely hypothetical basis, two quite contradictory theories have been developed. The less revolutionary theory is that the diamonds were formed by the shock of impact when the meteorite thudded into Canada. The other, bolder, theory, which is backed up with figures, claims that the meteorite's kinetic energy was so great that it pierced the earth's crust and reached the mantle, which splashed up to the surface, bringing diamonds with it.

There is yet a third theory, which, though somewhat neglected (perhaps because it is less sensational), derives some support from newly discovered data. Recent digging has revealed kimberlites in the Great Lakes region. So far they have proven unprofitable, but there is good reason to suppose that others, perhaps hidden beneath glacial deposits, may be the source of the diamonds in this area.

No attempt will be made here to advocate any one of these theories. History has shown that the explanation that appears most logical may be false, and that the wildest notions of science fiction may one day prove to be fact.

In his *Histoire des Minéraux* ("History of Minerals"), the great eighteenth-century naturalist Georges Buffon wrote, "There remains finally the vegetal and clay earth, which may be the home of the diamond and precious stones. This well-based assumption acquires the imprimatur of truth when we reflect upon two general facts which are likewise undisputed. The first is that these stones are found only in the warmest climates and that consequently excessive heat is required for their formation; the second is that they are found only on the surface, in the first layer of the earth or in the river sand." Farther on he added, "Every combustible matter only comes from organic bodies or their debris. Therefore the diamond, which nourishes itself on light and which we have had to class among combustible substances, can come only from the vegetal earth, which alone contains the combustible debris of organic bodies." Drawing practical conclusions from this hypothesis, he added, "It is more than probable that if research were undertaken in the hottest climates of Africa, we would find diamonds similar to those in the hottest climates of Asia and America."

Two centuries later, it is fairly easy to spot the traps into which Buffon fell by making predictions in a field with which he was necessarily unfamiliar. Logical reasoning applied to data far too fragmentary and hastily general-

Narcisse Janot, prospector for La Forminière, photographed in the Belgian Congo (now Zaïre) in August, 1911. *Sibeka Archives, Brussels.*

A prospecting expedition in Angola, 1972. *Photo René Delville, Brussels.*

ized led him to put forth a theory that has proven completely false. Yet despite its errors, its applications to Africa have been, in a sense, verified. Two centuries from now, what will remain of the current theories on the birth of the diamond?

Prospecting

From ancient times until the beginning of the twentieth century prospecting for diamonds, like many other techniques, was largely a matter of trial and error. Early methods were similar to those used today by the *garimpeiros* of Brazil and by other hopeful individuals in various parts of the world. In other words, there was an element of luck in every new discovery. Not until the early years of this century did large mining companies, equipped with advanced technology and backed by substantial financial resources, begin to make prospecting a systematic and scientific process.

One of the greatest problems inherent in diamond mining is that the object of the search is so small in relation to the material that surrounds it. The concentration of diamonds is extremely low, both in the alluvial gravels and in the primary sources of kimberlite. Another problem with diamonds, one that does not occur with many other valuable minerals, is that the diamond-bearing material cannot be subjected to industrial processes that will cause chemical or physical changes. The diamonds must be recovered intact, and thus the surrounding soil or gravel must be sorted with great care—in the final stages, grain by grain.

The modern techniques used in searching for diamonds were developed in Africa. It is possible to distinguish three methods, developed more or less independently in different situations. The characteristics of each one were determined by the physical environment in which the system first operated. The regions involved were British West Africa, the Belgian Congo (now Zaïre), and southern Africa.

The British Method. What may be called the "British" method was evolved during prospecting in the Gold Coast (now Ghana), where the material to be dealt with consisted of detrital deposits lacking in kimberlite minerals. A very direct method was used to locate the diamonds—large quantities of gravel were washed. Such a method is particularly well suited to the physical conditions of a humid, tropical region with a dense network of perennial rivers. The considerable drop in water levels during the dry season and the relative ease of movement in savannah country both favor alluvial prospecting—in the gravel of the actual rivers and on the ground that forms the riverbanks during the rainy season.

Rough diamonds found during a 1956 prospecting expedition in the northeast of what is now the Central African Republic. *Photo Jean-Claude Serre, Orléans.*

The originality of this method lies in its exploitation of natural weather cycles. During the dry season, the search can concentrate on specific points in the riverbed where sudden variations in flow or changes in direction of the current create natural "pots," or cavities in which the diamond-yielding gravel tends to accumulate. A major inconvenience, obviously, is that this method can be used only for comparatively short periods, from two to five months every year. Besides Ghana, the British method has been used most notably in Sierra Leone and in Guinea.

The Belgian Method. Conditions in the great basin of the Congo River are very different from those in Ghana. The "Belgian" method of prospecting has been governed in part by the sheer difficulty of movement and orientation in the rain forest, and in larger part by the equatorial climate, with its extremely heavy rainfall. Because there is virtually no dry season, the gravel lying on the riverbed is very difficult to reach. The system that evolved under the Belgians, at first in Kasai and later in the Bakwanga region of what is now Zaïre, is based on a grid: the area is marked in lines by men on foot, and then divided into squares. No special attention is paid to the river system. This may seem paradoxical, but in the Congo basin, where the diamond fields are dispersed over a wide area, the incidence of diamonds is comparatively uniform. Since diamonds are found in practically all the rivers, likely sites

in the valleys and on the old "terraces," where diamonds have been reconcentrated by the forces of erosion, have to be inspected. Wherever a line of the grid meets a watercourse—whether it is a tiny stream or a major river—samples of the gravel are taken, and holes are dug in the alluvial plain where deposits occur due to the flooding of the river. Like the British method, this is one of direct search for diamonds, not for the minerals associated with them. When favorable conditions appear at a particular spot, prospecting is continued both upstream and downstream, with lines of holes cutting through the valleys at intervals as short as 30–65 feet (10–20 m). With some modifications, the Belgian method has been utilized at Ubangi in the state now known as the Central African Republic, and in Gabon.

The Southern African Method. In southern Africa the targets are different, and the method therefore differs as well. The object is to discover the primary sources—the kimberlite pipes—from which the alluvial deposits derived. The southern African method, like the others, is largely dictated by physical conditions—in this case the dry, subtropical climate and the flat, arid plateau where rivers are relatively scarce and are generally dry for part of the year. Unlike the two methods described above, the southern African method is one of indirect search. The prospectors are not looking specifically for diamonds, but for the kimberlitic minerals that usually accompany diamonds. These minerals are quite abundant and can be detected in a much smaller sample than must be taken when diamonds alone are the object—a spadeful, more or less, instead of a truckload. This method has an additional advantage in that it need be applied only to a fairly shallow layer of soil. Since movement is easy in these dry, flat regions, an enormous area can be squared off in a regular pattern and swiftly prospected by taking small samples from the surface. The samples are then taken to a central washing station at the nearest available water supply. When an unusually high quantity of the kimberlitic minerals associated with diamonds (garnet and, less frequently, ilmenite) appears, the sampling grid is tightened by dividing the relevant area into smaller squares in order to localize the kimberlite from which these minerals were dispersed. Only then does the diamond itself become the object of the search, during the washing of large volumes of kimberlite or the eluvial deposits overlying it.

This method was used on a spectacular scale in 1958–60 in Tanganyika (now Tanzania), where an enormous network covered most of the country. In Botswana it led to the discovery of the Orapa mine in 1967 and, more recently, to the huge Jwaneng pipe under 130 feet (40 m) of Kalahari sand and calcrete.

The three methods described above may still be profitably employed where the physical conditions are nearly identical to those in which the methods were developed. They cannot be easily adapted to different environments. Nor will they function adequately if the aims vary slightly—if, for example, a dike is to be located instead of a kimberlite pipe. In general, diamond prospecting throughout the world has changed considerably over the past decade or two. Costs have risen so greatly and the political situation in many of the countries concerned is so unpredictable that only very large deposits justify the risks involved. In practice, this means that nowadays kimberlite deposits are actively prospected only by large mining companies. There are many smaller companies that are interested in the easily exploited detrital deposits, but in most cases what they undertake is not prospecting in the true sense of the word—that is, the search for previously unknown sources—but rather the investigation and evaluation of sites that are already known. Of course, the "wild" prospecting done by solitary individuals still continues in many parts of the world, and such people are little affected by the economic and political constraints that govern the big mining companies.

Prospecting in Zaïre. A geologist, with assistants and porters, making a path through the brush and (right) taking samples of gravel from a stream in the heart of the forest. *De Beers Archives.*

Prospecting in Zaïre. Washing gravel in a sieve and (far right) placing samples in packets for future analysis in the laboratory. *De Beers Archives.*

the customary digging of large pits in favor of small samples taken from the riverbeds. Finally, from southern Africa, the French took the technique of soil sampling, but only when less expensive techniques were impractical.

It should be emphasized that the basic principles have not changed with regard to the search for kimberlite—it is still a matter of de-

The French Method. In view of the risks, therefore, research today is focused almost exclusively on the known areas of kimberlite, and a modern method of prospecting has been developed that might be called the "French" method. Although many of the techniques are borrowed from other methods, some of the modifications that have made it more practical and easily utilized have come from French mining engineers. Undoubtedly the eclectic, adaptable aspect of the French character was important in refining techniques, but it should be added that their inventiveness was to some extent forced on the French by their sparse financial resources, which were much smaller than those of their competitors.

Thus the French method, generally speaking, seeks to obtain the greatest possible amount of information at the lowest possible cost. From the British it borrowed the method of prospecting alluvial deposits, which, when the sampling is carefully located, provide information about the whole area of the basin upstream. The French managed to lower the cost of this method by refining the techniques used to detect traces of kimberlite minerals in the gravel, thereby considerably reducing the volume of material to be treated. From the Belgian method the French adopted the system of moving along the lines of a predrawn grid, but here again costs were reduced by abandoning

tecting the minerals that *accompany* the diamond. Modern methods—magnetic, scintillometric, electromagnetic, and electrical—of photogeology, geophysics, and, to a lesser extent, geochemistry have also contributed tools useful in prospecting, from the reconnaissance of likely areas to be prospected to the exploration of the kimberlite pipes themselves.

From Photogeology to Geochemistry. The nature of the rocks underlying the soil in any region has considerable influence on the area's morphology—the nature of the terrain, the vegetation, the watercourses, and so on. Photogeology is based on the interpretation of these characteristics from photographs taken at different altitudes—by helicopter, airplane, and even space satellite—with different types of film—panchromatic, infrared, and others. With these aids it is often possible to make a reasonably accurate sketch of the structure of the region and, in particular, to locate the great subterranean cracks that indicate the presence of kimberlite. In addition to these general, regional data, photogeology can also detect the characteristic anomalies in vegetation that often betray the presence of a kimberlite pipe.

Radar images obtained from an airplane may be interpreted in the same way as aerial photographs. Radar has an additional advantage—it permeates clouds, so that radar images can be taken in all types of weather conditions and even at night. This is particularly helpful in equatorial or tropical regions, where a persistent haze makes it extremely difficult to achieve good photographic cover.

Magnetic methods, deriving from geophysics, consist of making a map of the earth's magnetic field and interpreting the variations in order to deduce information on the nature of the rocks that produce them. Measurements of the magnetic field are taken at regular intervals along parallel lines drawn on an imaginary map, either by moving across the terrain at ground level or from an airplane or helicopter. The results obtained differ widely, depending on which method is used—precision varies directly in proportion to altitude. A measurement taken at 3 feet (1 m) above the surface will be influenced chiefly by the rocks occurring within a 3-foot radius, whereas a measurement taken at an altitude of 3,000 feet (1,000 m) will be correspondingly influenced by the rocks occurring within a 3,000-foot radius. In the lat-

ter case, a small kimberlite pipe in the area may pass unnoticed, since the magnetic variations it produces will very likely be lost amid the variations produced by surrounding rocks, which occupy a far greater surface area. From a practical point of view, while the measurements taken from an airplane make it possible to cover large surfaces rapidly at a relatively low cost per square mile, they outline only the main features of the geology of the region and will reveal only rather large pipes with strong magnetism. Conversely, measurements taken at ground level will reveal very small pipes or dikes with slight magnetism, but since they require very close measurements taken along tightly spaced parallel lines, the cost per square mile is extremely high, and prospecting of this kind is inefficient for systematically covering realtively large areas. A compromise between these two extremes is offered by prospecting from a helicopter, at an altitude of, say, 300 feet (100 m). The cost is greater than that of prospecting from an airplane, but the data are more precise and a considerably larger area can be covered than from ground level.

Scintillometric, or radiometric, measurements record the radioactive radius of rocks along lines that are made either at ground level or from an airplane or helicopter. As with magnetic prospecting, the main object is to detect contrasts, but this method looks for zones of different radioactivity. Generally, scintillometry is used in conjunction with airborne measurement of magnetism. By combining the two operations on the same flight, additional useful information can be obtained at little extra cost. Scintillometry is therefore used rather frequently, even when the search is not for radioactive ore. The radiation used in this method has a low penetrative power, penetrating soil or alluvial deposits only to a depth of about a foot, so the usefulness of scintillometry, like magnetism, is highly dependent on the altitude at which the measurements are taken.

Electromagnetism is used in mineral prospecting by artificially producing an electromagnetic field and studying the modifications it undergoes when it passes over the terrain under inspection. A first-rate method in the search for certain mineral conductor ores, it is not in general particularly well adapted to the search for kimberlite pipes (though there have been some notable exceptions). It gives positive results only when combined with detailed measurements on the ground, especially for dikes that have become conductors because of water flow.

Electrical methods use electrodes that are placed in the soil at fixed intervals, the space between them varying according to circumstances. An electrical current is then intro-

Prospecting by MIBA in Zaïre in 1978: the site of a test pit. *Photo Guy Philippart de Foy, Brussels.*

netism, can be misleading. These techniques do not always work as well in practice as they do in theory, and they have sometimes failed entirely in the field. This is not so surprising when the wide variations in physical characteristics between one pipe and another are taken into account. Some pipes, for example, are highly magnetic, others not at all. It is worth emphasizing the important fact that geophysical methods cannot be used in all circumstances. The same rules do not apply in all conditions, and many other types of rock may produce anomalies similar to those caused by kimberlites. It is always necessary to investigate the recorded anomalies more closely, and, as a rule, this can only be done by expeditions on the ground. The efficiency of geophysical methods is virtually canceled out by the nu-

Aerial view of a prospecting site in Zaïre, 1978, showing the building where the gravel is washed and separated (right) with jigs operated by hand to the rhythm of an improvised tom-tom. *Photos Guy Philippart de Foy, Brussels.*

duced, and the current between the electrodes is studied. This method gives a picture of the "electrical resistance" of the terrain traversed by the current and thus provides information about the nature of the underlying rocks. Unlike the geophysical methods described above, this technique can be used only on the ground. Because it is comparatively slow and therefore expensive, its use is limited to the "tactical" stage of prospecting—for defining the outer limits of a kimberlite pipe that has already been located by other means.

The apparent efficiency of airborne geophysical methods, especially the use of mag-

merous checks that must be made of variations caused by surface features, which must be done on the ground.

Geochemical methods of prospecting look for certain chemical elements in the soil or in alluvial deposits. These elements often exist in very small proportions and are measured in parts per million (ppm) or grams per ton. A content "map" is made, showing significant variations in the distribution of the chemical element being measured. This method, frequently used in searching out metallic deposits, has given remarkable results in diamond prospecting. One type of kimberlite contains an average of 1,000 ppm of chromium and as much nickel—a high proportion, about ten times more than basalt and one hundred times more than granite. As the same content is found in the soil that derives from the kimberlite rock, geochemistry can be used to track down kimberlites. However, it is a slow and costly method, and geophysical methods, based on the search for kimberlite minerals, are generally preferred for covering large areas. But geochemistry is used in "tactical" prospecting in small areas that have been selected through other methods.

The Siberian Method. The relatively recent appearance of the Soviet Union on the world diamond market has attracted attention to the research undertaken by Soviet geologists prospecting the deposits of Yakutsk in Siberia. The Siberian method, not very well known outside the Soviet Union, apparently relies heavily on the old methods of prospecting alluvial deposits. However, climatic conditions have been an inhibiting factor, and airborne prospecting—using magnetism, scintillometry, and various kinds of photography—has been equally important. Results have proven the Siberian method effective, but it is characterized by a duplication of effort possible only in a socialist economy where there are relatively few constraints imposed by cost.

The Moment of Truth. Although each prospecting campaign is unique, if only because the physical setting varies, the primary operation is always a search for kimberlite minerals on alluvial or eluvial terrain. Once this is done, large-scale reconnaissance makes it possible during the so-called strategic phase to select from regions extending over tens of

Prospecting in Brazil, 1978, by the Tejucana Mining Company. Bottom: Drilling on the banks of the Jequitinhonha. *Photos Guy Philippart de Foy, Brussels.*

thousands of square miles the few thousand in which the search should be intensified. Often kimberlites are discovered solely by gradually intensifying the search in a decreasing area, but more frequently concentrating the search results only in isolating an area of a few square miles. Other techniques must then be used to locate the kimberlite itself. This is the "tactical" phase, in which geophysics incontestably plays the most important role—shallow soil samples are taken and test holes are dug. Then comes the "moment of truth," when the weathered kimberlite is washed to discover whether it contains diamonds or not. If these first tests prove positive, they are followed by a very careful evaluation of the reserves: pits are dug on a regular pattern of squares over the entire surface of the kimberlite area in order to obtain a representative sampling not only of the diamond content per cubic yard, but also of the average size of the stones. Sampling by automatic drills or "sounders" can penetrate as deep as hundreds of yards below the surface, making it possible to get an idea of the depth of the deposit. On the basis of the information thus derived, complicated calculations must be made to determine whether or not the deposit can be worked profitably.

All this may seem to be fairly simple, but mineral prospecting, and diamond prospecting above all, is a complicated affair. It is an art that demands the employment to the best advantage of a wide variety of techniques, whether derived from practical experience or scientific research. In the proper use of these techniques, nothing can replace experience.

Businesses in many countries are active today in diamond prospecting. In France the Bureau de Recherches Géologiques et Minières (Office of Geological and Mining Research, BRGM) has created a department specializing in this type of prospecting, and elsewhere there are many large mining companies, including of course De Beers, that are interested in diamond prospecting. Such companies generally remain highly discreet, and it is difficult to predict where the next important discovery is likely to occur. Although Africa has already been heavily prospected, active research is still going on there. A few years ago South America reentered the field, and considerable prospecting is under way there, especially in Brazil. The mining press periodically forecasts imminent discoveries in northwestern Australia, notably in a zone—can this be a portent?—called Kimberley. It may be that North America will one day have surprises for us, or perhaps China, where a press report from Peking in July, 1978, mentioned a diamond of 158.79 carats found by a peasant girl weeding on her commune.

Southern Africa

In 1929, when Sir Ernest Oppenheimer, who had founded the Anglo-American Corporation of South Africa Ltd. in 1917 and the Consolidated Diamond Mines of South-West Africa Ltd. in 1920, became chairman of De Beers Consolidated Mines Ltd., a new age began for the diamond industry in southern Africa: the major part of the industry was brought under a single management. Since then, the four De Beers mines in the Kimberley region—De Beers, Dutoitspan, Bultfontein, and Wesselton—and the coastal deposits in Namaqualand and to the north of the Orange River have been joined by three reopened mines: the Premier (of which Sir Ernest had been made chairman in 1927) in 1945; the Jagersfontein in 1949; and the Koffiefontein in 1971. Nearly all of the diamonds produced in south-

The principal diamond mines of southern Africa. *Burns Graphics, London.*

ern Africa since the Second World War have come from these mines.

When the Jwaneng mine in southern Botswana begins production in 1982, the total production of all the mines in the southern part of Africa will begin to rise from the current 25 percent of world production to as much as over 40 percent. The output from this area rose from 5 million metric carats (2,200 pounds, or 1,000 kg) in 1962 to 14 million in 1977, and it may rise to more than 22 million carats in the mid-1980's. This phenomenal growth has resulted from the discovery and development of new mines such as Finsch, Orapa, Letlhakane, and Koingnaas; from the reopening of Koffiefontein; and, currently, from a massive redevelopment of the Premier mine, a near-doubling of Orapa's rate of production, and from the new Jwaneng mine.

The mining companies have had to develop new technologies for open-pit and underground mining and for the recovery of diamonds from widely varying types of diamondiferous ore. The planning, design, construction, and commissioning of integrated mining operations in remote and difficult locations has exploited the skills not only of mining and mineral-processing engineers, but also of hydrologists; engineering geologists; civil, mechanical, and electrical engineers; architects; and town planners. A whole new way of life has developed for employees of the mining companies and their families, for both indigenous peoples and expatriates. In Botswana, the sale of diamonds is likely to account for more than half of the country's total foreign earnings within the next decade.

For the purposes of this chapter, southern Africa includes South Africa, Namibia (formerly South-West Africa), Botswana (formerly Bechuanaland), and Lesotho (formerly Basutoland). Swaziland, Mozambique, and Zimbabwe-Rhodesia have yet to produce diamonds in significant quantities. In South Africa there are a great many small- to medium-size diamond mines and diggings that do not fall under the control of De Beers Consolidated Mines Ltd. These include the fissure mines in the Bellsbank area north of Kimberley, the Swartruggens mine in the Transvaal, and the State Alluvial Diggings south of the mouth of

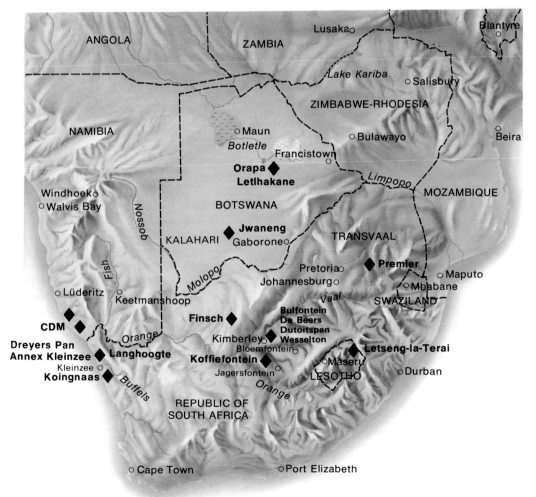

the Orange River in the western Cape. Their total production amounts to approximately 500,000 carats per year. However, this account will be confined to the discovery, development, and operation of those diamond mines in southern Africa in which De Beers has a major interest and which it manages.

Production

The table on page 101 shows the production of diamonds in thousands of carats from the major mines in southern Africa during the period 1962–78. The production of the Kimberley mines, once the cornerstone of world output, has dropped to about a million carats per year. These mines are now deep, and what were once large pipes on the surface are greatly reduced in area at the deeper levels. Jagersfontein, producer of some of the loveliest gemstones, finally closed down in 1971, a hundred years after its original opening: its bottom workings were some 2,515 feet (762 m) below the surface. The Finsch mine, currently producing 2.5 million carats a year and expected to rise to 3.5 million in the 1980's, began production in 1965; it will continue to be the largest producer of industrial diamonds in South

Africa for a number of years. The Koffiefontein mine was reopened by De Beers in 1971, and it produces about 400,000 carats per year. In the Transvaal, the Premier mine, which produced the famous Cullinan diamond, now has a new lease on life with the development of what is virtually a new mine under the gabbro sill (an intrusion of igneous rock) that at one stage appeared to form the bottom of the workings. Its annual production should increase to 2.5 million carats.

The production of fine gemstones will continue from the coastal workings north of the Orange River estuary—Consolidated Diamond Mines of South-West Africa (CDM)—and south of the river—the government's State Alluvial Diggings. Gemstones will also be produced by De Beers Namaqualand Division, which has mines on a number of farms, including Annex Kleinzee, Dreyers Pan, Tweepad, and Koingnaas. New processing plants should enable CDM to produce 2 million carats annually, mainly gemstones, and the newly opened Koingnaas will increase the Namaqualand mines' annual production to 1.7 million carats, again mainly gemstones.

In terms of production, the most remarkable achievement in this region is the development of the mines in Botswana. Orapa began full production in 1972 at 2.4 million carats per year; this is currently being increased to 4.5 million carats per year. The smaller Letlhakane mine should produce 400,000 carats per year for many years. It is thought that the new Jwaneng mine may well be capable of producing more than 6 million carats annually, including perhaps as much as 2 million carats of gemstones.

Lesotho has long produced diamonds sporadically from diggings high in the mountains. In 1977 the Letseng-la-Terai mine began production with 23,000 carats; this increased to 60,000 carats in 1978.

These are the main producing mines associated with the De Beers group in southern Africa. As long as diamond sales are maintained, the region certainly has the capacity to meet even an increased demand.

Recent Discoveries

The search for diamonds in southern Africa has continued uninterrupted since the first recorded 21-carat stone was picked up by fifteen-year-old Erasmus Jacobs in 1866 on a riverbank near Hopetown, south of present-day Kimberley. Exploration since those days has moved away from the gravels of the Vaal and other rivers and the pipes of Kimberley to the mountains of Lesotho and the semidesert of Botswana. Prospecting methods have become more sophisticated with the introduction of

The coastal terraces of Namaqualand: a general view of the Koingnaas installations. *De Beers Archives.*

Bottom: Aerial view of the Finsch mine, South Africa. The area of the pipe is 44.8 acres (17.9 ha) at the surface. *De Beers Archives.*

Treatment plant at
the Premier diamond mine,
South Africa.
Photo Explorer, Paris.

the reevaluation of known existing diamondiferous deposits.

The Finsch mine, 45 acres (18 ha) of kimberlite located on the Brits farm near Lime-acre, about 95 miles (160 km) west of Kimberley, was discovered by Alister Fincham and Ernest Schwabel in 1960. At the time they were prospecting for asbestos. The soil in the area had also yielded garnets, indicating the possible presence of kimberlite under the ironstone covering. In May, 1963, De Beers purchased the entire capital of Finsch Diamonds (the name is taken from an amalgam of Fincham and Schwabel) for 4.5 million rands (a rand is worth approximately a dollar). By July of 1963 preliminary boring had confirmed the profitability of working the region, and two years later, the Finsch mine began full-scale production.

In 1955 De Beers began prospecting for diamonds in Botswana, then known as the Bechuanaland Protectorate. Three small diamonds were found in the Motloutse River, a tributary of the Limpopo, near Francistown, but geologists were unable to trace their source. They did, however, find evidence of major tectonic movement in the area in fairly recent geological times, and this encouraged them to take the search westward. Soon good indications of kimberlite were found by the team headed by Dr. Gavin Lamont, De Beers' field manager, in the vicinity of Letlhakane. The Orapa pipe (275 acres, or 110 ha, in surface area), 145 miles (240 km) west of Francistown, was discovered in 1967. Of the numerous other kimberlite pipes in the area, two more, 9 miles (15 km) southwest of Letlhakane, were proven viable in 1973. The Orapa mine began production in 1971 and the Letlhakane mine five years later.

In southern Botswana other exploration

various geological disciplines—geophysics and geochemistry as well as straightforward geology.

Dr. John Williamson's discovery in 1940 of the large diamond pipe at Mwadui, in what is now Tanzania, was probably the first major find using modern techniques. In some ways Williamson motivated the systematic search that formed the foundation of prospecting and exploration of diamonds by large mining companies in Africa after the Second World War. The postwar era provided the economic potential for the development of new mines and for

[1]De Beers, Wesselton, Dutoitspan, Bultfontein (except 1972–73).
[2]Annex Kleinzee, Langhoogte (1965–71), Dreyers Pan (since 1966), Tweepad, Koingnaas (since 1978).
[3]Consolidated Diamond Mines SWA, plus coastal mining (1965–71).
[4]Orapa, Letlhakane (346,000 carats in 1977), Jwaneng (becoming operational about 1982).

Annual Production of Diamonds in Southern Africa (De Beers Mines) from 1962 to 1978 (in thousands of carats).

Year	1962	1963	1964	1965	1966	1967	1968	1969	1970	1971	1972	1973	1974	1975	1976	1977	1978	1985
Kimberley Mines [1]	1,479	1,532	1,523	1,627	1,620	1,603	1,378	1,428	1,438	1,100	888	905	885	1,010	1,051	1,085	1,081	1,100
Jagersfontein	85	73	59	69	78	102	107	99	82	22	—	—	—	—	—	—	—	—
Finsch	—	—	—	95	901	1,817	2,216	2,236	2,596	2,223	2,479	2,495	2,353	2,291	2,203	2,426	2,630	3,500
Koffiefontein	—	—	—	—	—	—	—	—	—	78	308	373	342	336	354	410	343	400
Namaqualand [2]	68	70	106	109	240	347	494	702	637	505	487	533	778	942	1,027	1,163	1,225	1,700
Premier	1,685	2,087	2,224	2,439	2,500	2,377	2,432	2,522	2,490	2,437	2,454	2,502	2,422	2,036	1,833	2,010	1,983	2,600
Total, South Africa (De Beers)	3,317	3,762	3,912	4,339	5,339	6,246	6,627	6,987	7,243	6,365	6,616	6,808	6,780	6,615	6,468	7,094	7,262	9,300
South-West Africa (Namibia) [3]	1,007	1,138	1,253	1,656	1,758	1,700	1,722	2,024	1,865	1,648	1,596	1,600	1,570	1,748	1,694	2,001	1,898	2,000
Botswana (Orapa) [4]	—	—	—	—	—	—	—	—	464	822	2,403	2,416	2,718	2,397	2,384	2,691	2,785	10,900
Lesotho (Letseng)	—	—	—	—	—	—	—	—	—	—	—	—	—	—	—	23	49	60
Total, southern Africa	4,324	4,900	5,165	5,995	7,097	7,946	8,349	9,011	9,572	8,835	10,615	10,824	11,068	10,760	10,546	11,809	11,994	22,260

teams, also under Dr. Lamont's direction, identified the Jwaneng pipe in 1973. This pipe is hidden under 165 feet (50 m) of barren Kalahari sands, silcretes, and calcretes. The discovery was the result of a systematic program of geochemical sampling that determined the pipe's position. The source, 90 miles (150 km) west of Gaborone, the capital, will be one of the world's major diamond producers when it begins production in 1982.

Colonel Jack Scott was granted a concession to prospect for diamonds in Basutoland (now Lesotho) in 1955. Two years later a 45-acre (18-ha) pipe was found at Letseng-la-Terai in the northeastern part of the country at an altitude of 10,000 feet (3,000 m). In all, nearly 2,000 carats were recovered from the workings before Scott decided that the pipe was not viable. Individual local diggers were then allowed to work there. After Mrs. Ernestine Ramaboa found a 601-carat stone in 1967, the Lesotho government decided that a systematic evaluation of the kimberlite was necessary, and in 1968 the Rio Tinto Mining Company began a premining feasibility assessment. Four years later they, too, decided that the pipe was uneconomical. Further negotiations took place, this time between Prime Minister Chief Leaboa Jonathon and De Beers chairman Harry Oppenheimer. On the basis of a reevaluation of the previous work, De Beers agreed to open a new mine in this remote and difficult location.

De Beers' decision was unique in that it was based on probability theory. The diamonds recovered during the original sampling were not expected to be representative of those that would be recovered during production over a longer period; for the mine to be considered viable, larger stones would have had to be recovered. So, twenty years after its discovery, the Letseng mine was officially opened in 1977. It is too early to tell whether expectations will be fulfilled.

During the 1960's it became apparent that the Jagersfontein mine in the southern Orange Free State was nearing the end of its long life. Koffiefontein, 20 miles (30 km) to the west, had lain dormant for nearly forty years after it had been mined as an open pit to a depth of 350 feet (100 m). Changes in technology, including the development of large earth-moving equipment, and new treatment processes, particularly the heavy-medium cyclone, suggested that it would be economical to reopen the mine. Production at the Koffiefontein mine recommenced in 1971.

The search for diamond deposits of a very different kind had been continuing along the west coast of southern Africa. Much of the work extended the known reserves of operations at Consolidated Diamond Mines on the north side of the Orange River and in Namaqualand to the south. Diamonds were first found on the Koingnaas farm, 35 miles (60 km) south of Annex Kleinzee, in 1962, and it was proposed that a mine to produce diamonds should be opened there in the early 1970's. However, the project was postponed because of unfavorable market conditions, and it was not until 1976 that the decision to mine was made. The Koingnaas mine began production in 1978.

Development of New Mines

The significant increase in diamond production in southern Africa since the mid-1960's has been a result of the development of six new mines as well as of the expansion of existing operations. The capital cost of these ventures, usually raised by De Beers, has risen dramatically over the period. The Finsch mine, the first of the new mines, located conveniently close to Kimberley, cost approximately 10 million rands to bring into production. Jwaneng, in a deserted part of Botswana, will have cost more than 200 million rands by the time it begins production in 1982. Apart from inflation, which has escalated all costs, the greater complexity of the facilities required at the start of production on the remote mines, and their

Industrial installations at the Letseng-la-Terai mine in Lesotho at an altitude of 10,000 feet (3,000 m). *De Beers Archives.*

Right: Construction of a processing unit for analyzing the first samples of ore at Jwaneng, Botswana, in the Kalahari Desert, 1979. The mine is expected to become operational in 1982. *De Beers Archives.*

A rough diamond crystal from Letseng-la-Terai, Lesotho. *De Beers Archives.*

lack of an initial infrastructure, resulted in expenditures that would have been unimaginable ten years earlier.

People sometimes wonder how De Beers has managed to achieve and maintain its virtual monopoly of the diamond industry in southern Africa. The simple answer is that De Beers has successfully demonstrated to the governments in the region its unique expertise in production engineering and diamond marketing. The various governments have of course gained financial concessions and a degree of control, reducing the effect of private—usually foreign—ownership, and the negotiations that preceded the agreements have often caused delays in starting construction and in eventual production. However, the ability of the governments of countries like Botswana and Lesotho to form viable partnerships with De Beers has been a major achievement. It has been the most important factor contributing to the expansion of the diamond industry in those developing countries.

The period between the decision to go ahead with a project and the day when the new processing plant and equipment are commissioned is a time of intense activity and excitement. This pioneering phase of a mine's life can last from two to four years.

The project team formed to effect the construction and establishment of a new mine under agreed cost and time constraints faces a complex task. Even though financiers and politicians have agreed on the terms of the overall operation, translating those terms into detailed plans, contracts, schedules, estimates, and drawings involves considerable work. The initial technical proposal—a short prefeasibility study in most cases—together with the legal documentation resulting from negotiations have to be converted into a form that can be used by engineers. Formal concepts have to be changed into practical details before millions of rands are spent.

Engineering plans are based on extensive investigations, often carried out after negotiations have been completed. Many disciplines are brought into play. Mining engineers require information concerning not only the shape, size, and grade of the ore body, but also the strength of the rock to be excavated and the effects of climate. In order to develop a flow sheet, mineral-processing engineers often have to conduct crushing, settling, and other tests on the ore: the diamonds themselves have varying physical properties that have to be identified before a recovery process can be designed. Locating water sources for both human and industrial purposes may entail a search for dam sites or drilling for underground reservoirs. Electrical power, the essential energy requirement, may have to be generated on the site or transmitted over high-tension lines many miles long. Communications, including telephones, telexes, and radios, have to be established, which often means that government engineers have to assess alternative routes. Their preparations must also include roads, airstrips, and railway sidings for the transportation of people and materials. Town planners need to match the housing and township requirements of the company with standards acceptable to the host country. All research must be both comprehensive and thorough.

During the geological exploration phase, access to prospecting sites, especially those in the more remote parts of Botswana or in the mountains of Lesotho, is often by four-wheel-drive vehicle on bush tracks or mountain paths. Communication is usually by radio, and accommodations consist of tents or prefabricated houses. One of the project team's first tasks, therefore, is to provide temporary roads and

Prefabricated buildings for the engineers and workmen constructing the Jwaneng mine in Botswana, 1979. *De Beers Archives.*

Sinking a sampling shaft, CDM mine. *De Beers Archives.*

housing for the construction workers. Improving the road to Letseng in the Maluti Mountains involved blasting hillsides, filling in swamps, and constructing bridges and fords. Even so, the journey by road to the mine site is hair-raising, and the alternative of flying in and landing on an airstrip carved into the top of a nearby ridge is usually considered preferable. When Orapa was built, the government constructed a 140-mile (230-km) all-weather gravel road from Francistown, with a telephone/telex link erected alongside it. Almost all early construction workers live in prefabricated houses brought to the site along the embryonic road system.

Providing water for a new mine is usually a major consideration, particularly with diamond ores that are treated with a wet process. The problem of water supply has been solved in many and varied ways. Finsch is supplied by water pumped out of a local asbestos mine as well as by a huge pipeline that brings water from the Vaal River. The Okavango delta in northwestern Botswana overflows annually, and water flows down two rivers, the Nghabe into Lake Ngami and the Boteti into Lake Xau and the Mgadigadi Pans. De Beers diverted water from the Boteti River into a reservoir in order to supply the Orapa mine. The water sources for the Letlhakane mine and the future Jwaneng mine are well fields in which bore-hole pumps are placed up to 650 feet (200 m) below the surface.

What might seem to be an unlikely problem with water supply occurs in extracting water from the sea for the coastal mines in Namibia and Namaqualand. The ferocious seas and moving sands jeopardize all but the most substantial engineering facilities. At CDM (Namibia) an undersea tunnel and concrete piers are used. At Koingnaas a lagoon has been constructed behind the high-water line, and water is pumped from there to the plant. When Koffiefontein was reopened, an irrigation canal was already passing through the mining lease: although negotiations with a farming-oriented government were difficult, good sense prevailed in the end, and the mine extracts the water it needs on the site.

The question of whether to generate or to transmit electrical power is usually decided by how much time it would take to make power available for the mine's operation. Overhead transmission lines covering hundreds of miles take years to construct and may not be the most economical method. Orapa has a diesel generating station, which also supplies the Letlhakane mine by overhead line. Finsch, Koffiefontein, Letseng, and Koingnaas are joined to the national electricity grid. By the time it begins operations, Jwaneng will have

CDM's Beauvallon farm at Oranjemund, on the Orange River at the edge of the Namib Desert. Employing the most up-to-date facilities, it was designed to provide for every possible need of the mining town.
De Beers Archives.

its own power station.

The design of mine townships has progressed from grid plans such as those found in Kimberley, Kleinzee, Oranjemund, and Finsch to layouts incorporating modern town-planning concepts. The Koffiefontein and Orapa mine townships, for example, include curved roads and cul-de-sacs. When the mine is far from other communities and there are few inhabitants, considerable attention is given to making the town attractive to employees and their families. Because the mines are generally the only significant economic activity in the area, the plans usually include not only houses and hostels, but also hospitals, schools, shopping centers, government administration offices, and recreational facilities. Even dairies and slaughterhouses may be set up, as part of extensive farms.

On the mine site the project's key facilities are usually constructed within a fenced security area. The mine, open-pit in all recent diamond ventures, requires offices, workshops, fuel bays, and explosives magazines. The processing plant, usually consisting of crushing, screening, heavy-media, and recovery plants, starts with a few survey pegs in the ground. Civil contractors construct concrete foundations. They are followed by steelwork erectors, equipment installers, and electrical contrac-

tors. Gradually, the steel skeletons are clad with sheeting, and conveyor gantries and pipes join the various sections. Workshops for the plant and for vehicles, mine stores, and yards, and security buildings and a power station or transformer station complete the mine complex. As soon as water is available and the equipment has been installed, commissioning begins and continues until everything is operating effectively.

The responsibility for coordinating these many activities falls to the project manager and engineer. The original planning estimates and schedules are fed into computers, which produce reports indicating where the project is on or off target. However, computers alone cannot do the entire job; the need for personal inspection and intervention remains.

So, after two to four years of intensive activity on site and in the supporting base offices, the mine takes shape. The training of staff and operators is put to the test as the plant is gradually started up. The day comes when the first mass of barren ground is gingerly tipped into the plant. Its progress through crusher, over screen, into sumps, and onto mini waste dumps is carefully watched. Then diamondiferous ground is fed in and processed until a concentrate appears. The recovery plant is put to the test, and the first diamonds are recovered.

Open-pit mining at Koffiefontein: blasting the ore with explosive charges. *De Beers Archives*.

A rubber-tired dozer cleaning up at Koffiefontein. *De Beers Archives*.

Modifications are necessary—a new chute here or a replacement screen-deck there—but gradually the contractors move off site. The time has come to prove what the geological sampling has indicated.

Open-pit Mining

The beginning of production at the Finsch mine in late 1965 marked a new stage in the mining of kimberlites in southern Africa. At that time, the Williamson mine in Tanzania was the closest similar operation. The massive seashore operations at CDM on the southwest coast, described below, were producing diamonds from marine gravels overlain by wind-blown sand dunes. At Finsch, De Beers' engineers were faced with the problems of designing an open pit. They made a number of visits to large mines in North America to evaluate experiences there.

The shape of a kimberlite pipe—usually circular or elliptical with nearly vertical sides—lends itself to a simple layout of benches or steps with connecting roads. The surface of the kimberlite is often weathered, which gives it a brownish-yellow color and makes it soft enough for direct digging or ripping. The deeper, unweathered blue ground is harder and tougher, and explosives must be used to break it up. The barren "country rock" surrounding a pipe varies with the geology of the district—it is ironstone at Finsch, shale and lava at Koffiefontein, and sand and calcrete on the surface at Jwaneng.

The factors to be considered in designing open mines include not only the local geology and the strength of the rocks, but also the type of equipment to be used. The stability of an open mine is an overriding safety consideration, but the average slope of the rock face is normally determined by the width and height of the benches being mined. Generally, for safety reasons, the slope is kept relatively flat during most of an open mine's operating life. Koffiefontein mine, now nearing the end of its open-pit life, has steep pit slopes of about 45 degrees.

Open-pit mining consists essentially of three activities—fragmentation, loading, and transportation of both ore and waste rock. After the direct digging or ripping phase, holes 4–6 inches (100–150 mm) in diameter are drilled downward in rows parallel to the bench faces. The holes are filled or charged with ammonium nitrate fuel-oil explosives and detonated in a prescribed sequence. At most of the mines, blasting operations are conducted at a fixed time every day, to minimize the disturbance caused by the necessary evacuation of personnel and equipment. One problem sometimes

encountered in blasting is the occurrence of large, unmanageable pieces of blasted rock that require further breaking. The introduction of hydraulic hammers capable of delivering hundreds of hammer blows a minute has almost eliminated the use of explosives in secondary blasting. Hydraulic hammers mounted on mobile cranes are a common sight at most open-pit diamond mines.

The loading of kimberlite ore or waste rock is performed by tracked power shovels or rubber-tired front-end loaders equipped with buckets having a capacity of 140–210 cubic feet (4–6 cu m). The first two electric power shovels at Finsch were put to work on the abrasive ironstone overburden in 1965. Their buckets had to be fitted with specially hardened magnanese steel tips, which lasted only one or two shifts. On rubber-tired loaders, the tires themselves can be damaged by the sharp edges of blasted rock. In one particularly hostile section of a De Beers mine, tires had to be changed after only ten hours. One of the problems of the early front-end loaders was the hydraulics system. Now, some fifteen years later, hydraulic equipment has been so greatly improved that some power shovels are hydraulically operated. The newest of the open mines at Letseng-la-Terai has such shovels as primary loaders.

Rear dump trucks with a capacity of 20–50 tons each are standard transportation vehicles. Inclined skipways and conveyor belts have been considered, but neither of these methods has the flexibility of the truck, whose performance has improved considerably over the years. Provided the open-mine roads are built with the right surface material and are kept graded and drained, trucks should enable open mines

Mining benches of the Koffiefontein mine. The mine roads are used by trucks transporting the ore to the processing plant.
Photo Vulcain-Explorer, Paris.

Opposite: Underground mining. Kimberlitic ore is scraped to a tip by an electrically driven winch. *De Beers Archives.*

to go to depths well in excess of 1,000 feet (300 m).

The diamond mines in Botswana, particularly Orapa and Jwaneng, will probably operate by open-pit methods into the twenty-first century. No doubt new technology will bring about modifications, but the mines will certainly become huge holes in the ground surrounded by immense dumps of waste rock and tailings from processing plants. The scenery of that country, generally very flat, will change dramatically and provide the opportunity for environmentalists both to criticize and to engineer a new landscape.

Underground Mining

Although there are some known examples of diamondiferous deposits of sedimentary origin occurring at depth underground, most diamond-mining operations in southern Africa are concerned with volcanic pipes and fissures that have already been worked at least in part from the surface. But a stage is reached in open-pit mining when, in order to maintain safety, so much waste side wall or country rock has to be removed with each ton of ore that it is more economical to extract the ore by underground methods. Koffiefontein is an example of an open-pit mine that has had to switch to underground production. The underground mining operations described below are mainly those of the four Kimberley mines—De Beers, Wesselton, Dutoitspan, and Bultfontein—and the Premier mine.

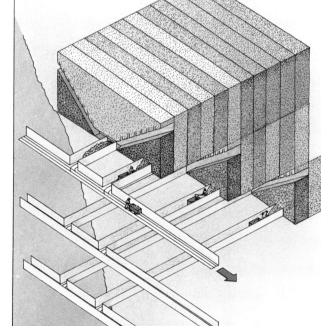

Underground mining: chambering. As successive chambers (blue) are mined out, the overlying waste rocks (brown) drop down. *Burns Graphics, London.*

The change from surface to underground mining has to be planned many years ahead, for two basic reasons. First, the grade and value of the kimberlite reserves at depth must be established. It is quite common for the average number of carats per ton and the size of the individual diamonds, as well as the area of the pipe, to decrease with depth.

The current practice is to sink a prospect shaft and develop tunnels on one or two levels up to 650 feet (200 m) apart in order to produce bulk samples. These samples generally also provide several hundred tons of material to be used for testing purposes. Based on the diamonds recovered, an estimate can be made of the quantity and quality of the diamonds in the pipe. To evaluate the diamonds and so predict the eventual revenue from production, it is customary to try to recover at least 5,000 carats of diamonds. This amount provides a sufficient range of stones of different size and quality for the sampling to be statistically valid. When there are lower-grade deposits, correspondingly larger samples must be taken.

The second reason for the preliminary underground exploration is to determine the factors that will affect the eventual mining operation. It is important to know the strength of both the kimberlite and the country rock surrounding it, because the tunnels that provide access for men, materials, and ore will be required to stand for many years. Geological faults, water fissures, and zones of weakness need to be dealt with well before the main flow of a productive operation begins, so that accidents may be avoided.

Water, in particular, is a significant hazard to underground mining of kimberlite, because it accelerates weathering and decomposition. In order to limit seepage into the workings within the pipes, the Kimberley mines have water tunnels driven around their circumference in the country rock. Drain holes are drilled into the roof of the tunnels to collect as much water as possible, and drains channel the water to the sumps at the shafts, where it is pumped to the surface.

Although this region of southern Africa is generally dry, there are occasional heavy rainstorms, and these are a factor to be considered in both surface and underground mining. In spite of elaborate precautions to prevent the seepage of water from the country rock around the sides of the pipes, rainfall inevitably finds its way into the workings. When the water mixes with shale from the side walls and kimberlite, the resulting mud poses a serious danger: on many occasions mud has poured into the workings, swamping both men and machinery.

The general means of handling the ore, once

it is mined, is similar in most of the De Beers mines. The mining operation reduces the ore to a size of under 25 inches (600 mm), which can be conveniently carried in trains of side-tipping trucks hauled by electric or diesel-driven locomotives. The broken ore is tipped down passes to a level where a jaw crusher is situated. The crusher reduces the ore to particles measuring less than 6 inches (150 mm). This is a suitable size for transporting on a conveyor belt and hoisting to the surface in skips in the main shaft.

The siting and design of the main shaft depends on a series of factors relating to the underground layout, the location of surface facilities, the eventual perimeter of the open pit, and the suitability of the ground through which the shaft is to be sunk. Usually, mining engineers plan the location of an eventual production shaft when the original mine plant is designed and positioned. In a few instances, inclined tunnels or ramps are used instead of shafts, but this is not yet common practice in the diamond mines where, as a result of partial open-pit operations, the highest part of an underground mine is as much as 1,000 feet (300 m) below the surface.

The main shafts are usually rectangular and consist of five compartments, two for hoisting rock (kimberlite and/or waste) in skips, two for lowering and hoisting men and materials in cages, and one that is used for services. The services include electric, signal, and telephone cables; pump columns; water and compressed-air pipes; and a ladderway or small service cage. The main shaft serves only the main levels of the mine, with stations at vertical intervals of about 650 feet (200 m). When it is necessary to have access to the workings at intermediate levels, underground vertical shafts are usually positioned specifically for this purpose. To ventilate the mine, fresh air is normally drawn in through the main shaft. The original prospect shaft remains in use as a return airway.

The basic underground excavations include sumps and pump chambers, workshops and stores, crusher stations and skip-loading arrangements, as well as the haulages and travelways between the shafts and the workings. The continued maintenance of these facilities is vital to the efficient operation of an underground mine. An excessive inflow of water into the workings at Dutoitspan in 1977 put part of the mine out of action for two months while imported emergency pumps drained the flooded areas. Mud rushes, collapsing support timbers in the tunnels, and occasional breakdowns in the shafts all can cause expensive delays and stoppages to the vital ore-winning operations.

Chambering. Chambering, introduced in the 1890's by Gardner Williams, then general manager of De Beers, was the first systematic mining method employed in the Kimberley mines. It has now been superseded in all the mines by block and sublevel caving (see below). Wesselton closed its last chambers in 1977. However, a modified system known as long-hole chambering has been adopted for early use at Koffiefontein.

Chamber levels were established from sub-vertical shafts at 40-foot (12-m) vertical intervals. Starting at the farthest point from the access tunnels and on the uppermost level, a series of 12-foot-wide (3.5-m) slots or chambers were mined from one level to the level above. These chambers were separated by 12-foot-thick back pillars and were so located that the back pillar of each level was directly over the chamber below it.

Mining in the chambers was done by drilling and blasting vertical holes. To give sufficient working space, the broken ground was lowered after each blast by means of hand-loading mine cars from loading points in parallel tunnels spaced 23 feet (7 m) apart (a process known as shrinkage stopping). As the chamber broke through into the level above, the overlying pillar was allowed to collapse into it. Loading continued until the kimberlite ore was so diluted by waste rock that it was uneconomical to continue. The ground was loaded into mine cars and pushed to ore tips feeding ore passes positioned in the country rock. It can be seen from the diagram on page 108 that the levels retreated in ranks, with the chamber on the lower level two or three cuts behind the upper one.

The advantages of chambering were safety and flexibility. It was the forerunner of block-caving, as it showed that the kimberlite would break up of its own accord. However, the excessive development costs and high labor requirements involved eventually made this method obsolete.

Block-caving. The need for a less labor-intensive mining method led De Beers mining engineers to look to the United States for a more productive and less expensive system than chambering. In the late 1950's an experimental block cave was established at Bultfontein, and the feasibility of the method was confirmed.

The principle of block-caving is simple. If a sufficient area of kimberlite is undercut, it will collapse and break up of its own accord, thus eliminating the need to drill and blast it. Provided the broken ground is removed, this fragmentation process can continue until all the kimberlite is drawn out. To design a block cave it is necessary to know the minimum undercut area that will bring about caving, the size of the broken rocks to be removed, and the effect of the loading, or weight, on the sides of the undercut. Although this method has been in use for more than twenty years, problems still exist and modifications continue to be made to improve each new block-cave layout.

In block-caving, development and mining operations are confined to within a few yards of the main levels, established at 600–650-foot (180–200-m) vertical intervals. The main level

Block caving. Caved rock falls through finger cones into parallel drifts cut in the kimberlite. Ore is scraped along drifts into mine cars. *Burns Graphics, London.*

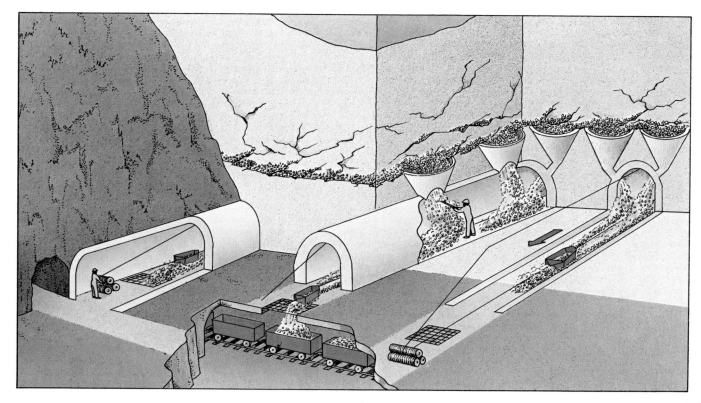

Underground open-bench mining as practiced in the Premier mine. *Burns Graphics, London.*

lined drifts appear to be stronger: their design has developed from a square cross-section to an arched one.

At 10–13-foot (3–4-m) intervals along the drifts, 4-foot by 4-foot (1.2 × 1.2-m) draw points are established with collection cones above them. The cave is made by undercutting the kimberlite, mining a slice 7 feet (2 m) thick across the block-cave area.

The block-caving operation consists of scraping ground from in front of draw points to drift tips, filling trucks, and hauling the ore to the shaft ore passes. However, particularly in a new cave, big rocks tend to jam in the cone and have to be blasted. This is a hazardous job, unless the rocks can be blasted by "bombs" consisting of a few pounds of explosives. Then miners have to enter the draw point and cone and drill and blast the rocks hanging above them. As the cave develops, some parts appear to break down too easily and care has to be taken to draw the whole block cave down evenly; otherwise sections of kimberlite can be left and the draw points fill with useless shale.

The most heartbreaking activity in block-caving is drift repairing. The distribution of weight from the cave has been mentioned. The control of the extraction of the kimberlite and the even lowering of all the ground, known as the "drawdown," must not only keep waste rock on top of kimberlite but must also prevent excessive weight on the drifts. If they are subjected to excessive weight, the drifts crush, close in, and become inaccessible. Drift repairing consists of replacing the destroyed concrete in an area where the kimberlite has already been crushed and weakened.

From the foregoing it can be seen that block-caving has not been without problems, and because of the collapse of entire sections of some mines, sublevel or intermediate caves have had to be established. These mini block caves have proven moderately successful.

Sublevel Open-bench Mining. One of the more successful underground mining methods, practiced at the Premier mine, is known as sublevel or open-bench mining. At the Premier mine, the consistently strong side walls of country rock permitted an open-pit operation to be converted into an underground operation fairly simply. The 130-acre (52-ha) Premier pipe is oval in cross-section—2,800 by 1,500 feet (850 × 450 m)—and split by a huge inclusion of quartzite some 200 feet (60 m) wide and 1,000 feet (300 m) deep. The pipe itself is split by a gabbro sill 247–264 feet (75–80 m) thick, which is some 1,270 feet (385 m) deep in the south and 1,500 feet (450 m) deep in the north. Until recently, operations were

is the haulage level, usually positioned a few yards from the pipe edge in the country rock and equipped with tracks and ore trains hauled by electric locomotives. Immediately above the haulage tunnel, parallel drifts (tunnels) are constructed 40–50 feet (12–15 m) apart, in kimberlite across the area to be mined. Behind that, in the country rock, chambers are cut for the winches that will pull scrapers along the drifts, drawing the ground into 6-ton side-tipping cars in the haulage. Behind the winches a tunnel provides access to the drifts.

Over the last twenty years methods of supporting and strengthening the drifts have changed. The Jagersfontein "2500" block cave (2,500 feet, or 770 m, deep) was equipped with steel arches and timber lagging. However, as the drifts took weight the arches distorted and soon became a tangle of steel and sticks. The pressure caused bolts to snap and nuts to ricochet about the drifts like bullets. Concrete-

planned to mine out the kimberlite only above this sill.

When the mine was restarted as an underground operation in 1945, a 46-foot-wide (14-m) slot was created from the bottom of the open pit at 610 feet (185 m) below surface level to ore-collection or cone levels 215 feet (65 m) below that. The current cone level is 1,170 feet (355 m) deep. With the slots serving as a free or unsupported face, benches have been established at 100-foot (31-m) vertical intervals. To break the ore, ring-drilling tunnels are driven at right angles to the slot 182 feet (55 m) apart horizontally on each bench level, from the country rock into the kimberlite. A ring or fan of twenty-nine holes is drilled 12 feet (3.6 m) back from the open-bench face up to the level above and halfway to the adjoining ring-drilling tunnel. After the holes are charged with explosives, they are blasted from a central blasting station. The benches are mined in such a way as to form an overall slope of 65 degrees. The slope enables the blasted rock to gravitate easily to the cone level.

The ore-collection system now consists of a grid of cones with their centers at 92 feet (28 m). The ore in the cones falls down onto grizzlies 50 feet (15 m) wide, allowing oversize rocks to be broken by hammering or blasting. The broken ore then falls through transfer passes to transfer slusher tunnels on the 1,270-foot (385-m) level. Here winches pull scraper scoops or slushers that collect the ore and tip it into ore passes, from which it falls to the main haulage level (1,700 feet, or 500 m).

Production from the Premier mine, 80 percent of which is by open-bench mining and the balance by block-caving, amounts to an average of 450,000 tons of ore per month, which makes it one of the largest underground mines in the world.

A modified form of bench mining will be used to mine the ore below the sill. Instead of being collected in cones, the ore will be loaded, using small load-haul-dump vehicles, from loading places with a layout similar to that

Mine tunnel supported by steel arches, with side-tipping mine truck in open or tipping position. *De Beers Archives.*

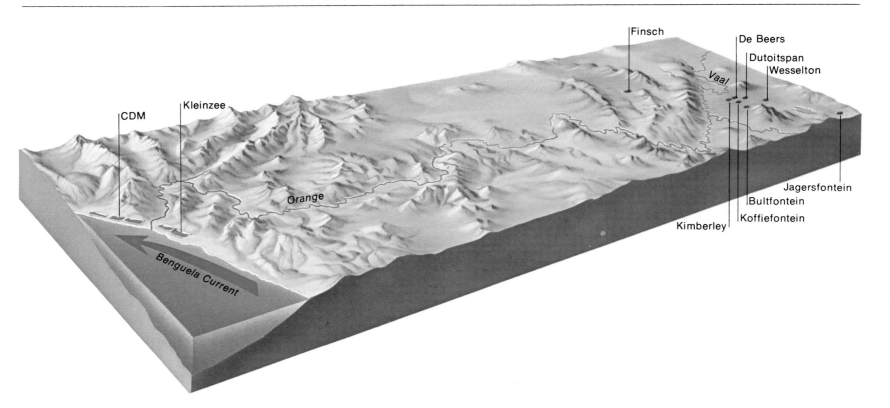

Location of the principal kimberlite pipes of South Africa, showing how, as a result of thousands of years of erosion, diamonds were carried down to the coast of Namaqualand by the Orange River. *Burns Graphics, London.*

used in chambering. A conveyor will carry the ore from the lowest excavation level—1,930 feet (585 m) below the surface—up to the crusher on the 1,700-foot (500-m) level. Initially, a large pillar will be left in the center of the pipe to serve as a retaining wall, but this will, eventually, be collapsed.

Mining on the Atlantic Coast

In 1908 diamonds were discovered by railway workers near Lüderitz in South-West Africa (now Namibia). A diamond rush followed, and the German colonial government proclaimed the *Sperrgebeit,* or "Forbidden Territory," that same year. A number of mining companies that formed during this short period continued to operate successfully in the vicinity of Lüderitz and along the coast. These firms were amalgamated by Sir Ernest Oppenheimer in 1920 when he formed the Consolidated Diamond Mines of South-West Africa, known as CDM.

Exploration continued along this lonely coast, normally inhabited only by seals and sea birds. At the end of 1926, Ernest Reuning and Hans Merensky discovered a rich diamond deposit at Alexander Bay on the south bank of the mouth of the Orange River in South Africa. This area is now mined by the State Alluvial Diggings. The occurrence of diamonds on the south bank prompted CDM geologists to explore the north bank of the river. They found diamondiferous gravels covered by sand dunes along 330 feet (100 m) of coast immediately to the north of the estuary. These major discoveries enabled CDM to develop what is now probably one of the world's largest integrated

earth-moving mining operations, currently producing nearly 2 million carats of gem diamonds a year.

South of Alexander Bay, in Namaqualand, prospecting started on the Kleinzee farm at the outlet of the generally dry Buffels River in 1926. Diamonds were found, and in 1928 Cape Coast Explorations Ltd. was incorporated, with Sir Ernest Oppenheimer as chairman.

With the depression of world trade in the 1930's and the outbreak of war in 1939, Cape Coast's operations were intermittent. It was taken over by De Beers' more powerful Consolidated Mines Ltd. in 1941, and mining recommenced in 1943. Adjoining farms, such as Annex Kleinzee and Dreyer's Pan and eventually those in the vicinity of Koingnaas 35 miles (60 km) to the south, were included in the operational area. In 1978, Koingnaas was opened as a satellite mine of the Annex Kleinzee complex. Together the mines of the Namaqualand division of De Beers produce approximately 1.5 million carats of gem-quality diamonds per year.

Origins of the Coastal Deposits. The origin of the diamonds that are now found in gravels and conglomerates under considerable thicknesses of sand along the Atlantic coast is presumed to be the kimberlites of Lesotho, Botswana, and South Africa in the central part of the southern African subcontinent. The weathering of the volcanic pipes and fissures, with the subsequent release of diamonds, has resulted in near-flattening of the interior.

Millions of years ago, huge quantities of soil were transported by rivers such as the Vaal,

Opposite: Part of
the Oranjemund mining
operations, the largest
enterprise of its kind in
the world, producing nearly
2 million carats a year.
De Beers Archives.

Working the coastal
deposits at Oranjemund
requires both manual labor
and highly sophisticated
modern technology. The
smallest cracks and holes
in the bedrock must be
cleared by hand. *Photos
Jacques Legrand.*

Bottom: General view of the
CDM works at Oranjemund.
De Beers Archives.

the Orange, and the Buffels down to the sea. Heavier minerals and diamonds, initially deposited at the estuaries, were distributed up and down the coast by wind and the action of the sea. The constant pounding of the sea eventually caused boart and poor-quality stones to disintegrate, leaving the better diamonds, mostly gemstones, lodged in the crevices and fissures that have been worn into the hard rocks of the shore. These rocks are pre-Cambrian schists, probably more than 800 million years old.

Fluctuations in the sea level, caused by the various ice ages, resulted in the formation of terraces of diamondiferous gravels that are now found up to 82 feet (25 m) above sea level and as far as 2 miles (3 km) inland. Some terraces are still below the high-water level, and diamonds are also found on the sea bed well offshore. The fact that fossils have been found in the terraces indicates not only that the terraces were formed relatively recently, but also that the climate was once far more favorable to animal and vegetable life than it is today. It is significant that the farther the diamonds are found from the Orange and Buffels rivers, the smaller their average size: this is additional evidence of the mechanism of their distribution.

At Koingnaas the ore bodies are irregular in shape and are overlain by overburden 17–100 feet (5–30 m) thick. The presence of water and

clayey material also adds to the difficulties of mining. The "marine terraces" were probably formed by coastal action and are similar to those that occur at Annex Kleinzee and CDM. As will be explained in the following section, the types of deposits, rocks, and minerals are significant in the processing for diamond recovery.

To summarize, the diamonds are generally found associated with gravels, pebbles, and boulders, sometimes cemented into conglomerates or clayey sandstones, in terraces that formed ancient marine beaches. They are now overlain by considerable thicknesses of mainly windblown sand. To locate these terraces, the normal geological practice is to sink pits on a grid covering the 1–2-mile-wide (2–3-km) coastal belt. Thereafter, at intervals ranging from 1,700 feet (500 m) to several thousand yards wide, trenches are excavated through the sand overburden and gravels to the bedrock. These trenches are cut at right angles to the coastline. The terrace material is loaded and transported to bulk sampling plants, where its diamond content is assayed. In spite of extensive exploration and sampling, the irregular nature of the base of the gravels and the seemingly random occurrence of the diamonds make evaluation of the deposits very uncertain. Thus, those responsible for the eventual production can never be sure that the geological expectations will be met. When diamond production falls significantly short of planned targets for several months in succession, there is an unmistakable tension among all employees, and the sampling methods are brought under repeated scrutiny.

The Operations at Oranjemund. The enormous earth-moving operation at CDM involves the mining of 60 million tons of sands and gravels in order to produce less than half a ton of diamonds in one year. The actual ratio is about 150 million to one, and at times it has been as much as 200 million to one. With more than three hundred large earth-moving machines, CDM operates a fleet of equipment nearly as large as that owned by the United States Army. Diamondiferous ground of varying composition is fed into four processing plants as well as into two large bulk sampling plants. The coordination of production is highly complex, and for many years computers have been used for day-to-day control and to simulate possible mining operations.

There are two mining methods, terrace and beach mining. Sea-mining operations are now minimal. Terrace mining takes place well above the high-water level, and up to 2 miles (3 km) inland. Beach mining, such as that conducted in the western block on the south end

of CDM's lease, involves mining on the beach with excavations up to 65 feet (20 m) below the high-water level. Among the many problems encountered in beach mining, one of the most critical is preventing the excavations from being inundated by sea water.

The removal of overburden 50–82 feet (15–25 m) thick from above the terraces is carried out in "cuts" or strips using huge bowl scrapers capable of loading, transporting, and dumping 60 tons of material at a time. Although some of these scrapers are self-loading, in normal practice tracked bulldozers push the back of the scraper while loading. During unloading and dumping, a plate in the back of the scraper bowl pushes material out and thus allows the machine to leave an even surface.

Once it has been exposed, the gravel terrace normally must be broken up and bulldozed into piles. Bulldozers equipped with tines tip and loosen those terraces that are cemented by clay, calcrete, or silica. When the ground is too tough, it has to be fragmented by drilling and blasting. The diamondiferous gravels are loaded by rubber-tired front-end loaders that fill rear- or side-tipping trucks, each one carrying 35 or 50 tons at a time to the treatment plants.

When the extremely tough and irregular schists of the old shore appear at the bottom of the excavation, large equipment can no longer be used. However, the gravels left in the potholes and crevices of the old shore contain most of the diamonds. Backtrenchers with small, powerful digging buckets gouge out the gulleys that are accessible, but the final operation is always done by hand. Workers known as bedrock cleaners drill, dig, and shovel out the ore, finally sweeping the base as clean as it was millions of years ago. For a brief time

the jagged paleo-coast is exposed, but very soon the unending stream of sand engulfs it once more.

In planning the beach mining of the western block, mining engineers were faced with two major problems. A large proportion of the diamondiferous gravels lay up to 65 feet (20 m) below the high-tide level, and the total amount of overburden exceeded 300 million tons. The block varied in width from 1,300 to 3,600 feet (400–1,100 m) at right angles to the shoreline. It extended 10 miles (15 km) along the coast, with depths of overburden varying from 33 to 82 feet (10–25 m).

The decision to use a large bucket-wheel excavator was based on the successful use of similar but smaller machines during the 1950's. Today's operations involve the construction, from overburden, of huge sea walls using bowl scrapers. These walls, which are more than 65 feet (20 m) wide at the top, are continually being eroded by the sea. On the inside of the walls hundreds of well points—pipes with hoses—drain the sea water from the bank. Pumps then collect the water and return it to the sea.

While this continual combat with the sea is being fought, the bucket-wheel excavator, capable of excavating 1,800 tons per hour, digs into the overburden and loads a mobile conveyor. The conveyor transports the sand across the mined-out area and stacks its load beyond it. As soon as the gravels are exposed, the loading and cleaning operations described above begin. A sense of urgency and even danger is apparent throughout this part of the CDM operation. Should the sea wall be breached, there is the risk of men being drowned and equipment lost. There is no time for finesse with grade control now. All ground is collected

At the CDM works at Oranjemund work goes on in most sectors night and day; the protecting banks are under constant attack by the sea, and time is precious. *Photos Jacques Legrand (left); De Beers Archives.*

General view of the top of a mined-out kimberlite pipe and treatment plant at a mine in Kimberley. Below: Trucks delivering ore to the main tips at Koffiefontein. *De Beers Archives.*

Following pages: Hydraulic power shovels are employed in modern diamond mines like Letseng-la-Terai, in Lesotho. *De Beers Archives.*

as speedily as possible.

Over the past twenty years attempts have been made to recover diamonds from the sea bed off this coast. Barges equipped with suction dredges prospected for and eventually produced diamonds. The positioning of the barges was critical to avoid duplication of mining the sea bed, and considerable problems were encountered during the gale-force winds in an area known as the Skeleton Coast. The last operating barge, called *Pomona*, had a crew of twelve men and communicated with the shore by helicopter. The evaluation and recovery of diamonds by this method has been difficult and generally uneconomical. However, the age of undersea mining for other minerals has begun, and the experience gained so far in the development of suitable technology may yet prove this source of diamonds to be viable.

Treatment and Recovery
The methods of processing diamondiferous ores to produce diamonds are determined by both the mineralogical composition of the ore and the physical characteristics of the diamonds therein. In most cases, geological exploration only identifies the boundaries of the

kimberlite or gravel that is to be mined and treated. The mining of this ground often involves the removal of considerable quantities of waste, such as the wall rocks at Finsch and Koffiefontein and the sand overburden at CDM. Processing normally is divided into two stages: the treatment, which reduces the ore to a con-

Mine or Group of Mines Exploited by De Beers	Quantity of Ore (in tons)	Diamond Production (in carats)
De Beers, Kimberley Mines	4,509,000	1,085,000
Finsch	3,416,000	2,426,000
Koffiefontein	3,721,000	410,000
Premier	7,074,000	2,010,000
Letseng-la-Terai	659,000	23,000
Consolidated Diamond Mines	14,906,000	2,001,000
Namaqualand	4,067,000	1,163,000
Botswana-Orapa and Letlhakane	4,343,000	2,691,000
Total for 1977	42,695,000	11,809,000

centrate with a volume about one-hundredth that of the original mass, and the recovery of diamonds from that concentrate. The final classification and evaluation of the diamonds is not usually conducted at the mines in southern Africa and therefore falls outside the scope of this chapter.

The table above shows the tonnage treated in 1977 by the various mines or groups of mines of the De Beers companies. The largest single plant is that at the Premier, which treated 7 million tons to produce 2 million carats (900 pounds, or 400 kg) of diamonds. In all, the mines processed 42.7 million tons of ore to produce 11.8 million carats, or just over 2 tons of diamonds, an overall ratio of 18 million to one.

It is only the diamond's unique physical properties that allow its recovery from such vast quantities of waste material. The treatment process is directed at taking the mined ore and isolating the diamonds by utilizing one or more of these properties to separate it from the waste.

It is important to realize that diamonds in different deposits—and sometimes those in the same deposit—have different characteristics such as size range, wettability, and fluorescence when irradiated by x-rays. Thus, for each mine, processes have had to be designed for the most economical extraction of "different" diamonds from different ores. The mineral process testing of an ore body is therefore critical.

Treatment or Concentration. When a diamondiferous ore is evaluated or when a process to recover the diamonds is designed, one of the first factors that must be considered is the size range of the diamonds to be recovered. The value of diamonds increases geometrically with their weight, and therefore it is highly undesirable to destroy a large diamond by crushing. However, with the exception of the Premier and Letseng mines, where very large diamonds are recovered, most kimberlites contain diamonds that rarely exceed 1.2 inches (30 mm)—that is, they will pass through a screen with a 1.2-inch mesh. At the lower end of the size scale, it is not uncommon to recover diamonds as small as .06 inches (1.65 mm). The west-coast mines do not recover any diamonds less than .08 inches (2 mm), because the sea apparently carries smaller stones away from the gravel currently being mined.

However, in most kimberlites and sedimentary deposits the diamonds are locked in the volcanic rocks, conglomerates, or clays. The initial process then is to take the run of mine material and reduce it to a size of 1.2 inches to 1 inch (30–25 mm). This is usually carried out in two stages. The primary crushers are positioned at the bottom of the main rock shafts of the underground mines or close to the perimeter of the open pits. The product of these crushers that is below 6 inches (150 mm) is generally "dry," but the next stage involves the addition of water. Secondary (and tertiary) crushing is carried out by cone crushers, which reduce the ore to a predetermined maximum size. This size is controlled by both the gap setting on the crushers and the openings in the screens.

In the case of mines that have ores containing a great deal of clay or weathered kimberlite, scrubbers (large rotating drums) wash and break down the material. This is done at the new Koingnaas mine. The main purpose of the scrubbing is to make this type of ore amenable to further crushing; the clays are eventually discarded.

An interesting variation on the initial stages of treatment is found at CDM, where conglomerates and boulders are mixed. The large pieces are fed by conveyor belt so that they drop onto a steel plate. The more bouncy (and barren) boulders jump over a plate that stops the softer conglomerate. These boulder bounce plants are designed to replace some of the hand sorting, in which the products are separated by visual examination.

Up to this stage, the processes have generally been determined by the size range of the diamonds and the nature of the ore. The next stage involves separating the diamonds (along with other heavy rocks and minerals such as ironstone and ilmenite) from the lighter material, and takes advantage of the diamond's high specific gravity, which is 3.52. There are three common methods of gravity concentration—jigs (seldom used now in southern Africa), pans, and heavy media.

Kimberlite partially breaks down and forms a viscous "puddle" with water, and rotary washing pans have been used for concentrating diamonds since their introduction at Kimberley in 1874. The pan, shaped like a shallow saucepan about 13 feet (4 m) in diameter and less than 3 feet (1 m) high, has rotating arms to which tines are fitted. The tines are set so that their tips are a few millimeters from the pan base and are aligned to move any gravelly material gradually outward. Thus, as the arms rotate, the heavier minerals settle and move to the outer rim of the pan. Here the "concentrate" is extracted. The lighter "float" material overflows through the center and is eventually discarded.

Pans have been used in the Kimberley central treatment plant at Koffiefontein and at Finsch, where they are now being used in the fine diamond circuit, recovering stones smaller than .16 inches (4 mm). The rotary-pan operators now use modern instruments to measure the electric current drawn by the pan motor and determine the puddle's density and viscosity, but in earlier days they would have looked at the wakes of the rotating tines and felt the puddle between thumb and forefinger to gauge its density.

There are two main types of heavy-medium plants—cones and cyclones. The medium normally used is magnetic ferrosilicon ground into a fine powder and mixed with varying quantities of water to give different densities. Magnetite is also sometimes used. In the cone system the material is fed into the top of the cone. The medium's specific gravity is set at about 2.6, and the lighter rocks float off the top while the heavy minerals sink to the bottom of the cone, where they slide to the discharge point. In the cyclone the pulp is pumped into the top tangentially. This causes centrifugal force to speed up the separation process. A cyclone occupies considerably less space than a cone of equivalent capacity. To recover the medium, both "float" and "sink" are passed over magnetic drums that attract the ferrosilicon while the other products continue moving. The ferrosilicon is returned to the medium circuit. Often a secondary cyclone is employed to reconcentrate the primary sink, using a higher-density medium.

Considerable quantities of water are used to transport material in treatment plants. Water-recovery circuits utilize fine screens and thickeners. The waste products from such plants are often split into coarse material, which is stacked in dumps known as tailings dumps, and fine slimes, which are pumped into slime dams where the solids can settle.

Recovery. When diamonds are separated from other heavy minerals, physical properties other than density are used to make the distinction. One of these properties was known to the early miners of Golconda, in India, who noted that when diamondiferous gravel was poured through a greased wooden trench, the diamonds adhered to the greasy surface while the accompanying minerals did not. In other words, diamonds—particularly those from fresh, unweathered kimberlite—are not "wettable."

On the basis of these early observations, a method of diamond recovery was developed in 1896; it is still in use today. Vibrating grease tables, consisting of a series of steps covered with a lubricant similar to axle grease, were

The crushing station in a processing plant. Premier mine, South Africa. *Photo Vulcain-Explorer, Paris.*

Diamonds are recovered on grease belts, as at the Kimberley mine (below), or by means of x-ray sorters (right). *Photos Jacques Legrand.*

devised to separate diamonds from the other heavy minerals that accompany them. The tables were generously sprinkled with the gravel, and at the end of each shift the grease was scraped off the table and melted down, freeing the diamonds.

Grease belts have now largely replaced the tables: as the belt moves slowly across the flow of concentrates, it collects the diamonds. The grease is continuously scraped off the end of the belt, and the diamonds are recovered, again by melting. This method is used on a large scale at the Premier mine. However, it is relatively ineffectual at a mine like Finsch, where the kimberlites have been broken down by climatic forces.

The fact that diamonds luminesce when exposed to x-rays was discovered by Soviet scientists in 1958. In South Africa the Diamond Research Laboratory and a firm that manufac-

One day's production at CDM, Oranjemund. *De Beers Archives.*

tured seed sorters joined to develop the first of a number of x-ray sorters. Optical or natural-light sorters were tried at Finsch in 1966 but were soon replaced by the more accurate x-ray machines.

The principle of the x-ray sorter is simple. Dry, sized particles—diamonds and other minerals—are fed onto a fast-moving belt that projects them through an x-ray beam. The diamond's fluorescence is detected by a photo-electric cell, which triggers a valve to release a puff of compressed air that blows the diamond into a separate container. The original machines were capable of handling only a few tons of concentrates a day, but recently developed multibelt and broad-belt machines can sort several tons per hour. Finer concentrates, however, take a good deal longer to be processed than coarse ones, for this method of sorting essentially involves the identification of each particle.

The modern recovery plant, such as that constructed at Letlhakane, consists of a drying and sizing section followed by two to four x-ray sorting circuits that extract the diamonds. Zircons, ilmenites, and garnets often accompany diamonds all the way to the sorting table, where they are generally separated by hand. The diamonds are cleaned by being treated with one or more acids—hydrochloric, nitric, or hydrofluoric—and sometimes by boiling as well. The final cleaned product is then weighed and put into a safe, where it remains until shipment.

Recovery plants usually operate only during the day. Occasionally there is a flurry of excitement when a large diamond is discovered among the coarse concentrates. The stone is weighed, and semiprofessional estimates of its value are made. The Premier Rose (353.9 carats rough), which was recovered in 1978 from the Premier mine, is believed to have been sold for more than $5 million.

Security

Because of its small size and high value, as well as the relative ease with which it can be sold, the gem diamond is an ideal target for thieves. Diamonds are fairly easily concealed in clothing or on the body. There are illegal buyers around mine areas who buy and resell, forming a link in an illegal chain that extends all over the world.

Illicit diamond buying, or IDB as it is commonly called, is one of the major problems of the diamond industry. In some countries the industry has been virtually ruined by it. In southern Africa a combination of extremely heavy penalties and ever-vigilant police forces make IDB unattractive; nevertheless, the mines' security arrangements are continually

reviewed to ensure that diamonds do not enter the chain. The future of developing countries such as Botswana depends largely on the revenue generated from the legal production and sale of their diamonds.

Diamond mines are surrounded by fences, located to provide different levels of security and to control the entry and departure of personnel and equipment. A standard security fence is 8 feet (2.5 m) high and has an overhang that makes it difficult to climb over. Two parallel fences can create a no man's land, guarded by a security staff or dogs. At CDM the desertlike conditions of the "Forbidden Territory" create a barrier that is probably more effective than a barbed-wire fence. Control of personnel is maintained at the gates through which employees and visitors enter the mining areas. At most of the mines' exit gates, employees are selected at random for a physical search. Equipment and people can also be x-rayed with low-intensity x-ray equipment. Security guards patrol the mine area and fences on foot, on horseback (camels were used in the past), in trucks, or by helicopter. During processing, security barriers and guards prevent diamonds from being removed from the plant. For plant operators, the guards and the locks on concentrate bins and x-ray sorters may often seem to be something of a nuisance, but they are recognized and accepted as a necessity.

Special security regulations apply to employees and their families living in townships within the security area. The following examples are taken from a mine booklet written a few years ago:

"Employees (and families) wishing to leave town will be required to obtain a permit from the Personnel Office. . . .

The life of a mine is necessarily limited. Above: Offices of the Premier mine, fringed by flowering jacaranda trees, a picture of prosperity. Below: The old Kolmanskop mine, near Lüderitz in the Namib Desert, half submerged by drifting sand. *De Beers Archives.*

"Under no circumstances may pigeons be brought into the township [to prevent the use of carrier pigeons].

"No person not being a resident may enter 'the town' without the necessary security clearance. . . .

"The possession of radio-control model boats and aircraft on the company's property is strictly prohibited."

Most employees accept the security regulations as part of their lives. As the mines are often in remote locations, any movement away from them requires planning that naturally includes passing the security clearances. Recently some mines have become less restrictive, and access to the mine townships has become somewhat easier.

The key to the security of diamond mining is the industry's employees' commitment to preventing theft. Most employees rarely think about security, let alone talk about it. The mining companies are moving away from employing people on short-term contracts. People with a long-term commitment and ties to an organization are less likely to jeopardize their livelihood and their retirement pensions by stealing diamonds.

IDB and diamond security have inevitably been the subject for thrilling novels, and the business does have its excitement. But most security work is repetitive; it consists largely of guarding fences, controlling gates, searching personnel, and watching television monitor screens.

Craftsmen in a Communal Enterprise

Today, just a little more than a hundred years after the first diamonds were discovered in South Africa, new mines are being exploited (or are about to be), and unprecedented developments such as the sites at Oranjemund are evidence of renewed drive and vitality. Thousands of men are engaged in a multitude of activities—prospecting the land, extracting minerals, working in the treatment plants, maintaining equipment, and so on. These thousands are part of a communal enterprise that derives its power from each one of them. The daily operation of a mine requires the solution of technical problems and the development of new activities. As it creates new wealth, each mine—and its satellite town—becomes an individual entity, with its own history and population.

After the geologists have spent months carrying out exhaustive research, the construction workers arrive to lay the foundations for the future operation; they do not normally settle in one place, and most of them leave the site when their job is completed, never to return. A way of life is not really established until the mine finally comes into commission: three shifts per day, six days per week.

Because the mining companies fulfill so many of the essential needs of the employees and their families, providing accommodations, schooling, health care, and leisure activities, they inevitably appear to be somewhat paternalistic. In the newly constructed towns, which are often geographically isolated and consequently rather parochial, a society is created in which everyone knows everyone else and each person feels he or she belongs to one big family, with all the advantages and disadvantages such an arrangement can have. Generations often succeed each other in the same location: in this way a past is created, and a collective memory is formed.

But the life of a mine is highly vulnerable. When work is finally terminated, the site is left to the mercy of the sand and the wind. The only signs of its past importance are the huge tips that stand out against the horizon. The earth has given up its treasure, and silence has returned. But somewhere else a new life has already begun.

Tanzania

The Williamson Mine

"Every geologist dreams of discovering an important diamond mine. Everybody wants to own one outright. Only one man, Dr. John Thorburn Williamson, B.A., M.Sc., Ph.D., D.Sc., the discoverer and founder of the now famous Mwadui Diamond Mine in Tanganyika [Tanzania], has ever achieved both ambitions." Thus begins an unpublished manuscript, *The Williamson Story*, by G. J. Du Toit, who spent two decades at Mwadui working for "the Doctor" and his successors.

"Jack" Williamson was born at Montfort in the Canadian province of Quebec in 1907. In 1924 he entered McGill University in Montreal to study law. However, he had a passionate interest in natural science, and on one of his vacations he joined a student exploration trip to Labrador. Whether it was this trip or a lecture by a visiting professor that caused him to transfer from law to geology is not important. He changed disciplines during his third year, and in his final exams he received the highest marks that had ever been given in geology at the university. He remained at McGill to take his master's degree and, in 1933, his doctorate.

Though reserved by nature, Williamson nevertheless had a sense of humor and was an excellent sportsman—he boxed, was an expert marksman, and was the university's fencing champion. Possibly because of an unhappy romance during his student days, he never married. After earning his doctorate, he joined the Quebec Gold Mining Corporation as a geolo-gist. His interest was soon captured by the mineral discoveries in central Africa, and in 1934 he was recruited for the Anglo-American Corporation of South Africa by its chief geologist in Northern Rhodesia (now Zambia), Austin Bancroft, who had formerly been a professor of geology at McGill.

No doubt Williamson dreamed of the riches that lay undiscovered in the African continent, and perhaps, as he set out, he was already thinking of finding diamonds. In 1935 he accepted the position of geologist with the Tanganyika Diamond and Gold Development Company, familiarly known as "Tank Diamonds," which operated three small diamond mines at Mabuki, Kisumbe, and Nzega, near Lake Victoria. He discovered a number of small pipes, but all of them proved to be unprofitable. In 1938 the company decided to abandon its operations in that region, and Williamson took over, on his own behalf, the Kisumbe workings, near the town of Shinyanga, about 95 miles (150 km) south of Mwanza. After a frustrating year in which he made only minimal discoveries, he was bankrupt and on the point of giving up to join the army. He was saved by a loan from a prospector named McNaughton, but even this held him for only a short time. At the beginning of 1940 Williamson, after paying his debts, was left with just £100 and very little hope.

On the evening of March 6, 1940, Williamson's right-hand man for most of his time in Tanganyika, Bundalla, arrived at Kisumbe with a soil sample that had been taken from an abandoned geological survey trench near the village of Mwadui, about 12 miles (20 km) northeast of Shinyanga. Bundalla was excited because the sample contained ilmenite, one of the minerals that often indicates the presence of diamonds. At that hour all the workers had gone home, so Williamson and Bundalla decided to process the sample themselves. They were rewarded with a beautiful, 2-carat octahedral diamond. The following morning they recovered several more stones from the trench. Williamson immediately obtained an exclusive prospecting license from the district commissioner in Shinyanga.

By systematically digging sample pits and trenches and using a magnetometer to measure

Typical landscape of northern Tanzania: Serengeti National Park. *Photo H. Veiller-Explorer, Paris.*

General view of the Williamson mine in Tanzania. *Photo Hallower and Johnston, Sheffield.*

John T. Williamson, discoverer of the mine that bears his name. *Photo Tanganyika Information Services.*

magnetic fields, Williamson outlined a massive kimberlite pipe and associated diamondiferous gravels. The ancient intrusion, hidden for millions of years, had been exposed through the persistence and skill of one geologist and a small team of workers. The business of developing a mine now had to be undertaken, and here Williamson received invaluable help from a Dublin-educated Punjabi lawyer, Iqbal Chand Chopra, who had a practice in Mwanza. It was he who set to work to establish Williamson Diamonds Ltd. At that time industrial diamonds were needed for the war effort, and this helped to ease the inevitable logjams of colonial government bureaucracy. The shortage of supplies for the new mine was more of a problem than the shortage of money to pay for them, but Chopra's persistence ensured that the "Doctor" received more than his quota of materials.

Had Mwadui been established thirty years later, Williamson would have been confronted by irresistible political and financial forces that would have prevented him from retaining control of his discovery. The circumstances of war, the absence of a nationalistic government, and the fact that diamond production offered high revenues with low operating costs enabled Williamson to finance the growth of the mine out of its own profits. Williamson built a township for several thousand employees and their families, complete with schools, clubs, and shopping facilities. Huge reservoirs and an 8-megawatt power station were constructed, and a 3,000-ton-per-day processing plant was opened in 1956. Sadly, just when the mine joined the ranks of the world's largest, Williamson became seriously ill. He died early in 1958.

Williamson's heirs decided to sell the Mwadui mine jointly to De Beers and the Tanganyika government. After Tanganyika gained its independence in 1961, the mine was nationalized. Thanks to the abilities of George Hunt, the general manager, the transition was made without serious problems. Today the Williamson mine is a wholly Tanzanian company affiliated with the Diamond Corporation. Its huge crater has produced several million carats, about half of them of gem quality. Among the finest stones was a rough diamond of 54 carats, which was cut into a gem of 26.6 carats. The jewel was mounted in a brooch and presented to Princess Elizabeth, now queen of the United Kingdom, on her marriage in 1947.

Most of the richer reserves at Mwadui have now gone. A shaft sunk to 1,320 feet (400 m), from which sampling tunnels were driven, revealed that the kimberlite was insufficiently rich at that depth for the mine to be worked much longer. Soon the Mwadui mine will join "the Doctor" as part of Tanzania's history.

Zaïre

When in January and March of 1914 the Antwerp press mentioned the arrival of two consignments of diamonds from Kasai in the Belgian Congo (now Zaïre), no one outside the trade was very interested, and even among diamond merchants only a few were sufficiently well informed to judge the significance of the event. The two batches, which were put up for auction at the headquarters of the Société Générale de Belgique, amounted to only 6,795 and 5,000 carats respectively. No one could have known that these diamonds were the first fruits of what would become one of the greatest diamond producers of modern times.

The Congo had been acquired by the Belgian state only in 1908, when King Leopold II, who had taken possession of the territory in his own name in 1885, bequeathed it to the nation. Through this acquisition, in less than a quarter of a century, Belgium was able to wrest from South Africa the first place among diamond producers. The preeminent position of the Congo was further strengthened in the 1930's, and today the republic of Zaïre produces an annual total averaging between 11 million and

The beginnings of the industry in the Tshikapa region, 1917–18: washing and grading diamondiferous gravel with rocking screens. *La Forminière Archives, Brussels.*

14 million carats, which makes it the world's leading diamond supplier, just ahead of the Soviet Union and South Africa.

This may seem surprising, as few people even now realize that Zaïre is a major diamond producer. The reason is that Zaïre produces mainly industrial diamonds. Though industrial diamonds represent about 80 percent in volume of world production, they account for no more than 15 percent in value. It is true that about 40 percent of the diamonds mined in the Tshikapa region, in southern Zaïre, are of gem quality, but they represent scarcely 5 percent of the country's total production. The remainder comes from Mbuji-Mayi, where almost all the diamonds are of industrial quality.

Obviously, in early 1914, when the diamond trade was wondering rather anxiously about these first batches of diamonds from an unknown source, none of this was known, not even to the prospectors who had located the deposits, and any speculation about the future was highly uncertain. There would certainly have been more curiosity about the mysterious source if the outbreak of the First World War in August, 1914, had not swept all such questions aside. It was only after the war, during the 1920 international trade fair held in Brussels, that the existence of diamonds in the Congo was revealed to the general public.

The Creation of La Forminière

The discovery of diamonds in the Belgian Congo was not made in one day; it was the result of several years of geological prospecting, conducted under extremely difficult conditions. The organization responsible was the Société Internationale Forestière et Minière, known as La Forminière, a concessionary company established in 1906 by Leopold II.

Acting as sovereign of the Congo state, Leopold had, in 1896, drawn up a set of plans to explore the Congo basin. An international association had been created to carry out this exploration. Anxious to ensure the Congo a future in accordance with his own ideas, Leopold created a number of companies, such as the Union Minière du Haut Katanga, that were given vast concessions to develop the country's natural resources. Before any such development could be undertaken, it was essential to make a systematic inventory of the mineral and forest resources of the immense territory. Leopold wanted this task to be assigned to an organization with sufficient resources to permit a policy of long-term development that would bring no immediate rewards. In this spirit La Forminière was founded with the assistance of the American Ryan-Guggenheim group, chosen because of its financial capacity and, more important, its great mining experience. This group provided 25 percent of the registered capital (50 percent of the paid-up capital), which was established at 3.5 million Belgian francs. The balance came from various Belgian individuals and from the Société Générale de Belgique, the large financial-industrial conglomerate. The Congo state and the Belgian Royal Foundation received, gratis, half the shares issued, or to be issued, in compensation for the rights granted.

Leopold's emphasis on the long term proved

Below: Transporting gravel in wheelbarrows, Mulamba, 1918. Right: After initial sifting in the trommels, the gravel is concentrated in hand-operated joplin jigs. *La Forminière Archives, Brussels.*

justified. No less than five years of constant effort and many prospecting expeditions were required before La Forminière succeeded in finding, among other valuable minerals, diamondiferous deposits.

Commissioned in May, 1907, the first expedition spent two years covering the huge concessionary territories, devoting special attention to Maniema, a highly mineralized region that seemed to merit detailed study. Some worthwhile scientific knowledge was gathered, and scattered traces of iron and tin were found, but not on a large enough scale to justify commercial operation. During the next two years additional expeditions were organized, more restricted in their aims and concentrating on smaller areas. One relatively profitable result was the discovery of gold deposits in the basin of the Tele River, a tributary of the Itimbiri, which produced some 50 pounds (23 kg) of gold in 1911. Although this was encouraging, it was not nearly enough to compensate for the expenses incurred up to that time, and La Forminière's situation became rather precarious: the original capital had long since been absorbed, and new loans were necessary. In 1912 the advances made by the American group and the Société Générale de Belgique totaled almost 3 million Belgian francs. The future appeared highly uncertain, and there was a serious possibility of liquidation.

Then, suddenly, the existence of diamond fields in Kasai was announced. It was of course too early to estimate the size or the nature of the deposits, but considerable encouragement

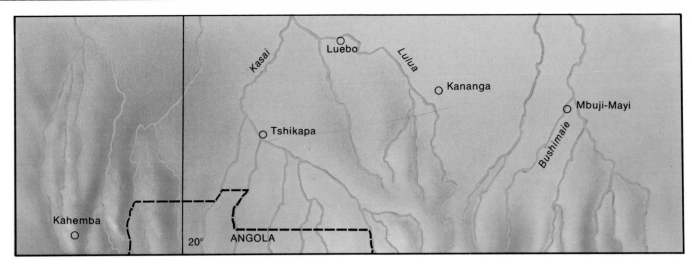

The diamondiferous
regions of Zaïre: Tshikapa and
Mbuji-Mayi.
Burns Graphics, London.

Below: Diamondiferous
gravel receiving initial sorting
in a hand-worked trommel,
about 1920. *La Forminière
Archives, Brussels.*

125 days were spent traveling with a small bodyguard of armed men along narrow trails through country that was often hostile. The men explored the region downstream from Port-Francqui, systematically examining the many tributaries of the Kasai, the Lulua, and the Luebo. Even the smallest streams were inspected by careful sifting of sand and gravel. The great hope that nourished every member of the expedition during this exhausting task was that they might discover gold. As time went on, hostile encounters with local tribes increased. This was not surprising, for the area was virtually unexplored—it was only thirty years since H. M. Stanley had led his beleaguered expedition down the Congo to the sea—and this column of white men, followed by many porters bearing loads of mysterious equipment, not unnaturally created anxiety among the inhabitants.

Before leaving the unfriendly Kasai and heading north—with little to show for their endeavors—Richard Mohun and the geologist Sydney H. Ball, who was in charge of technical operations, instructed three members of the team to make a brief inspection of the central Kasai. The men appointed were an experienced Belgian prospector named Narcisse Janot; Millard King Shaler, an American geologist; and R. B. Oliver, a surveyor. Their caravan included 140 porters, 20 soldiers, and a dozen others. On the evening of November 4, the caravan was resting at the village of Mai-Munene, on the right bank of the Kasai. In an atmosphere dominated by the impressive roar of the Kasai River as it plunged over the splendid Pogge Falls nearby, Shaler noted the events of the day in his working journal: "This morning Janot prospected the stream of Tshiminina, about 300 meters upstream from the place where the track crosses it. Here he found a golden color in the gravel, about one meter deep. Because of rain, he could not continue his prospecting. In a sieve trough, Janot found a small transparent stone, with a greater bril-

could be derived from the fact that in only a few months, and with no tools other than their sieves, the society's prospectors had found more than five hundred diamonds. Though they were little more than mineralogical specimens, they held great promise for the future.

A Clue Not Followed
The events leading up to the first shipment of diamonds from the Congo followed some circuitous and improbable paths, but the story is an interesting one, worth recounting briefly. It began early in 1907, when an American, Richard Mohun, who was familiar with the problems in Africa, and especially those in the Congo, joined with nine other men in a Forminière expedition that sailed from Antwerp on May 30, 1907. They reached Leopoldville (now Kinshasa) with no trouble, but after that progress was slower. It took thirteen days to travel up the Congo River and then the Kasai River to Dima, where the Kasai Company, a Belgian general trading firm, had its main office. They arrived there on July 2. The next

liance than the diamond sample in my collection tube and, according to all appearances, with diamond crystallization. I put this stone aside for later inspection, as we have no means to determine the specific weight and the stone is too small to determine its crystallographic characteristics with a small magnifying glass." Placed among other panning samples in one of the test tubes every geologist carries in the field, the stone that Shaler described was actually a diamond weighing a tenth of a carat.

The next day the Shaler column moved on. They traveled through the region of Tshikapa, passed the Wissmann Falls a few miles below the confluence of the Kasai and the Lovua, and eventually reached the post at Luebo, at the junction of the Lulua and Luebo rivers. In January, 1908, Shaler, Janot, and Oliver rejoined the main expedition at Maniema, where they spent fifteen months exploring the soil and rivers before returning to Europe. Mineral deposits of many kinds had been identified, but the diamond found in Kasai was forgotten.

A Missing Label and a Wooden Box

While searching for India, Christopher Columbus found the Americas. Because of the accidents of history, the new-found continent was named not for him, but for Amerigo Vespucci, whom the geographer Waldseemüller credited with the discovery. A similar sort of

twist of fate occurred in the discovery of the Congo diamonds. The "Indies" so ardently sought by Shaler and Janot had escaped them, and a third man was required to recognize, identify, and name the "continent" they had unexpectedly touched on. This man was a Belgian mining engineer, Prosper Lancsweert. Entrusted by La Forminière with a prospecting expedition, he made elaborate preparations before leaving Brussels, studying all the available published material on the subject (there was not a great deal), reading reports of former expeditions, and carefully examining the numerous mineral samples preserved in the offices of La Forminière. One day in September, 1909, he opened Shaler's test tube containing the still-unidentified diamond. The label, unfortunately, had been lost. But among many other samples of no interest, Lancsweert was attracted by this tiny crystal. He examined it with a magnifying glass, then under a microscope, and finally tested its hardness. He had no doubt then that this was a diamond. His analysis was confirmed by Henri Buttgenbach, professor of mineralogy at the University of Liège.

The revelation produced a flood of questions. Where did this diamond come from? In which stream, in what gravel of the huge Belgian Congo, was the valuable evidence found? Narcisse Janot, who was in Brussels at the time, recalled that it might have been shipped from Maniema. Shaler, the expedition leader, was questioned. He turned to his notebook and found the lines written on the evening of November 4, 1907. One fact was now established: *one* diamond had been found in Kasai. Certainly it would have been too bold—indeed, false, as later experience would prove—to assume that the region explored in 1907 was a workable diamond area. Consequently, although geologists and prospectors were informed of the find, no change was made in the programs of expeditions then in the field or under preparation.

In 1910, not long after Lancsweert's mineralogical discovery, he and Janot sailed for Africa. More than a year passed before other evidence was found indicating the existence of diamondiferous fields. Janot's work first took him to Kwango, and he did not reach Kasai until August, 1911. As can be imagined, it was with great zeal that he began to inspect the riverbeds. On August 6, at the junction of the Kasai and Kabambaie rivers, about half a mile (1 km) from Bantua-Sanki, where the Kasai Company had installed a trading post, he discovered several diamonds. In the following days the amount rapidly increased. On September 10 the expedition leader cabled the Brussels headquarters that 242 stones had been

In the waiting room at the Tshikapa buying offices, and (below) an original method of weighing diamonds: bottle tops and matches stand in for scales and weights.
De Beers Archives.

A modern washing plant in the Mbuji-Mayi region, built close to the mine. It produces concentrate from the rough ore. *Photo Guy Philippart de Foy, Brussels.*

A giant excavator that can remove up to 585 cubic yards (450 cu m) of material in an hour, in the Mbuji-Mayi mine. *Photo Guy Philippart de Foy, Brussels.*

scribes how these prospectors, as they followed the rivers upstream, also discovered diamonds in Angola, whose border was only some 90 miles (150 km) to the south. The origin of the Angolese diamonds is closely linked with that of the diamonds of Kasai.

The first diamonds destined for the Antwerp market arrived in Europe on October 28, 1913, in a small wooden box carried by C. W. Boise, an engineer for La Forminière. The stones came from a decidedly rudimentary work site on the left bank of the Tshikapa, near its junction with the Kasai. Compared with what had been found in South Africa at the close of the nineteenth century, this parcel of 6,795 carats was a rather poor trophy. So far, the results of much patient labor were still uncertain. Developments in the Belgian Congo were vastly different from the violent diamond rush in South Africa in 1866, when, in less than a year, ten thousand searchers with a taste for adventure were attracted to the banks of the Vaal from every part of the globe. In the remote regions of the Congo, where access was difficult, there were serious problems of transport, labor, and food supply, and the discovery was not on a large enough scale to generate the interest to solve these problems. However, new sites were opened, notably in the Longatshimo and Kasai valleys. By late 1913, about 15,000 carats had been extracted.

The outbreak of the First World War obviously did not make things easier. Production reached only 127 carats in December, 1914, and during the first months of 1915 it was down to zero. Once links with the company were reestablished—its headquarters had been transferred to London during the war—the indispensable supplies to keep the struggling work sites going came from the United States. Thanks to the work of fourteen engineers and agents and about three thousand Africans, production recovered: from 3,000 carats in May, 1915, it reached 50,000 carats in 1916, 100,000 in 1917, and more than 160,000 in 1918.

The Deposits of the Tshikapa Region
It soon became apparent that these deposits were only of the alluvial type; consequently, the diamonds found there were dispersed in the river gravels or in the conglomerates of the old river terraces. The prospecting teams estimated the area at more than 8,000 square miles (20,000 sq km), a considerable territory, much of it covered with thick forest. Given the prevailing social conditions, a large labor force was required during the early period. The gravel was transported in cane baskets, which the workers carried on their heads. Wheelbarrows were not seen until 1918. They were followed by small wagons,

found, and more kept turning up. Ten diamonds were found at Tshikapa, seven near Pogge Falls, and nine in a small tributary of the Tshikapa River. Another company prospector, a Scotsman named George S. Young, working in the neighboring valley of the Longatshimo, discovered 237 diamonds in a few days in December, 1911. The company decided to concentrate the prospectors' efforts in this area. On March 5, 1912, the expedition stopped at the Tshikapa site, at the junction of the Tshikapa and Kasai rivers, and built a hut with a roof of leaves. This was the first headquarters of La Forminière in Kasai. A prospecting area was laid out, and by late 1912, 2,540 diamonds had been collected. The following chapter de-

Opposite: Part of the works at Mbuji-Mayi. The yellowish area on the right is one of the newly discovered kimberlite pipes. *Photo Guy Philippart de Foy, Brussels.*

which were either pushed by hand or drawn by cables. Much later, as work developed, belt conveyors came into use to transport the gravel to the washing plants and, after washing, to the dumps. For the washing process, a device was developed on the site which is still used by prospectors today. Known as a rocking screen, it both grades the gravel and removes the sand. It consists of a series of screens, one above the other, mounted on a rocking device that is vigorously shaken by two men working in unison. It delivers the gravel graded into three categories. African workers gave it an appropriate name, *bukebuke,* which perfectly conveys the noise it makes when shaken. Obviously, its efficiency is somewhat limited. After the First World War, a mechanical sieve called a joplin jig was introduced. Its screens, when agitated in water, made it possible to sort the component elements of the diamondiferous gravel according to their density. Because diamonds are heavy, they form, along with the few other minerals that have a similar density (known as "join elements"), a relatively homogeneous mass that falls to the bottom. The joplin jig,

The processing plant at Mbuji-Mayi. Below: Part of a pan in which diamonds are separated. *Photos Guy Philippart de Foy (right), Jacques Legrand.*

first employed in the 1920's and, like the rocking screen, still used by some prospectors today, soon proved insufficient and was replaced by pans of much greater capacity, which are adequate for present industrial requirements.

Although the diamonds recovered were small, the high proportion of gemstones among them encouraged La Forminière to begin a series of mines in the area, each with its own washing plant (in 1957 there were no less than fifty-three of them), from which the concentrated gravel is collected and sorted in the central plant at Tshikapa.

The gradual impoverishment of the deposits, as well as the difficulties caused by the political events of recent years, considerably diminished industrial production and finally ended it altogether. One by one, La Forminière's installations closed, and today only local digging is carried on. This method of production is the only one that is worthwhile, since the diamond content of the gravel does not justify industrial operations.

There is a buying office at Tshikapa, operated by Britmond (British-Zaïre Distribution Ltd.), a Zaïre-based company affiliated with the Diamond Corporation. It negotiates for the production of the diggers and tries as best it can to keep diamonds from leaking to other countries where a more favorable monetary system tempts diggers with higher profits. Current transactions, amounting to a total of about 600,000 carats a year, would seem to contradict statements about the impoverishment of the deposits. The explanation must be that either there are a great many more diggers active than the authorities suppose, or, more likely, that some of the diamonds reaching the Tshikapa buying office come from illicit digging beyond the border, in Angola.

The Mbuji-Mayi Deposits

Although the First World War prevented operations from starting in the Tshikapa area, systematic exploration of the Congolese subsoil continued. In addition to La Forminière, a number of other companies were active. The Compagnie du Chemin de Fer du Bas-Congo au Katanga (Bécéka, or BCK) organized an expedition led by the Scottish geologist George S. Young, who had previously worked at Tshikapa. After a long investigation of the basin of the Lulua River, Young's expedition headed east and reached the Bushimaie River. The gravel there proved unexpectedly fruitful: by December, 1918, some 8,400 stones had been collected. Subsequent investigations led to the discovery, not far from Bakwanga (now Mbuji-Mayi), of a deposit that eventually turned out to be one of the largest found since the great Kimberley days in South Africa. It was this

deposit that made the Belgian Congo the world's largest diamond producer (67 percent of world production in 1939). Unfortunately, the stones proved to be of poor quality; most were of industrial quality only.

In January, 1920, Bécéka asked La Forminière to work the deposit. La Forminière had already proven its capacity at Tshikapa, and its experience in diamond mining was second to none. This arrangement continued until the Belgian Congo gained its independence in 1960. At that time, the Bécéka mining company (which had since been renamed Sibeka)

A conveyor belt carrying the rough ore from the mine directly to the central recovery plant at Mbuji-Mayi. Below: Washing diamondiferous gravel before the final sorting.
Photos Jacques Legrand (top), Guy Philippart de Foy.

created the Société Minière de Bakwanga, better known as MIBA. In 1973, when the republic of Zaïre nationalized all foreign companies, MIBA came under local control. But the situation steadily deteriorated, and after five years of decline the former shareholders were reassigned 20 percent of their capital in return for accepting the obligation to restore and modernize the mining installations.

The work accomplished by La Forminière in the 1920's required investments that were all the more substantial because the region was totally without means of communication, and before the work could begin on a large scale, a costly infrastructure had to be created virtually from scratch. To make the enterprise possible, it was decided that the first deposits to be attacked should be those that would

bring swift and valuable returns. Such deposits were to be found in the alluvial fields bordering the wide slopes of the Kanshi and Bushimaie valleys. A careful study of the morphology and of the deposits themselves soon convinced the geologists that there were still primary deposits that remained to be found, and the search was extended to the slopes of the hills bordering the alluvial deposits. The geologists noted the presence of strong diamondiferous belts that all converged on the heavily flattened spur of Disele, west of Bakwanga. However, it was not until 1946 that a few deep pits were sunk in this area to provide access to a diamondiferous kimberlite mass. In time, ten other kimberlite sources were discovered. Laid out like a string of beads over several miles, these primary deposits cut into two more or less equal parts the angle formed by the Kanshi and Bushimaie rivers. The sites being worked there today form a triangle about 5 square miles (14 sq km) in area. Another diamond area was recently identified 20 miles (35 km) southwest, up the Katsha River.

The opening of the first mines confirmed what surveys had foretold: the deposits were large and rich, but the diamonds were almost exclusively of industrial quality. More precisely, they were mostly the variety of industrial diamond known as crushing boart, or bort, which is suitable only for grinding into powder. This type of diamond was at that time a doubtful proposition for investment; it was only during the Second World War that the demand for it greatly increased and it became—as it still remains—an important industrial material. In 1939, before the demands of war had changed the picture, the Diamant Boart (a Belgian company created two years earlier to study and promote the use of crushing boart) held stock exceeding 30 million carats. This surplus was rapidly absorbed within the next few years, and during the postwar period new markets were opened that gave an unprecedented stimulus to the working of Mbuji-Mayi. In less than fifteen years, it became the largest diamond mine in the world. A production record was set in 1961 with 18 million carats, of which only 2 percent was gem quality. (Though a small proportion, at 360,000 carats this quantity was far from insignificant.) The general run is between four and eight stones to the carat.

The region of the Mbuji-Mayi alluvial deposits is essentially a large plateau, about 2,300 feet (700 m) above sea level, where the rivers are wide and meandering, often with no clearly defined banks. One of the distinguishing features of the deposits is the considerable depth—often as much as 100 feet (30 m)—of the layer of barren soil covering the diamondiferous gravel. The first task is to remove this barren layer. In the past, powerful water hoses broke up and cleared the surface soil, but in the early 1950's the hoses were replaced by mechanical shovels, 22-ton bucket trucks, and bulldozer-scrapers. Still more powerful machines followed, including a huge excavator weighing more than 600 tons, whose scoops cleared an area 180 feet (54 m) wide and 50 feet (15 m) deep, removing an average of 580 cubic yards (450 cu m) of soil in an hour.

Today the alluvial gravel is still shifted by mechanical shovels. Depending on the site of

Two views of the mining city of Mbuji-Mayi. *Photos Guy Philippart de Foy, Brussels.*

Below: Isolating a section of the Katsha River at Senga-Senga, about 17 miles (28 km) south of Mbuji-Mayi. *Photo Guy Philippart de Foy, Brussels.*

the mine, the gravel is either washed on the spot in a modern washing plant or carried directly by conveyor belt to the central plant at Mbuji-Mayi. The treatment depends on the type of material recovered. The kimberlite naturally requires different treatment from the gravels recovered from alluvial deposits. Generally, all kimberlite is conveyed to the main plant, while gravel is washed and sorted in a local washing plant near the site of mining operations. The concentrates, regardless of whether they come from kimberlite or alluvial gravel, are moved to the sorting plant, where the diamonds are extracted by the same methods as those used in South African mines. The final sorting is usually done by x-ray.

Today the Mbuji-Mayi plant is fully automated. All the operations are controlled from a central control room, where a large chart displays the various processes through which the gravel passes. Cameras are placed at strategic points, and the whole operation can be monitored on screens in the control room.

The immensity of the task of removing the barren soil, and the huge quantity of heavy equipment required for this operation, have led prospectors and engineers to channel their efforts into the direct working of the gravel from the numerous rivers that drain the region. But since the winding courses of the rivers in Zaïre and, more important, the shallowness of their deposits make it impossible to use dredges, other means have been adopted, recalling those of the Brazilian diamond diggers of the eighteenth century, though on a much greater scale. The most dramatic method consists simply of diverting the course of the river by digging a drainage canal to isolate one of the loops of the river. If the topography makes this impossible, several dams are constructed and the riverbed is drained in stages, so that the greatest amount of gravel can be collected while the riverbed is dry. In practice, these methods have proven exceptionally profitable. For example, at Senga-Senga, 17 miles (28 km) south of Mbuji-Mayi, in a drained section of the Katsha River, 5 million carats were recovered in less than one year, the ratio being 40 carats per cubic meter of gravel. The record to date is 1,500 carats from a single pit in the riverbed 100 feet (30 m) deep.

The Future

The work begun by La Forminière at Tshikapa, in the very heart of the bush, was not confined to the exploitation of mineral wealth. At the same time that technical development was going on, a genuine town was created, which, in addition to general services, provided housing for the European and African staff. Hospitals, maternity wards, schools, theaters—everything was built entirely by the company. At Mbuji-Mayi, an airport and a hydroelectric power station were also constructed. As many as 300,000 persons were employed, all in one way or another directly dependent on the diamond industry for their livelihood.

During the 1970's the situation changed considerably. The country's chronic instability facilitated the increase of illegal dealing in diamonds. Clandestine diggers often operated within a few hundred yards of the official installations.

The entire legal production of Zaïre diamonds is sold to Britmond at Kinshasa, which grades and evaluates every batch of stones it receives. The prospecting of the whole region, made by teams of geologists who take samples on a systematically defined grid, has continued for several years, and the fabulous wealth of the deposits they have surveyed suggests that the mines may be profitably worked for a long time to come. Despite the problems, the future of Zaïre's diamonds seems assured.

Illegal diggers at work on the territory of the official concession, only a few hundred yards from the main works. *Photos Guy Philippart de Foy, Brussels.*

Angola

The central African state of Angola and (right) the diamond region in northern Lunda province. *Burns Graphics, London.*

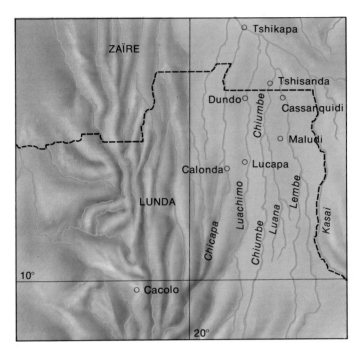

The discoveries made by the Janot team in the Tshikapa region of the Belgian Congo toward the end of 1911 encouraged La Forminière's prospectors to continue active searching on a large scale. Their program, dictated by the nature of the river system of the region, was to examine very carefully the principal rivers that, running in roughly parallel courses to the north, flowed into Kasai from sources far south in Angola. This meant that the prospectors had to enter the Portuguese colony, which was not divided from the Belgian Congo by an obvious frontier.

The first official finds in Lunda, in northeastern Angola, were made by Donald Steel, prospecting the Maculo and the Monji, two tributaries of the Luembe, in July, 1912. These and subsequent discoveries led to the formation of a Portuguese mining company known as the Companhia de Pesquisas Mineiras de Angola (PEMA), founded in September, 1913. Its principal shareholders were the Société Générale de Belgique (already involved in La Forminière), various banks in Lisbon and Paris, and the American Ryan-Guggenheim group, also involved in La Forminière. The first base camp was established at Tshisanda, and a few workings were soon in operation. On October 16, 1917, PEMA founded the Companhia de Diamantes de Angola (Diamang), with its registered offices in Lisbon. Diamang's operational center, at first located in Tshitatu, was later moved to Dundo, a stone's throw from the frontier and only about 85 miles (140 km) from Tshikapa. At first all workers and supplies came from Tshikapa, because La Forminière was responsible for operations and works management. Within several years, however, the railway line being constructed between the port of Lobito and Katanga reached Vila Luso (now Luena), and a 360-mile (600-km) road was completed between Vila Luso and Dundo. These connections enabled Diamang to become self-sufficient and autonomous.

On May 14, 1971, the contract that gave Diamang exclusive mining rights expired, and the company had to be content with selecting reserved mining areas, the total area of which was limited to 20,000 square miles (50,000 sq km). The remainder of the old concession was granted to a consortium known as the Consor-

cio Mineiro de Diamantes (Condiama), whose members included the Angolan government, De Beers, and Diamang itself. On July 10, 1976, eight months after Angola declared its independence, Diamang's head office was moved from Lisbon to Luanda. Finally, on August 28, 1977, the independent state of Angola took over the operation of the company by acquiring 60 percent of the stock. During the late 1970's production was seriously disrupted by political events, and mining came to a standstill. Nevertheless, everything remained ready for resumption.

A High Yield of Gemstones

The first alluvial mines, though small, proved remarkably fruitful. The work in the river flats was soon supplemented by mining of progressively higher terraces, then of much older conglomerates totally independent of the current river system. In some places, the courses of large rivers were diverted. This made it possible to explore thoroughly the twisted rocks of the riverbeds, which often concealed sizable cavities that held astonishingly rich deposits of stones. Some deposits yielded a comparatively low diamond content, but as compensation very high proportions—an average of 70 percent—were of gem quality. Annual production from 1959 to 1974 regularly exceeded 1 million carats and reached a peak of 2.4 million carats in 1970.

The Hunt for Kimberlites

Since it appeared that the diamonds were transported and distributed primarily by the rivers, the discoveries made in Kasai in the Congo and in Lunda gave rise to the belief that the stones there had been brought by the numerous streams running north through Angola. Therefore, geologists concluded, the primary deposits from which the diamonds derived would be found in the Portuguese colony. As soon as mining had started in Angola, a vigorous hunt for the kimberlite sources began. Not until 1952 was the first of the elusive primary deposits finally found. In the interim numerous and often contradictory theories had been advanced. There was much at stake, for the quality as well as the quantity of the stones being found suggested that the Angolan mother rock, if and when it were found, would prove unusually rich.

The immense territories of northeastern Angola were practically virgin land at the beginning of the twentieth century. When Donald B. Doyle, an American geologist, was hired by PEMA in 1914 to make the first geological survey of the region, the only information he had to go on was the superficial description given a century earlier by the Portuguese explorer Henrique de Carvalho and a few reports made by the *pombeiros,* Afro-Portuguese intinerant merchants who regularly traveled from one village to another. Doyle covered the entire region and found, beneath the light surface soil and gravel of some valley slopes, the prevalent occurrence of a soft, layered, diamondiferous conglomerate in sandstone formations. He inferred that because of the gradual destruction of the conglomerate by the flow of the present rivers, all the gravel of the region had been—

and was still being—sown with diamonds. In short, Doyle founded what may be called the "basal conglomerate theory." Many geologists reshaped his theory to suit their own conclusions on the age of the conglomerate and on the direction in which to search for the source of diamonds. At Xatuca, a southern mine near a little tributary of the Luembe called the Maludi Caquece, which marked the southernmost diamond discoveries, a South African expert, B. F. Werner Beetz, noted a much coarser diamondiferous gravel beneath the normal gravel of a terrace deposit. The coarser gravel was packed with unusual pebbles of a rose-pink, granular quartzite. The rock formation from which they derived was known only on the River Luana, between Maludi and Xatuca. On the basis of this and other clues, Beetz formed the belief that kimberlite existed somewhere south of Maludi, and in 1930 he propounded an ingenious theory to account for it. He suggested that during the Pleistocene epoch, periods of intensely heavy rainfall had created a violent, sporadic torrent called a "run," which had attacked this kimberlite and the quartzite outcrop. In a series of mighty rushes it carried off quantities of debris—and diamonds—northward in a muddy mass. This primeval flux then separated into two branches. One, running northwest, had accounted for the few isolated diamond deposits on the Luana and middle Chiumbe rivers; the other, much greater, branch had supplied all the mines of the Luembe and the lower Chiumbe and, fanning out beyond the frontier, had finally created the diamond fields of Kasai.

The new theory of the "run" aroused much interest; however, no kimberlite had yet been found. An American geologist, A. C. Veatch, taking up Beetz's ideas in 1935, suggested a different explanation. He questioned the supposition that the two branches of the flux ran from south to north on the grounds that at the period when this was happening the general slope of the terrain was not from south to north, as it is now, but in the opposite direction. He believed that the kimberlites would be found in the Congo.

Ten years later, in 1945, a Portuguese geologist and director of Diamang named C. Freire de Andrade devoted about nine months in Lunda to a demanding research program aimed at solving the mystery of the kimberlite sources. He made the first comprehensive geological map of the region between Maludi and the Congo border and correctly assigned to the Upper Pre-Cambrian the outcrop of rose-pink, granular quartzite mentioned above, which he named the Luana formation after the river that crosses it. More important, he identified a fracture zone north of Maludi, which he thought

A temporary washing station set up by prospectors in Lunda, September, 1972. Boxlike rocking screens are being used to sift the unsorted gravel (right) and, partly visible in the left foreground, gravel is being separated into three grades in jigs. *Photo René Delville, Brussels.*

The bed of a large river after the water has been diverted. Lunda, September, 1972. Right: After removing the layer of silt, diamondiferous gravel is extracted from a "pot." *Photos René Delville, Brussels.*

might contain kimberlite eruptions. He recommended searching this area in case of failure in the work south of Maludi, especially in the valley of the Maludi Caquece creek, which he, like Beetz, considered more promising. Freire de Andrade came close to a correct solution, but he was unlucky. All the searching he recommended was in vain, probably because of the inferior means of investigation available at the time.

The Lucapa Theory

In 1950 the author of this chapter, then an engineer employed by Diamang since 1934, was leading a prospecting expedition upstream on the Chiumbe and Luachimo rivers. As no very significant deposits had been found, instructions were issued by the management to abandon the search. However, there were two small and supposedly uneconomical deposits on the Chiumbe that were something of an enigma: their total isolation was scarcely compatible with either the basal conglomerate theory or the "run" theory. Even more significant was the discovery on the Chiumbe of an outcrop of the Luana formation that lay in a direct west-southwest line through the two outcrops of the same formation located by Freire de Andrade on the Luana and the Luembe. Moreover, the two small deposits on the Chiumbe could be linked with current mining sites on the Luana and the Luembe by a straight line following a similar west-southwest direction, parallel with the Luana outcrops but a few miles away. Instead of leaving as ordered, the prospecting team concocted an excuse to remain on the Luachimo. At first the results were even poorer than on the Chiumbe. A few weeks later, however, when the prospectors reached the point at which the river met the apparent line of deposits indicated by the map, their hopes were fulfilled. Two small, isolated deposits were found, one on each bank of the Luachimo. A few miles downstream, a hitherto unknown outcrop of the Luana formation was also found—exactly as anticipated.

Geological and mineralogical evidence suggested that the prospectors had come upon a continuous fault that in all probability was responsible for the presence of diamonds in these widely dispersed deposits. Moreover, since diamonds had been found all along the supposed fault wherever the lower layers of gravel had been inspected, it was expected that the fault would turn out to be mineralized along its entire length. It was decided in secret to conduct an inspection on the next major river in this sequence of northward-flowing streams, the Chicapa (about 20 miles, or 35 km, west of the Luachimo), at the point where it intersected the west-southwest line representing the fault. There the prospector Alberto dos Santos Champlon found, as hoped, a new outcrop of the Luana formation. It was now, if not conclusively proven, at least highly probable that all these outcrops of the Luana formation along a straight line, in the midst of much older rocks, were the last visible evidence of a *graben,* or rift valley. This would have been formed before the present river system, subsequently partly leveled by erosion, and then obliterated by more recent overlying formations now under attack by current watercourses. To name it, the term "Lucapa" was coined from a combination of the names of the two rivers (*Lu*embe and Chi*capa*) between which the fault lay.

At this stage the theory seemed almost too good to be true. Since a *graben* by definition includes two faults, one at each side, the southern fault, similar to the northern one and running parallel to it, remained to be found. But where in this little-known territory should

the search for the southern fault begin? In the absence of other clues, it seemed that a logical place to begin was at the most southerly known deposits, those of the little stream of Maludi Caquece. If this did indeed mark the southern fault line, the space between it and the northern fault was about 7 miles (12 km) and encompassed the entire fracture zone mapped by Freire de Andrade north of Maludi. On the basis of these assumptions, a line was drawn on the map to indicate the presumed fault line. The search began at the point where this line met the Chicapa and its tributaries, about 75 miles (125 km) from the Maludi Caquece. At the chosen spot the assumed fault was straddled by a creek called the Calonda. The first pits there produced magnificent diamonds.

Yet still no kimberlite was found in the bedrock. Work continued at a feverish pace along the Chicapa itself northward toward the northern fault. On May 27, 1952, only a few miles from the Calonda, the long-awaited discovery was made. In a prospection pit, Champlon came across a much-altered diamond-bearing rock of a distinctive greenish color. A sample was immediately taken to Dundo. After some weeks of cautious hesitation, geologist F. Real confirmed that the rock was indeed kimberlite.

Thus, at last, some proof had been obtained for the "Lucapa theory," which states that any exploitable alluvial deposit is derived from a mother rock situated less than 6 miles (10 km) away, that this mother rock is associated with a fracture, often dating to the Mesozoic era, and that it has been relieved of its diamonds either by direct erosion or through the medium of a conglomerate (the above-mentioned basal conglomerate and "run"). This conglomerate, called Calonda formation, is simply a piedmont, more or less reshaped by water, stemming from the erosion of the fault scarp itself.

Even before identification of the first kimberlite had been confirmed, the Lucapa theory was successfully applied to other regions of Angola where Lucapa-type *grabens* were detected beneath more recent overburden. Once a start had been made, discoveries of both kimberlites and alluvial deposits followed one another in quick succession. Most were apparently connected with the suspected faults that caused the *grabens.* More than five hundred primary deposits have been found to date. Though many seem to be uneconomical, surface mining of some of them has been highly profitable. It is now established that the pipe found on the Chicapa is one of the largest in the world. Angola holds much promise and will play a greater role in the diamond industry in the future. It is significant that the capital of the new mining province of Lunda Norte is called Lucapa.

Sketch illustrating the Lucapa theory. The parallel fault lines mark the *graben*; diamond deposits are shown in black, Luana formation shaded. *Burns Graphics, London.*

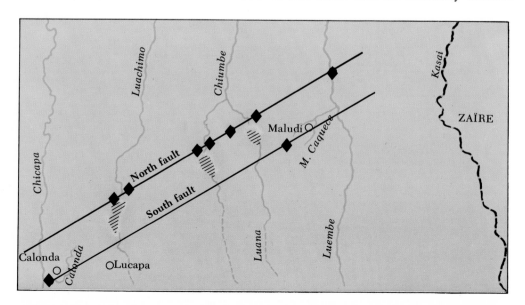

Mining the bed of a large river in Lunda, September, 1972. The "pot" is so deep that a mobile crane is needed to winch out the diamond-bearing gravel. *Photo René Delville, Brussels.*

Sierra Leone

The greatest annual amounts of diamonds in Africa come from South Africa and Zaïre, and in these countries diamond mining is a large, well-established, and well-organized industry. There are other countries in Africa that produce diamonds, though on a smaller scale. They include the Central African Republic, Tanzania, Ghana, Guinea, the Ivory Coast, Liberia, and Sierra Leone. In these countries, the diamond is not a long-established source of wealth, and in many of them it has been responsible for considerable upheaval and confusion. One reason for this is the sheer ease with which diamonds can be collected, which makes diamonds a tempting commodity for illicit dealers. It is hard to imagine an illegal trade involving, say, 40,000 tons of iron ore, but smuggling 300 grams of diamonds—the equivalent in value—is a great deal simpler, especially when there are plenty of buyers prepared to make deals outside the authorized channels. The illicit diamond trade has substantially reduced the revenues of these countries, which, as developing nations, can ill afford such losses.

Circumstances naturally vary from country to country, but Sierra Leone offers the best example of the difficulties encountered by governments—most of them established fairly recently—in their efforts to control and systematize diamond working. Moreover, the high reputation of the gems produced by this small West African state, the importance of diamonds in the economy, and the way in which the diamond market evolved there make Sierra Leone a particularly interesting example to investigate.

Wedged between Liberia and Guinea on the west coast of Africa, Sierra Leone covers an area of 28,700 square miles (71,740 sq km). Its capital, Freetown, on the coast, is so named because it was originally settled by freed slaves in the late eighteenth century. The coastal settlement became a British colony in 1808, and a British protectorate was established over the entire country in 1896. Sierra Leone became independent in 1961.

Apart from the generally flat and in places marshy coastal belt, the country consists basically of a large granite plateau cut by numerous deep valleys. In the tropical climate, vegetation is generally dense. Rainfall is heavy, about 88 inches (219 cm) annually, and seasonal; the dry season extends from mid-November to mid-April.

The country processes varied mineral resources, including bauxite, rutile, and iron ore. (Production of iron ore ceased, perhaps temporarily, in 1975.) But these resources pale into insignificance when compared with diamond production, which at 1.2 million carats (530 pounds, or 240 kg) in the early 1970's accounted for no less than 60 percent of the country's revenue. In some years it accounted for as much as 75 percent. The drama of Sierra Leone's diamonds might be reduced to this simple equation: 530 pounds of goods = 60 percent of national revenue (though the proportion has recently declined somewhat).

Discovery

In 1930 a British geologist named J. D. Pollett, sent on a mission by his government, discovered the first Sierra Leone diamonds on the banks of the Gbobora, a tributary of the Bafi, in the Yengema-Koidu region. He had no idea, of course, that he had found one of the most valuable diamond deposits in West Africa, a deposit that, over the next forty years, would produce more than 50 million carats of

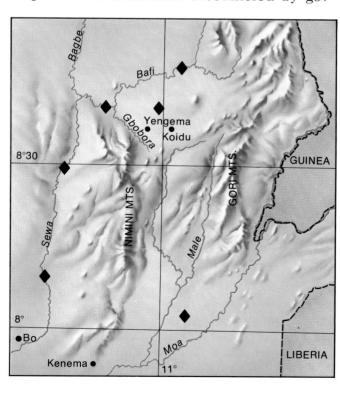

The diamondiferous region of Yengema-Kenema, Sierra Leone. *Burns Graphics, London.*

Comparative levels of erosion of some well-known mines in relation to the original kimberlite pipe. *Burns Graphics, London.*

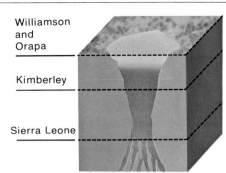

Williamson and Orapa

Kimberley

Sierra Leone

The River Sewa during the dry season. *Photo Guy Philippart de Foy, Brussels.*

diamonds, approximately half of them gemstones of the finest quality.

What are the geological phenomena that brought this remarkable situation into existence? That question was asked long before any precise answer could be given, and even today there are some points that remain unexplained. The first diamond fields discovered by Pollett were essentially alluvial. It was not until some time later that a whole group of diamond-bearing dikes was discovered, and the first kimberlite pipes were not found until 1948. As was explained earlier, in the chapter on geology, these pipes were the evacuation tubes of kimberlite formed by exploding magma that penetrated the earth's crust and finally took the form of craters. Toward the base of the pipes a network of fissures, or dikes, was formed, like errant roots of a plant. Filled with kimberlite, they varied in width from a fraction of an inch to several yards. An important characteristic of the Sierra Leone diamond sources is that they are composed of these "roots" of old pipes that have been weathered and worn away by erosion at the top. Moreover, these pipes must have been exceptionally rich, for even though a considerable part of their treasure was carried off to the sea, the diamond content of the remaining area is high.

The Nature of the Deposits

The diamond-bearing area found by Pollett measures about 50 by 60 miles (80 × 100 km), bounded on the east by the frontiers of Guinea and Liberia and on the west by the River Sewa (which is formed by the junction of the Bafi and the Bagbe). In the north it extends some 20 miles (30 km) beyond Yengema and in the south to the Liberian border south of Kenema. The landscape is made up of rounded hills divided by valleys. There are many streams and rivers, and the heavy rainfall has accelerated the process of erosion: in many places the underlying rock is exposed, because water has swept away the soil and vegetation. There are two principal mountain chains, running north-south and about 22 miles (35 km) apart: the Nimini Hills in the west and the Gori Hills in the east. These hills are basically schistose rocks, relatively resistant to erosion; the peaks are about 2,500 feet (750 m) above sea level. The intervening plain, of granitic rocks whose coarse grain has facilitated weathering, is about 1,300 feet (400 m) above sea level. Over thousands of years this landscape has been sculpted by the varying effects of erosion. The kimberlite dikes were themselves deeply eroded along with the surrounding rocks, and the diamonds were gradually freed to feed the alluvial deposits of the River Sewa.

This evolutionary process explains the presence of diamonds in the old banks from which the river has long since receded, as well as in the alluvial plains. Indirectly it also explains why the River Bagbe, a main tributary of the Sewa, is diamond-sterile. Flowing roughly north-south, the Bagbe drains a region in which there is no kimberlite. The Bafi, on the other hand, is fed by streams flowing from the hills around Yengema, which pass through kimberlite regions.

All this is clear enough. Less easily explained is the presence of extremely high concentrations of diamonds in the Sewa, downstream from the Bafi. It is possible that there is another network of dikes, as yet undiscovered, that produced this aggregation. A less exciting but perhaps more likely explanation is that the more gentle flow of the river in this section permitted the accumulation of alluvial deposits—and diamonds—that would otherwise have been swept downstream.

As for the deposits of the Tongo region, between the Nimini and Gori hills, they clearly derive from kimberlites that also fed the Moa and Malo rivers. The Moa and its tributaries also brought diamonds into the area south of Kenema. What is quite certain is that masses of diamonds have been lost, carried down to the coast and out into the Atlantic Ocean, where they lie on the sea bed amid vast accumulations of sand and gravel. The prospecting that has been done so far suggests that the reconcentration of marine deposits into workable diggings, as occurred in South-West Africa, has not happened here.

Early Developments

When the first diamond discoveries were made in Sierra Leone, the British firm of Selection Trust was already well known for various mining activities, especially in iron and copper. Since 1922 it had also been interested in diamonds, and in that connection it had created the Consolidated African Selection Trust (CAST), with its main office in London. De Beers had subsequently bought shares in CAST.

The moment the existence of diamonds in Sierra Leone became known, prospecting teams were sent out to the region from the CAST mines in the Gold Coast (now Ghana). As early as 1932, 750 carats were found, and in the following year the total soared to 32,000 carats. In 1934, when the profitability of the deposits was confirmed, CAST decided to create a London-based subsidiary called the Sierra Leone Selection Trust (SLST), devoted exclusively to diamond operations in Sierra Leone. Early results were encouraging, especially in view of the simple methods then in use, and the high proportion of gemstones in relation to industrial diamonds—roughly 40 percent—was a crucial factor in the success of the company. However, before making the huge investment required to build a processing plant in the heart of the rain forest, SLST required guarantees. On October 29, 1934, it concluded an agreement with the government that gave it exclusive working rights throughout the Sierra Leone territory.

The apparent generosity of this contract is explained by contemporary world economic conditions. This was the period of the Great Depression, and demand for diamonds was at its lowest. Demand had sunk so low, in fact, that De Beers had decided to reduce production in its South African mines. Moreover, the region to be worked in Sierra Leone was wild and remote; everything needed at the site had to be transported there with great difficulty, for communications with Freetown were minimal. Finally, the extensiveness of the site and the way in which the diamond deposits were dispersed promised to make surveillance a major problem. In fact, it proved a worse problem than even the most pessimistic forecasts had predicted.

While ordinary hand-working methods continued, the first years of SLST operation were devoted to constructing a processing plant at

Manual work on a large scale on the terraces beside the Sewa, about 90 miles (150 km) from the present banks of the river. The unproductive upper layer is being removed under the supervision of the site boss. *Photo Guy Philippart de Foy, Brussels.*

Industrial installations of Diminco at one of the central sorting plants, west of Kenema. *Photo Guy Philippart de Foy, Brussels.*

Yengema. A number of washing stations were also set up close to the principal deposits. As methods and facilities improved, production increased. Heavy machinery was brought in to clear the forest and remove the barren upper layers so that the diamond-bearing gravel could be recovered.

An increase in production was recorded in 1942, when the armament industries spawned by the Second World War demanded increasing quantities of industrial diamonds. In 1944, however, a decline began because of the labor shortage that followed the intensive recruitment of West African regiments. The men who joined the army and subsequently fought in various theaters of war abroad returned with different ideas on a great many matters, including diamonds.

Clandestine Digging and Illegal Trade

The SLST geologists and prospectors naturally made use of local labor. As most of the alluvial deposits lay near the villages, the people were able to observe at their doorsteps the most appropriate methods for extracting the little crystals that were causing such upheavals in their country. In the past, they had not paid much attention to diamonds. The stones were not particularly attractive in their rough state, and the people had no use for them. Now, however, the diamonds did at least provide opportunities for work and the means to buy various consumer articles that seemed useless to people living in the bush but were apparently prized by their friends in Freetown.

Things changed when the soldiers serving in the British army returned after the war. During their travels they had seen what value people in Europe and other parts of the world at-

tached to the stones that could be picked up so easily near their own homes. Subsequent events followed a predictable pattern. Every man began to work for himself. Rumors of sudden and incalculable wealth spread rapidly. Workers left their jobs, convinced that a fortune lay within easy reach. Diggers from other parts of Sierra Leone and from Guinea and Liberia descended in great numbers. By the early 1950's, a diamond rush was under way.

The situation was beyond the control of the authorities, and the exclusive rights granted to SLST were difficult to safeguard. A 1936 law that forbade search for, possession of, and trading in diamonds was ineffective. It was estimated that by 1954 more than thirty thousand people were engaged illegally in the diamond business. SLST complained to the authorities about the pillage of its reserves; even its actual work sites were invaded by illicit searchers who shamelessly profited from the earthworks performed by the company's machines. Although police detachments were stationed at Yengema and Motema, they could hardly do more than make a few token arrests. Drastic action of any kind would result in a direct conflict with the searchers.

The facts had to be recognized: it was practically impossible to stem the rush. Communications between local leaders and the authorities in Freetown were unsatisfactory, sometimes nonexistent. Some people took advantage of the lack of organization. Searchers formed bands, posting lookouts to watch for the security patrols. The security guards were unarmed, and when they did encounter illicit searchers they could only report them to the police. By the time police arrived, the place would be deserted, but when they left the searchers would reemerge from the forest and continue their work. On a few occasions armed police did succeed in surprising the searchers, and the latter sometimes resorted to violence to prevent police intervention.

Between 1954 and 1956 the rush of illegal diamond searchers reached such proportions that the national economy was imperiled. Farmers neglected their crops and livestock to such an extent that the government had to import commodities like rice, which in normal times Sierra Leone exported. Instead of enriching the country, diamonds were threatening to ruin it. In the region of the diggings there was a severe shortage of food, and prices rose to dizzying heights. The cost of a chicken, for example, was at one point twenty times higher than it had been a year earlier.

New Legislation

In 1955 it was estimated that more than a million carats of diamonds were taken by illegal diggers, a staggering loss by any standards. In the context of Sierra Leone's economy, the seriousness of such a drain can be gauged by the fact that, five years later, a million carats of diamonds, valued at the official rate, were equivalent to 43 percent of the country's total trade. In view of this situation, the government decided in February, 1956, that the only feasible solution was to legitimize the searchers by granting them licenses. This, of course, violated the contract that granted exclusive rights to SLST, and lengthy negotiations with the company were undertaken with a view to canceling that agreement. SLST made substantial concessions, amounting to 480 square miles (1,200 sq km) of its assigned territory. The SLST working areas were confined to the Yengema mining areas and to the Tongo region (25 miles, or 40 km, north of Kenema), where a new deposit had recently been identified. In return for its territorial concessions, SLST received compensation of £1,570,000.

For the government to control the situation on the ground and—equally important—to ensure that the diamonds produced were legally exported and taxed, it seemed advisable to set the price of a searcher's license fairly low, at £9 a year. Besides this, searchers were asked to pay a ground rent of £10 a year for a plot of land 400 feet (120 m) square. Each searcher was entitled to employ a maximum of twenty assistants, provided they were registered.

In terms of licenses granted, the new arrangement was a great success. Some fifteen hundred authorizations were issued in the region of Bo alone in just two months, February and March, 1956. Since each licensee employed the maximum twenty workers allowed by the law, about thirty thousand individuals hitherto engaged in a clandestine activity became, at one stroke, properly licensed diamond searchers.

Another problem was the presence of large numbers of foreigners in the region, many of whom came from neighboring countries under French control. The issue of licenses was specifically restricted to natives of Sierra Leone, but foreigners exploited a loophole in the law by getting themselves hired as workers. The diamond regions were therefore declared "forbidden areas" to non-natives, and all foreigners were ordered to leave. While the world's attention was focused on the dramatic events occurring in Hungary and the Suez at the time, the British and French governments, already associated in the Suez affair, combined to evacuate as discreetly as possible thousands of so-called undesirables from Sierra Leone. This potentially explosive move was defused by a decision to expel only those who had resided in the region for less than six years. Anyone who could prove that his activities did not include searching for diamonds was likewise immune. Within three weeks, however, about 45,000 people were forced to leave the country. They had come to make a fortune, but most of them left no richer than they had arrived. Their huts were burned after they had gone. With the number of searchers considerably reduced, prices rapidly fell from their inflated levels. By December, 1956, prices had returned to normal in the region of Kenema. The whole episode had been handled with minimal publicity and was, in fact, almost entirely ignored outside the area affected.

Legalizing the searchers and expelling the excess foreign population nevertheless failed to solve the government's problems. During 1956 taxes were paid on only 127,000 carats from official searchers, although total production was estimated at over a million carats. The bulk of this, representing some £15 million, continued to vanish into illegal channels.

Dealers and Traffickers

Bo, Yengema, and Kenema are the chief settlements of the diamond regions of Sierra

Above: Large areas of land denuded by illegal digging in Sierra Leone. Right: Washing gravel at a small nonindustrial site. *Photos Guy Philippart de Foy (above), Jacques Legrand.*

Washing and grading the gravel with foot-rocking screens, made locally. They consist of layers of sieves with successively finer meshes. Two men agitate the sieves by simple leg movements while balancing on top. *Photo Guy Philippart de Foy, Brussels.*

Leone. They are typical African overgrown villages, with a main street and a large market. The houses on the outskirts are of the traditional wattle-and-daub construction, but the buildings in the center, some of them two stories high, are of more durable materials. Outside such places, people live in groups of huts arranged in a circle in an open space in the forest or the savannah. Agriculture is the main activity, and slash-and-burn methods are commonly practiced. From the air the landscape resembles a huge green carpet with a random pattern of black patches.

When in the 1950's the inhabitants of this forest became diamond seekers, merchants immediately appeared among them. At first, no doubt, the merchants had little idea of how to go about their business, but they soon learned. By the end of the Second World War, several hundred Lebanese had settled with their families in West Africa, particularly in Freetown. They were merchants born and bred, and their main activity in West Africa was the importing and distribution of such common consumer products as cigarettes, clothing, and tools. Once they became aware of what was happening in

Panning gravel in Sierra Leone. The circular sieve is shaken with a rotating movement, which results in the larger material being gathered at the center. The gravel is then turned out on the bank and inspected carefully. *Photos Guy Philippart de Foy, Brussels.*

apparent relation to the next. Moreover, when a clandestine searcher found a diamond, he was anxious to dispose of it as quickly as he could. Possession of it made him, in principle, a criminal, and besides that he was driven by a natural desire to know the worth of his find as soon as possible. The earliest transactions were therefore the most fruitful for alert buyers. The seller, even if he knew that he was not getting as much as he could, generally had little desire to keep his stones: they burned his fingers, he ran the risk of losing them, and, above all, he feared that they might be stolen from him.

For the first traffickers this was a golden age. The boldest of them unhesitatingly traveled through the forest to isolated huts scattered here and there, and they often returned with their pockets filled with diamonds worth a fortune. But to make such purchases they had to have large financial resources and be prepared to invest their profits immediately. Much richer than the local merchants who were often their clients, the Lebanese had long been accustomed to traveling to Kenema, Bo, or Yengema to sell their merchandise. Familiar figures, they did not attract much attention, and they had the added advantage of being able to deal with the diamond searchers by barter, exchanging their ordinary trade goods for the stones. Obviously, diggers living in the heart of the forest would prefer to sell their diamonds to the same man who supplied them with clothing, tools, pots and pans, and hair lotion; bank notes were not much use to them. Inevitably, the Lebanese gained control of the illegal diamond market.

The Monrovia Market

If purchasing stones at the digging site posed few problems, getting them to outside markets was another matter. Freetown was the meeting point of all illegal traffic, and while policemen were rare in the forest, in the capital they were numerous and well organized. To prevent the escape of illegal diamonds, they only had to keep a careful watch over activities in the port and airport. The police made some handsome seizures, but the smugglers succeeded in some equally profitable evasions. Both sides used every means available: what the smugglers most feared was not a prison sentence but the confiscation of their diamonds, which could mean ruin. In a year and a half the Freetown police officially confiscated more then £300,000 worth of diamonds, but the figure obviously does not include the many sub rosa deals that were made between police officials and smugglers. It was during this period that Lebanon, without producing a single diamond or, according to offi-

the forest, it was inevitable that they would play a part in the fast-developing diamond rush. The opportunity to make large profits was too tempting to pass up. There were, of course, certain risks in illegal diamond transactions, but they were more than justified by the potential profits, which were especially large at first because of the comparative ignorance of the diggers. Prospectors had taught the diamond diggers to recognize quartz, but their familiarity with diamonds was superficial; the gems were of many diverse forms, and each stone had a value that bore no readily

cial figures, importing any, managed to export considerable quantities of the stones.

The strengthening of security and currency controls at Freetown forced the defrauders of the government to seek new routes. The proximity of the Liberian border to the diamond-producing areas favored the establishment of a shipping route to Monrovia. The capital of Liberia offered several advantages. As the crow flies, it is scarcely 120 miles (200 km) from Kenema, but to avoid patrols in the border area, the traffickers took a more roundabout route via Guinea in the north and then south through the whole length of Liberia. Though the way was longer, it had an incidental advantage in that a good road was available.

Until 1954 there were few restrictions on the diamond trade in Liberia, apart from a 15 percent tax. This tax, however, was high enough to encourage fraud, and the following year the government decided to reduce it to 9 percent. At the same time, a licensing system was introduced for the diamond business. Licenses were easy to obtain, but the taxes to be paid were calculated on the basis of declared value rather than on an administrative valuation. Obviously, the declarations made were as low as possible, and it is estimated that the taxes paid never exceeded 1 percent of the real value of the exported stones. That was a small price to pay to stay within the law.

Diamond dealers and cutters from Antwerp and elsewhere headed for Monrovia, where there was free currency and banking transactions could be made in dollars. (In Freetown, there were strict currency controls and all transactions had to be made in sterling—these were major inconveniences to the illegal traffickers.) Gradually the traffickers took on the role of intermediaries between the diggers in Sierra Leone and the buyers in Monrovia. But as the searchers' experience increased and the number of dealers, most of them working alone, multiplied, the dealers' profits dropped. Much

Two diamonds are removed from the pile: one is of gem quality, the other industrial. *Photo Guy Philippart de Foy, Brussels.*

Below right: The Star of Sierra Leone, the largest alluvial diamond of gem quality ever discovered. Weighing 969.8 carats, it was found at Yengema on February 14, 1972. *De Beers Archives.*

now depended on the evaluation of stones whose size or quality made them exceptional. Because the slightest error in assessing a stone could result in a disastrous loss, the dealers held back from forming associations: any association might collapse if one of the partners made even one serious error. However, the buyers in Monrovia had great experience. These men, most of them from Antwerp, Amsterdam, or New York, were professionals, often cutters, and they were capable of making very

Opposite: Buying diamonds at a village in the bush. *Photo Guy Philippart de Foy, Brussels.*

Workers showing their finds to the site boss. *Photo Guy Philippart de Foy, Brussels.*

Having returned from their trips into the bush, itinerant buyers from Kenema wait for the DCWA buying office to open. *Photo Jacques Legrand.*

accurate evaluations of large stones.

The importance of the Monrovia market could no longer be ignored. In 1955 more than a million carats were negotiated there, in spite of the fact that Liberia produced almost no diamonds of its own.

The Creation of Buying Offices

By 1955, illicit activities had reached crisis proportions and were responsible for a serious loss of revenue. To persuade searchers to sell their diamonds on the official market rather than to the illegal dealers, it was necessary to offer them the same advantages and facilities they enjoyed when dealing with the latter. At the very least, prices had to be comparable and an organization had to be created that, like the illegal dealers, would send qualified buyers to visit the searchers in their village, preferably in the evening, when they gathered to calculate the results of their digging. The British colonial office invited the minister of mines of the Sierra Leone government-elect, Siaka Stevens (now president of Sierra Leone) to London and began discussions aimed at solving the problem. Sir Philip Oppenheimer and the SLST participated in the talks as well. A joint decision was made to license diggers to work within an agreed concession area, provided that De Beers was able to investigate the diggings, and to authorize the Diamond Corporation of Sierra Leone (DCSL) to set up a buying office. This buying office, established in 1956, was responsible to the government for the purchase of all production from the diggers and for all export and mining taxes. These arrangements did much to reduce smuggling.

The government buying office's aim was to buy diamonds from licensed searchers and to resell them in London to the Diamond Trading Company, which would redistribute them on the world market through its Central Selling Organization (CSO). The decision to buy on the spot was a radical departure from usual practices and indicated the profound misgivings of the Diamond Corporation in the current situation. Previously, it had been content to buy systematically the entire production of important mines, such as those in Tanzania and Zaïre. Its sales contacts had been built up over a period of many years, and prices were set according to strict standards negotiated in London with the general managements of the firms involved. These global purchases satisfied both parties: the mines sold their stones without having to bother about creating a sales service, while the Diamond Corporation gained virtual control of the world market and ensured price stability by adjusting supply to demand. But to maintain this position it was essential that the percentage of world production not controlled by the Diamond Corporation should be very small. The Monrovia market threatened this balance, particularly since the stones from Sierra Leone had acquired such a reputation for high quality that many of the best-known diamond dealers were traveling to Monrovia.

The great novelty of the new arrangement was that diamonds were bought individually in the forest. This manner of doing business could hardly have been more different from the standard transactions of the Diamond Corporation, which took place in well-appointed offices with payments made by bank transfers. Those who did the buying had to possess

rather unusual qualities. They had to be not only expert in judging rough diamonds, but also young and fit enough to be willing to leave their comfortable cosmopolitan environment and set off for the heart of an unknown tropical forest with little more than a knapsack filled with bank notes. They had to deal with African searchers whose outlook bore little relation to that of the people they normally dealt with, and as they were dependent entirely on their own judgment, they had to be capable of handling transactions amounting to thousands of pounds without making any unfortunate mistakes. But their greatest difficulty was that they had to work in the same place as the experienced illicit dealers, who were not at all inclined to surrender their lucrative monopoly. There were many diamond sorters in London, but how many of them would meet the necessary criteria and be prepared to accept the

risks of such a mission? To provide its employees with a certain amount of comfort and security in the forests of Sierra Leone, the DCSL built lodgings equipped with many of the conveniences of modern European living.

The first buying office was opened in Bo in 1956, and licenses to negotiate with the buying office were made available to those dealers who applied for them. First results proved rather disappointing: the buyers from London applied the rates dictated to them, but they were required by law to deduct export duties and alluvial-diamond-mining taxes amounting to 7.5 percent. The illicit buyers had no such restrictions and tended to offer higher prices initially, in order to "hook" the diggers. Consequently, the searchers were inclined to continue selling directly to the traffickers. Moreover, there were hundreds of traffickers and only a handful of London buyers. Despite the existence of an official buying office, it is estimated that in the five years after the creation of the DCSL, fraud accounted for at least the following quantities (the true figures were probably higher):

Views of Kenema and its environs, and (below right) two local beauties.
Photos Jacques Legrand (below left), Guy Philippart de Foy, Brussels.

1956: 950,000 carats
1957: 800,000 carats
1958: 640,000 carats
1959: 500,000 carats
1960: 200,000 carats

The improvement in 1960 was probably a result of the government's decision to change the status of the DCSL when it became obvious that the persistence of illegal purchasing was largely due to the fact that the prices the Diamond Corporation imposed on its buyers were too low. Accordingly, a new firm was created, the Government Diamond Office (GDO). Its management was entrusted to the Diamond Corporation, but purchasing prices were fixed by a committee of five persons, including an important diamond dealer from Antwerp not connected with the Diamond Corporation, capable of influencing prices to present the Monrovia market with effective competition. At the same time, since the searchers had increased their efforts along the River Sewa, a decision was made to open a new buying office at Kenema. The government export tax was then 5 percent, and a government official was stationed with the buyers in order to verify their evaluation of the diamonds and to collect the tax on the spot. The new organization was immediately successful. In forty-two months, the DCSL had negotiated for the sum of $18 million; in its first twenty-three months the GDO's figure was $60 million.

In this situation, the risks attached to illegal dealing were no longer worthwhile, and more and more dealers began requesting licenses to

Far left: An itinerant buyer selling diamonds to a Lebanese broker. Left: In the DCWA buying office at Kenema, a price is negotiated for a packet of diamonds, while (below) other vendors await their turn in the waiting room reserved for them. *Photos Guy Philippart de Foy, Brussels.*

negotiate with the official buyers. Once they were licensed, they could sell all their stones without fear or anxiety to offices where they were received with great consideration. After all, they accomplished the most dangerous part of the buyer's mission, for the idea of walking through the forest carrying large sums of cash appealed to no one. Moreover, the negotiators, almost all Lebanese, were thoroughly familiar with the terrain, attuned to local customs, and in frequent contact with the searchers. For these Lebanese dealers, there was no problem in estimating the weight of a stone in matches,

a primitive system developed by the Africans that always inspired grave mistrust among the London buyers. All things considered, the profits made by the Lebanese were commensurate with the work they performed, and an equilibrium was established to everyone's satisfaction. After thirty years, Sierra Leone was finally making an equitable profit from its diamond resources.

When Sierra Leone's independence was proclaimed, in 1961, the Diamond Corporation of West Africa (DCWA) was established, a Sierra Leone company whose management was entrusted to the Diamond Corporation. This arrangement continues to the present day. Naturally, clandestine searchers still remain in the forest, but their activities are no longer of much importance. Illicit operations chiefly involve very fine stones, those that can be sold quickly and offer rewards that justify the risks.

Industrial Production

In 1970 the government took control of the SLST diamond mines and a new company was created, the National Diamond Mining Company (Diminco). The government held 51 percent of the shares of Diminco in return for gradual reimbursement of the former owners, while SLST held 49 percent. The capital of the new company was fixed at £5 million, equivalent to SLST's assets at the mines. Three mines are now worked by Diminco, at Yengema, Koidu, and Tongo. Operating methods are technologically up-to-date and essentially do not differ from those used in the mines of

In the offices of the DCWA all payments are made in cash, and as the current bank notes are of relatively low denomination, one small packet of diamonds is exchanged for many large bundles of notes. *Photo Guy Philippart de Foy, Brussels.*

Constructing an earth dam to isolate a section of the river at a small hand-worked site on the Sewa. *Photo Guy Philippart de Foy, Brussels.*

South Africa and Zaïre. Although there was a serious drop in production in 1976–77, it is believed that the development of new working methods will result in a satisfactory yield for many years to come. The Koidu field has proven to be one of the richest in the world. It has produced almost 10 million carats from an area only 3 miles (5 km) across, and it was here, in the midst of the dike network, that relatively important pipes were found in the late 1940's. The average yield is 6 carats per square meter, but it often reaches 80 or 100 carats. Eventually, underground work will probably be undertaken.

Until 1961 all diamonds were automatically sold to the Diamond Corporation. Today Diminco sells its production at prices set by the Diamond Trading Company and agreed to by the Sierra Leone government. Sales are held three times a year, usually in April, July, and December. The diamonds are classified in about 250 different categories (the number varies from year to year) independently of their weight. Half the production is sold to the Diamond Corporation and the rest is divided among four buyers selected by the government. The prices of stones larger than 14.7 carats are negotiated separately.

The largest alluvial rough diamond ever discovered, the 969.8-carat Star of Sierra Leone, was found in the Yengema mine on February 14, 1972. It was bought by Harry Winston of New York, who had it cut into seventeen stones, thirteen of which are absolutely flawless. The two largest cut stones, which are

pear-shaped and emerald-cut, weigh 53.96 and 32.53 carats respectively.

Production by Local Diggers
Alongside the industrial installations, individual diggings by numerous local searchers continue; in fact, their output is equal to the production of the Diminco mines. Over 30 miles (50 km), in the heart of the forest, the River Sewa is thoroughly searched along its entire course. The type of work varies according to the season. In the dry season, three methods are currently in use.

The first consists of attacking the broad strips of land that remain on either side of the riverbed when the river recedes. It is here that the best-equipped men work, for bulldozers are required to remove the layers of mud covering the gravel. These machines are usually owned by Lebanese, who, in addition to their role as silent partners in the digging operation, provide some technical supervision and can exploit their knowledge of stones to negotiate sales with the DCWA. Once the mud has been removed, the gravel is recovered and washed by hand. As in Zaïre, prospectors here sometimes use joplin jigs or, more often, locally made foot-rocking screens for the washing process. The foot-rocking screen consists of a series of screens, one above the other, each with successively finer mesh; the last screen is the finest. The uppermost screen has two long bars on each side on which two men can stand, balancing each other. By moving their legs, they shake the screens. With constant washing, the

Making a U-shaped dam with a bulldozer on the banks of the Sewa River. *Photo Guy Philippart de Foy, Brussels.*

gravel passes from one screen to the next and the coarser items are separated out. Obviously, the diamonds are most likely to accumulate in the last screen, and the final selection is made by hand.

The second method, which has been practiced for a long time, consists of isolating part of the riverbed by building a U-shaped dam out from the bank. Here, too, a bulldozer is needed. When the dam is completed, pumps are used to drain the enclosed area, which must be dried out before the gravel can be recovered and sorted. This method, though more rapid than the first, is less efficient because it frees less gravel.

The last method, adopted during the early days of the rush, is the most expedient. It consists of literally diving for diamonds. What could be more efficient than locating the gravel right at the bottom of the river and inspecting it on the spot? However, this method, which at first used very rudimentary equipment—the divers' oxygen was supplied by a hand pump—was extremely dangerous, and after a number of divers were killed it was forbidden for many years. Now that better equipment is available it is once again in use. The water is very muddy, and the diver's main task is to locate the areas of gravel. When he finds such an area, he uses his legs to point a suction pipe, driven by a motor pump, in its direction. Today divers generally work in teams and take turns, each remaining underwater for several hours. This system, which is highly efficient when the men are lucky enough to find a "pot," makes it possible to explore the central bed of the river, whereas the dam technique is confined to the edges and banks.

When the rainy season arrives, the rising water sweeps away the dams, and the strong current prevents the divers from working. Generally, riverbed exploration must be aban-

doned, and the search is diverted to the slopes of the valley where the river ran in earlier times. The work here is more difficult and less profitable. Divided into small groups of four or five men each, the searchers dig holes several feet deep until they reach the gravel bed. The gravel is washed on the spot by any means available. Scarcely efficient, this method has the major drawback of leaving the gravel intact between the various excavations, and it transforms the area into a ghastly kind of lunar landscape where nothing will be able to grow for a long time.

On the site it is difficult to distinguish the licensed searcher from the illegal one. Those working systematically are usually licensed, while most hole-diggers are unlicensed. One fairly simple way to determine who is who is to fly over the region in a helicopter: those who flee for the nearest hiding place are illegal; those who remain on the spot and wave in greeting are usually authorized.

The passion for diamonds is acquired young, and large numbers of children keep themselves busy searching the ground on the outskirts of the villages. The few diamonds they find are sold to authorized searchers, who simply add them surreptitiously to their own production. Illegal searching no longer threatens the country's economy, and the authorities sensibly ignore it unless it is done in regions granted to the official mine.

The diamonds obtained by hand-working are sold to the DCWA's buying office at Kenema. Today there are still local dealers who visit the searchers in the forest, collect the production of small workings, and sell it directly to the DCWA—or to a Lebanese dealer, if they think he will offer a better price. Numerous Lebanese are themselves involved in this activity, and they make regular visits to the buying office, often with excellent stones for sale. Although these transactions take place in the heart of the bush, they are made according to the very strict rules that characterize the profession throughout the world. As each stone must be analyzed and evaluated separately before an overall offer can be made, negotiations over price often take some time. The seller may leave the buying office empty-handed, then return two or three days later to discuss the final offer. No one would dream of asking for a receipt, or of profiting by this lapse of time to make off with even a single stone. Any kind of malpractice is unthinkable, and all transactions are based on absolute mutual confidence. Payments are always made in cash. It is not uncommon to see a man enter the buying office with a few grams of diamonds and leave some time later carrying a suitcase packed with bank notes worth thousands of pounds.

The Sewa River seen from the air. From the platforms on which the suction pumps are mounted, divers (below) descend to inspect the riverbed. The gravel recovered by the pumps is poured into two large tanks on the bank, where preliminary concentration takes place. *Photos Guy Philippart de Foy (right), Jacques Legrand.*

Venezuela

The existence of diamonds in the Venezuelan state of Bolívar, south of the Orinoco River, can best be explained by viewing the geology of the country in the context of the geological evolution of the two American continents. During the Cretaceous period, the great Atlantic ditch gradually opened and the two continental blocks that were to form North and South America began to drift slowly westward. Eventually their movement was halted by a stationary oceanic plate that formed the bottom of the Pacific Ocean. At the close of the Cretaceous and beginning of the Tertiary period, this vast, slow impact gradually threw up the immense mountain chain that extends along the western rim of the Americas from Alaska to Tierra del Fuego. However, the two continental blocks did not drift in perfect unison; their lines of drift diverged, creating friction in the area of contact—the present Central American and Caribbean region. This, of course, is merely a brief summary—the actual process was far more complex—but it provides a broad explanation of why the great north-to-south mountain chain in this region divided into two branches. The western branch descended through Central America and the Isthmus of Panama, while the eastern branch formed a long arc through the Caribbean islands, northern Venezuela, and Colombia, where it rejoined the western branch. From the beginning, these mountain chains were subjected to heavy erosion, and the resulting alluvial deposits filled the hollows and spread out over vast areas in the form of plains.

Venezuela contains examples of all three of these large geological units. In the north and northeast, the Merida Cordillera and the Sierra de Perijá originated with the folds of the Cretaceous period. At the foot of these mountains, on the northern plain of Maracaibo and the *llanos* region that covers the center of the country between the Cordillera and the Orinoco River, there are deposits derived from the material eroded from the mountains. Often very deep, these deposits are of great economic importance, for they contain enormous oil reserves. Finally, the entire region south of the Orinoco is a huge relic of the original continental shield. The most ancient rocks here are more than 3 billion years old, and the region has remained geologically stable.

It is in this third region, which contains the famous Angel Falls, the highest natural waterfall in the world, that most of Venezuela's diamond activity is concentrated. As was explained in the section on the geology of the diamond, the stones tend to be found near the center of old continental shields, and Venezuela's diamonds provide an example of this tendency. There is no known indication of diamonds north of the Orinoco. In fact, the presence of diamonds is linked more or less directly to the sandstone and the conglomerate formation known as Roraima that extends into the state of Roraima in Brazil and, more noticeably, into Guyana (formerly British Guiana). The depth of the sandstone deposits is considerable, often extending to 6,500 feet (2,000 m). The distribution of diamonds, however, is not uniform: they seem to exist only in some layers.

The conglomerates themselves are not worked—extraction and processing are too difficult, and results are disappointing—but the eluvial and alluvial deposits are generally enriched by natural forces. As they descend the rivers and leave the conglomerates behind, the deposits become less rich and the average size of the diamonds decreases, but this disadvantage is balanced by the large accumulations of gravel, especially along major rivers like the Orinoco, which justify the use of dredges.

There is no doubt that the Roraima diamonds already had a long history when they were deposited in the gravel from which conglomerates were formed more than 1.5 billion years ago. Where did they come from? From the African shield (which was then quite close)? Or from the Brazilian shield? Knowing their origin would be helpful in the search for the kimberlite mother rock, but there is little hope that a conclusive answer will be found.

The remaining diamond area, Guaniamo, is located in the west, quite remote from the Roraima plateaus. Geological maps indicate remains of the Roraima formation in this area, but the maps are based on aerial photographs, which are not altogether reliable. In any case, such remains would not explain the high concentration of diamonds. Moreover, the Guaniamo diamonds are of quite a different type from those found elsewhere in Venezuela. It

The shanty town of Guaniamo in the Venezuelan jungle, a product of the diamond fever. The photograph was taken just as the block in the foreground collapsed after being undermined by water. Two miners can be seen hastily seeking a less precarious situation. *Photo Guy Philippart de Foy, Brussels.*

is almost certain that they are of a different origin. Is there kimberlite in the region, or are there conglomerates in the folded mountains of Cuchivero? Perhaps one day the research being conducted by the Venezuelan government will provide an answer.

Miners in the Jungle

Ciudad Bolívar, with a population of about 100,000, is the nearest sizable city to the diamond fields. So far, the difficult access and the irregular nature of the deposits have prevented even tentative attempts at industrial operations. Roraima is the finest remaining reserve for the wandering digger and the adventurer eager to make money quickly. Almost anything that happens, or could happen, in this part of Venezuela is an adventure. Although the environment is not particularly hostile, the region is almost impenetrable and for the most part bears no traces of the activities of man. The climate is tropical, and the temperature rarely falls below 85° F (30° C). The many rivers running in different directions through the forest would provide excellent means of access were they not repeatedly interrupted by waterfalls and rapids that make navigation impossible, even for small boats. Rapids are not the only problem. When the rivers are in flood, powerful and unpredictable currents are a constant hazard. On the other hand, the dry season changes many of these rivers into long strips of rocky carpet. The few trails by which the traveler may venture into the forest were all hacked out by hand; they are so narrow that two people cannot walk side by side on them. The trails link the scattered Indian villages whose inhabitants live in peace, undisturbed by the "benefits of modern civilization."

This environment was naturally attractive to individual prospectors. However, until recently, the rules and regulations imposed by government authorities were very strict. Working permits allowed each miner only a very small area—12 square yards (10 sq m)—and it had to be worked within eighteen months. Moreover, all heavy equipment was forbidden, so the plots had to be worked by hand. With these limitations, only a small amount of gravel could be worked, and it was impossible to work out the bedrock on which the gravel lay.

The first mining began in 1926 and was quickly concentrated on the Río Caroní, a major tributary of the Orinoco that runs from the heart of Roraima, not far from Santa Elena on the Brazilian border. The alluvial deposits that border the Río Paragua and the Río Cuyuní were also worked. As the years went by, about fifteen sites were worked on the Caroní alone, advancing along the course of the river as new discoveries were made.

From the start, working methods have been much the same as those used in Sierra Leone and other parts of western Africa. The method of conveying the diamonds to market, however, is different. Important mining villages like Santa Elena have laid out landing strips for light airplanes in the forest. The risks taken by the pilots are so great that no insurance company will cover them, and the price of a ticket is accordingly high. The diggers charter

The main geological units of South America. *Burns Graphics, London.*

Stable shield dating from the Pre-Cambrian

Tertiary and Quaternary sedimentary deposits resulting from erosion of mountain chains

Folded mountain chains, formed at the end of the Cretaceous and beginning of the Tertiary period

Sedimentary and volcanic deposits, not folded, dating from the Pre-Cambrian through the Cretaceous
1. Paraná basin
2. Xingu basin
3. Maranhão basin
4. Amazon basin

Oceanic plate, Pacific

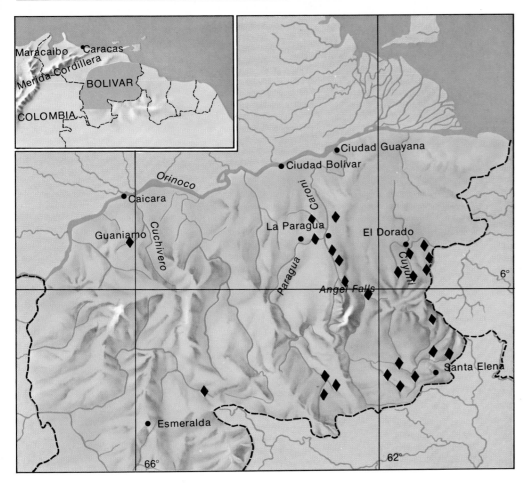

The region of Guaniamo and Roraima, Venezuela's diamond zone. *Burns Graphics, London.*

Maurice Siebenberg, one of the first prospectors in the Santa Elena region of Venezuela, about 1926.

these airplanes and make regular trips to Ciudad Bolívar, where they declare their finds to the Ministry of Mines. A 3 percent tax must be paid, based on the value of the stones as determined by a government evaluator. When the tax has been paid, a certificate is issued permitting export of the goods. The owner of the diamonds then merely contacts buyers in New York, Amsterdam, or Antwerp and waits for them to arrive. (In Venezuela, unlike most other diamond-producing countries, the stones are sold not through the Diamond Corporation in London but directly on the open market by dealers who acquire them in their country of origin.) This system works well largely because the region is so difficult to get to. It is impossible to reach the area' by any means other than airplane, and flights from the south are strictly controlled. Moreover, a special travel permit is required. Although the quality of the stones is generally very high, especially in the region of the Río Caroní, the chances of a miner making his fortune here are rather slim. The proportion of industrial stones ranges between 30 and 40 percent, and the weight of gemstones is generally only about a quarter of a carat; a stone weighing 5 or 6 carats is extremely rare. The one find of real importance was the 155-carat diamond known as El Libertador, found in El Polaco mine, near Santa Elena, in 1942.

Over the past twenty years, production fig-

ures have remained stable, rarely exceeding 100,000 carats a year. But in 1970 a considerable jump was made after the discovery of the Guaniamo diamond fields in the state of Bolívar, some 180 miles (300 km) west of Ciudad Bolívar. As noted earlier, these fields are something of a mystery, since they are far from the Roraima plateaus and yield diamonds of a demonstrably different type. Their origin has yet to be explained.

Guaniamo and Diamond Fever

The history of Guaniamo offers an example—probably unique—of strange and anachronistic events, of a town that in the second half of the twentieth century has fallen prey to the kind of diamond fever associated with South Africa a century ago. If a new deposit were discovered tomorrow in a similarly remote place, no doubt the same improbable scene would be reenacted there.

The story began in 1970, at the beginning of the dry season. An adventurous prospector was sailing up one of the many rivers of the region in a canoe. Equipped with only a washing trough and sieve, he was pursuing the wild dream that lies in the heart of every South American prospector: to find gold or diamonds in a quantity that would buy him every conceivable luxury. It is hard to imagine the force of the ambition behind such dreams, the intense drive that characterizes the prospectors who roam through the country. These men make up an army that attacks the savannah and the forests, the marshlands and the mountains, an army of hopeful *conquistadores* who ignore the existence of political boundaries. Nothing stops them. In fact, the dangers and difficulties they face often seem to enhance the attraction of the search. It is worthwhile to try to identify with one of these wanderers of the bush in order to understand the significance of this type of "wild" prospecting, the results of which never appear on any map or in any report, for it is almost always these men who are responsible for new discoveries.

This particular prospector in 1970—his name has already been forgotten—was going up the river in his boat, occasionally washing the gravel of a few "pans," those natural traps that retain the passing diamonds. He had had no luck, but he had encountered a promising array of the heavy minerals that often accompany diamonds, and this encouraged him to continue. At length luck, or the instincts of the good prospector, intervened. He decided to leave his boat to explore small tributaries upstream. He reached the farthest end of the most distant ravine, crossed the crests, and, without realizing it (he had no map), crossed the basin of the Río Guaniamo. Before him lay

"El Milagro," the main street of Guaniamo, at 5 A.M. *Photo Guy Philippart de Foy, Brussels.*

Opposite top: "El Milagro" from the air. Mining has diverted the river from its original course and turned it a dirty yellowish color. Bottom: The beer cans will remain when the buildings have disappeared. *Photos Guy Philippart de Foy, Brussels.*

a nameless ravine, later called El Candado, that empties into what is now the Quebrada Grande, or Quebrada Las Minas.

Suddenly the prospector's dream was on the verge of fulfillment. Although there was very little gravel in the almost-dry bed of the ravine, what there was proved wonderfully rich in diamonds. In a few days he extracted several hundred carats. With this encouraging start, he decided to head for town to buy some necessary equipment and food, and to gather a few trustworthy friends. His plan was to return with them to make the real fortune he was certain lay waiting for him.

A prospector with money in his pockets is a rare sight and never passes unnoticed. This man was no exception. He was feeling happy and rich; his money practically begged to be spent. He bought drinks for all his friends—and he suddenly had a great many friends, all prepared to join him and profit by his discovery. He had failed to realize that when his secret ceased to be a secret, his fine dream would come to an end. A new rush, a *bulla* or *bomba* as it is called in Venezuela, began, probably the greatest in the country's history.

In a few days the rush was at its height. The Río Guaniamo attracted every adventurer in search of a fortune—not only Venezuelans, but also Brazilians eager to find a less inhospitable land than their native Nordeste, Colombians exasperated by the increasing difficulties of the clandestine search for emeralds in their own country, escaped convicts from the French penal colony on Cayenne Island, and a host of

unclassifiable men with dubious pasts, who simply turned up at the site—no one knew where they came from or how they got there.

The development of a rush of this kind is a strange, emotion-packed phenomenon, and it is surprising that no sociologist or economist has been tempted to study it. In it one can see, in miniature, the full development of a society, passing through every stage from prehistory through social maturity to decline, decadence, and finally disappearance. The entire process occurs rapidly, within a remarkably brief period, like a grotesquely speeded-up movie.

At first there is total anarchy. This is the pioneering period, dominated by rough individualists who know no law but that of the jungle. Every man must conquer and defend his claim, and disputes are settled with fists or knives. The miners work very hard, using almost absurdly inadequate tools—picks, shovels, and sieves—to extract gravel from the diamond fields. They work under extremely hazardous conditions, excavating between loose blocks of granite or drilling vertical pits from which, despite the risk of rock falls, they carve horizontal passages into the richest layer. The gravel they manage to extract must often be transported several miles to the nearest water source for washing.

There is little time to hunt, fish, or cultivate a plot of land, yet the miners must live, so other people arrive to provide the necessities of life. Commerce begins. The extent of its development depends on the wealth of the deposits. It is at this stage that those entrepreneurs with a "sixth sense" decide whether or not to gamble and make their investment before others arrive.

As one might expect, prostitution is one of the first trades to appear. The women are often paid in diamonds, and it is said that skill in evaluating a rough stone is an essential part of their business. Some of them, in fact, have allegedly gained such experience that they have given up trading in sex and now trade in diamonds instead.

At first, simple transactions with merchants are made on the basis of straight exchange, but eventually barter is replaced by cash deals. The cash is brought in by the buyers who come to exchange their bank notes for diamonds. The first commerce is in basic necessities only—food and tools—but it soon diversifies. Much money circulates around rich mines like Guaniamo, and it changes hands easily. In a short time, every economic opening is filled, and competition begins. If the proprietor of a restaurant wants to continue earning money, he must be prepared not only to serve meals at any hour of the day or night, but also to satisfy the whims of his customers by providing such things as fans to stir the humid air, a little music (if only to drown out the din from the neighboring bars), or a "night club" in the back room where a lonely prospector can find the solace of female companionship.

Life is no easier for the barber. In the early days of the rush a miner may agree to be shaved in a hurry, seated on a stool, but the situation changes when money starts flowing freely. Then the barber who wants to keep his customers must furnish his shop with comfortably upholstered armchairs, so that being shaved becomes a pleasure.

These tradesmen and shopkeepers reveal an extraordinary taste for taking risks and an equally remarkable sense of enterprise. It takes a good deal of audacity to build a movie theater in the heart of the bush, to set up a poolroom, or to open a jeweler's shop. Yet all these things exist at Guaniamo, and all seem perfectly natural.

The most crucial requirement in the early days of a rush is to establish effective means of travel and communication. The diamond buyer who moves about carrying large sums of money in this "Wild West" setting and does not wish to be held up stagecoach-fashion, the shopkeeper who must rapidly replenish his stock, and the lucky miner who wants a few hours of extravagant relaxation amid the luxuries of the town all agree on the urgency of the communications problem. In the early stages, building a road is not even considered, for it would be usable only several months of the year. Consequently, the first link to the region is by air. The nearest convenient stretch of reasonably flat savannah is crudely laid out as a landing strip, and in no time it is in frequent use by *avionettes* (light airplanes). Helicopters provide, at "diamond" prices, a relay to the rocky peaks or hard-to-reach ravines.

Once it has become possible to transport heavy equipment to the work sites, the method of working the deposits is gradually modified. The miners form groups to pool their claims and their labor, and they set up small share companies with more substantial means than one man could raise alone. Such joint efforts have enabled them to attack the vast alluvial deposits of the Quebrada Grande. The gravel is immensely rich there—it is not unusual to extract stones worth $5,000 from one cubic meter of gravel. However, this layer of gravel is seldom more than about 8 inches (20 cm) thick, and it lies beneath 30, 50, or even 70 feet (10, 20, or 30 m) of totally sterile mud. Therefore it can hardly be reached without relatively heavy equipment, particularly various pumps—some that break up and disperse the mud layer with a powerful spray, others that pump out the mud and dump it in areas that have already been worked, and still others that

extract the gravel so that it can be stored on high ground, safe from the river in flood, and behind a barbed-wire fence, safe from thieves. The general rule in this region is to collect as much gravel as possible during the dry season. Washing is postponed until the rainy season, when high water makes extraction impossible.

Eight years after the first discovery, seven years after the first big rush, and only three or four years after the best *bulla* years—when annual production exceeded 1 million carats and some $50 million in cash flowed into Guaniamo—daily life in the mining area had become relatively routine and monotonous. The administration, consisting of the army, police, and officials of the Ministry of Mines, was maintaining firm control at Guaniamo and had set down rules and regulations to eliminate the chief causes of conflict. Weapons were forbidden, as was strong drink, but it would be a mistake to suppose that either disappeared completely. The Ministry of Mines banned the old method of digging vertical pits and horizontal galleries off them. Though this method was, to be sure, very dangerous, it was the only one available to individual miners. When it became illegal, the individual miner really had no choice but to become a salaried laborer for one of the many small companies.

Other than these constraints, the administration took very little concrete action. Although

Far left: Working seventeen hours a day in these conditions is no joke. *Photo Guy Philippart de Foy, Brussels.*

Left: A fence of chicken wire is swiftly erected to protect the mounds of diamond-bearing gravel. *Photo Guy Philippart de Foy, Brussels.*

A temporary plant for separating gravel and sand, made of wooden posts, pipes, metal sheets, and empty drums. *Photo Guy Philippart de Foy, Brussels.*

Unproductive layers of mud are dispelled by powerful hoses or monitors. Time is precious during the dry season, and everyone works straight through, despite the unpleasant conditions. *Photo Guy Philippart de Foy, Brussels.*

Guaniamo. When the unproductive layer, which is sometimes more than 30 feet (10 m) deep, has been removed, the gravel is carefully collected and put into sacks for sorting later. Pumps help to drain the work site and permit access to the gravel. When there are diamonds to be found, no one minds getting wet and dirty.
Photo Guy Philippart de Foy, Brussels.

the Office of Radio Communication broadcast to every remote spot—loudspeakers were sometimes mounted on trees in the forest—no schools or medical dispensaries were set up, and the construction of an all-weather road that could be used throughout the year seemed about as likely as the Second Coming. During election campaigns, the latent discontent attracted the attention of political candidates, whose visits—and promises—multiplied.

Today the Guaniamo rush is virtually over. Of course, on Saturday night, women wearing long gowns and adorned with jewels can still be seen on their way to the dance halls, and it is not uncommon to see a miner paying for

his coffee at the counter with a high-denomination bank note taken from a case filled with bundles of such notes. Nevertheless, the scene has changed. Excitement diminishes as the available reserves are depleted and extraction becomes more difficult; old dreams fade away. Production has begun to decline, and there is a hint of decay in the air.

Judging from the example of earlier rushes, the end will probably not be sudden and brutal. Rather, it will be a slow death. One by one, the most adventurous and enterprising miners will leave to pursue elsewhere the dream that the current situation at Guaniamo denies them. Soon only the old, the sick, and the handicapped will remain. Doubtless there will be a few bursts of enthusiasm—for example, when the Ministry of Mines decides to break up the original landing strip and permit mining there. In the enthusiasm of the great days of the rush, this strip was created on a level area of the Quebrada Grande in a section that later proved to be one of the richest in the valley. An estimated 12,000 carats remain to be extracted from under the buildings of the village. But after that has been done, Guaniamo will finally

Above left: This miner once drove a bus in Paris. He was living in Guyana when he felt the lure of Guaniamo and made his way there on foot. *Photo Guy Philippart de Foy, Brussels.*

Above: Buying office at Guaniamo, where the miners come in the evenings to sell the day's finds. Left: Almost anything can be bought in Guaniamo, but it costs three times as much as anywhere else. *Photos Guy Philippart de Foy, Brussels.*

A brief moment of relaxation before work resumes. Below: The tough but hopeful face of Guaniamo miner. *Photos Guy Philippart de Foy, Brussels.*

pass into history and legend, and the forest will slowly reassert its dominion. Soon it will be left to the historians to examine the story of Guaniamo in the glorious period when there was so much money to be earned that the wildest risks were taken, and to rediscover the monuments of that adventurous era when aircraft landed almost anywhere they could put their wheels down. Such monuments include the DC-3 that lies, almost intact, in the Cuchivero savannah; the almost unrecognizable remains of a small aircraft placed on four empty oil drums like some striking, surrealistic sculpture; and the twisted remains of a helicopter in El Candado ravine. Archeologists may one day study the strata of the mountainous rubbish dumps in order to establish the chronology of successive periods: the era of canned beer—the earliest, when all transport was by air and weight was a major consideration—and the later period, the era of bottled beer, which followed the construction of the long-awaited road.

However, all this anticipatory nostalgia may be misplaced. It is said that history never repeats itself, and maybe Guaniamo's fate will be different from that of other diamond towns. Some geologists in Venezuela think there may be kimberlites near Guaniamo; that would explain the exceptional richness of the deposits. But no one has discovered them yet, and it is likely that they were dispersed long ago. The speculation that they still exist may be no more than a scientific cloak for the old dream of every diamond prospector.

A Solitary Dredge on the Paragua

Some people feel the tug of diamond fever but do not relish the kind of life encountered in Guaniamo, and it is possible for them to try their luck in comparative solitude. Among those who have done so are Frank Taube and the few people with him who operate a dredge installed in the Río Paragua, the chief tributary of the Caroní, at a spot difficult to pinpoint on any map. In Ciudad Bolívar this little band is known as the "forest hermits," and their story bears comparison with those of explorers of an earlier time. Few people have ever met them, so it is difficult to know how many of the stories told about them are true. Still, it is possible—though not easy—to visit them. To find an airplane and a pilot to fly to Santa Elena or Guaniamo, which is expensive, is one thing; to persuade the pilot to fly over the ill-mapped forest in search of a dredge and then to land nearby is something quite different. But it can be done.

In the early 1970's Frank Taube, an American in the prime of life, was running a garage in Miami, Florida. He seemed content with all the comforts that modern civilization provides—and in Miami it provides plenty. Taube, however, is a man of instinctive enterprise and daring, and he was growing bored with the routine of daily life. He dreamed more and more of freedom, adventure, and a life in the wilderness. He had heard about Venezuela and its rivers that carry diamonds in their gravel, and he was at least vaguely aware that this gravel was pumped and sorted more or less mechanically with the aid of dredges. Of diamonds themselves, he knew little more than what he had gathered by glancing at the fine stones displayed in jewelers' windows.

One day he decided he had had enough of life in Miami, and he resolved to make a drastic change. He sold everything he owned, collected his savings, and left for Venezuela. He did not consider that a license was necessary for diamond mining, nor did he worry about various other technicalities. His mechanical ability enabled him to build a large floating platform and to install diesel-driven pumps and a sorting tower for the gravel. His plan was

simple, original, and effective. He attached five giant tanks to the sides of his dredge, containing enough fuel to last more than a year. He installed a generator on board and took on a refrigerator, a few pigs, a thousand bottles of beer, and some camping equipment. All these preparations were completed in the village of La Paragua, on the banks of the river, among miners exhausted from searching the river and the immediate neighborhood. Taube fixed his departure for the next rainy season: in high water he would be able to go up the river and reach places that had never been worked.

Since then, Frank Taube has lived in the heart of the South American forest, with an Indian woman as his companion. He has no contact with the outside world, not even a radio. He has been joined by a German sailor, Werner Jaap, and by a cook from San Francisco,

A small prospecting dredge used by Frank Taube, a former garage owner from Miami, to locate gravel deposits in the Río Paragua. It is easier to maneuver than the big dredge, a virtual floating factory that he built for his lonely operations. *Photo Guy Philippart de Foy, Brussels.*

who also has a dredge, though much smaller than Taube's.

There is nothing unique about the dredging operation. The dredges used in Venezuela are usually equipped with a suction pipe 4 inches (10 cm) in diameter, which enables the crew to process about 72 cubic yards (55 cu m) of gravel an hour and, if the site is ideal, to recover from 35 to 60 carats of diamonds a day. This is how Frank Taube works. However, this type of dredge is less common than the smaller machines called *chupadoras*, equipped with a pontoon with a compressed-air pump, on which gravel extract is sorted by hand in large concave sieves known as *surucas*.

There is something attractive in the simplicity of the life of these men. Certainly, it was the diamond that brought them here, and the search for diamonds occupies most of their time, but they work in freedom, taking orders from no one. When they run out of beer, they drink river water and find themselves none the worse for it. They eat vegetables grown in their own plots and pork from the pigs they raise. Their relations with the Indians are excellent. If it were not for the noise of the diesel engines, they would hardly be noticed at all, since the dredge, floating heavily in the middle of the river, is often obscured by the trees that overhang the banks.

During the dry season, work is necessarily restricted to a short stretch—1 or 2 miles (2–3 km)—of the river, as rocks in the bed of the stream prevent much progress up or down. The gravel is difficult to extract. It is often covered with a brick-colored layer of laterite, which has a tendency to crumble in the hole made by the searching head of the suction pipe. As handling the large dredge is a very delicate operation, finding the precise location of the gravel beds is most important. A diver, a local man working from a small dredge, performs that task. He descends 65 feet (20 m) or more and works at that depth for four or five hours without interruption. The success of the operation depends entirely on his work, for he not only locates the gravel—he must also direct the suction pipe into the holes in the rock where the diamond concentration is greatest. Despite the importance of the diver's job, the equipment he uses is, to say the least, rudimentary. Frank Taube's diver wears a diving helmet and a shirt with the sleeves open at the elbow. This arrangement is ingenious but not without danger. It keeps the diver in an air bubble, the volume of which depends solely on the pressure maintained within the helmet. The water is relatively warm and the work is tiring. When the diver becomes thirsty, he raises an arm, allowing the air to escape from his sleeve and causing the water level to rise

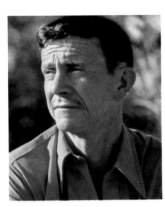

Frank Taube's camp on the Río Paragua. Top: George Leroy. *Photos Guy Philippart de Foy, Brussels.*

Right: The sorting tower on the big dredge assembled on the spot by Frank Taube. *Photo Guy Philippart de Foy, Brussels.*

to his lips. To reduce the water to a more comfortable level, he merely lowers his arm—simple in theory, but, as can easily be imagined, less so in practice.

Apart from the noise and throbbing vibration of the machine itself, life around the dredge is quite peaceful. Inevitably, there are breakdowns, but these are accepted with a fatalism doubtless fostered by the calm magnificence of the natural setting. Not surprisingly, the results achieved by the well-managed dredges are far more impressive than those obtained by solitary miners on land, but there is a corresponding difference in the cost of equipment and operation.

Visiting Frank Taube and his friends, one soon observes that the lure of making a fortune is perhaps less marked than the men's taste for the type of life they have chosen. Once a year, during the rainy season, they head downriver with their empty tanks and their harvest of diamonds. There is no sign of any pressure to achieve success as great as that won by another American, George Leroy, a former cowboy from Oklahoma who led the same life on a dredge before he discovered enough diamonds to spend the rest of his life in a luxurious hotel near Angel Falls. But who knows? Perhaps one day Frank Taube and his crew will have their turn, too.

Brazil

Though Brazil held a virtual monopoly on diamond production for almost 150 years, it is now only a third- or fourth-rate producer. The decline is due not to the gradual exhaustion of resources, but to the nature of the reserves themselves. As described in an earlier chapter, Brazil's diamond deposits are widely dispersed and the diamond concentration is low, so that, with one exception (the Tejucana mine), industrial operations are unprofitable. It was only the labor of thousands of slaves, forced to search every patch of ground by hand, that permitted the Portuguese governors to achieve significant diamond production in the eighteenth and early nineteenth centuries.

The tourist who visits Brazil today is invariably told of the country's wealth of precious stones, and the windows of countless jewelry shops contain rich displays of aquamarine, tourmaline, topaz, and amethyst, as well as emeralds, rubies, sapphires, and of course diamonds. However, it seems certain that at least some of these beautifully displayed diamonds are not of Brazilian origin at all, but are imported, for the evidence suggests that the 400,000 carats produced annually are no longer sufficient to meet local demands.

The retail shops are an obvious sign of the Brazilians' love of gems; what is less obvious is the mythic fascination the diamond still holds for so many people. It is this fascination that motivates the persistent efforts of more than thirty thousand *garimpeiros* in their search for the rarest and most precious of precious stones. So powerful is the diamond's pull that, in certain regions, people spend their Sundays searching for diamonds, just as Europeans and Americans spend their weekends fishing.

Although two and a half centuries have passed since the discovery of the first Brazilian diamonds, the origin of the stones remains a mystery. They can be found in every region except the Nordeste (Rio Grande do Norte, Ceará, Pernambuco, and Alagoas), the extreme south (Rio Grande do Sul, Santa Catarina), and the central Amazonian region. Every new discovery in Brazil has proven to be an alluvial field, and therefore a secondary deposit. In spite of the endeavors of some of the most eminent geologists, no primary source of diamonds has yet been located.

The Origin of Brazilian Diamonds

Brazil occupies an area about nine-tenths the size of the United States and comprises almost half of the South American continent. The geological evolution of the country is therefore inseparably linked with that of South America as a whole (see page 159). Basically, Brazil's deep bedrock consists of extremely ancient formations; their geological history is highly complex, but they have remained comparatively undisturbed since the Pre-Cambrian era, experiencing no later folding. Depressions were formed on this stable substratum, and as they gradually filled, they sank under the weight of the sediment. This process continued more or less uninterrupted from the Pre-Cambrian until the Cretaceous period—essentially, before the separation of Africa from America—and some basins accumulated sediment several thousand yards deep. The similarity of these deposits in the continents on both sides of the Atlantic, and of the fossils found in them, was one of the first and strongest arguments in favor of the theory of continental drift.

After the uplifting of the Andean chain in

The principal diamond regions of Mato Grosso and Minas Gerais, Brazil. Burns Graphics, London.

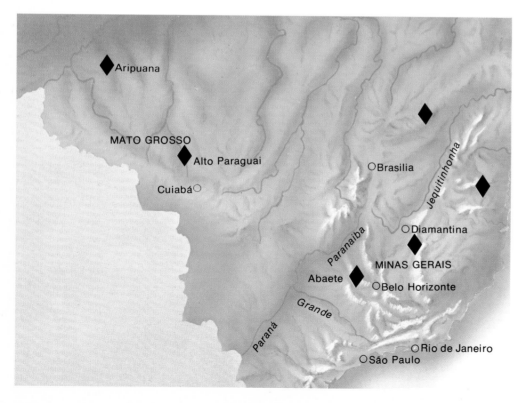

Mining site in the region of Alto Paraguai in Mato Grosso: removing the unproductive layer on the old terraces. The main problem is water supply, and the water used is constantly recycled through a closed system of pipes and conduits. *Photo Jacques Legrand.*

A Pre-Cambrian conglomerate, particularly rich in diamonds, near Sopa, a small village 9 miles (15 km) from Diamantina, in Minas Gerais. *Photo Jacques Legrand.*

the Cretaceous period, the ensuing erosion of the mountains helped continue the filling in of the Amazon basin. The other sedimentary basins, which were no longer being fed, were themselves subjected to erosion. Where are diamonds to be found in this geological system? There is no doubt that some of them have a very long history. The diamonds in the conglomerates of Roraima, Diamantina, and Morro do Chapeu date from the remote Pre-Cambrian era. At Paraná and in the southern part of Mato Grosso they seem to have come from the Carboniferous or Devonian sandstone erosion of the Paraná's sedimentary basin. Elsewhere, in Minas Gerais, Goiás, and the Alto Paraguai region of Mato Grosso, they seem to have a more recent origin—the Cretaceous sandstone layers of the same Paraná basin, which fed the rivers with diamonds. A great deal of field research, especially in the Coromandel region (known for its unusually large diamonds), was under-

taken in the hope of tracing the diamonds to their source. In 1968 a team of French and Brazilian geologists discovered kimberlite in this region, but after extensive sampling it proved to be barren. The hypothesis that currently seems most probable is that most Brazilian diamonds are very old, dating from the Pre-Cambrian era, and that they were successively reworked during later geological periods, with the process continuing right up to the present. Their wide dispersal throughout most of the country, as well as the low concentration of the deposits, can no doubt be attributed to this successive reworking and redistribution. There remains some hope that, at sites so far unknown, diamondiferous kimberlites may be found, directly feeding certain rivers with diamonds.

Geology and Psychology: The Brazilian Diamond Seeker

The nature of the Brazilian deposits, especially their wide dispersal and low concentration, along with the occasional appearance of very large stones, have all helped to form the temperament of the *garimpeiro*, the local diamond searcher whose exact equivalent cannot be found in any other country. The *garimpeiro* is inspired by the hope of making a discovery that will bring him enormous riches, yet he has a fatalistic nature that is seldom seen elsewhere. His Venezuelan counterpart at Guaniamo or Santa Elena knows that the gravel he is working will provide at least some

Top: The cabin of a *garimpeiro* in Minas Gerais. *Photo Guy Philippart de Foy, Brussels.*

Above: An Indian diamond searcher of Mato Grosso, and *garimpeiros* from Minas Gerais. *Photos Jacques Legrand (left) and Guy Philippart de Foy.*

Diamond dealing in the village of Alto Paraguai. The only instruments used are a small lens and a portable precision balance. *Photo Jacques Legrand.*

return, even though it may not bring a sensational profit. As he pumps out the mud and separates the ore, he is almost certain to find some diamonds in the final sorting, after all the gravel has been extracted. He generally shows no particular anxiety or excitement as he works. The only surprises come with an unexpectedly large haul of diamonds, or unusually large individual stones, in the final sorting.

In Brazil, however, everything is governed by chance: the search for diamonds is a gamble. Though the gravel is washed daily, weeks can pass when nothing appears at the bottom of the sieve. On the other hand, a magnificent stone may appear at any time, justifying in a single moment years of exhausting labor. Except for the few thus favored by luck, most *garimpeiros* are poor and live in primitive conditions. The *garimpeiro* lives by faith, faith

that is constantly reinforced by stories of the wealth enjoyed by those before him who have found the crystal he so diligently seeks.

The Deposits of Mato Grosso

Bordered on the west by Bolivia and Paraguay, Mato Grosso extends northward into the Amazonian forest, crossed by many rivers on their way to join the mighty Amazon. Its central and southern part, quite different in character from the north, borders on the western edge of the Paraná basin and is drained chiefly by the Rio Paraguai. *Garimpeiros* are still quite numerous here, but their numbers appear to be diminishing every year.

Prospecting for and mining of diamonds are free in Brazil; to obtain a prospecting license one need only register with the authorities. The license is free of charge, on the condition that the holder work alone, without the use of mechanical devices. In practice, the *garimpeiros* almost always form cooperative groups, using commonly owned pumps as well as some mechanical tools. The authorities turn a blind eye to such practices, since the deposits are generally so poor that the *garimpeiros'* accumulated production has no significant effect on Brazil's economy. Moreover, the *garimpeiros* are actually doing the government a service by conducting a relatively systematic search of the likely areas. There is no risk of important resources being stripped, because it is impossible to conceal a major discovery for long.

Because of the difficulties of the search and the rather remote chances of major success, the *garimpeiros* often form joint ventures that have no precise equivalent in other diamond-producing regions. The purchase of equipment is generally financed by a "silent partner" who supports the searcher, or searchers, and provides staples such as food and tobacco. The owner of the land, if there is one, is also a partner in the enterprise and shares in any profit. The *garimpeiro* contributes his labor and his practical experience. When a find is made, the production is sold by common agreement and the proceeds are shared among the partners on a percentage basis agreed on in advance. The *garimpeiro's* share ranges between 40 and 80 percent.

The work on the actual banks of the rivers is similar to that done in other countries, especially Venezuela. But when it comes to mining the *manchaoes*, the terraces to which the searchers retreat when the rainy season sets in and the riverbanks become unworkable, methods are different. Paradoxically, the main problem is the organization of the water supply, which is indispensable for the work. An artificial hollow has to be made from which water can flow through the entire mining area and then be taken back to its point of departure. The water is first propelled through powerful hoses to break down the sterile soil; the same water is then used to pump the gravel and carry it through conduits and canals to the towerlike washing station, which consists basically of a wooden crate covered by a coarse strainer. The coarser gravel is rejected, while the finer gravel enters the crate, where the diamonds, because of their weight, gradually sink to the bottom. This shaky structure, with its flexible pipes and pumps, does allow some small diamonds to escape, but it is perfectly efficient for extracting the larger ones.

This type of mining, which is done in the outlying regions of Alto Paraguai, requires a small community of six or eight people, the rhythm of whose life is dictated by the tempo of the diesel pumps and the need to keep them functioning properly. Accidents are not infrequent. A rupture in a pipe may suddenly release a reddish-colored torrent, while the pipe sweeps about crazily. One of the motors may stop, or the tower may collapse after the sup-

The sorting tower of a small mine in Mato Grosso. The larger pebbles are discarded while the smaller ones (together with the diamonds), which pass through the mesh of a sieve, are washed into a tank by the flow of water. In the tanks, the force of gravity causes the diamonds to sink gradually to the bottom. But in this type of rough-and-ready operation, many diamonds are lost. *Photo Jacques Legrand.*

Manual work in a small stream of the Diamantina region, Minas Gerais. *Photo Guy Philippart de Foy, Brussels.*

porting posts have been loosened by the flowing water. Each day ends with the inspection of the crate that should contain the booty. Children participate in the work by checking the gravel rejected by the sorting tower. They are trained to handle a sieve when very young, and they spend hours on end eagerly inspecting the washing trough. It is not unusual for a child of ten to be able to estimate the weight of a stone without using any measuring instruments, and to calculate its value with remarkable accuracy. The youngsters' patience is often rewarded, if not by diamonds, which are rare, then by an occasional find of gold nuggets.

In addition to the field of Alto Paraguai, there are a few alluvial deposits in Mato Grosso, like those of Paranatiga, northeast of Cuiabá, and Rondonia in the Amazon region. Almost two thousand *garimpeiros* live in the village of Alto Paraguai alone, about 120 miles (200 km) north of Cuiabá. Here the stones are purchased by dealers who have set up shop in the area and await the miners' visits. The houses of the dealers can be distinguished from the others not only by a certain degree of luxury, but more obviously by the high protecting walls that surround them. The only in-

Diamantina: The church of Chica da Silva, and the market. *Photos Jacques Legrand (top), Guy Philippart de Foy.*

struments used by these dealers in evaluating rough diamonds are a small magnifying glass and a simple balance. The price is agreed on with little difficulty, as both parties are knowledgeable and experienced. The dealers sell the stones to cutters in Rio de Janeiro.

The "Mining Triangle" of Minas Gerais

The section of Minas Gerais sometimes called the "Mining Triangle" extends like a wedge into the neighboring states of Goiás and São Paulo. Here the powerful Paranaíba flows southwest, joining the Rio Grande to form the

Paraná. The Paranaíba is the region's chief river but certainly not its only one. Those of particular interest from the point of view of diamond production are the southern tributaries of the Paranaíba, which are particularly rich in alluvial deposits. At the beginning of the twentieth century, several small companies were still working the river gravel on a semi-industrial scale. They gradually disappeared, leaving the region to the *garimpeiros*.

Some diamond fields in the area, like that of Abaeté, have been known since the second half of the eighteenth century. The reputation of Coromandel, on the other hand, has been made within the past fifty years, and there is no doubt that it has been a major inspiration to the persistent *garimpeiros*. In this region alone, between 1935 and 1965, they discovered sixteen stones weighing more than 100 carats each, and another nine that weighed more than 200 carats. These included the famous President Vargas, a 726.6-carat stone found in 1938 on the Santo Antonio do Bonito. Sold by its first owners for $56,000, its price increased tenfold within a year, when the famous New York jeweler Harry Winston bought it for $600,000. In 1941 he had it cut into twenty-nine stones, most of them emerald-cut; the largest weighed 48.26 carats. On the same river, five stones with an average weight of 320 carats were recovered in less than five years from a single stretch a few miles long. It is not hard, then, to understand the excitement of the diamond seekers who have settled in that part of the country.

To cope with the special problems of this region, the local *garimpeiros* have devised some rather unusual working methods. These methods provide further evidence of the love of gambling that is a marked feature of the *garimpeiros'* character.

The most efficient method consists of diverting the river from its course by means of a canal that cuts off a bend. The technique, also used in Venezuela, is known as *virada*. It requires the construction of dams at two points in the river, work that may involve more than two hundred people, all of whom contribute to the effort without recompense. This cooperativeness dissolves, however, as soon as the construction has been completed and before draining begins. The isolated stretch of river is divided up into as many sections as there are participants, and lots are drawn to determine who gets which section. The pumping of the water then begins, and everyone waits to see if he has been fortunate in the lot he has drawn. The formation of the riverbed is variable, and gravel deposits occur irregularly; in some parts there are none at all. A man whose section has no gravel can go home and forget

Above right: The Jequitinhonha River and the dredge *Chica da Silva* (which belongs to the Tejucana Mining Company, Minas Gerais) in the dry season. The massive operations of the giant dredge have considerably enlarged the riverbed, which was originally not much more than 330 feet (100 m) wide. Above: The bucket scoops of the dredge, which recover the diamond-bearing gravel. *Photos Guy Philippart de Foy (above right), Jacques Legrand.*

about it. But if he has been lucky enough to draw a section with a "pot" of deep accumulated gravel, he may make a fortune.

When, for one reason or another, it is impossible to divert the course of the river, it is necessary to go diving. The price of the costly diving suit and equipment is shared among a group of five or six. Each man takes his turn diving, returns to the surface with his bag of gravel, and then helps operate the pump while one of the others dons the diving suit. The whole operation is organized cooperatively, with the important exception of washing the gravel. Each man washes his own gravel, and any profits that may accrue are his alone.

Diamantina

Scientists agree that the deposits of the Diamantina area are geologically the oldest in Brazil; they date from the Pre-Cambrian era. They were also the first to be discovered—in the early eighteenth century—and are situated farthest east, which made them more accessible to the Portuguese arriving in the country. They have been worked since 1729, and the fame of Diamantina long ago spread beyond the borders of Brazil. Its past production was enough to stimulate wild fantasies of wealth, and as recently as 1950 the area produced about 100,000 carats annually, including a good number of perfectly transparent stones. Although the quantity of diamonds handled there today is negligible, the village of Diamantina has not lost its picturesque character.

Located about 120 miles (200 km) north of Belo Horizonte, Diamantina is spread out lazily on the slopes of verdant hills, at an altitude of some 3,960 feet (1,200 m) above sea level, in the northern part of the Serra do Espinhaço. Its steep, narrow streets still have their original paving stones. Each quarter has its own church, one of which is said to have been built for the notorious Chica da Silva.

But those who hope to find at Diamantina an echo of the glorious days of the diamond's past will be disappointed. Only the name of the town and the presence of a diamond museum suggest that the people here have a more than usual interest in the most precious of all gems. Yet diamond dealers do live here, and there are still some traditional marketplace transactions, in which the object of the trade is concealed within a small, crumpled piece of paper. Some dealers are licensed and receive their clients—buyers as well as sellers—at home. Others can be found parked in the main square, which has become their meeting place; they often conduct their business without leaving their cars. There are also two or three small cutting shops discreetly hidden in houses that are outwardly identical with the other buildings. The activity of the *garimpeiros* is hinted at by the many shops that sell gravel sieves along with groceries. The sieves are stacked in piles, much as shrimp nets are stacked outside shops in European seaside resort towns.

The actual mining now done in the district is on a very modest scale. According to the season, the *garimpeiros* work the *cascalho* (river gravel) or the *gorgulho* (alluvial gravel of the old terraces and the plains) within about 18 miles (30 km) of Diamantina. The techniques they use are similar to those described in the preceding sections, but one phenomenon peculiar to the region is the presence of a rich conglomerate known as Sopa, named after a small village 9 miles (15 km) west of Diamantina. Sopa is a formation of very old, rounded pebbles held together by a claylike cement. It is broken up with a pick and falls apart easily, since the old pebbles have become as crumbly as the clay that binds them.

The Tejucana Mine

At the northern end of Diamantina, a poor road leads out of the town and plunges into the broad, windy valley of the Jequitinhonha River. Forty-eight miles (80 km) downstream from this point are the dredges of the only industrial mining company operating in Brazil. Its workshops and administrative buildings are in the village of Lavrinha, 12 miles (20 km) from the river, in a setting of wooded hills.

Before an industrial operation can be undertaken, careful sampling and measuring of the alluvial gravel—always a delicate operation in

The conveyor belt of the dredge *Chica da Silva,* which carries away the coarser gravel. *Photo Guy Philippart de Foy, Brussels.*

Final grading at the offices of the Tejucana Mining Company in the village of Lavrinha. *Photo Jacques Legrand.*

the middle of a river—is necessary in order to determine the concentration of diamonds. If the content is too low, the project would obviously be a wasteful investment. Some twenty years ago a bold gamble was taken by a Brazilian engineer, Alexander Misk, who decided, despite the extremely low content of the gravel (.01 percent), to install a dredge on the Jequitinhonha. To compensate as much as possible for the poverty of the gravel, it was necessary to use a bucket dredge with sufficient capacity to excavate the ore directly in large masses instead of using pumps. Consequently, a gigantic machine weighing 2,700 tons was ordered. Made in California, it was transported to the heart of the Brazilian forest in pieces and assembled on the site. Assembly took more than a year, and it did not begin operation until 1967. Thanks to ingenious adaptations that enable it to be floated on the river, the dredge can process 650 cubic yards (500 cu m) of gravel per hour and requires a crew of only four. Named the *Chica da Silva,* this machine has made Alexander Misk's gamble pay off.

The task of removing the first, barren layers is performed by a suction dredge, which pumps the sand from the river before vacating the site for its more powerful colleague. A chain of seventy buckets, each with a capacity of 78 gallons (300 l), collects the alluvial gravel and tips it into a huge rotary drum, which washes and sifts it, rejecting stones more than 1 inch (25 mm) in diameter. The remaining stones pass through a series of jigs, from which 8 tons of concentrate are produced daily. The concentrate is shipped to Lavrinha for final processing, and there, after a series of further refinements, the final concentrate is sorted by hand. Annual diamond production amounts to about 80,000 carats. There is also a significant by-product in the form of gold—more than 380 pounds (140 kg) are produced per year. The great dredge, a prisoner of the part of the river in which it is located, advances along the path it digs in front of it and fills in the path behind it by ejecting oversize material. Naturally, production could be greatly increased if the locations of high diamond concentration were determined in advance, but that is not easily done. A "pot" is rarely detected, but one that was found in 1974 resulted in the extraction of 45,000 carats in a few days.

The stones produced by the Tejucana mine are generally very small—they average twelve stones to the carat—but 80 percent are of gem quality. Owned by the Belgian Sibeka group, the Tejucana mine now has three main dredges besides the suction dredge. The stones are marketed independently of the Diamond Corporation, and sales take place regularly in the company's main office at Belo Horizonte.

The gravel removed from the riverbed by the scoops of the dredge is passed through a rotating drum, or trommel, where it is washed with powerful water jets and sieved. All stones more than 1 inch (25 mm) in diameter are ejected; the remainder is graded and concentrated. *Photo Guy Philippart de Foy, Brussels.*

Other Producers

India

No one needs to be reminded of what the diamonds of India represent. Sparkling with unquenchable fire, their mystery enhanced by the myths and legends that still surround them, the stones that have graced the regalia of Oriental and European courts have been known for centuries. Museums that are fortunate enough to possess one of the great Indian diamonds value them above all other natural treasures and reserve for them the same honors—and security precautions—that are given to the rarest masterpieces of the art world.

Some of the most famous diamonds of history, like the Koh-i-Noor, the Orlov, and the Regent, came from the mines of Partial and Kollur in the ancient kingdom of Golconda. The kingdom was destroyed by its legendary wealth, and the capital was sacked in 1687, after the Mughal emperor Aurangzeb had emptied the treasury of diamonds. But the Mughal rulers were themselves eventually overthrown, and in 1739 Nadir Shah pillaged Delhi. The gems he took were the foundation for the extraordinary collection of diamonds in the Persian treasury and provided the sumptuous gifts Nadir Shah presented to monarchs he wished to honor. In 1829, less than a century later, one of the most curious stones of the Persian treasury, a diamond called the Shah, was sent to the Russian court as compensation and a token of regret after the Russian ambassador, Aleksandr Griboiedov, was assassinated in Teheran. This stone, weighing 88.7 carats, is interesting for several reasons, not the least being its appearance: it is bar-shaped and only partly polished. It is also one of those rare stones that bear engraved inscriptions, made possible by its unusual shape. There is good reason to believe that it came from the Golconda mines. From the first inscription, "Bourhan-Nizam-Shah-II-1000," it can be dated to the year 1000 in the Muslim calendar (1591 in the Gregorian calendar); the name is that of the governor of Ahmadnagar province. The second inscription, which reads "Son of Jahangir Shah, Jahan Shah, 1051," reveals that the stone belonged to Shah Jahan, third son of Jahangir, who ruled from 1628 to 1658. When Tavernier visited the court of the Great Mughal in 1665, he described one stone in sufficient detail for it to be identified as the Shah diamond. The third inscription refers to "Kadjar Fath Ali Shah," who was the shah of Persia in 1824, and from this we can conclude that the diamond was almost certainly one of the jewels seized by Nadir Shah in 1739.

Of all the stories associated with Indian diamonds, that of the Shah is one of the most straightforward. It offers evidence of the traditional fondness Oriental princes had for precious stones, and of the continuation of the tradition over a long period: in the nineteenth century the maharajahs adopted the tradition established by the Mughal emperors, and to this day the temples of India contain many splendid diamonds, the finest of which derive from the ancient Golconda mines. There were, of course, many other mines that were less famous. Active mining continued for some time near Wairagargh, in central India, then was carried on in the southeast, near Sambalpur, and finally in the Panna district, where India's largest working mine is to be found today.

Throughout the first half of the twentieth century Indian diamond production continued

The historic Shah diamond, weighing 88.7 carats. It is unusual not only because of its shape, but also because it is one of the few diamonds with an engraved inscription. Soviet Diamond Collection, Moscow. *Fotokhronika Tass, Moscow.*

In the past, diamonds were extracted from very old conglomerates formed of quartzite, jasper, and soft, clayey schist, as well as from the alluvial deposits that derived from the erosion of the conglomerates. In the Panna district, the Rewa site appears to be one of the most thoroughly worked: remains of ancient mines have been found there spread out over distances of more than 50 miles (80 km). Geological studies of this area were the source of many arguments, and it was not until 1930 that the first diamondiferous kimberlite was discovered, just 14 miles (24 km) from Panna. The pipe, which is more than 1.1 billion years old, is now mined by Majhgawan Diamond Mines. The mine, surrounded by security barriers manned by fully armed troops, is 40 feet (12 m) deep and about 1,000 feet (300 m) in diameter. It has already produced more than a million tons of kimberlitic ore. Some 140,000 tons were processed in 1976–77, and 29,586 diamonds, with a total weight of 18,278 carats, were extracted. The proportion of gemstones is roughly 40 percent, which means that about 20 tons of ore have to be processed to obtain 1 carat of gemstones. The operation would hardly be profitable were it not for the occasional discovery of outstanding individual stones. One example, found in 1978, weighed 18.5 carats and, according to the management of the company, was worth 500,000 rupees. The diamonds shown to visitors to the mine are mainly hexoctahedrons with rounded sides, varying in weight from .5 to 3 carats. Most of the stones are yellow, reddish-brown, dark brown, yellowish-green, or grayish; there are, of course, also some very handsome colorless stones. Some stones from the mine appear to have a milky green color, but they have perfectly colorless, limpid, interiors and may be fashioned into gems of the finest water.

Annual production of the mine during the 1970's was as follows:

> 1970–71: 15,815 carats
> 1971–72: 15,642 carats
> 1972–73: 16,247 carats
> 1973–74: 17,705 carats
> 1974–75: 18,114 carats
> 1975–76: 16,542 carats
> 1976–77: 18,278 carats

When the mine reached a depth at which unweathered kimberlite was encountered, two pits were dug with a number of lateral galleries leading from them in order to determine the shape and dimensions of the pipe.

Ore is transported to the processing plant, not far from the mining site. The plant handles approximately 400 tons of ore per day, recovering about 100 diamonds. The methods of recovery are similar to those used in South Af-

Fath Ali Shah, emperor of Persia. About 1805. His name was engraved on the famous Shah diamond. Musée du Louvre, Paris. *Photo Réunion des Musées Nationaux, Paris.*

uninterrupted, though on a small scale. The known deposits were not quite worked out, and, more important, the occasional discovery of a particularly fine stone encouraged thousands of peasants to try their luck at searching for diamonds, in the hope of escaping from their extreme poverty.

A *tangguk*, an oval bamboo basket of the type used in Borneo for carrying ore. *Photo Guy Philippart de Foy, Brussels.*

At Umpung, in Borneo, workers wash gravel in a shallow, cone-shaped dish called a *linggangan. Photo Henri-Jean Schubnel, Paris.*

rica. The kimberlite is unloaded from trucks, and the larger blocks are broken up by pneumatic drills before being passed on to a horizontal, wide-mesh screen. Below the screen, the jaws of a crusher further reduce the ore. It is then transported on a conveyor belt to open-sided buildings, where it undergoes the various processes designed to separate the heavy minerals with which diamonds are concentrated. One of the classic operations is the use of vibrating grease tables. The diamonds adhere to the greasy coating of the tables, and the other heavy minerals in the concentrate, which do not adhere, are discarded.

There is a small cutting center at Panna, where both imported and locally produced stones are fashioned. However, it is a small operation compared with the cutting centers of Bombay and Surat (see page 242).

Borneo

It has often been said that India was the only source of diamonds before the discoveries in Brazil in the early eighteenth century, but that is not strictly true. Diamond mines have existed on the island of Borneo, the third largest island in the world, from a very early date, although production has always been small. It is impossible to say when the mines were first opened, nor do we know much about early working methods. The evidence suggests that the technique used for washing the ore was borrowed from the Chinese, who were present in Borneo at least as early as the Sung period (960–1279), and possibly at the end of the T'ang dynasty in the early tenth century. The numerous fragments of Sung porcelain found on the site indicate that, at least as early as the twelfth or thirteenth century, there was a regular exchange between Chinese trading stations and the people of Borneo, who supplied the Chinese with highly prized products of the island's forest. It was not until the sixteenth century that the Europeans arrived on the coasts of Borneo, and in the following century they made Borneo the object of their commercial rivalries. The Portuguese were the first to arrive; they were ousted by the Dutch and the English, who eventually divided the island between themselves. Tavernier mentions that in the seventeenth century Borneo paid an annual tribute to the emperor of China, part of it in diamonds. In addition, it is certain that close contact existed with India as early as the third century, and people from southern India invaded the island in the fifth century. It was probably from the Indians that the people of Borneo learned how to cut diamonds.

Nowadays the northern part of the island, which is part of Malaysia, is open to tourism on a large scale, but the central and southern part, known as Kalimantan and under Indonesian control, is relatively unknown to the outside world. It is in Kalimantan that diamonds are found. Far removed from the international airports that serve Java and Bali, it is a comparatively remote country that still offers challenge and adventure to explorers.

There are two main diamond areas. The first is in the western part of the island, in the area of the Landak River, close to the equator. The second and more significant area is in the southeast; it consists of alluvial fields scattered around the Bobaris Mountains, about 24 miles (40 km) east of Banjermasin, the capital of Kalimantan. These fields are not far from the small town of Martapura, where there are diamond-cutting workshops. The primary source, the Pamali kimberlite pipe, was discovered after the First World War in the mountains some 24 miles (40 km) east of Martapura. The diamonds thus derive from the weathering of kimberlitic sources in the mountains, from which they were dispersed by erosion and the action of the rivers. The diamondiferous alluvial deposits being mined today are found in the heart of the rice fields at Umpung, not far from

Alat Membarsinkan.

During the summer of 1977 about three hundred people could be found working there, even on holidays, half a mile (1 km) from a path that is often underwater. The mining pits are not very deep, from 13 to 26 feet (4–8 m), and they are securely shored up against collapse. A major problem here, as in other parts of Southeast Asia, is pumping out the water that drains into the pits from the surrounding rice fields. Operations here are somewhat more sophisticated than those in similar alluvial mines for precious stones in countries such as Sri Lanka and Thailand. There are no cranes or hoists to assist in the removal of the diamondiferous ore, but there are many water pumps, and the muddy gravel is washed in a series of separate operations.

The tools and equipment used are characteristic of the country and are worth a brief description. Once the ore has been roughly washed in a nearby stream, it is carried in a *tangguk*, a large, oval bamboo dish, to the *takungan*, a rectangular wooden tank measuring about 80 by 16 by 16 inches (200 × 40 × 40 cm) and hewn from a single tree trunk. It has handles at either end so that it can be moved easily from one place to another. In this tank, the diamondiferous material is soaked in water and broken down by two men who vigorously trample it. The muddy, semiliquid material that results from this process is then shoveled out and passed through an oval bamboo screen with a .3-inch (8-mm) mesh inside a second

takungan alongside the first. The coarse gravel is discarded after careful checking, for a diamond of more than .3 inches, though rare, does occasionally turn up. The finer gravel, which has passed through the screen, is washed in a trough called a *linggangan*. The *linggangan* is conical in shape and similar to the standard Chinese washing trough, except for one addition: inside it, near the rim, there is a small cavity covered by an aluminum plate pierced with a hole. In this cavity the daily yield, averaging two crystals per miner, is placed.

At noon the sun is very hot, and the workers labor beneath canopies or large parasols mounted on bamboo poles and stuck into the riverbed. Some old myths about the diamond linger on here. If a man finds a small stone, for example, he may place it on the upper rim of the washing trough and hammer it violently with a rock. If it shatters, that proves to him that the stone is not a diamond. As many others have done for centuries, he is confusing hardness with unbreakability and believes that nothing can break a diamond except another diamond.

At Martapura, not far away, there is a diamond-cutting shop that contains 96 cutting lathes. There is another shop across the street that once had 144 cutting lathes, but it is now abandoned. As in India, the diamond cutters sit cross-legged on simple wooden benches covered with mats or cushions. Although they use mechanical dops (a dop is a tool that holds gemstones while they are being cut or pol-

A work site at Umpung on the island of Borneo. In the center is a *takungan*, a wooden tank cut from a tree trunk, in which the diamond-bearing soil is broken up; on the left, washing away the mud. *Photo Henri-Jean Schubnel, Paris.*

ished), the cutting is not of the highest precision. The stones worked consist chiefly of irregular cubes, octahedrons with grooved faces (most of them somewhat misshapen, though some are well formed), rounded dodecahedrons, and some little crystals that resemble grains of rice. Current production is probably between 20,000 and 30,000 carats annually. In the eighteenth century it was undoubtedly greater. Like India's production, it declined toward the end of the nineteenth century because of the sudden and tremendous competition from South Africa. As in some other areas of comparatively low production, the business has been kept going largely because of the occasional discovery of individual stones of extremely high quality. In the late 1960's, for example, a stone was found that weighed 166.8 carats before cutting. It was called the *Trisakti,* or "Three Principles," named for the watchwords of the new Indonesian republic— nationalism, religion, and unity. The government sent the stone to the well-known firm of Asscher in Amsterdam for cutting, and the end result was an emerald-cut gem of perfect pu-

rity weighing 50.53 carats. It was sold in Europe to a buyer whose identity has never been revealed.

The Jakarta Museum contains many splendid treasures that bear witness to the luxurious past of the sultans of Borneo. Among thousands of jewels there are many diamonds of more than 10 carats cut in the old-fashioned manner. The throne of the Banjermasin sultans, which is completely studded with diamonds, outshines even the shimmering gold of the museum's marvelous collection of exquisitely worked Malay ceremonial daggers.

The Soviet Union

During the Second World War, the Russians found themselves seriously handicapped by their lack of an independent supply of industrial diamonds. When peace was restored in 1945, they began prospecting various regions of their vast country in the hope of discovering diamond fields. A few deposits were already being worked in the Ural Mountains at Krestovoz-Dvichensk, northeast of Perm, where the first Russian diamonds had been accidentally discovered by gold diggers in 1829–30. But these deposits produced only a small number of stones. The prodigious development of the Soviet steel industry required several million carats of industrial diamonds per year, and a search was undertaken on an unprecedented scale, involving huge financial investments.

In the late 1950's, new alluvial deposits were discovered 180 miles (300 km) north of Perm along the River Vichera. Whatever the ultimate importance of these deposits, however, they cannot be compared either in number or richness with those discovered at almost the same time in Siberia. Gold diggers had also found a few stones there, in the upper

Mining diamondiferous ore in the frozen earth of Yakutsk in the Soviet Union. *Photo APN, Paris.*

A workers' camp at the *Aikhal* ("Glory") mine in Yakutsk, soon after the mine's discovery in 1960. This source has proved even richer than the *Mir* pipe. *Photo APN, Paris.*

A 25.52-carat gem from the Yakutsk diamond fields, now in the Diamond Collection of the Soviet Union, Moscow. *Fotokhronika Tass (photo Gende-Rote), Moscow.*

basin of the Yenisey, in 1898, but the site of these discoveries was more than 600 miles (1,000 km) away from the actual deposits. Geologists had reason to believe that the entire region, especially the rocky central Siberian platform between the Yenisey and the Lena, would reveal previously unsuspected wealth. It took eight years of prospecting before the first serious indications appeared in the Viliouj basin in 1953. Hundreds, if not thousands, of geologists and prospectors must have crisscrossed a territory four times the size of Texas under extremely difficult conditions in one of the harshest climates in the world—the ground remains frozen throughout the year up to 1,000 feet (300 m) deep, and only 7–10 feet (2–3 m) of this thaws during the hot, but short, summer. The effort eventually proved worthwhile. Within twenty years, the Soviet Union became the world's second largest producer of industrial diamonds after Zaïre and the second largest producer of gem diamonds after South Africa. The geologists' original hypothesis was verified: the central Siberian platform, anchored to the ancient Pre-Cambrian cores, was indeed a source of exceptional wealth.

By the late 1970's, 250 to 300 kimberlite pipes had been discovered. Radiometric dating, using potassium-argon, shows that their eruption was spread throughout a vast stretch of geological time, ranging from the Cambrian-Ordovician through the Devonian and Carboniferous up to the Upper Jurassic period. Although their structure is the same, it would seem that the kimberlitic eruptions intruding

in the level rocky layer of the Siberian platform are much older than the kimberlitic intrusions in most other regions of the world.

Working the deposits posed serious problems. For six to seven months of the year the temperature in Siberia ranges between $-22°$ and $-76°$ F ($-30°$ to $-60°$ C), and communications are very difficult. The Trans-Siberian railway comes no closer than 600 miles (1,000 km) from the deposits in northern Yakutsk.

One of the first kimberlite zones to be discovered was that of Daaldinsk. Found in 1954, it is situated 960 miles (1,600 km) north of Irkutsk and 36 miles (60 km) west of Shologontsi. The pipes here are between 100 and 2,000 feet (30–600 m) in diameter. One of the largest, known as *Udatchnaya*, "The Lucky One," is also the richest in diamonds; it was discovered in 1955. Situated farther south, and therefore more accessible, is the most interesting diamond field from an economic point of view, the little Batuobiya field in the upper basin of the Marka, a tributary of the Viliouj. The great pipe known as *Mir*, or "Peace," was discovered here. Its unusually rich eluvium contains as much as 2 carats of diamonds per cubic meter. Very wide in area (1,617 × 1,056 feet, or 490 × 320 m), the pipe has been drilled to a depth of 3,300 feet (1,000 m). It has produced exceptionally handsome octahedral crystals of 40–100 carats that are among the most limpid and best formed of all the diamonds displayed in the diamond collection of the Soviet Union in the Kremlin. Besides its wealth of several million carats in large gem diamonds, this splendid collection also contains the ancient jewels once worn by the czars, including the famous Orlov and Shah diamonds.

The Soviet Union publishes no production figures, but, judging by the quantity of large Siberian stones exhibited in the Kremlin, there is little reason to doubt the western experts who estimate that the Soviet Union has already produced at least 100 million carats. The largest stone to be discovered recently is the Star of Yakutsk, which weighs 232.1 carats and is brownish in color. It was found in 1973 in the Mirnyi field, at the very place where, only three months earlier, another diamond of nearly the same weight had been found and named, somewhat unbecomingly, the Fiftieth Anniversary of Aeroflot.

Although production figures remain secret, it is estimated that the quantity of gem diamonds produced in 1965, for example, was close to a million carats. For 1973–75 it was estimated at 1.9 million carats of gems and 7.7 million carats of industrial diamonds. Among the few hard facts that were revealed for those years, the proportion of gem to industrial diamonds was given as 18.5 percent.

According to an agreement made in 1960 between the Soviet Union and De Beers, the latter committed itself to buying the entire production of rough diamonds that the Soviet Union exported to western markets. This agreement was modified in 1972, when, after long negotiations, De Beers surrendered its purchasing monopoly of rough gemstones, and Russalmaz, a Soviet-Belgian company, was created to sell both gem and industrial diamonds from the Soviet Union on the Antwerp market. Given the large Soviet reserves of diamonds, as well as of gold and platinum, it seems probable that the country may, in the coming years, develop mass production of jewelry for export.

Other Countries

Besides Zaïre, Sierra Leone, and the large diamond producers of southern Africa, there are a few other African states that are known for their production of diamonds. In 1914 alluvial deposits were discovered in Ubangi-Shari (now the Central African Republic). On the basis of this discovery, explorations have been continued, with relatively good results, up to the present. There are two main productive regions—one in the west, in the area of Berberati (which encompasses the entire length of the Lobaye River), and the other in the northeast, in the Kotto basin. Diamonds are the country's principal resource, and they are hand mined by some fifty thousand miners. The total output so far has been about 4 million carats. In 1919 the Gold Coast (now Ghana) entered the diamond market. Alluvial deposits

dating from the Pre-Cambrian period were discovered in the Birim valley, in the Akwatia region midway between Accra and Kumasi. These are still being mined. Even though annual production in this region is about 3 million carats, diamonds play a relatively small part in the nation's economy, for about 85 percent of the stones are of industrial quality. Comparable to Ghana's diamonds are the small stones found in the diamond fields of the Ivory Coast. The first alluvial deposits, discovered at Tortiya around 1930, were of Pre-Cambrian origin. In the region of Séguéla, however, deposits deriving from a more recent mother rock were found, and these generated considerable interest. Total production there was about 3 million carats, and about 60 percent of the stones were industrial. Between 1957 and 1962 numerous clandestine miners entered the region, and it became necessary to form a miners' union, the Saremci. A trait shared by all three countries is that no one has yet found the primary deposits from which the diamond fields derive.

The situation in Guinea is similar to that in Sierra Leone. Diamonds were first discovered in Guinea in 1932, in the Macenta region. They originated directly from kimberlite dikes and probably dated from the Cretaceous period. Most of Guinea's diamonds weigh about 1 carat each, but there are a certain number of large, transparent octahedrons that may weigh 30 carats or more. In 1956 Guinea was invaded by some thirty thousand illegal miners who had been expelled from Sierra Leone. A large part of the country's production, therefore, has been accomplished by clandestine means. It is estimated that some 4 million carats have been extracted to date, about 35 percent of which are of gem quality.

Outside Africa, diamonds have been found in Australia, where, between 1884 and 1957, more than 200,000 carats were mined in the diamond fields of New South Wales. Active prospecting is done by several different organizations. In 1976 deposits were found in the west, outside Nullagine, in the Kimberley district. In the United States, the kimberlitic pipe of Murfreesboro, Arkansas, is well known to mineralogists. The stones mined here, added to those found in the glacial deposits of Lake Michigan, have given the United States a total production of several thousand carats. There is no recent information concerning diamond production in China. Deposits are located near Shantung, where brown stones in excess of 100 carats were found near the beginning of the twentieth century, as well as in Hunan. Experts believe that when the day comes when a systematic search can be made in China, there will be many surprises for us.

The Saremci works in the Tortiya mines, Ivory Coast. *Photo Michel Desjardins-Top Réalités, Paris.*

World Production

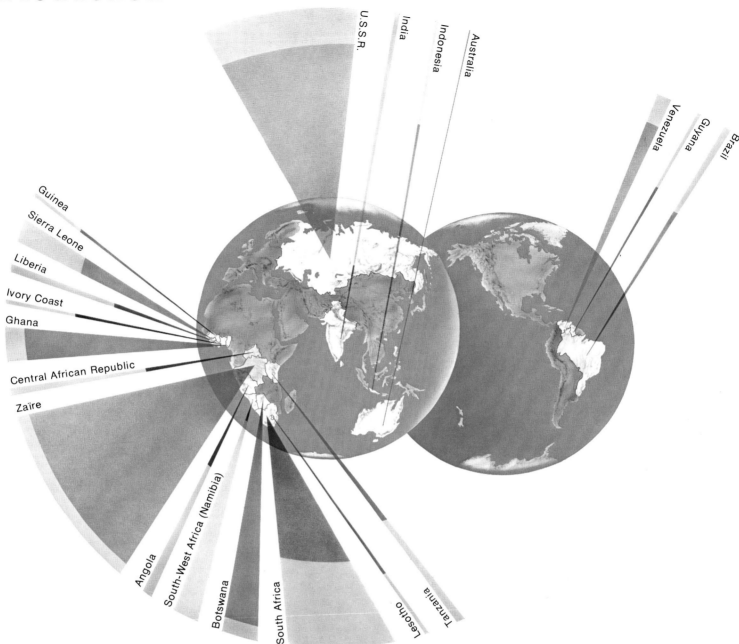

Guinea

Sierra Leone

Liberia

Ivory Coast

Ghana

Central African Republic

Zaïre

Angola

South-West Africa (Namibia)

Botswana

South Africa

Lesotho

Tanzania

U.S.S.R.

India

Indonesia

Australia

Venezuela

Guyana

Brazil

World diamond production, showing the proportion of gem-quality diamonds (lighter shade) and industrial diamonds (darker shade) for each producing country. *Burns Graphics, London.*

Anyone attempting to compile a precise table of the world's annual production of diamonds faces two major difficulties. First, some countries decline to publish their production figures. Second, it is impossible, for obvious reasons, to determine the exact quantity of diamonds mined illicitly. It is therefore necessary to resort to estimates for these figures. One of the most reliable sources of information is the United States Bureau of Mines. According to that institution, world production in 1977 was approximately 39,678,000 carats, or nearly 18,000 pounds (8,000 kg). This can be broken down into stones of gem quality (10,481,000 carats, or 26.3 percent) and stones of industrial quality (29,197,000 carats, or 73.7 percent). These figures represent an increase of about 1 million carats over the figures for 1976 but are on a level with the figures for 1975. Inter-

estingly, the quantity of diamonds mined in the past two thousand years is estimated at 260 tons (1.3 billion carats), and of this total more than 140 tons have been mined during the past eighteen years. This remarkable rise is due partly to the exploitation of new deposits in various countries, most notably the Soviet Union, and partly to the modernization of production processes. Finally, it should be reemphasized that industrial stones, while they account for 73.7 percent of world production, constitute a far smaller proportion in terms of value than stones of gem quality. Gem diamonds, though they comprise only 26.3 percent of the total by weight, command market prices at least twenty times higher than industrial stones. It is for this reason that the proportion of gem-quality stones is so important in calculating the profitability of a mine.

The Central Selling Organization

Between the two world wars, Sir Ernest Oppenheimer developed a central marketing organization to ensure the stability of world trade in rough diamonds. The events that led up to this development have been described in an earlier chapter and need not be repeated here. Oppenheimer's system proved well suited to its purpose, and in the past half-century it has saved the diamond market from a good number of threatening situations. It still operates today to the general satisfaction of all involved, although the domination of the world diamond market by a single organization inevitably attracts outside criticism from time to time.

The diamond marketing system is illustrated in diagram form below.

The power of the Central Selling Organization, or the CSO, a group of companies based in London, lies in its control of 80–85 percent of world production of rough diamonds. Whether or not they have been sorted previously, and regardless of their place of origin, diamonds of gem quality are classified by the Diamond Purchasing and Trading Company in one of more than two hundred categories according to weight, color, clarity, and shape. Stones that come from the Diamond Corporation's various buying offices are revalued in-

dividually, which incidentally provides a check on the abilities of the Diamond Corporation's buyers.

Once it enters the system, each diamond acquires many technical specifications and loses something of its original identity, since its country of origin and the circumstances of its discovery are deliberately suppressed. (However, the expertise of an experienced buyer would probably enable him to identify the origin of a large proportion of the diamonds in any lot.) Industrial diamonds are dealt with separately. These stones are classified and marketed through De Beers' Industrial Diamonds Division.

In offering to purchase the total production of "foreign" producers as well as that of the big South African groups, the CSO provides a guarantee that all the producers' diamonds will be sold. At the same time, it relieves the producers of the need to create large and costly marketing divisions. It is the responsibility of the CSO to dispose of all these diamonds. While very fine stones can obviously be sold quite easily, it is more difficult to find buyers for those with more limited potential. Such stones may be stockpiled, perhaps eventually to be sold for comparatively low prices. Problems of this kind can be solved only by a monopolistic system. It was necessary to create an organization that would benefit the trade worldwide and ensure the prosperity of all producers. The CSO plays an essential role in guaranteeing the producers a regular outlet at stable prices. By holding stocks of diamonds, it is able to adjust supply according to the fluctuations of world demand. The financial strength of the companies that constitute the CSO enables it to withstand crises that no other system could survive.

The solution provided by the CSO to the problem of fluctuating supply and demand is unique in the commercial world and worthy of closer examination. During the past fifty years, with the aid of certain brokers, the CSO has chosen some three hundred diamond companies around the world with proven reputations and sound financial status, capable of dealing with the exigencies of a new kind of market. Guided by these brokers, the appointed "members," who are usually important dealers

Chart illustrating the marketing of diamonds through CSO channels. Gemstones are indicated in blue, industrial diamonds in red. *Burns Graphics, London.*

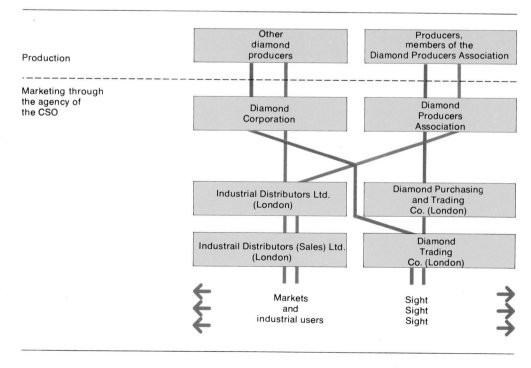

Production

Marketing through the agency of the CSO

| Other diamond producers | Producers, members of the Diamond Producers Association |

| Diamond Corporation | Diamond Producers Association |

| Industrial Distributors Ltd. (London) | Diamond Purchasing and Trading Co. (London) |

| Industrail Distributors (Sales) Ltd. (London) | Diamond Trading Co. (London) |

Markets and industrial users

Sight
Sight
Sight

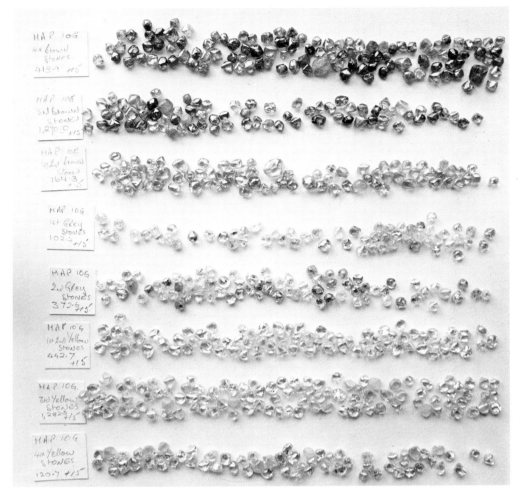

Diamonds sorted and classified in the offices of the Diamond Purchasing and Trading Company, London. *De Beers Archives.*

Top right: A sorting box with screens. Above: "Sights" on arrival at the Antwerp Bourse. *Photos Michel Plassart, Paris.*

or cutters, become in effect the wholesalers of the trade. Ten times a year they submit their requirements for rough diamonds to their respective brokers, who pass the information on to the CSO. Subsequently they are invited to London, where the CSO provides them with their allocation at a "sight." They will not receive exactly what they have asked for, and sometimes they will be allocated quite unsuitable stones, but the parcel, or sight (the word is applied to both the meeting at which the diamonds are offered and to an individual parcel, or box), cannot be divided, and there can be no argument about the price. A box must be accepted as it is. It is possible to refuse—but only once. The prices of stones of more than 14.7 carats are not included; they are negotiated separately.

The value of a single parcel may be considerable. Some may be less than $200,000, but others may reach $3 million. The average price is probably about $1 million. After it has been inspected and accepted, the box must be paid for within a fixed time. Once the check has been received in London, the box is dispatched to the purchaser with all appropriate security measures.

Clients of the CSO have offices in the main exchanges throughout the world, notably in Antwerp, Tel Aviv, Bombay, London, Amsterdam, New York, and Idar-Oberstein. South Af-

rican clients only are supplied in Johannesburg, and "melee" (very small diamonds), the chief resource of the Israeli market, is distributed in Lucerne. Most of the CSO's approved dealers are manufacturers, and most have specialties according to the capacity and costs of their respective establishments. They retain only those diamonds that are suitable for their own operations and resell the remainder to dealers or cutting factories interested in other types of diamonds.

Through this system the CSO is effectively able to control virtually the entire world market by careful monitoring of fewer than three hundred companies. What might be regarded as the world's most exclusive club is governed by strict regulations, and—noblesse oblige— any infringement means instant, on-the-spot expulsion. There is a long waiting list of firms eager to join—further evidence of the success of the system.

The 15–20 percent of world production that is not controlled by the CSO is sold directly by the other producing countries, such as Ghana, Brazil, or Venezuela, which naturally benefit from the stable prices ensured by the official system. Those "free" diamonds that are not sold directly to manufacturers or cutters eventually turn up at the various diamond exchanges, where they become indistinguishable from those that originated with the CSO.

III

From Rough Stone to Polished Gem

Mineralogy and Crystallography

First mentioned in the Vedic texts as early as the end of the second millennium B.C., the diamond has been the subject of a great many scientific studies. The first of its characteristics to be recognized was its hardness, though, especially for westerners, another quality—its rarity—was equally responsible for the many rash speculations that grew up around the diamond over the centuries. Strangely, the first experimental research into the nature of the diamond was aimed at finding a way in which it could be destroyed, as if its ages-old reputation for "invincibility" nourished the desire to disprove a quality so hard to believe.

Pure Carbon
It is said that the first man to succeed in combusting a diamond by subjecting it to very high temperatures was the Irish-born scientist Robert Boyle (1627–91), best known for his formulation of "Boyle's Law" concerning the behavior of gases. Two Italians, Tragioni, of the Accademia del Cimento, and Averani, tutor to the son of Grand Duke Cosimo III of Tuscany, successfully destroyed diamonds in Florence in 1694 and 1695 by focusing the sun's

rays on them through a burning glass. Much later, around the middle of the eighteenth century, the German emperor Francis I of the Holy Roman Empire witnessed an experiment demonstrating that diamonds were combustible in a furnace. Thereafter, experiments became more numerous. In 1766 Jean d'Arcet reported that a diamond heated in a crucible gave off "a sort of black smoke with nearly the same weight as the diamond itself." Five years later, Pierre Joseph Macquer observed that a diamond being burned was enveloped in a bright flame, like phosphorus. Antoine Lavoisier (1743–94), the "father" of modern chemistry, proved in 1772 that diamonds were combustible only in the presence of air, and that a gas very much like carbon dioxide was given off during burning. Lavoisier came close to stating, without quite proving, the now well-known fact that diamonds are pure carbon. It was left to the English chemist Smithson Tennant (1761–1815) to reveal the surprising nature of the most famous of precious stones. In 1797 he burned a diamond and a piece of coal in a gold tube that was closed at one end and discovered that the quantity of carbon in the

Below left: The position of the eighteen carbon atoms in the cubic lattice, each atom situated at the center of a tetrahedron formed by the four closest atoms. The atoms within the cube are shown in gray. Right: Three-dimensional model of the cubic, face-centered structure of the diamond. *Alain Midan, Paris (left); Burns Graphics, London.*

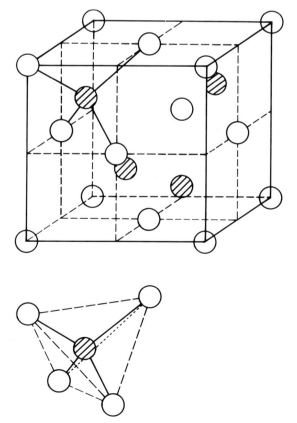

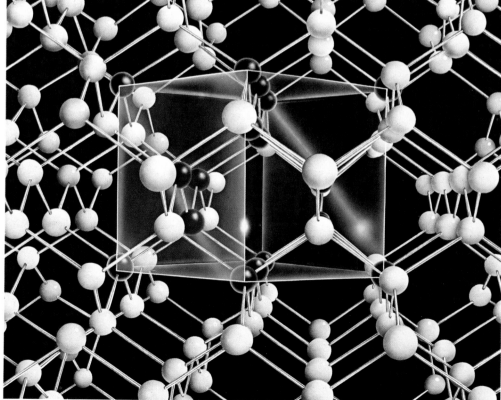

Diamond crystals of various colors and shapes, including twinned crystals, macles, etc. Above: A diamond crystal of gem quality joined to an industrial crystal. Museum national d'Histoire naturelle, Paris. *Photos Guy Philippart de Foy, Brussels.*

carbon dioxide recovered after burning was identical for both the diamond and the coal.

Cubic Structure

At the beginning of the twentieth century Max von Laue discovered, through the diffraction of x-rays in the crystal, that the atoms within the diamond crystal are linked together in a regular, three-dimensional lattice. Because of its simple chemical composition, the diamond was naturally one of the first minerals to be studied by the x-ray method. William Henry Bragg and his son Lawrence were among the early users of the technique in 1913. Other physicists, including Hull, Debye and Scherrer, Mohr, and Huggins, undertook a series of radio-crystallographic studies. They established the cubic, or isometric, system of crystallization of the diamond, in which the basic unit, represented by two face-centered cubes penetrating each other, contains eighteen carbon atoms. Fourteen of these atoms are distributed among the eight apexes and the center of the six faces of a "cube" of 3.56 angstrom units.* Four atoms are situated in the interior

of the cube and are surrounded by four others, each group of four making an imaginary tetrahedron. One atom is situated on an apex of the cube and the other three are at the center of the three faces adjoining that apex (see drawing). The bonds between the atoms are "covalent," or linked by shared electrons. Relatively short (1.544 angstroms), the bonds are very strong, which explains the diamond's great hardness. Similarly, the basic lattice structure of the eighteen atoms is responsible for many of the stone's other properties, such as the orientation of macles and the planes of cleavage, as well as the shapes of rough crystals.

Hardness: 10

Once they discovered the diamond's extreme hardness, the ancients used the stone for cutting and engraving other gems. On the comparative scale of hardness established by Friedrich Mohs in 1822, the diamond occupies the tenth and highest degree. This characteristic is often used in mineralogy as an identifying test. As the hardest of minerals, the diamond can scratch all others but can be

* An angstrom is a unit of length equivalent to one-tenthousandth of a micron; it is used in measuring atomic dimensions as well as wavelengths. However, it was recently decided that the latter should be expressed in nanometers. A nanometer is equivalent to one-thousandth of a micron, or ten angstroms.

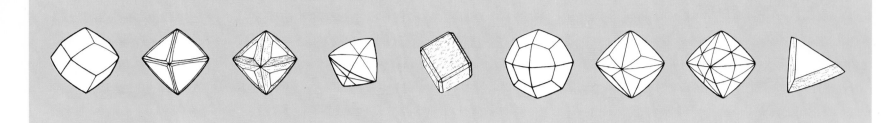

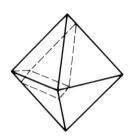

scratched only by itself, although some of its faces are harder than others (octahedral faces are harder than cubic faces). This, however, does not preclude the possibility of diamonds breaking. A few synthetic minerals, such as the carbide of boron and the silicide of titanium, are comparably hard. But these minerals bear little resemblance to diamonds when cut, so the diamond's extraordinary hardness remains the most obvious criterion for distinguishing it from imitations. In practice, however, when polished gems are in question, the hardness test is rarely used, and identification is increasingly based on tests of optical qualities.

Density: 3.52
Although its specific gravity is remarkably constant and is usually given as 3.52 (that is, 3.52 times as heavy as an equal volume of water), diamond's density does vary slightly, usually between 3.506 and 3.524. The higher the density, the purer the diamond: certain Australian diamonds have been measured at 3.56; very impure industrial diamonds may have a much lower-than-average density.

Conductivity

The diamond is a poor conductor of electricity, a fact observed by Guyton de Morveau in 1799. However, there are some types of diamond, notably Type IIb, that have semiconducting properties. Diamonds are excellent conductors of heat, approximately four times better than copper, a quality exploited in some advanced technological operations. This combination of poor electrical conductivity and good thermal conductivity is very unusual.

Crystalline Shapes of Diamond
The diamond takes many forms in nature. The different crystallographic types can be inspected in many museums of natural history, such as that in Paris, where the crystals were first measured and classified by René-Just Haüy (1743–1822), who propounded many of the principles of crystallography. The crystalline shapes most frequently encountered are the octahedron, hexoctahedron, dodecahedron, and, in industrial-quality stones, the cube. These shapes may often be combined in the same crystal, resulting in curved faces.

Cleavage
A diamond cleaves perfectly in layers in four directions, parallel to the faces of the octahedron. Diamond cutters take advantage of this property when splitting large stones into two or more pieces. The existence of the planes of cleavage, however, renders the diamond relatively vulnerable to knocks.

Macles
Often two or more crystals are closely joined along one face; this is called twinning, and such twinned stones are known as macles. Because the orientations of the crystals are different, macles can be very difficult to cut.

Optical Properties
In his famous work *Optics* (1704), Isaac Newton gave the refractive index of diamond as 2.439 (it is now generally given as 2.417) and pointed out that this is the highest index encountered in a colorless body. Dispersion, which is the difference in the refractive index over the visible spectrum, is also described as high, though in fact it is not particularly high in relation to the refractive index. Dispersion is responsible for the "fire" that gives the cut and polished diamond its unique charm.

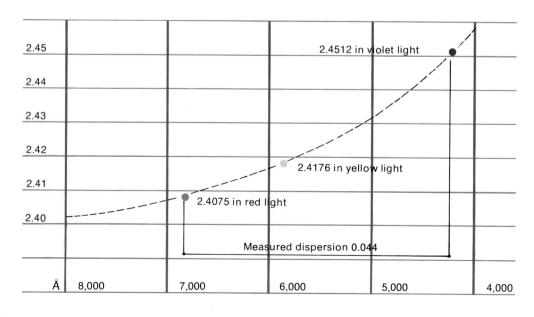

Variation in the Refractive Index of Diamond

2.4512 in violet light

2.4176 in yellow light

2.4075 in red light

Measured dispersion 0.044

Å   8,000   7,000   6,000   5,000   4,000

The *refractive index* of diamond for violet light is higher than it is for red, and white light is split into the different colors of the spectrum by the prismatic effects of the stone. The diagram opposite shows the variation of the refractive index for the different wavelengths: from 2.4075 for red (686.7 nanometers) up to 2.4512 for violet (430.8 nanometers); the index for yellow light is 2.4176. Normally, diamonds are singly refractive, but some diamonds display slight birefringence, or double refraction.

The *phosphorescence* of diamonds was described for the first time by Robert Boyle in 1672. In 1902 Chaumet noted that phosphorescence was brighter after diamonds had been exposed to ultraviolet light, which can also cause some degree of *fluorescence* in certain stones. Very white specimens generally display no fluorescence at all. The *luminescence* of diamonds when exposed to x-rays is a property utilized in recovering some stones.

Physicists distinguish among several types of diamond, according to the transparency of the stones in ultraviolet light. Type I (recently divided into Types Ia and Ib according to the way in which nitrogen atoms are distributed in them) transmits ultraviolet light down to 330 nanometers only. Type II, more transparent, transmits it down to 225 nanometers. The latter category has also been subdivided into Types IIa and IIb. Type IIb diamonds are distinguished from all others in that they are electrical semiconductors.

Color

Diamonds occur in many colors, from the palest to the most vivid, and the origin of their coloring is explained by some rather complicated physical theories. When a diamond is absolutely pure, it is absolutely colorless, absorbing no light from the visible spectrum. The presence of chemical impurities, such as nitrogen, has an important effect on coloration. A small proportion of nitrogen (one nitrogen atom for 100,000 carbon atoms) results in a yellow color. If there is a higher concentration of nitrogen, the stone will be green or greenish-

black. The color of blue diamonds is due to the presence of boron in very small proportions (one boron atom for 1 million carbon atoms).

It has been known since the early twentieth century that diamonds can be colored artificially by irradiation: Sir William Crookes did it successfully, using radium, in 1904. Diamonds treated in this way usually turn a shade of green. If irradiation is followed by prolonged heat treatment, the stone will turn yellow or brown. However, no commercial method has yet been found to reverse the process—that is, to make a colored diamond colorless, or "white." The distinctive rose tint so greatly admired in some diamonds is nearly always natural; it is seldom obtained by irradiation. An artificially produced color in a diamond can usually be detected with a spectroscope.

Absorption Spectra

The spectroscope is used a good deal in gemology. Diamonds have characteristic types of absorption spectra, the following in particular: (a) In diamonds of the Cape series, which are colorless or very slightly yellow, there is an intense band at 415.5 nanometers in the violet zone of the spectrum, with less distinct bands at 435, 452, and 478 nanometers. (b) In brown to green diamonds, there is a band at 504 nanometers in the green zone, with less distinct bands at 491, 515, and 531 nanometers. (c) In artificially colored diamonds, especially yellows and browns, there is a band at 592 nanometers accompanied by bands at 496 and 504 nanometers. In some cases the band at 592 is not easily visible, but it almost never occurs

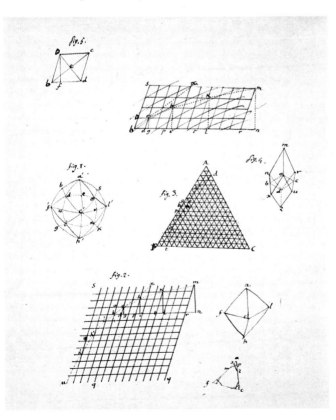

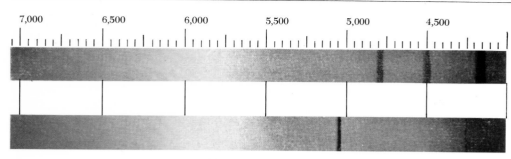

Absorption spectra of a diamond of the Cape type (above) with a line at 4,520 angstroms (452 nanometers) and of a brown diamond (below) with a line at 5,040 angstroms (504 nanometers).

at all in naturally colored stones.

If naturally colored diamonds and diamonds whose color has been modified by irradiation are submitted to luminescence tests with ultraviolet light, or to spectroscopic examination, the differences in their optical properties become apparent. For example, naturally blue diamonds are transparent to ultraviolet light down to 225 nanometers, but diamonds whose blue color has been induced by irradiation are not transparent beyond 330 nanometers and have a different absorption spectrum.

Inclusions and Flaws

Small inclusions and flaws of crystallization may be desirable in precious stones in general because they are a guarantee of authenticity. In the diamond, however, if they are too visible they affect the clarity of the cut gem and make it less valuable. The current preference is for specimens that are clear under a 10× loupe. But many experts anticipate that in a few years, when white synthetic diamonds may appear on the market, studying a stone's inclusions will be an important means of determining whether a diamond is natural.

Apart from the various flaws of crystallization that are described by such self-explanatory terms as "fractures," "feathers," "graining," and so on, and the small dark brown or black spots or cracks that were once erro-

neously called carbon spots, inclusions of small crystals, single or grouped, also appear. They are sometimes surrounded by fine tension fissures caused by disparities in growth rate between the inclusions and the diamond that enveloped them during crystallization.

The inclusions found in diamonds are made of various kinds of small crystals that formed in the mother rock at the same time as the diamond. They include olivine, diopside, chromiferous pyropes, and iron and nickel sulphides. The study of inclusions is very important, for it provides information on the environmental conditions in which diamonds, especially industrial diamonds (80 percent of total production), were formed. It was once impossible to analyze inclusions *in situ*, but in the early 1960's a great step forward was taken with the invention of the electron microprobe, which made it possible to identify inclusions of 2–3 microns. Since 1976 a new method of studying inclusions has been perfected at the University of Lille, thanks to the invention of the Raman laser microprobe. This instrument has two important advantages: it requires no special preparation of the sample, and it leaves it completely intact.

Crystallization and Synthesis of Diamonds

The hypothesis of a volcanic origin for diamonds was suggested as long ago as 1856. In 1890 Auguste Daubrée wrote that "the diamond originates in infragranitic regions at a considerable depth where peridot is dominant . . . it arrived near the surface accompanied by this mineral, and . . . its formation required great pressure and high temperature." This theory gained ground, and in 1914 Damiens, through thermodynamic experiments with the allotropic forms of carbon, confirmed that these were indeed the conditions under which diamonds were formed and that synthetic production was therefore possible.

In fact, several scientists had already attempted to manufacture diamonds. James Ballantyne Hannay of Glasgow claimed to have produced tiny diamond crystals in 1878, but his experiments proved unrepeatable. Henri Moissan made a similar claim in France, but crystals later produced by his methods were found, with the aid of more modern techniques of identification, to be silicon carbide or other material. Sir Charles Parsons reported success in 1918, but this claim was never satisfactorily confirmed, either. It was not until 1953 that B. von Platen in Sweden achieved a successful— that is, repeatable—synthesis of diamonds, producing fourteen crystals less than .04 inches (1 mm) in size, by maintaining a pressure of 50,000–100,000 atmospheres at 2,900° F (1,600° C). Within a few years Von Platen's firm had

Photograph of an inclusion taken with a Raman laser microprobe at Lille University, 1978. *Photo Henri-Jean Schubnel, Paris.*

a production capacity of 2 million carats. Sweden was swiftly followed by the United States (1955) and South Africa (1959). These and other countries have since devoted enormous resources to the production of synthetic industrial diamonds as a hedge against a shortage of natural diamonds, which would have disastrous effects on industry throughout the world.

Diamond Simulants in Jewelry

Because of its great value, the diamond is the most frequently imitated precious stone. Substitutes include the "doublet," made of two flat diamonds cemented together with the help of a thallium salt, and various artificial simulants endowed with a high refractive index and strong dispersive power. The table below lists the principal properties of the most important simulants. Besides doublets made of two diamond fragments, which are comparatively rare and which are obviously less valuable than a gem cut from a single stone, there are much more common doublets consisting of a thin plate of garnet cemented to a glass material called strass (paste), which protects it. Of all the older simulants, strass, named after a Strasbourg jeweler, Joseph Strasser, who perfected it in the eighteenth century, is by far the most successful. It is a colorless lead glass with a dispersive power that produces particularly convincing effects. Stones that are too dispersive, however, are betrayed by their highly colored iridescence: they are too flashy. For about half the common simulants—all those that measure less than 7 on the Mohs scale—the hardness test is a good one. They scratch easily and show signs of damage with everyday use (scratches, rubbing, frosting of the facets, and so on). A diamond, more than any other stone, retains the pristine quality of its

cut. Examination with a loupe can reveal simulants that show birefringence—a double image of the bottom facets is seen. The higher the birefringence, the greater the doubling effect. Colorless diamond substitutes are easily detected by their low refractive index: they simply lack the luster and fire of the diamond. Finally, the most common diamond simulant is, of course, ordinary cut glass, with the bottom given an ultrathin reflective coating of silver or gold.

The Principal Properties of Diamond and Diamond Simulants

* Natural and synthetic ** Artificial	Hardness	Density	Refractive Index	Birefringence	Dispersion
Diamond	10	3.515	2.417	none	.044
Corundum*	9	3.99	1.760–1.768	.008	.018
Zirconium oxide**	8.5	5.68	2.177	none	.065
YAG (Yttrium aluminum garnet**)	8	4.57	1.834	none	.028
Topaz	8	3.56	1.610–1.620	.010	.014
Spinel*	8	3.64	1.727	none	.020
Zircon	7.5	4.70	1.926–1.985	.059	.039
Quartz	7	2.65	1.544–1.553	.009	.013
Rutile*	6.5	4.25	2.613–2.900	.287	.280
Demantoid	6.5	3.85	1.89	none	.057
Lithium niobate**	5.5	4.64	2.210–2.300	.090	.120
Strontium titanate**	5.5	5.13	2.410	none	.190
Scheelite*	5	6.10	1.918–1.934	.016	.026
Lead glass**	5	3.75	1.635	none	.031
Sphalerite	3.5	4.10	2.370	none	.156

History and Evolution of Diamond Cutting

In order to describe the history of the techniques involved in fashioning gem diamonds, it is essential to begin with a precisely defined terminology. Over the centuries the same words have often been used to mean different things, and even nowadays technical terms may be used in a slightly different sense by different authorities. This is not the place for a long semantic discussion, but it is necessary in this chapter to use terms that are precise and unambiguous. Thus the term "fashioning" in the present context covers all the steps leading from rough diamond to gemstone. It is preferable to "cutting" or "polishing," which are more strictly applicable to particular steps in the fashioning process.

Cleaving

A diamond can be split in the same way as a piece of wood is split with a wedge and mallet, for like wood, the diamond has a natural grain. It can be split in any one of four directions, but the split must be made precisely along a cleavage plane. A kerf, or notch, is first made in the stone at the point where it can be successfully cleaved.

There are two reasons for cleaving a diamond—to obtain two or more stones from a single rough stone, or to remove minor irregularities or impurities. In the early days of diamond working, in India, for example, cleavage was performed only on octahedrons that had become cloudy during the formation of the crystal or as a result of alluvial drifting. Inter-

nal defects that were aligned in a plane of cleavage could also be eliminated or at least exposed on the surface, where they could be removed during later stages of fashioning.

The technique of cleavage was probably introduced into Europe from India, where it apparently was invented more than two thousand years ago. There are ancient Indian sources that describe stones "with six points, of perfect transparency, without flaw, with sharp edges, and of good color [and] flawless exterior . . . lighting up the room with the reflection of the fire of a rainbow."

Before the Renaissance, Europeans believed that a diamond would lose its magical powers if its original shape or aspect were changed in any way, so naturally anyone involved in manipulating diamonds tried to keep his activities secret. During the superstitious Middle Ages the longstanding belief that a diamond could be divided only if it were first soaked in the blood of a ram or a he-goat no doubt provided a useful cover for diamond cutters anxious to keep their techniques to themselves. This belief, which provided Christianity with much apt symbolism, seems to have originated with a mistranslation of Pliny. What Pliny actually said was that if a steel blade—not a diamond—were tempered by being soaked in goat's blood (the best hardening agent known at the time), the blade would be able to cleave a diamond.

In the past, the slices removed during cleaving, if reasonably transparent and without major flaws, were themselves often fashioned into small odd pieces, shaped according to some specific design, for the embellishment of monograms, crosses, or rosettes. Cleaving is, however, a hazardous operation: if the craftsman fails to judge the directions or planes of cleavage correctly, his blow may shatter the diamond instead of parting it cleanly.

Sawing

A diamond can be cleaved only along its planes of cleavage. To be divided in other directions, it must be sawn. For example, if one wanted to remove the apex of an octahedron to obtain either a table-cut stone or a half-octahedron, sawing would be the method to use.

The first gem saw was probably the bow saw used in China for cutting jade, with garnet

A diamond-cutting shop in the 18th century. Engraving from the *Encyclopédie* of Diderot and d'Alembert. The first craftsman is rubbing one diamond against another, the second is treating the scaife with oil-soaked diamond powder, and the third is moving a beam to and fro, which turns the large wheel to drive the scaife.

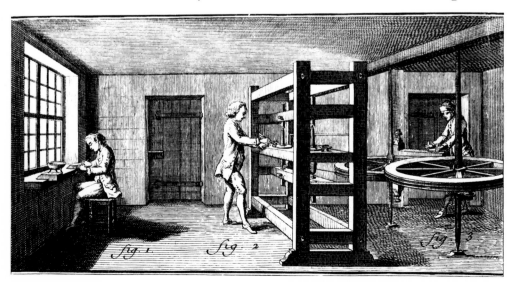

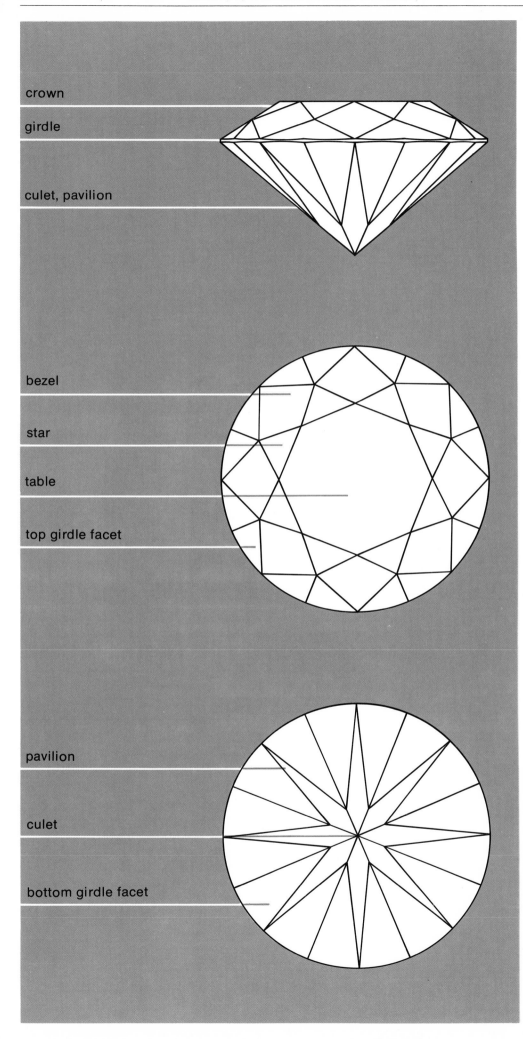

crown

girdle

culet, pavilion

bezel

star

table

top girdle facet

pavilion

culet

bottom girdle facet

powder as an abrasive. In the first century A.D., according to Pliny, marble was sawn with sand as an abrasive, and in the sixteenth century iron was cut by copper wire impregnated with oil and emery. In the early nineteenth century John Mawe described the diamond saw as a fine brass or iron wire attached to a length of cane or whalebone, with diamond powder pressed into the wire blade to give it "bite." The wire was probably held in a frame like that of the fret saw used today. As in cleaving, a notch or kerf was first made in the stone and was then filled with a mixture of oil and diamond powder. According to Mawe, it took eight to ten months to saw through a large stone; a full year was needed for the Regent.

The toothless rotating saw was patented in England in 1833 but not introduced into the diamond trade until about 1900, when a saw produced specifically for the diamond industry came on the market. A similar saw—extremely thin, circular, and made of phosphor bronze—was reportedly patented in the United States in 1910. Since then sawing has been used more than cleaving for dividing rough stones and for removing objectionable parts.

Rubbing

The rubbing process was described by Benvenuto Cellini in 1568 and was presumably a common technique at that time. The process consisted simply of rubbing two diamonds together by hand: each was fixed to the end of a stick, and a box was placed underneath to collect the diamond dust. It was strenuous work, requiring great physical exertion as well as skill. The craftsman's hands, though usually protected by leather gloves, often became swollen and painful.

Rubbing was an essential part of the fashioning process: fancy shapes, drops, roses, brilliants, and designs like those of the Sancy and Yellow Florentine could not have been achieved by any other method. The modern equivalent is bruting, which is done on a lathe. One stone is fixed to the lathe, and the other, on a stick or a dop, is held against it as it revolves. When used in fashioning brilliants, this process is called girdling.

Grinding

Grinding permits a more regular shape and greater control over proportions than other methods. A stone can be given many different shapes by grinding, but there are two major limitations: the resulting surfaces are all flat, not rounded; and in certain specific directions the diamond completely resists any abrasive.

A stone that is to be ground is fixed in a dop that can be turned in any direction and is held against the grinding wheel. The wheel, often

Bruting (left) and faceting.
From John Mawe, *Treatise on
Diamonds and Precious
Stones*, 1823. Some of the
instruments in use at that time
can be seen in greater
detail in the photographs on
this page and the next.
Bibliothèque Nationale, Paris.
Photo Hubert Josse, Paris.

called a lap or scaife, is a cast-iron disc impregnated with a mixture of diamond powder and oil. Coarse powder is used at the start of the process, finer powder toward the end.

According to the physican Anselmus de Boot of Bruges, writing in the early seventeenth century, it took about a week to grind a facet with the wheel only—an indication that grinding alone was used at that time in fashioning diamonds from the rough. Also in the seventeenth century, Tavernier wrote that in India "a large wheel was operated by four blacks." De Boot also mentioned a pewter wheel driven by a treadle that was worked by the craftsman.

Later, donkeys or horses supplied the power, then water wheels, and, in the nineteenth century, steam engines. Today the wheel is powered by electricity.

In modern usage the term "grinding" has been replaced by "faceting."

Polishing

In the present context the term "polishing" applies only to the final process in fashioning a diamond—achieving the fine finish of the surface of a facet. The method is exactly the same as grinding except that an even finer powder is used, and it is done on the same

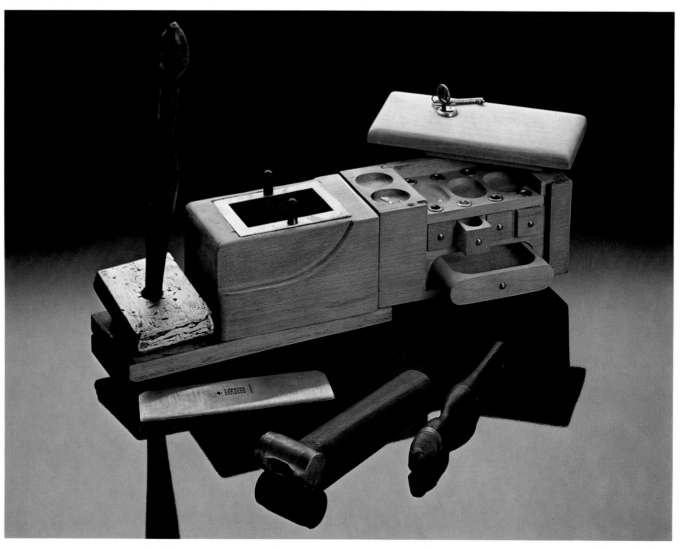

Tools used in the past for cleaving and bruting (cutting). Left, the cleaving stick, balanced with a lead weight; foreground, a steel blade and mallet to cleave the diamond, together with a bruting stick (seen in use in picture at top left); center, the box in which diamond dust was collected during bruting, and (right) the little chest with containers in which the diamonds were kept. *Photo Michel Plassart, Paris.*

Tools used in the past for diamond polishing. When bruting had been completed, another craftsman known as a vesteller prepared the diamond for polishing by fixing it to the end of a dop, a cup on a metal stalk, in a lead-based cement or solder. It was repositioned for each facet, the solder being softened by heat so that the diamond could be adjusted. The dop was mounted in a tang, a wooden arm ending in a metal clamp. *Photo Michel Plassart, Paris.*

Pincers used in the 18th century for measuring diamonds. Engraving from David Jeffries, *Treatise on Diamonds and Pearls*, London, 1751.

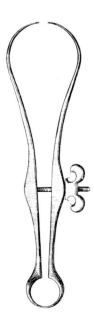

wheel, which has one area for grinding and another for polishing. Each facet is usually ground and then polished before the dop is turned to grind the next facet.

Cut

The cut of a diamond is the "geometry" of the finished gem and the pattern of its facets—point cut, table cut, brilliant cut, emerald cut, and so on. The diamond cutter is the craftsman who fashions gem diamonds, and the term "cutting" is often used for the fashioning process as a whole as well as for certain steps in the process.

Make

In diamond terminology, the total effect of the cutter's work—proportions, symmetry, and finish—is called the make. However, the skill of the cutter is not necessarily reflected by the quality of the make. From the commercial point of view, it is often preferable to produce a make of medium quality or even a rather poor one in order to preserve the size of a large gem, rather than to aim for perfect make at the cost of greatly reducing the stone. In the early days, diamond workers were more concerned with preserving as much of the original weight as possible, since weight was the most important consideration. They either retained the shape of the crystal, if it was attractive, and eliminated only the worst irregularities, or, if

the rough was irregular, they transformed it into another shape, using a great deal of imagination to select one that would preserve the maximum amount of weight. In shapes such as those illustrated on page 208, symmetry, light effects, and weight had only secondary importance. Size was the primary factor. Only when the new type of rose cut and the brilliant cuts became accepted were fire and luster requested, and well-balanced, harmoniously "unsymmetrical," beautifully sparkling diamonds were produced. Make became a quality factor, and there was an intelligent appreciation of the overall beauty of the diamond, without an exaggerated examination of details.

Fire and Brilliance

The play of colors created by the dispersion of light in a diamond is called fire. Brilliance is the total effect created by both reflected and refracted light. The brilliance of a diamond depends solely on the extent to which white light entering from above is reflected back to the viewer from the pavilion, or base facets. The more light reflected and the less refracted out of the stone and lost in the surrounding medium, the greater the diamond's brilliance.

Foiling and Tinting

If the pavilion of a diamond is well proportioned and the angles are correct, it has per-

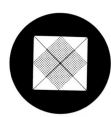

fect brilliance. In the past, if the pavilion was too shallow or some similar imperfection existed, efforts were sometimes made to eliminate refraction and improve brilliance by applying foils or tints to the base. Similar means were used to improve the color of rubies, sapphires, emeralds, and other stones. Various substances were used in attempts to make the pavilion a better reflector. Cellini boasted of his own expertise in the use of foils, and other writers described similar methods. Many rosettes, point cuts, and table cuts, for instance, were set in a bed of pitch; black silk was used under very thin table cuts and tablets. People involved in restoring and resetting the jewelry in old treasuries have sometimes had the disconcerting experience of seeing a splendid pink color, for example, disappear during cleaning. It was not a rare and beautiful natural color at all, but merely the result of a tint applied to the base of an ordinary brownish-yellow stone.

The History of Diamond Cuts

Diamond design has always been dependent on taste and demand, and to some degree on supply. It is therefore impossible to describe the evolution of diamond fashioning in an orderly chronological sequence. However, the stages outlined below represent the general trends in the development of diamond cuts.

Until the early fourteenth century the only diamonds known in Europe were natural crystals, or rough stones. India was the only source of such stones, and because diamonds were highly appreciated in their country of origin, comparatively few reached Europe.

Very few rough diamonds are naturally regular, smooth, and transparent. While they all conform to the isotropic system of crystallization, they occur in a variety of related shapes, and their geometry is often highly irregular. The shape that occurs most frequently is the octahedron, a crystal with eight faces, resembling two pyramids joined base to base. The

common term "diamond-shaped," used to describe, for instance, the diamonds on playing cards, refers to the outline of this form. Octahedral stones, if reasonably symmetrical and attractive, were highly valued in India from the time when people first began digging for diamonds in the dry riverbeds sometime between 1000 and 300 B.C. Another attractive shape is the dodecahedron, with twelve equal, rounded, rhombic faces. Besides these, intriguing combinations of the octahedron and dodecahedron and shapes based on the hexahedron, or cube, were also greatly appreciated in Europe, where rough diamonds were used as talismans or symbols of power and were frequently mounted in religious objects or personal jewelry.

A popular travelogue written in the fourteenth century by "Sir John Mandeville" (apparently a physician from Liège named Jehan à la Barbe), who seems to have had personal knowledge of precious stones, if not of all the places he claimed to have visited, contains a reference to diamonds: "...and sume ben 6 squared, sume 4 squared, and sume 3, as nature schapethe hem." Because naturally handsome stones were in short supply, the only way to meet demand was to improve unattractive stones by some kind of fashioning. This involved breaking the barrier of superstition by defying the popular belief that a diamond would lose its mystical powers if it were in any way altered by man. Commercial demand proved stronger than superstition, and craftsmen learned how to improve the appearance of octahedrons by cleaving them in order to remove unsightly or otherwise undesirable fragments. Cleaving was already being practiced on other kinds of precious stones, so it merely had to be adapted to the much harder diamond. The origins of cleaving, however, are still a mystery: the craftsmen of the time carefully preserved the secrets of their art, and documents provide no help at all in determining whether the beautiful octahedral surfaces of a particular stone are the work of nature or of man.

A natural octahedron is, in fact, rarely perfect. When viewed vertically, for example, the outline is seldom perfectly square. It is more often rectangular, sometimes very elongated. The octahedral gem diamond was called a "diamond point" or, more correctly, a "natural point." Such a diamond is easily recognized by the dark, square reflection that extends to the girdle.

Rhombic dodecahedrons, twin crystals, and all the other appealing shapes in which diamonds may crystallize were used in their natural form, but only very small stones of such shapes are found in museums and treasuries

Detail of the bracelet on the preceding page. Some of the diamonds are simply cleaved and polished, others are rose-cut or "Mughal"-cut. *Photo Guy Philippart de Foy, Brussels.*

today. The larger ones have all been reshaped according to the prevailing fashions of intervening periods. One of the few surviving examples of a famous piece of jewelry set with natural diamond crystals is the late-fourteenth-century crown once worn by Princess Blanche of Lancaster, now in the treasury of the Residenz in Munich.

Refinement of Natural Forms

As diamonds became more widely known in Europe, the demand for stones of various specific shapes increased. Diamond craftsmen endeavored to beautify the surfaces and geometry of a stone without changing its basic natural shape. One method was to file the flat surfaces of a regular octahedron to obtain distinctly rounded faces. The file was wooden or copper, with a diamond-powder abrasive. Other, more laborious, methods may also have been used, including rubbing and subsequent polishing with leather or another soft material impregnated with diamond dust, as described by Pliny in the first century A.D.

With the help of the wheel and the dop, craftsmen of the late Middle Ages were able to improve the appearance or symmetry of a diamond without sacrificing too much of its original shape and weight. They soon learned to reduce the angles of pyramidal stones to obtain the first point cut. From this basic form, via the table cut, the Baroque cut, the Peruzzi cut, and the Regent cut, the modern brilliant cut ultimately developed.

The Gothic point cut was the predominant form during the Renaissance, so much so that in the inventories and wills of the time the word "diamond" was used without further qualification to mean a point-cut stone. Other cuts were described as squares, triangles, round, faceted, and so on. In portraits and illustrations of jewelry of the period, point-cut diamonds can often be recognized by the dark reflection previously mentioned as characteristic of the natural crystal, which in point-cut stones, with their reduced proportions, does not reach the girdle. From the size of this reflection it is possible to determine how much the original height of the stone was reduced.

The exact date at which the point cut was introduced cannot be determined, but a masterly example of this cut certainly existed very early in the fifteenth century. This was the diamond in a famous jewel known as the Three Breathren, owned by Charles the Bold of Burgundy and first mentioned in an inventory of 1419. The stone measured about two-thirds of an inch (16 mm) and weighed about 30 old carats. (An old carat weighed slightly more than the metric carat used to measure diamonds today.) This large and splendid diamond was apparently inspired by the shape of the trisoctahedron (twenty-four faces, three for each face of an octahedron) and fashioned from a rather irregular octahedron. The available illustrations and documentary references, and the drawings based on them, show not only that the height of the rough stone was lowered, but

Painting on parchment
by Hans Muelich, dated 1551,
showing examples of
different cuts. Bayerisches
Nationalmuseum, Munich.
*Photo Bayerisches
Nationalmuseum.*

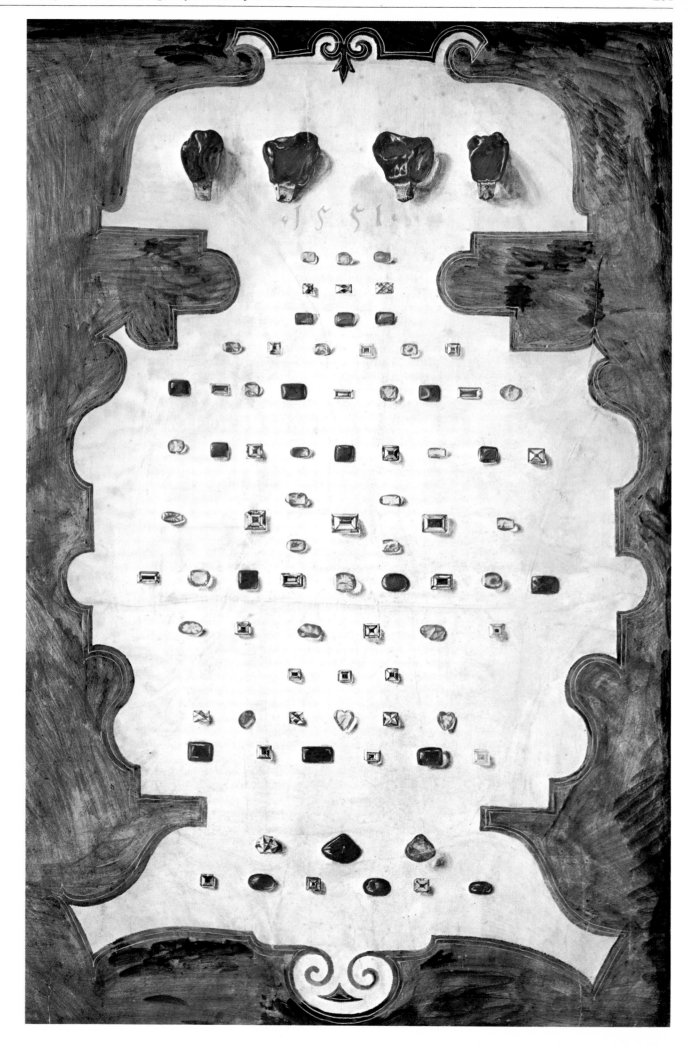

also that the main, octahedral faces were replaced by low, three-sided pyramids, resulting in a design closely resembling a trisoctahedron. In addition, a narrow facet was placed on each edge. Such cuts are encountered in the later fifteenth century and, more frequently, in the sixteenth century, but the diamond of Charles the Bold proves that the art of fashioning at will was known very early in the fifteenth century. Moreover, there are examples of differently faceted point cuts dating from about this time.

The Three Brethren jewel took its name from the three beautiful "balas rubies," or red spinels, surrounding the central diamond. Colored gems had a greater appeal at that time, and diamonds, being of less interest, were often mentioned more or less in passing. The diamond from the Three Brethren was subsequently refashioned several times, and in the nineteenth century it was acquired by an American whose name has never been revealed.

Renaissance craftsmen were capable of fashioning point cuts from shapes other than octahedrons. Diamonds have been found in settings with the exposed pyramid higher than octahedral proportions and with the base pyramid, which is concealed by the setting, excessively shallow. These stones were fashioned from triangular rough. There is a particularly fine example in a ring in the Grünes Gewölbe in Dresden. Another example, with all its surfaces exposed, is in the Hermitage in Leningrad. Miniatures by Hans Muelich (1516–73), now in the Bayerische Staatsbibliothek, Munich, show several similar diamonds, which once belonged to Duke Albert V of Bavaria.

Dodecahedrons were especially suitable for cuts that resembled the modern brilliant cut but had a point in place of the optically important top facet, or table, of the brilliant. These were also called "faceted points." A notable example is the stone in the Burgundian goblet, made about 1450, in the Kunsthistorisches Museum in Vienna. Another appears in a miniature of the Aigrette or Feather Jewel of Charles the Bold, now in the Kunstmuseum, Basel. A contemporary description of such stones referred to them as "round and mirroring." The type may justly be described as Burgundian brilliant cut, since it was the prototype of the oval or near-round brilliants popular from the mid-seventeenth century on.

Fancy Cuts

It soon became necessary to create new cuts that would enable craftsmen to make use of the many different kinds of rough that arrived at their workshops. In the early Renais-

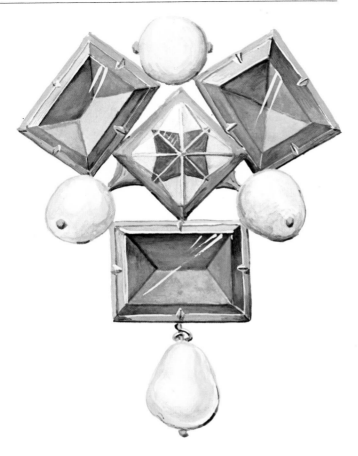

Above: The famous piece known as the Three Brethren, which belonged to Charles the Bold. Reconstruction based on research by Herbert Tillander.

Below: A pendant with six "natural points." Painting by Hans Muelich, from the *Livre des joyaux de la duchesse Anne* (wife of Albert V of Bavaria), 1560. Bayerische Staatsbibliothek, Munich. *Photo Bayerische Staatsbibliothek.*

sance, fashionable jewelry usually consisted of a large central stone combined with many small diamonds, but the small fragments obtained by cleaving could be used in pendants, brooches, crucifixes, monogrammed rings, and similar items that were made in large numbers. The ways in which craftsmen used these sometimes extremely small fragments are proof of their remarkable skill. A good example is the diamond rosette, which appeared around the middle of the fifteenth century. The simple diamond rosette was made up of four to nine cleaved fragments; the more intricate double rosette required between twelve and twenty pieces. Each fragment had to be ground and polished with the utmost precision in order to fit into the final composition. This was assembled in the shape of a rose, with the tiny diamonds fashioned into petal and leaf shapes radiating symmetrically from the center, where they were fixed by a "pistil," often set with a small emerald or other gem. Rosettes were sometimes mounted individually in rings, but they were also combined with other gems in jewelry and religious objects of the greatest splendor.

By the middle of the fifteenth century there were more than two hundred different cuts in existence, most of them achieved by the use of the wheel alone. This fact ought to dispel once and for all the claim that diamond cutting was invented—or even significantly improved—by Lodewijk van Berckem in 1476. On the contrary, it might almost be said that the evolution of diamond fashioning had ended by that time, for no fundamentally new design or cut has been invented since. Modern cuts are merely elaborations of the basic forms that had been developed by about 1450. The craftsman's equipment has improved, but his work is essentially the same as it was five centuries

ago. A modern diamond cutter, in fact, could sit down in a medieval workshop and produce intricate fancy shapes, or indeed any modern cut. Moreover, several of the old fancy cuts have survived to the present. They differ from today's cuts only in their proportions, for the modern craftsman has somewhat different aims, seeking an attractive combination of maximum fire and brilliance (though with greater emphasis—regrettably, some may think—on brilliance, as well as on apparent size).

The Thick Table Cut

Burgundian inventories from about 1400 use the terms *plat* ("flat") or *carré* ("square") to describe certain diamonds. Somewhat later, they refer to diamonds *en table* ("table-cut") or *en façon de mirouer* ("mirroring"). These terms indicate another trend in jewelry, in which relatively uncomplicated, square stones came to be preferred to fancy cuts and richly faceted gems. Point cuts remained popular, but they were gradually confined to smaller and smaller stones and eventually were used only as subsidiary ornamentation in jewelry. Table-cut stones became the most fashionable and remained so for about two hundred years. The original table cut, the "thick stone" or knob cut, was made by grinding—and to some extent rubbing—an octahedral rough. The main faces were made fairly symmetrical, and the apex, which was frequently damaged, was ground to a horizontal facet called the table. By the end of the sixteenth century, ideal proportions for this cut had been established. The steps by which these proportions were achieved were described as follows.

First the upper point of the octahedron was ground down to a quadrangular plane (the table), following the shape of the rough. The opposite point was similarly ground, but to a

A "faceted point" cut. Detail from the Burgundy Goblet, 1425–50. Prototype of the brilliant cut, derived from a dodecahedral crystalline shape (see drawing). Kunsthistorisches Museum, Vienna. *Photo Kunsthistorisches Museum.*

Far right: A diamond rosette. Detail from the Host of Maximilian I, late 15th century. The rosette is made up of fourteen cleaved diamonds (see drawing). Harburg Castle, Swabia.

The Great Cross of diamonds of François I, with mirror-cut stones on the cross and four rose cuts below. Reconstruction by Herbert Tillander according to Germain Bapst, *Les Joyaux de la Couronne de France*, 1889.

Right: An early 16th-century brooch in the form of a figure of St. Michael in diamonds. Grünes Gewölbe, Dresden.

Below: Brooch of Catherine Jagiello, daughter of Sigismund I of Poland, dated 1546. The monogram "C" is formed from small table-cut diamonds. Uppsala Cathedral, Sweden.

much smaller plane (the culet). The sides of the opposing pyramids were ground down until the angle at which they met was a perfect right angle (their angle of inclination to the plane of the girdle, therefore, was 45 degrees). The width of the stone at the girdle was twice its width at the table; the height of the crown (the top part) was one-third the total height, or half the depth of the pavilion (the bottom part). The area of the culet was one-fifth the area of the table.

These figures were, of course, approximate, and over the centuries they varied somewhat. However, examination of jewels of the period shows that, contrary to the reports of most writers on the subject, the majority of table-cut diamonds have angles well below the "divine" ones of the natural octahedron (nearly 55 degrees), and in a surprisingly large proportion they are very close to the ideal angle of 45 degrees. Moreover, the other specifications appear to have been followed with only slight variations. These proportions, of which a large culet was an essential part, were perfect according to contemporary ideas of the laws of optics, and they were still valid in the nineteenth century for brilliants of particularly fine make.

Table-cut stones often had rounded outlines, because many octahedrons have convex faces. As in the point cut, corners were often left blunt to preserve the size of the stone. This defect, referred to by the term *coins manqués* in wills and inventories of the period, could be concealed by skillful setting or by applying facets to the corners. For small ornamental stones, this design soon developed into what is known today as the single cut, or 8/8 diamond, and the Swiss cut, or 16/16 diamond (also known, for obscure reasons, as the Mazarin cut).

The Mirror Cut

The term "mirror cut" will not be found in other books today, but it is not a new invention. It was frequently used in old wills and inventories, and it appears in the names of several historic diamonds, such as the Mirror of Portugal and the Mirror of France. It is a variety of the full-bodied, or thick, table cut, though the latter was always recognized as the superior design. In gemological literature and books on historical jewelry the mirror cut is erroneously called the "thin stone" or "thin table" cut, terms that should refer to very thin stones.

The mirror cut, actually a spread table cut, was developed in response to the great popularity of the thick table cut before the seventeenth century. (In the 1600's the table cuts were gradually displaced by the rose cut and

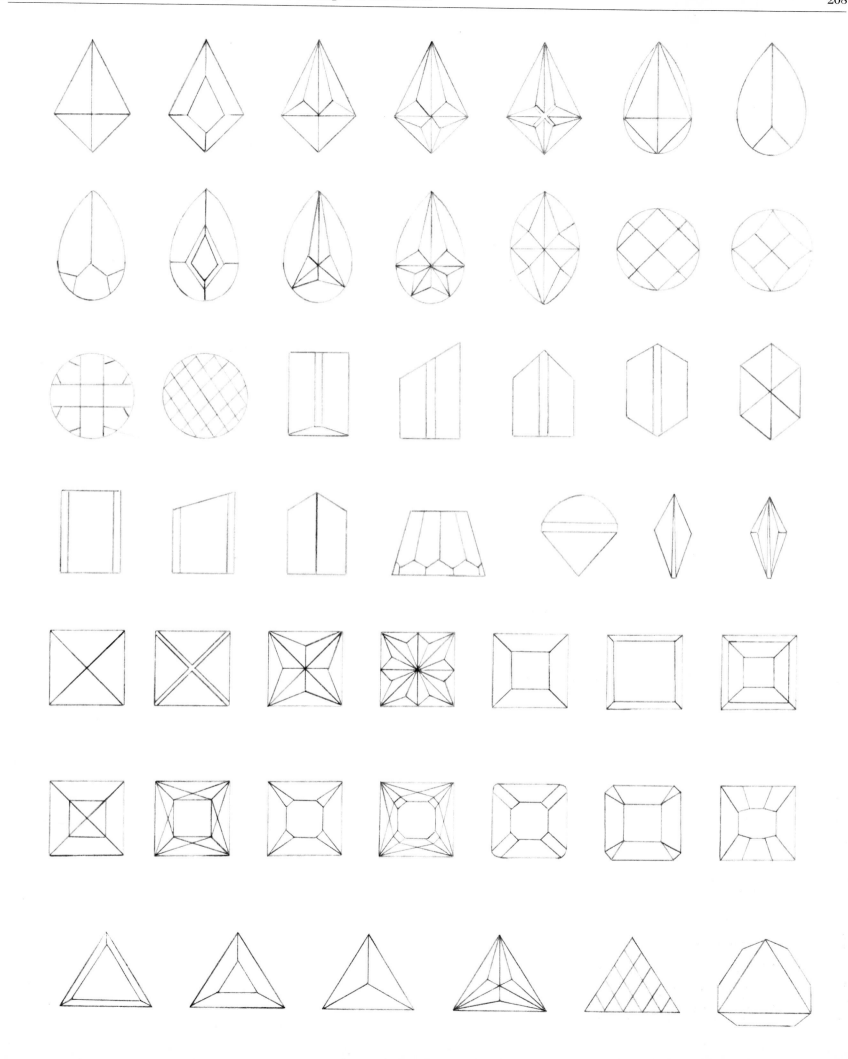

the brilliant cut.) The general geometry of the mirror cut is similar to that of the thick table cut, but the proportions are different. The deep pavilion with its relatively small culet is the same, but the crown is very low and consequently the width of the table constitutes as much as 80 or 90 percent of the total width. This large facet is highly reflective and acts literally as a mirror. In addition, strong reflections from the pavilion facets through the crown enhance brilliance. Gems of this type could be fashioned quite easily and with relatively little loss in weight from fairly thick, triangular rough stones (twinned crystals), which were readily available and less expensive than octahedrons. Mirror cuts were mostly square or rectangular in outline, but the cutters' efforts to preserve as much of the original weight and form as possible led to some rather fancy shapes.

When the brilliant cut came to be recognized as the finest cut, the popularity of the table and mirror cuts naturally declined. Many diamonds, in fact, were recut as brilliants. The table-cut diamonds bequeathed by Cardinal Mazarin to the French crown in 1661 are a well-known example: they were recut as brilliants in the Netherlands in the 1780's.

The step-cut diamonds of today are in principle simply modern versions of the historical table cut with new proportions—a pavilion angle reduced from 45 to 41 degrees, with vary-

ing proportions for the crown, and a culet that is hardly visible at all.

The Tablet Cut and Lasque Cut

A mirror cut with a very shallow pavilion and a culet about the same size as the table is called a tablet cut; it totally lacks brilliance and fire. Lasque-cut diamonds were fashioned from thin slices obtained by cleaving irregular octahedrons. They are practically all table and culet, with tiny irregular facets applied all around. The very thinnest were often used as covers for miniature portraits set in jewelry and are therefore sometimes called portrait stones.

The Rose Cut

Benvenuto Cellini's remarks in 1568 about faceted diamonds give the impression that the rose cut had been invented not long before. Alternatively, several authors have credited Cardinal Mazarin with its invention, but this belief stems from a statement by the Marquis Léon de Laborde (1807–69), who was well known for his tendency to ascribe all artistic innovations to Parisians. Mazarin was certainly a great admirer and collector of precious stones and did encourage the diamond trade in Paris, but there is very little evidence that he influ-

Opposite: A heraldic piece, the imperial two-headed eagle of Austria, in gold, rubies, pearls, and diamonds in a variety of cuts. Probably Venetian, about 1550. Residenz Schatzkammer, Munich. *Photo Residenz Schatzkammer.*

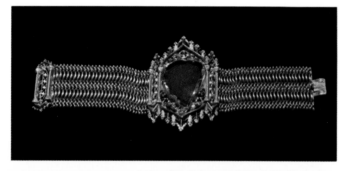

A "portrait stone" on a gold bracelet, in Neo-Gothic style, early 19th century. A miniature portrait could be slipped under the diamond, which weighs about 25 carats. Diamond Collection of the Soviet Union, Moscow. *Photo APN, Paris.*

enced the actual fashioning of diamonds.

The classic shape of the rose cut in fact dates from the fourteenth century. Because it was created from fragments cleaved from trisoctahedral or hexoctahedral faces, or from fragments of a rough indicating crystallization into a cube, it had a shallow profile. The rose had a domed crown with triangular facets meeting in a point at the center, and the base was flat, usually corresponding to the plane of the original cleavage. When set in jewelry, the base was of course hidden in the mount. The most common type had only three or nine facets and straight or rounded sides. There were also many fancy designs with names like *Oeil, Fusée, Crête de Coq, Fer de Lance,* and *Écu.* Obviously, the shape of the rough diamond and the desire to preserve weight influenced the cutter in his choice of design. Drop shapes were also popular, and among them the double rose is especially distinguished. One particularly attractive double rose was the Sancy cut, which became popular in the sixteenth century, primarily because it could be fashioned without visually reducing the "size" of the rough. Rose-cut diamonds in the classic form were simply called "faceted," unless exceptional size or value earned them a special name.

Jewels had an important function in the lavish decoration of the court of Louis XIV, the Sun King, at Versailles in the second half of the seventeenth century. It was soon noticed that candlelight enhanced the appearance of diamonds, and diamond cutters anxious to exploit this effect began to experiment with a new type of rose cut. They had as an example the Indian Mughal cut, which they reproduced in a somewhat less intricate form. From these experiments the high, round, oval, and drop-shaped multifaceted modern type was created. It was given the name rose cut because it resembled a rosebud.

The proportions of the rose cut were first studied in scientific detail by Marcel Tolkowsky at the beginning of the twentieth century. He demonstrated that this cut did not favor light dispersion—in other words, that it lacked fire. This unfortunate characteristic had in fact been observed some two hundred years earlier and accounted for the rose cut's decline in popularity. Over the years, high roses were refashioned as brilliants, and today there are very few full-bodied high roses left. Some can be seen in the Grünes Gewölbe in Dresden and in the royal castle of Rosenborg in Copenhagen, and there are surely others in private collections. Beginning in the eighteenth century only very thin and small rose cuts were made—the Amsterdam or Dutch and the Antwerp or Brabant roses—along with some very irregular shapes. Today, the rose cut has disappeared altogether.

The Brilliant Cut

The true history of the brilliant cut is far more interesting than the well-known stories that credit Van Berckem, Mazarin, or Peruzzi with its invention, stories that owe more to human imagination than to historical research. The prototype of the brilliant cut can be found in Burgundy at the beginning of the fifteenth century. It was derived from both octahedral and dodecahedral stones. The oldest and finest example of the former is the central gem in Charles the Bold's Three Brethren piece, mentioned earlier. A number of other early faceted diamonds are known from paintings of about the same period. The scissor cut, as seen for example in the sixteenth-century double-

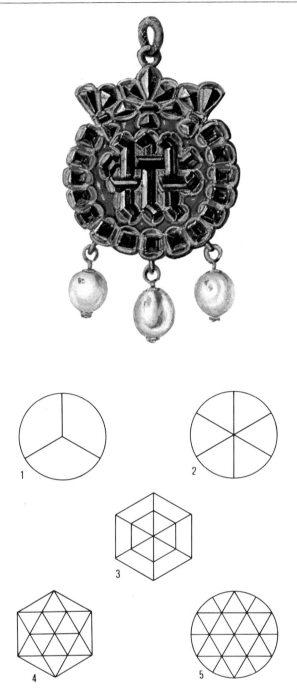

headed eagle in the Residenz Schatzkammer
in Munich, is very close to the brilliant cut.

The term "brilliant cut" did not come into
general usage for some time, and this alone
suggests that the cut was not invented at one
stroke by a single individual. More likely, it
was the result of many years of development
by craftsmen seeking to heighten the optical
effects of the gem. A very early mention of a
"brilliant" occurs in an inventory of a Hanau
jeweler, Daniel de Hase, in 1614. Several brilliants are mentioned among the jewels belonging to the future Mary II of England in 1668.
In 1673 Louis XIV ordered the recutting of the
Tavernier Blue diamond into a "modern European shape," and we now know that this was
the heart-shaped brilliant cut. (The Blue diamond was later recut again and is known today
as the Hope.) The Wittelsbach Blue diamond,
35.56 carats, was cut as a brilliant no later than

1664, but it was not called a brilliant at that
time.

The evolution of the modern brilliant cut
continued with the appearance of a few richly
faceted, pyramidal stones inspired by the hexoctahedron, and of table cuts with various additional facets—sometimes scissor-cut but more
often cut in steps, frequently with small facets
replacing the edges. Contrary to earlier belief,
there was no direct development from the
table cut through the old single (8/8 facets) and
double (16/16 facets) cuts to the triple, or full,
cut with 32/24 facets. Those cuts were used
only on very small ornamental stones. Rather,
the Baroque brilliant cut, both oval and round,
developed quite logically from the dodecahedral rough. The drawings on pages 212–13 illustrate more clearly than words how the earliest commercial brilliant achieved its final
design simply through the addition of one row

of facets after another. Because of the eclectic nature of this process, there was never any formulation of the ideal proportions. Fine proportions were often achieved nevertheless: beautiful example of perfect make can be seen among the jewels of Augustus the Strong (1670–1773), now in the Grünes Gewölbe in Dresden.

The brilliant cut was so popular that craftsmen were obliged to consider ways of adapting it to the ample supply of octahedral rough stones without sacrificing too much weight—or expending too much effort. The result was the almost square brilliant. This represented a reversion in style from the Baroque to the Renaissance. The shape was not new; it was clearly inspired by the classic figure of a four-pointed star covering the whole surface, a design familiar in religious art such as floor mosaics and stained-glass windows.

The perfect symmetry of the square brilliant cut is easily recognized. Each facet edge of the crown is parallel to one of the sides of the star, the corners are sharp, and the edges are slightly convex. The correct measurements were given with great precision by David Jeffries in 1750, and many nineteenth-century authors emphasized the importance of strictly adhering to them: the slightest deviation would destroy the symmetry. Experiments with rock crystal have shown, however, that excellence of symmetry is not affected by modified depth proportions.

The square brilliant was certainly known as early as the beginning of the eighteenth century. In the nineteenth century it was given the name Peruzzi cut, and although books frequently refer to one Vincenzo Peruzzi of Venice as the inventor of this design, there is no historical evidence that such a man ever existed. However, the name has now become so firmly established that there is no point in changing it.

During the eighteenth century an intermediate design was introduced, known as the Regent cut after the famous diamond that is part of the French crown jewels. The Regent had

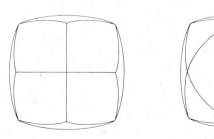

Opposite: The "Dresden Green" mounted in an epaulette. Probably of Indian origin, it was bought by the elector Frederick Augustus II of Saxony (Augustus III of Poland) in 1743 at the Leipzig Fair. The largest-known green diamond, it is pear-shaped and weighs 41 carats. Grünes Gewölbe, Dresden. *Photo Claus Hansmann, Munich.*

long been considered a masterpiece of correct proportioning, and close examination of the stone, in which the main facets of crown and pavilion meet at the girdle in a perfect right angle, confirms its reputation. The similarity with the Peruzzi cut is striking, but the Regent cut has attractively rounded corners and its symmetry is less strict: the star does not extend to the limits of the girdle. It was therefore easier to fashion.

Another development on the way to the completely round, standard brilliant cut of today can be discerned in what modern terminology calls the European and English round-cut brilliants. Certain experimental designs, such as the Lisbon and Caire cuts, can be passed over, but attention should be drawn to the enormous number of poorly proportioned old brilliants. The trouble here derived partly from the act of cleaving, which inevitably resulted in pavilions that were too shallow. That is why the ideal proportions of such beautiful designs as the Peruzzi and the Regent cuts were so rarely achieved, and it may explain why many people preferred the old square brilliant and Baroque round cuts, which retained their admirers until the end of the nineteenth century.

Mechanical rounding on a lathe and machine sawing were introduced into the diamond industry only in the late nineteenth and early twentieth centuries, although similar machines had been in use in other industries for some time. The new methods led to changes in the proportions of the cut. In 1916 E. F. Wade wrote in detail of the many factors involved in achieving perfect symmetry while retaining as much weight as possible, placing great emphasis on light dispersion. His work has been almost totally ignored, yet it provided the foundation on which modern standards for analyzing the color, clarity, and cut of gem diamonds are based. Marcel Tolkowsky studied brilliants fashioned in London and 1919 published his theoretical work *Diamond Design*, describing how the finest brilliance and dispersion were attained in such cuts. While ad-

mitting that slight deviations were acceptable, he calculated specific proportions and found that they were close to the finest on the market in London. Since then his design has been modified: the culet, clearly visible in Tolkowsky's original version, is now omitted; pavilion facets are longer and narrower; and the table is larger (Tolkowsky listed this as a variant). This modernized version is known in the United States as the American ideal cut and in Europe as the Tolkowsky cut. However, it is seldom produced, mainly because of the prohibitive cost and the ever-increasing popular prejudice in favor of maximum brilliance, at the expense of fire, in brilliants. These fashionable contemporary diamonds may be said to have "practical proportions," but the old name for them is spread cut, or overspread. In their proportions, the old spread table or mirror cut can be seen once more.

The beauty of a given diamond is of major importance in the evaluation of the quality of cut. It is determined by the combination of the light effects—fire, brilliance, and scintillation—for which the American ideal cut provides the mathematically best-balanced criterion. Today, American diamond experts cite the Scan.D.N. standard cut as equally good and even superior in that it is much less expensive to fashion from normal rough.

Proportions, however, are only one part of the problem. Lack of symmetry alone may substantially reduce the quality of a diamond, since it causes disturbances in the light effects. The words of an author of about 1900 still bear repeating: "A well-cut diamond lights up almost equally all over, even when viewed from different distances and in different positions." Unfortunately, no diamond certificate describes the combined light effects, and the consumer must therefore consult his local expert jeweler in order to find out if a particular diamond compares in make with what can reasonably be requested.

It is evident, then, that the make is of major importance both for the beauty and for the price of a diamond.

 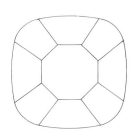 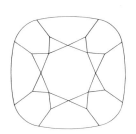 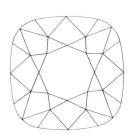

Successive steps in fashioning a rhombic dodecahedron into a Baroque brilliant. *Herbert Tillander.*

The Modern Brilliant Cut

Today, as in the past, the diamond cutter's task is to achieve the finest result, or to get the best economic return combined with maximum beauty, from the stone he is cutting. His first job is to make a close, detailed study of the crystal, or portion of a crystal, that he is to transform into a fashioned gem. On the basis of that examination he will decide what steps he must take to achieve his objective. This inspection reveals vital information on the structure of the crystal; without this information he could not usefully start work. Analyzing small stones is fairly straightforward. Larger stones demand closer attention, which is justified by their greater value.

In order to locate inclusions within the stone, the diamond cutter polishes a small facet of the

pear to be where they are not. Properly oriented windows eliminate this problem.

Thus, one of the main purposes of the initial inspection is to find the exact location of inclusions, which will largely determine the most suitable shape to be cut from the rough stone. It may be best to fashion it into a single stone, or the cutter may decide that dividing the rough into several separate pieces would be more advantageous. The problems at this stage are extremely subtle: weight, clarity, and color must all be taken into account, along with other commercial considerations. The table on page 283 in the appendix will help to clarify the complex—and exciting—situation of the diamond cutter confronted with a valuable rough stone.

Above: Opening a "window" in a diamond to examine the interior. *Photo Guy Philippart de Foy, Brussels.*

Center left: Marking a stone with India ink to indicate where it should be cleaved. *Photo Guy Philippart de Foy, Brussels.*

Left: Lazare Kaplan, a master cleaver and cutter with an international reputation, preparing to cleave a diamond. Below: Positioning the blade in the kerf; the cleaved stone. *Photos Dunning Inc., New York.*

stone, creating a little "window" that will give him a view of the stone's interior, allowing him to inspect it at leisure. This operation, performed on the wheel, is necessitated by one of the diamond's special properties—the ability to "bend" light as it enters or leaves the crystal. This property is responsible for the diamond's great brilliance, for it allows the properly cut diamond to return light up to the viewer's eye. However, it also creates a problem for the cutter by causing inclusions to ap-

It is true that a small inclusion in a fashioned diamond will reduce the value of the stone, but it is also true that a large stone is rarer and therefore worth more than a small one. However, these statements are relative: the value of a gem diamond is not strictly proportional to its weight. At the same time, it must be borne in mind that weight loss during cutting can be considerable. How much weight is lost depends, of course, on the final shape. With the brilliant cut, weight loss may be 60 percent or more, which means that a rough stone of 2.5 carats may end up as a brilliant of only about 1 carat or even less. There is, therefore, an understandable temptation to remove only the minimum amount from the stone. It is always possible to plan to create two quite different gems from the same rough stone: a relatively small but perfectly shaped diamond, or one that is larger but less well proportioned and finished and, therefore, less beautiful. It is basically a decision between emphasizing beauty and emphasizing size. Choosing between the two is far from easy, and what might be called the "emotional" value of the diamond becomes a significant factor: two dealers may

mercial chain. As a rule, cutting factories sell their fashioned diamonds to retail jewelers, who are the only ones in direct contact with the consumer. In the final analysis, the aim is to create a gem that will be in highest demand and will bring the highest possible price, and the diamond cutter, the sole judge, chooses and fashions his stones with this goal in mind. Standards change, of course, according to changing tastes and market demand.

When the examination of the stone, which in some cases may take weeks, is completed, the diamond is marked with India ink to show the best cleavage plane, if it is to be cleaved, or to indicate where it should be sawn. There

Sawing. Whereas a stone is cleaved in the direction of the "grain," sawing is done against the grain. Modern machines have a phosphor bronze disc that rotates at about 5,500 rpm. *Photo Guy Philippart de Foy, Brussels.*

view the same rough stone in entirely different ways, each one honestly convinced that his own judgment is correct.

When very large or otherwise extraordinary stones are involved, cutters sometimes make models in lead, plaster, or plastic in order to experiment with various plans before beginning cutting. This, however, is the exception rather than the rule. Cutters buy their rough stones with no knowledge of the identity of the customers who form the last link in the com-

are four cleaving directions and nine sawing directions. In a large and complicated stone, the possible combinations of these are almost infinite, and it takes a lot of exacting work and great imagination to make the best choice. Diamond marking is a job that requires a great deal of skill and expertise, and outstanding stones are usually marked by the most experienced man available. Once the stone has been marked, the preparations are complete. The fashioning of the diamond can begin.

Bruting imparts the desired roundness. *Photo Guy Philippart de Foy, Brussels.*

The facets are checked at frequent intervals. *Photo Guy Philippart de Foy, Brussels.*

Modern Fashioning Techniques

Cleaving and sawing are quite different operations, but both have the same aim—to reduce the rough in such a way that its maximum potential as a gem will be realized. The main purpose of both processes is to divide inclusions or flaws so that the resulting parts will be "clean." As explained in the preceding chapter, the difference between cleaving and sawing is that the former follows one of the four planes of cleavage that every crystal possesses, regardless of its shape, while sawing must be done in directions other than that of the cleavage planes.

Cleaving has always been done in the same way. Among the cleaver's tools is a special "cleaver's stick" about 10 inches (25 cm) long. The diamond to be cleaved is fixed to the end of this stick with a special cement, something like sealing wax, the composition of which varies according to individual preference. Other, sharp-edged, diamonds, also held at the end of a stick, are rubbed against the mark that indicates where the stone will be cleaved, making a small notch or kerf. This is done over a special box or tray that catches the precious diamond dust as it falls. As the kerf gets deeper, successively sharper-edged diamonds are used. When the kerf is finally deep enough, the cleaver, holding the diamond upright, sets the stick in a hole in a lead block on his workbench. He then carefully sets a rectangular, square-edged steel blade in the kerf. With a small mallet, he gives the back of the blade a sharp tap, and the diamond splits very smoothly in two along the cleavage plane. This may appear to be a very simple operation, but in fact it demands great experience, a sharp eye, a steady hand, and strong nerves. The slightest error could ruin the stone forever and, in a large stone, cost a fortune. When very valuable stones are to be cleaved they are sometimes sent thousands of miles to an acknowledged master of the craft.

Since the mechanical, toothless, rotating saw was introduced into diamond workshops around the turn of the century, cleaving has gradually been replaced by *sawing*. (Cleaving, of course, remains an important operation—

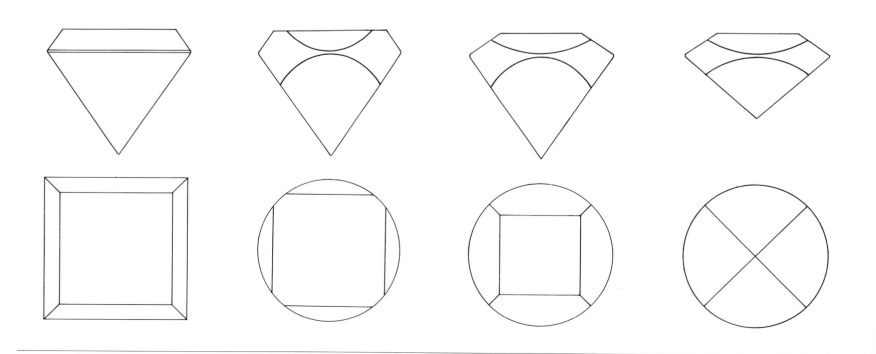

Faceting four diamonds simultaneously. The scaife revolves at about 3,000 rpm and diamond paste is applied to it frequently, sometimes with the thumb. The diamonds are held in clamps, and the mechanical dops are adjustable, so that several facets can be ground consecutively without the necessity of removing the diamond each time. *Photo Michel Plassart, Paris.*

Stages in fashioning a modern brilliant from an octahedral crystal that has first been sawn. *Herbert Tillander.*

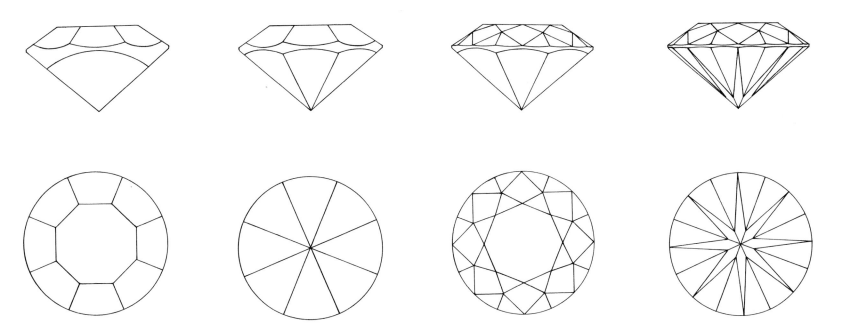

The principal diamond cuts (left to right and top to bottom): emerald, round brilliant, pear-shaped brilliant or pendeloque, marquise or navette, baguette, oval brilliant, heart-shaped brilliant. *Photo Michel Plassart, Paris.*

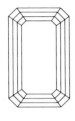

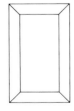

some goods can be cut only by cleaving.) The great majority of stones are sawn in the cubic direction, which results in the most efficiently shaped segments. The stones may be divided in several directions in order to create a more workable shape or, for example, to obtain two brilliants from a single octahedron. The blade of modern sawing machines is a phosphor bronze disc about 4 inches (10 cm) in diameter, which rotates at between 4,500 and 6,500 revolutions per minute. Two steel discs hold it rigidly in a vertical position, and the sawing edge is coated at intervals with a paste made from an olive-oil and diamond-dust base. The diamond is held by clawlike clamps at the end of a mechanical arm; its position in relation to the disc, as well as the pressure exerted, can be adjusted. Sawing is a slow process: the rotating disc cuts into the diamond at the approximate rate of only one-twentieth of an inch (1 mm) per hour.

Formerly, sawing was done right in diamond-cutting workshops; now it is an entirely separate operation. There can be as many as one hundred mechanical saws in a sawing factory, usually mounted in rows so that one craftsman can comfortably supervise a dozen or so machines at once. It takes a very long time to saw through even a relatively small diamond, and each machine must be given fairly frequent attention. The diamonds must be inspected at regular intervals with a loupe, the abrasive paste must be reapplied to the cutting edge, and worn-out discs must eventually be replaced.

Nowadays the *bruting* or *girdling* process is done on small lathes like those used in precision engineering or, indeed, by jewelers. Unless the diamond to be bruted is a rough of a shape that does not require preliminary cleaving or sawing, it is first worked on by the cleaver or sawyer. In preparation for bruting, the diamond is cemented onto a conical dop, or stick, which is mounted on the lathe and rotated at high speed. A second rough diamond, cemented onto a hand-held dop, is placed against it as it spins and is held there until the desired roundness is achieved. In fact both diamonds are being bruted at the same time: when the first one is ready, the second replaces it on the lathe, a third stone is held against it, and the process is repeated. Any diamond dust produced during bruting is gathered in a strategically placed dish. The bruting lathe may be used again at a later stage to perfect the roundness of the gem.

The tools used in *faceting* have changed very little over the past few centuries. Considerable improvements have been made in efficiency, but the principles remain the same. The main piece of equipment is of course the grinding wheel or scaife, a cast-iron disc about 12 inches (30 cm) in diameter and about an inch (2–3 cm) thick. It is normally used by one craftsman at a time, though it can accommodate two people sitting opposite each other, and in the labor-intensive cutting shops of India as many as five or six workers may sit side by side around the same scaife. The wheel turns at about 3,000 revolutions per minute, and an abrasive paste of olive oil and diamond dust is applied to its surface at frequent intervals. The bruted diamonds are held in clamps attached to a wooden arm, or tang. Their position against the scaife can be adjusted so that several facets can be ground consecutively without remounting the diamond each time. As a general rule, the outer part of the scaife is used for grinding, the inner part for smoothing or polishing. In spite of the use of diamond dust, the surface of the scaife soon shows signs of wear. After about a week's use, scratches begin to appear

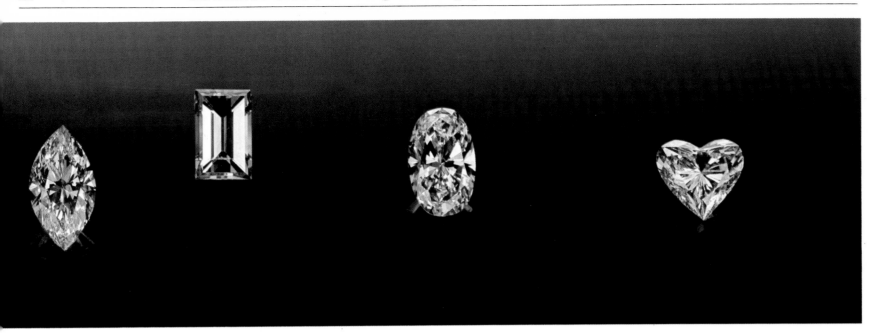

and the wheel has to be rescoured. It can be reused many times until it becomes too thin.

Faceting

Since the brilliant is by far the most popular cut today, the steps by which it is achieved should be described in some detail. Applying fifty-eight facets on a stone that may be minuscule is no easy task, and faceting is a job for the skilled elite.

When the table has been ground and checked, the first facet can be applied on the crown. The placement of this first crown facet is determined by the grain of the stone. It must be positioned with the utmost precision, for the entire symmetry of the finished brilliant depends on it. The remaining fifteen facets are then applied in the following order: three on the crown, so that they form directly opposing pairs in relation to the first crown facet; four on the pavilion, again directly opposite each other, two by two; four more on the crown; and four on the pavilion, similarly in opposition to each other (see the drawings on pages 216–17). Before further faceting is done, the stone is returned to the bruter, who corrects the girdle and the roundness of the stone. It is then returned to the wheel, where the facets already ground are polished to exactly the right size and then smoothed.

Forty smaller facets remain to be applied, twenty-four on the crown and sixteen on the pavilion. The grinding of these facets is called brillianteering and is usually performed by a different craftsman. One of the trickier parts of this delicate work is to get the facet junctions of four or five facets to meet in exact points, while at the same time keeping perfect symmetry all around the stone. Great delicacy of touch as well as patience are required.

Although so-called automatic machines are used in several larger workshops today, the word "automatic" should not be misunderstood. There is no way a rough diamond can be put in at one end of a machine and, with the touch of a button, emerge as a fully finished gem at the other end. The machine consists of an ordinary scaife with four arms around it. The arms end in clamps that pivot automatically as soon as each facet has been ground and polished. Even with this equipment, a master cutter must keep constant watch and inspect each stone with a loupe. This type of equipment is used primarily on smaller stones, usually less than one-fifth of a carat.

Drilling and Sawing by Laser

Since the earliest days of diamond fashioning, it has been possible to cut diamonds only by using other diamonds, and only in certain "soft" directions. Recent technological advances, however, have changed the situation somewhat.

Recently, lasers, originally used to drill holes in industrial diamonds for wire drawing, have been used to drill down colored or opaque inclusions in gem diamonds. The inclusion is located by the use of cross hairs in a microscope, and then a thin laser beam drills a fine hole down to the inclusion along the same line of sight. The intense light of the laser heats the diamond and turns it to graphite. (Since this is done by heating, hardness is not a factor, and the diamond can be drilled in any direction.) A strong chemical oxidizer is then forced under great pressure through the laser hole into the inclusion. The inclusion dissolves and becomes transparent and less visible; the diamond, therefore, becomes more attractive and more valuable.

When parallel holes are drilled, the diamond can be sawn by laser, and this is possible in

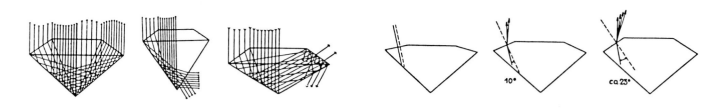

Diagrams illustrating the laws of refraction and reflection that explain the brilliance of a diamond. When the proportions are perfect, all light entering the stone is reflected by the table or the facets of the crown. If the pavilion is too deep or too shallow, light rays escape through the facets of the pavilion and are "lost" to the eye viewing the stone from above. Brilliance depends largely on the angle of the facets of the pavilion, "fire" on the angle of the facets of the crown.

any direction and in any size diamond. This has become a useful technique for the diamond cutter.

Standards of Appreciation

Of the four criteria used in determining the value of a diamond, that of the make, or cut, is not the least important. Naturally, there can be no dispute about the weight of a diamond, and as we shall see in the following chapter, the standards relating to clarity and color are becoming so rigid that there is not much room for argument in those areas, either. But when it comes to assessing the type or quality of cut, there is more scope for subjective opinions. In this area, fashion has always played a significant role, for popular taste throughout the ages has favored different types of cuts at different times and in different places. Today the round brilliant holds undisputed sway, and fancy cuts are less appreciated. This is not surprising, considering that most fancy cuts are made from roughs that, because of their shape, would have lost a great deal more weight if they had been brilliant-cut. Therefore, modified brilliant-cut diamonds (marquise, pear, heart, oval, and so on) are also less appreciated than round brilliants, which are the most highly prized of all. Modified brilliant cuts are, however, considered superior to the step cuts (emerald, square, baguette), which do not exhibit as much brilliance.

The round brilliant owes its preeminence not so much to its shape, perfect though it is, as to its outstanding light-reflecting ability, unequaled in any other cut, which permits it, if perfectly fashioned, to display an unsurpassed combination of brilliance and fire. Several centuries of labor by highly skilled and experienced diamond workers, whose pursuit of perfection led to the gradual refinement of the proportions of the round brilliant, have resulted in precise standards for the "geometry" of the cut. But what was true yesterday is no less true today—an ideal cut is a rarity. The combined qualities of brilliance, fire, luster, and scintillation can be considered ideal only if the symmetry and dimensions of the crown, table, pavilion, facets, girdle, and culet all adhere to strict standards.

However, since individual conceptions vary,

there has never been total international agreement as to what those standards are. The customer buying a diamond in a jeweler's shop depends on the jeweler's expert advice, especially on how greater weight may adversely affect the beauty or light effects of a diamond. The customer cannot interpret the technical documents and certificates issued by laboratories. These refer specifically to weight, color, and clarity; the figures given for proportion, however, mention the quality of the cut only summarily and therefore provide no direct guide to the beauty of the stone.

The physical principles governing the phenomenon of brilliance are fairly simple and are based on well-known laws of refraction and reflection. A perfectly proportioned diamond catches the maximum amount of light through the crown and returns it to the viewer only after it has been reflected several times inside the stone. As shown in the sketch above, any serious error in proportioning of the pavilion or the crown leads to some loss of brilliance and fire. However, minor proportional faults have less bearing on the beauty and harmony of the effects of light than imperfect symmetry. A really poor cut is usually the result of an attempt to retain too much of the original stone. It has always been accepted that quality of cut must be sacrificed to some extent to preserve size or weight.

It is now easier than ever to recognize the quality of a cut. Apart from having a gem checked by specialized laboratories such as that of the Diamond High Council of Antwerp (see page 236) or that of the Gemological Institute of America, there are several ways in which a jeweler can obtain advice on behalf of his customer. Special organizations throughout the world offer courses in diamond grading, and manuals are published to assist the jeweler in classifying a stone himself or in interpreting the laboratory certificates issued for it. The jeweler who takes advantage of these resources is well equipped to assume the responsibility of selling valuable gems.

People are becoming increasingly conscious of the beauty of well-cut stones. Such awareness should be encouraged by diamond cutters, who deserve the appreciation of the public for the splendid work they do.

Clarity and Color

The fundamental attributes that distinguish precious stones from all other minerals are beauty, rarity, and durability. The diamond possesses all three of these cardinal virtues to an exceptional degree—that is why it is the most precious of precious stones. Thanks to its extraordinary hardness, a diamond will last and retain its fashioned form far longer than any other gem; virtually nothing can mar the precision of its contours or dull the sharpness

Inclusion of two small olivine crystals in a parallel position inside a cut diamond. Enlargement × 20. *Photo Eduard Gübelin, Lucerne.*

Ruby-tinted pyrope (alumino-ferrous garnet), rich in chrome. The presence of chrome indicates that the mother rock of the diamond with the pyrope inclusion resulted from metamorphic processes at great depths. Enlargement × 50. *Photo Eduard Gübelin, Lucerne.*

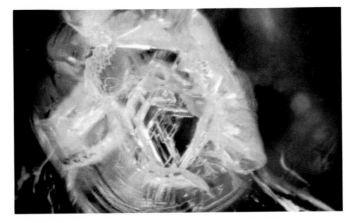

Two small chromiferous diopside crystals, whose allomorphic crystallization assumes that of the diamond in which they are included. Enlargement × 30. *Photo Eduard Gübelin, Lucerne.*

of its edges. Although it is by no means the scarcest mineral on earth, the strict standards regarding clarity and color to which the diamond must conform to be selected for jewelry unquestionably give it the quality of rarity. As for its beauty, that depends not only on its remarkable optical qualities (its adamantine luster and high refractive index and power of dispersion, which are responsible for the scintillating fire of a cut diamond), but also on its incomparable limpidity and its marvelous colors—"white," black, and all the colors of the spectrum from red to violet. No other gem can boast of so many desirable properties, and therefore the diamond is graded according to strict criteria, particularly in the areas of color and clarity. Though the full beauty of a diamond is revealed only by a perfect cut, its value is nevertheless largely determined by its clarity and color. They are the factors considered when rough diamonds are sorted and the vital decision regarding their future is made—whether they will become simple industrial stones, or marvelous jewels giving pleasure to countless future generations and, perhaps, representing a prime financial security as well.

The study of the clarity, or purity, and the color of diamonds is an especially rewarding subject in gemology. It reveals the close association between the king of precious stones and the history of our planet, making the diamond a highly valuable source of geological information.

Clarity and Inclusions

The degree of clarity is one of the essential factors in the evaluation of a diamond. Perfect clarity means that no inclusions—no internal features—are discernible when the stone is examined under a 10× lens corrected for chromatic and spherical aberration. Inclusions that can be detected only under greater magnification are disregarded. Flaws that are visible under a 10× lens reduce the value of the diamond; just how much the value is reduced depends on the size and number of the inclusions, their influence on optical properties, their degree of visibility or position in the crystal, and their potential effect on the firmness (which may be weakened by fractures) of the diamond. Obviously, inclusions that are

Black grains of chromite in a cut diamond. Like all other chromiferous inclusions, they indicate formation at great depth in the earth's crust. Enlargement × 20. *Photo Eduard Gübelin, Lucerne.*

Iron-rich, grayish-green, omphacitic diopside below the table of a brilliant-cut diamond. Guest and host crystal originated in an eclogite. Enlargement × 40. *Photo Eduard Gübelin, Lucerne.*

Almandines (alumino-ferrous garnets) and grossularites (alumino-calcic garnets) inside a cut diamond. Ferrous garnets indicate an eclogitic mother rock. Enlargement × 35. *Photo Eduard Gübelin, Lucerne.*

easily visible count more than those that are barely discernible, and colored mineral inclusions count more than inclusions of the same size that are colorless and transparent. Colored inclusions as well as "clouds" and cracks have a deleterious effect on optical properties, diminishing brilliance. Obviously, too, inclusions situated in the heart of the cut stone, directly under the table, are more significant than those under the facets of the crown or close to the girdle, which are less visible. Inclusions that are repeated through reflection by neighboring facets are likewise more serious. Finally, the presence of cracks or cleavages usually leads to lower grading than tiny crystalline inclusions or cloudiness, for cracks may be enlarged by some physical mishap such as a fall, a blow, or a sharp change in temperature, and may even cause the diamond to fracture.

In the eye of the professional dealer or dia-

mond cutter, the internal flaws of a diamond merely diminish its beauty and its value, but the gemologist may judge them differently. To him, the inclusions are interesting, because they render each stone unique. This view is really the more justified one, since diamonds that show perfect clarity under a 10× lens are extremely uncommon, far rarer than most people imagine. It would be absurd to exclude from the trade or from jewelry making diamonds that happen to contain minute flaws or impurities. It can even be said that, in a sense, an inclusion increases the worth of a diamond by giving it individuality, setting it apart from millions of others. However, anyone purchasing a diamond with an eye to its investment value would be wise to choose one that is "loupe-clean" or flawless. This is the category that has shown the steepest rise in value over the years.

The Gemologist's View of Inclusions

Diamonds containing flaws or inclusions have a lower value because they are less rare. Nevertheless, it would be wrong to dismiss all inclusions as simple defects lodged in the heart of a high-priced stone. The gemologist sees them as eloquent witnesses of the diamond's mysterious creation, as incontrovertible signs of its authenticity, and indeed, depending on their type and shape, as independent works of nature's art.

The process by which the diamond was formed in the inaccessible interior of the earth millions of years ago is illuminated by the character of its inclusions, and the number and variety of "guest" minerals the inclusions represent suggest a highly complex evolution. Because it is inert, the diamond has given the crystalline inclusions it shelters in its adamantine heart perfect protection from external influences. As a result, the inclusions have retained, unaltered, their original chemical composition and thus provide accurate information on the physical and chemical conditions prevailing at the time of the diamond's crystallization. The external appearance and evident perfection of these crystals indicate that diamonds grew in an ultramafic, carbon-rich silicate melt during its solidification. A quantitative analysis of the principal chemical elements of the inclusions suggests that they crystallized from a picritic magma, rich in water and carbon dioxide, in the presence of immiscible iron, nickel, and copper sulphites. In the course of this highly reactive phase, while the rocks themselves were undergoing several changes and before the intrusion of kimberlite in the earth's crust, the diamond and its guest minerals crystallized. Through these immense tectonic reactions in the magma, the diamond

A crystal of rutile, prismatic in form, included below the girdle of a cut diamond. Rutile is a secondary mineral typical of eclogitic rocks. Enlargement × 25. *Photo Eduard Gübelin, Lucerne.*

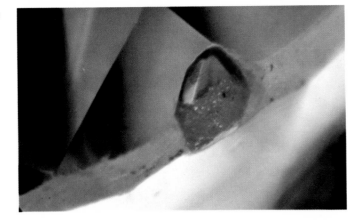

A diamond crystal with black marks that have the appearance of combined crystals, included in a younger diamond. Enlargement × 32. *Photo Eduard Gübelin, Lucerne.*

A slightly distorted octahedral diamond with a broken lower point. This type of inclusion proves that diamonds are formed over many generations. Enlargement × 35. *Photo Eduard Gübelin, Lucerne.*

was formed along with such inclusions as olivine, garnet, chromite, diopside, enstatite, rutile, cyanite, ilmenite, coesite, graphite, and various sulphides. The favorable conditions in which the diamond crystallized enabled it to grow more rapidly than its associates, and they became integrated in the diamond in minute particles before they could achieve an independent existence. The complex occurrences at its birth left additional traces in the developing crystal, in the form of planes of growth, and of tension cracks often lined with thin films of pyrrhotite or graphite. The concurring chemical composition of the external with the internal paragenesis (mineral association) of the diamond inspires the conclusion that the diamond crystallized during the metamorphism mentioned above. On the other hand, the different chemistry between the guest minerals in the diamond and the mineral components of the kimberlite indicates that the dia-

mond was not formed in the kimberlite—at least not during its later stages (that is, during its ascent and volcanic eruption through the earth's crust). The diamond, though itself composed of pure carbon, forever retains within its body evidence of its formation in the earth's mantle, each feature being unique and unrepeatable. Because of these characteristics, each individual diamond may at any time be recognized and reidentified.

Inclusions in diamonds have aroused man's curiosity for a long time, though the first written reference to them occurs only in the seventeenth century. The diarist John Evelyn reported in 1645 that he had found "a pretty ruby inside a diamond" (the "ruby" was undoubtedly a garnet). In 1676 Jean-Baptiste Tavernier mentioned the presence of "black marks and knots" in Indian diamonds. Since then much research has been done, and experts have reached general agreement on the distinctions between cleavage cracks (or "feathers"), mineral inclusions (often of one precious stone in another), structural phenomena ("clouds," distortions, and so on), irregular striations caused by parallel growth lines, and twin planes.

To the gemologist, mineral inclusions—the mysterious phenomena of crystals within crystals—are the most interesting type. They exhibit an extraordinary variety of forms and colors. Any shape is possible, from perfectly regular, ideal crystals to elongated, distorted, rounded, flattened, as well as club- or onion-shaped resorbed or corroded crystals. This diversity is explained by their origin—specifically, by the time they were formed in relation to the crystallization of the host diamond: before, during, or after development of the diamond crystal. So-called protogenetic inclusions—those that formed before the crystallization of the diamond—include iron sulphides (pyrrhotite), but the most common examples are of diamond itself, small diamonds enclosed by another crystal that developed later and grew larger. Syngenetic inclusions—those that formed simultaneously with the host gem—occur when the embracing crystal grows faster than the other. They appear to be the most common. As in the first category, diamond itself is a frequent syngenetic inclusion. The third type, epigenetic inclusions, which penetrated the host diamond after it crystallized, entered through cracks or cleavages. In a cut brilliant, they are usually eliminated.

The minerals most often found as inclusions in diamonds have been listed above. A few of them, notably garnet and chrome-diopsides, can be identified by their characteristic color, but the majority are either black or colorless. The presence of olivine and chromiferous min-

A loupe-clean diamond, which displays no inclusions or internal blemishes and corresponds to the highest degree of clarity—internally flawless. *Photo Eduard Gübelin, Lucerne.*

The photomicrographs on this page and the next conform to the international rules for judging the clarity of diamonds and were taken at 10× magnification.

vvs clarity grading: very, very small inclusions. Left: Pinpoints of light color included deep inside the stone. Right: A minuscule colored crystal under the table. *Photo Eduard Gübelin, Lucerne.*

vs clarity grading: very small inclusions. Left: A line of minute dots and a very small crystal under the table. Right: A very slight crack under the girdle. *Photo Eduard Gübelin, Lucerne.*

si clarity grading:
small inclusions.
Left: Several small crystals
below the table and the facets
of the crown, invisible to the
naked eye. Right: Several
small crystals below the table,
invisible to the naked eye.
*Photo Eduard Gübelin,
Lucerne.*

p1 clarity grading:
inclusions hardly discernible
to the naked eye,
which do not affect brilliance.
Left: Several inclusions
below the table and the crown
facets. Right: Cracks
under the table and the
facets. *Photo Eduard
Gübelin, Lucerne.*

p2 clarity grading:
larger and/or more numerous
inclusions, which slightly
diminish brilliance.
Left: A large group of cracks
or feathers, reflected in the
opposite facets and visible to
the naked eye. Right: A large
black inclusion below the
crown and the table, visible to
the naked eye. *Photo Eduard
Gübelin, Lucerne.*

p3 clarity grading:
large and/or numerous
inclusions visible to
the naked eye, diminishing
brilliance.
Left: Numerous cracks, brown
marks, and black spots
distributed throughout the
diamond, considerably
diminishing brilliance. Right:
Numerous inclusions,
light-colored cracks, and black
marks, considerably
diminishing brilliance. *Photo
Eduard Gübelin, Lucerne.*

erals (garnet, pyrope, diopside, enstatite, and chromite) proves that the diamond was formed from an ultramafic mother rock far below the earth's crust. Sodium, present in nearly all garnet inclusions, testifies to formation under very high pressure, and so does coesite, a variety of quartz formed in similar conditions. That a rapid cooling occurred after the formation of diamond crystals is confirmed by the presence of a relatively large nickel content in inclusions of pyrrhotite.

These are just a few of the signs from which the conditions prevailing during the birth of diamond may be inferred, clues pointing toward a solution of some of nature's deepest mysteries.

The Jeweler's View of Inclusions

What delights and fascinates the gemologist and the research scientist is often irritating to the diamond dealer and to the jeweler and his customers, for whom inclusions are simply defects likely to reduce the quality and value of an extremely valuable object. That is why the question of clarity is so important. International standards have been established for the commercial classification of clarity. Diamonds with the highest degree of clarity are described as "loupe-clean": they reveal no internal peculiarities under 10× magnification. In the United States and some other countries the term is "internally flawless," usually abbreviated **if.** Diamonds displaying very, very

small inclusions only just detectable with a 10× loupe are classed as **vvs;** this group may also comprise stones with very fine cracks or minute "fringes" (radial cracks from the girdle inward, a so-called bearded girdle). As in the highest category, the inclusions must be transparent and all but colorless. Diamonds with this degree of clarity or purity (the word preferred by the CIBJO) are of great value; the features mentioned are of course totally invisible to the naked eye. In **vs** diamonds (very small inclusions), the inclusions, still difficult to see even with a 10× lens, must also be light in color. Diamonds in this category are still very valuable, especially if their color is good. The next category is **si** (small inclusions), in which inclusions are relatively easy to find under 10× magnification; if they are situated under the table they must be light in color. They must, however, not be visible to the naked eye through the crown. Within this category are diamonds with inclusions that are few enough or isolated enough to be examined and analyzed individually.

All diamonds with blemishes more or less visible to the naked eye are classified as **piqué,** subdivided into **first, second,** and **third piqué.** In a diamond classed as **p1** (first piqué), the inclusions, though discernible, must be difficult to see with the naked eye when viewed through the crown and should not reduce the brilliance of the stone. In **p2** diamonds, the inclusions are either more numerous or relatively large; they can easily be seen with the naked eye through the crown and generally have a slightly deleterious effect on brilliance. In **p3** diamonds the inclusions are large, are easily seen when viewed through the crown, and, by their size or number, seriously impair brilliance. Diamonds with inclusions that threaten to fracture them are also classed as p3.

The table shown here, worked out by a joint committee drawn from international associations of the diamond trade, summarizes and defines the different degrees of clarity.

The highly discriminate nature of the categories of clarity should be emphasized; visibility under 10× magnification is a particularly exacting criterion. The minuscule inclusions of the vvs and vs categories have no effect on the beauty of the diamond, and even in a brilliant classified as si, the inclusions have no influence at all on the appearance of the stone, as they are invisible to the naked eye.

Colors of the Diamond

Whatever the importance of the clarity of the gem diamond—and it is considerable—the color of the stone is an even more vital factor. The diamond is not the only colorless precious stone; rock crystal shares this attribute. But the

Degrees of Clarity		The clarity of a diamond is determined under a 10× lens, corrected for chromatic and spherical aberration, under normalized light, by an experienced professional.
CIBJO Grade	**GIA Grade**	**Criteria for Grading**
Flawless	Flawless	Examination with a 10× lens reveals absolute transparency and no inclusion or external blemish.
vvs	vvs$_1$ vvs$_2$	Very, very small inclusion(s), very difficult to see with a 10× lens.
vs	vs$_1$ vs$_2$	Very small inclusion(s), fairly difficult to see with a 10× lens.
si	si$_1$ si$_2$	Small inclusion(s), easily visible with a 10× lens, but not visible to the naked eye when viewed through the crown.
p1	I$_1$	Inclusion(s) hardly discernible to the naked eye through the crown, not affecting brilliance.
p2	I$_2$	Larger and/or more numerous inclusion(s), easily visible to the naked eye through the crown and slightly diminishing brilliance.
p3	I$_3$	Large and/or numerous inclusion(s), very easily visible to the naked eye and diminishing brilliance.

Rough diamonds selected for their diversity of color, with some cut diamonds in the center. Muséum national d'Histoire naturelle, Paris. *Photo Guy Philippart de Foy, Brussels.*

The diagram on page 192 shows how each carbon atom occupies the center of a tetrahedron formed by the four closest atoms in the diamond's cubic lattice. Here, several tetrahedrons are grouped together (for the sake of simplicity, not all the tetrahedrons possible are shown). The arrows indicate the position in the crystalline lattice of the nitrogen atoms responsible for yellow coloring.

diamond is infinitely superior not only because of its hardness but also because it possesses unparalleled brilliance and fire, displaying all the colors of the rainbow—qualities that rock crystal, whose vitreous luster is not particularly attractive, cannot equal. The diamond is a symbol of immaculate colorlessness to such a great extent that the average layman is completely unaware of the fact that it is found in a great variety of colors.

Before examining in some detail the chemistry of the color of diamonds, those gems that are apparently colorless must first be discussed. In gemologists' jargon, they are known as "Cape" diamonds, a reference to the stones from the Cape province in South Africa, most of which are in fact slightly yellowish rather than totally colorless or "white." Just as a loupe-clean diamond may be called "optically pure," one might suppose that a diamond described as colorless is "chemically pure"—that is, composed exclusively of carbon. In reality, this is seldom true, for absolute chemical purity is extremely rare. Most diamonds used in jewelry contain slight traces of elements other than carbon, and it is some of these substances that give them their color. The varying yellowish shades of the Cape series are caused by the presence of nitrogen. Since the shades can range from pure white to a fairly obvious yellow coloring, an international scale has been established. This is printed on page 228, in three languages, together with the corresponding scale of the Gemological Institute of America and the traditional color-grading terms still often used informally in the trade.

The table is sufficiently explicit to require no further comment. The greatest value, obviously, is given to "exceptional white" stones, and from there downward the yellowish tint becomes stronger and the value declines. A layman looking at a stone in the category "tinted color[4]" would recognize the yellowish shade without difficulty, but even here, at the bottom of the scale, it is still a comparatively faint tint rather than a definite yellow. The new international scale of colors evolved from consultation among professional associations throughout the world, and its use became mandatory in 1978.

The traditional terms, listed in the third column of the table, refer to the diamonds' origins; some of them were derived from the names of old mines. The term *River* described a color said to be "blue white," *Top Wesselton* a "pure white," *Wesselton* a "white," *Top Crystal* a "slightly tinted white," *Crystal* a "tinted white," *Top Cape* a "slightly yellowish" diamond, *Cape* a "yellowish" color, *Low Cape* or *Light Yellow* a "faint yellow," and so on. Besides those listed here, there were a number of other terms in use as well. The description "blue white" has always been a source of confusion: the diamonds so described were in fact never blue, but colorless. What gave them their apparent bluish hue was the well-known phenomenon of fluorescence, caused by the ultraviolet rays of the sun. The term *Jager* (from the Jagersfontein mine) is still sometimes used to denote white diamonds with a strong blue fluorescence. The name *Premier* is occasionally applied to diamonds with blue fluorescence but a yellow tint.

The perception of color is a subjective matter, so how is it possible to determine precisely the infinitesimally subtle shades of difference in the color of diamonds? The quality of the cut is measurable, and clarity can be judged according to fairly exact standards with a lens, but how can these delicate tints be judged? They may be determined by an electronic color-measuring instrument, or they may be graded by comparison with the colors of sample diamonds used as standards. The international scale introduced in 1978 represents a considerable advance over earlier dissensions. It is based on a range of Master Diamonds selected by mutual agreement as standards. A diamond to be appraised is compared with the models and placed in the category of the diamond closest to it. The examination must be done in normalized artificial light equivalent to northern or southern daylight (excluding direct sunlight) in the northern or southern hemisphere, respectively.

The Origin of Diamond Colors

As everyone knows, ordinary white light,

International Scale of Colors			GIA	Traditional Terms
exceptional white[+]	blanc exceptionnel[+]	hochfeines Weiss[+]	D	River
exceptional white	blanc exceptionnel	hochfeines Weiss	E	
rare white[+]	blanc extra[+]	feines Weiss[+]	F	Top Wesselton
rare white	blanc extra	feines Weiss	G	
white	blanc	Weiss	H	Wesselton
slightly tinted white	blanc nuancé	leicht getöntes Weiss	I	Top Crystal
			J	
tinted white	légèrement teinté	getöntes Weiss	K	Crystal
			L	
tinted color[1]	couleur teintée[1]	getönt[1]	M	Top Cape
			N	
tinted color[2]	couleur teintée[2]	getönt[2]	O	Cape
			P	
tinted color[3]	couleur teintée[3]	getönt[3]	Q	Low Cape (or Light Yellow)
			R	
tinted color[4]	couleur teintée[4]	getönt[4]	S–Z	Yellowish to Yellow

Top: Some "fancy" diamonds, showing the variation in shade possible for each color. From left to right, pink, yellow, blue, brown, and green diamonds. Above: A black diamond. *Photos Claude Mercier, Geneva.*

whether natural or artificial, is a mixture of the colors of the solar spectrum, corresponding to strictly defined wavelengths (between 400 and 700 nanometers). A diamond that is chemically pure does not alter white light; that is, it absorbs none of the waves passing through it and transmits the same light it receives. Where, then, do the colors come from? For a long time the mystery remained unsolved, but eventually it was discovered that most of the colors could be traced to "impurities," called "allochromatics," which are dispersed throughout the diamond crystal lattice. Alternatively, these gorgeous colors can be due to the presence of minute traces of a chemically alien element.

And in fact, if diamonds of the Cape series (which includes not only colorless stones but also very pale yellow ones, even saturated yellows) are submitted to spectroscopic analysis, they all display characteristic absorption spectra, with bands in the blue region at 390, 401.5, 415.5, 423, 452, 465, and 478.5 nanometers; the principal band, which determines the color, is at 415.5 nanometers. The diamond's absorption of light waves in the blue zone causes accentuation of the complementary color. In other words, the more light the diamond absorbs in the blue section, the more yellow it becomes. Now, it has been proven that the number and intensity of the absorption bands are strongly dependent on the proportion of nitrogen in the diamond. Totally colorless ("exceptional white +" or D) diamonds that contain no nitrogen whatsoever and are therefore chemically pure can be recognized by the absence of the band at 415.5 nanometers in their absorp-

tion spectrum. If, moreover, diamonds of the Cape series are submitted to ultraviolet light, they will invariably display blue fluorescence.

But besides the white, grayish, and other faintly tinted diamonds, there are gems that are truly colored. On the color scale these "fancy" diamonds begin where the slight glint of pale yellow, pink, green, mauve, or blue gives way to a sustained, pronounced coloration. If the color saturation is strong, these gems are of unusual splendor, and their rarity makes them especially valuable. Some of the costliest jewels in the world are fancy diamonds. They are regarded both as natural curiosities and as collectors' items. What is true of the great majority of apparently colorless minerals is equally true of colored diamonds—foreign elements are responsible for the coloring. Recent research has made it possible to distinguish between two broad classes of diamond, those that contain nitrogen (Type I) and those that do not (Type II).

Each type has been further divided into two subcategories. In Type Ia the nitrogen/carbon ratio is relatively high (1:1,000), and the nitrogen atoms aggregate to form minute "platelets," which somehow slip within the interstices of the lattice structure of the crystal. Such diamonds are, despite their nitrogen content, colorless. In Type Ib, on the other hand, in which the nitrogen/carbon ratio is usually less than 1:1,000, the nitrogen atoms merely take the place of occasional carbon atoms: nothing is changed in the general structure of the crystal. Yet it is these diamonds that, drawing energy from the blue wavelengths of the impingent light, show a yellow color (see figure on page 227). Depending on both the nitrogen/carbon ratio and the distribution of the nitrogen atoms within the crystalline structure, yellow, brown, or green diamonds may result. Among the yellow diamonds, the "canary" yellow is by far the most attractive color; it is also extremely rare. Under spectroscopic examination, these diamonds display a spectrum quite different from that of the Cape series, and for a very good reason: their much-admired hue has nothing to do with the presence of nitrogen, but results from voids—so-called color centers—in the crystalline lattice; under ultraviolet light they emit intense yellow luminescence. The diamonds of the brown series often have a secondary tone ranging through coffee, cognac, cinnamon, bronze, sherry, and even extending to orange or reddish-brown. Most of them are characterized by some degree of green fluorescence. Brown diamonds, as well as the spectroscopically allied green specimens, can have acquired their color as a result of uranium irradiation over the course of several million years. It was knowledge of this that made it possible, as long ago as 1904, to color diamonds artificially by plunging them into radium salts.

Type II diamonds, which are generally devoid of nitrogen, are also subdivided into two categories. Type IIa diamonds are chemically the purest: they contain no nitrogen and are therefore colorless. The presence of slight traces of manganese gives a rosy tint, and the spectrum of a truly pink diamond shows a band at 550 nanometers. Depending on the strength of this band in the green region of the spectrum, there is a corresponding modification of the complementary color, red, producing shades from palest pink to ruby.

Diamonds of Type IIb contain boron, which gives them their blue color. The boron atom has one electron less than the carbon atom, which results in the creation of an electromagnetic field of tension drawing from white light some waves in the yellow part of the spectrum. Consequently, the stone shows the complementary color, blue. The color ranges from a pale sky blue (as in the Idol's Eye, a famous diamond recently bought by the collector Laurence Graff), passing through steel blue (as in the Wittelsbach diamond), to a dark, inky blue (as in the Hope).

A particularly precious variety is the so-called chameleon diamond, which changes color according to environmental conditions. When it is heated to temperatures of 120° to 212° F (50–100° C) it takes on a beautiful yellow color, which it retains as long as it is kept in the dark. If it is reexposed to daylight, it gradually turns green, and remains so unless it is heated again.

Artificial Colors

Since the 1930's it has been possible to irradiate diamonds. Irradiation by electrons damages the surface of the diamond; irradiation by neutrons affects the crystal lattice. Depending on the length and intensity of treatment, varying shades of green result. If, after irradiation, the diamond is heated to between 900° and 1,650° F (500–900° C), the damage is partially "repaired," and the diamond turns a strong yellow or brown, depending on its original shade and the applied treatment. This kind of process is used when a deeper color is desired. For example, light yellow diamonds of the categories "tinted color¹" to "tinted color⁴" may be irradiated in order to obtain a darker color than the original natural shade, which increases their value. But while such an

The Condé, a rose-pink, pear-shaped diamond weighing 9.01 carats, is one of the most remarkable of historic gems. It was acquired in 1643 by agents of Louis XIII, and given by the king to the prince de Condé in gratitude for his services during the Thirty Years' War. It remained in the Condé family until 1892, when it was bequeathed to the state by the duc d'Aumal. Since then it has been kept at the Musée Condé, Chantilly.
Photo Giraudon, Paris.

The Wittelsbach, a blue diamond of 35.32 carats, came from India. It was owned by Philip IV of Spain, who gave it to his daughter, the future wife of Emperor Leopold I, in 1664. It passed into the Wittelsbach family when Archduchess Maria Amelia married Charles Albert of Bavaria in 1722. In 1931 it was put up for sale by Christie's in London, together with other Bavarian crown jewels, but was withdrawn unsold. It reappeared in Antwerp in 1961 as the property of I. Komkommer, a diamond merchant, and was sold to a German collector in 1964. *Photo Ernst A. Heiniger, Zurich (Le Grand Livre des Bijoux, 1974).*

Left: The Tiffany, the best-known yellow diamond. It was found in the De Beers mine in Kimberley in 1878 and weighed 287.42 carats. The following year it was bought by Charles Lewis Tiffany, the famous Fifth Avenue jeweler, and was cut in Paris as a cushion-shaped brilliant with 90 facets, weighing 128.51 carats. *Photo Tiffany & Company, New York.*

artificially colored diamond is worth more than it was in its original state, its value is only about one-tenth that of a naturally colored diamond of identical hue. Artificially colored diamonds must be designated as "treated colors."

Some of the most famous gems in the great collections of the world are fancy diamonds. Among them are some fabulous blue diamonds, including the Hope, the Wittelsbach, and the Idol's Eye. This last gem, a semiround diamond that weighs 70.2 carats, supposedly was the eye of a sacred image in an Indian temple. In 1607, the East India Company accepted it from Prince Rahab of Persia as payment for his debts. It has since changed hands several times. Another legendary blue diamond is the Brunswick, a pear-shaped stone of 13.75 carats that once belonged to the duke of Brunswick. In 1874 it was put up for sale in Geneva, where it was purchased by the Paris firm of Ochs Brothers. One of the rarest and most notable fancy diamonds is the Dresden Green. Some of the loveliest fancy diamonds are the pink ones, such as the Darya-i-Nur ("Sea of Light"). According to tradition, this stone was one of the eyes of the famous Peacock Throne of the Mughals and was carried off to Persia by Nadir Shah after his sack of Delhi in 1739. It has remained in the Iranian treasury ever since. The Elizabeth II was found in October, 1947, by Dr. J. T. Williamson in his mine at Mwadui in Tanzania. He presented it to Princess Elizabeth on the occasion of her wedding in November, 1947, as a rough crystal of 54 carats. She had it cut to a brilliant and its present weight of 23.6 carats. The deep yellow Tiffany (128.51 carats) and the golden-yellow Red Cross (205.07 carats), the largest yellow diamond known, are probably the best-known yellow diamonds in the world. The latter, a cushion-shaped brilliant, was cut from a 375-carat rough found in 1901 in the De Beers mine, near Kimberley. The great Cullinan (3,106 carats rough) and the Big Rose (137.02 carats, cut from the 353.9-carat Premier Rose, which was found in the Premier mine in 1978) are Type IIa diamonds of the finest quality.

Radiating an intangible beauty and dazzling color, these unique gems are perfect symbols of the inexhaustible magnificence of nature.

Exchanges and Cutting Centers

Antwerp

Of the sixteen diamond exchanges now in existence, four are in Antwerp, contributing to the city's status as the world's leading diamond center. The Antwerp dealers regularly receive an abundance of rough stones via the "sights" approved by the CSO, and about 70 percent of all cut diamonds are produced here. The city owes its unique position as much to its centuries-old tradition of craftsmanship as to its commercial experience, and its present prosperity would have been impossible if the conflicts that sometimes exist between the diamond manufacturing industry and the diamond trade had not been reconciled. Of course, the economic structure of the industry has changed enormously over the ages. Though it is hard to imagine, in the eighteenth century the Antwerp diamond trade was flourishing while the cutting workshops were experiencing what seemed to be an irreversible decline. This paradoxical situation remained unchanged through the early nineteenth century, and even as late as 1865 stagnation was so prevalent that the creation of a new cutting factory in Antwerp by merchants from Paris was regarded as a crazy enterprise.

The "Antwerp Mondays": Prosperity and Abundance. Within a few months during 1870–71 the massive influx of rough stones from South Africa provided work for thousands of craftsmen. The swift revival of diamond cutting in Antwerp was further stimulated by the ever-growing demand for gemstones. The mood in the trade was euphoric. Wages increased so dramatically that it became customary for diamond workers who had celebrated too heartily on Sunday, their day off, to spend the following day recovering. These were the famous "Antwerp Mondays," which gave the diamond workers their reputation as *bons vivants.* In the next decade, however, there was a devastating reaction to the renaissance in the diamond industry. The market became saturated, leading to an alarming drop in prices and a sharp rise in unemployment.

In an effort to counteract the uncertainties of employment in the industry, the Algemene Antwerpse Diamantbewerkersvereniging was founded in 1887 to unite the workers, regard-

less of the religious or political differences that divided them. This initiative had only limited success, but it provided the impetus for further efforts at labor organization, and in 1895 the Antwerpse Diamantbewerkersbond (ADB) was founded. It is still active today, under the name of the Algemene Diamantbewerkersbond van België (Amalgamated Union of Belgian Diamond Workers). As the diamond trade's first real labor union, the ADB was instrumental in bringing about improved working conditions and in establishing generally accepted standards of employment.

The Diamond Club. Diamond merchants and dealers were just as seriously affected by the upheavals in the industry in the 1870's and 1880's. With the market declining as rapidly as it had expanded a few years earlier, they recognized the need for better information and more reliable forecasting. In 1886 a group of diamond merchants began meeting fairly regularly at the Café Flora in Aneessenstraat to exchange views and discuss their business affairs. After some time, they decided that these informal meetings were not enough: what was really needed was some kind of formal institution that would protect their common professional interests without restricting their commercial freedom. Thus the Diamond Club was founded in 1893. Housed in a new building near the central railway station in Pelikaanstraat, it soon attracted some four hundred members, including dealers from all over the world. It was the world's first diamond exchange, and although many more have arisen since, it is still revered by diamond dealers as a pioneer.

Development of an Industry in Campine. Following the discovery of the Premier mine in South Africa in 1902 and, more important, of alluvial deposits in South-West Africa in 1908, diamonds began flooding the free market, outside the London "Syndicate." To avoid bankruptcy, some merchants were forced to sell their stocks at low prices. There were also some unexpected consequences for the diamond dealers of Antwerp. The fact that most of the diamonds coming in were very small (fifty to eighty stones to the carat) favored the

A poster for the 1923 Festival of Antwerp announcing a "procession of jewels" through the city, with some 2,000 people dressed in period costume, fifteen richly decorated chariots, and 600 animals—horses, mules, camels, zebras, and elephants. Expenses were paid by local businessmen, diamond merchants especially.

An Antwerp craftsman and a diamond-cutting and polishing factory. With its 250 factories employing nearly 15,000 highly trained people, Antwerp is by far the world's foremost cutting center. *Photos Guy Philippart de Foy, Brussels.*

Far right: A page from E. Jensen, *Begrippen over Diamantkunde en Diamantbewerking* ("Observations on the Art and Craft of Diamond Working"), Antwerp, 1929. Staatsbibliotheek, Antwerp. *Photo Staatsbibliotheek.*

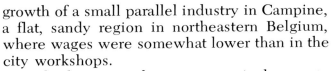

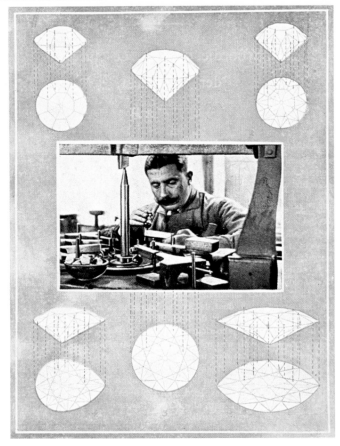

growth of a small parallel industry in Campine, a flat, sandy region in northeastern Belgium, where wages were somewhat lower than in the city workshops.

In the long run, these comparatively remote operations gave Antwerp a big advantage over Amsterdam in the diamond industry. By 1908 there were sixty-six small workshops on the outskirts of the city, with 1,184 grinding wheels and 1,500 employees. Wishing to distinguish themselves from the ADB workers, who had socialist tendencies, the Campine workers formed a new union, the Christelijke Belgische Diamantbewerkersbond (Belgian Union of Christian Diamond Workers).

The Creation of New Exchanges. Within a few years the diversification of industrial and commercial activities gave rise to several new institutions. First, in 1904, the Beurs voor Diamanthandel (Diamond Trading Bourse) was set up. It still exists today and, along with the Diamond Club, is one of the pillars of the Antwerp diamond trade. The Fortuna N.V. Society, housed in a sumptuous building at the corner of Vestingstraat, was founded in 1910 and was followed the next year by the Vereniging voor Vrije Diamanthandel (Association For Free Diamond Trade).

The First World War blocked Antwerp's trade with the United States, and many diamond merchants fled to Holland, which had remained neutral. But the temporary advantage thus acquired by the Amsterdam market was short-lived. After the war, when the self-exiled dealers returned, Antwerp recovered rapidly. Business prospered still further with the income from the newly discovered alluvial deposits of the Belgian Congo, which were just beginning to be exploited. When they returned to Antwerp, the dealers continued to base all transactions on the Dutch florin, which, they decided, should be equivalent to 20 Belgian francs regardless of monetary fluctuations. This curious but practical custom continues to this day among the dealers of Antwerp, though it is gradually declining as the number of foreign buyers increases.

The COFDI. The Depression of the 1930's hit the diamond trade hard—the cutting shops were sometimes shut down completely for several weeks at a time. The situation remained difficult until the outbreak of the Second World War: in 1929, according to the official statistics, there were 27,000 diamond workers employed; in 1936 there were no more than 13,000.

When the storm finally broke in 1939, many Jewish businessmen in Antwerp, aware of the fate of German Jews at the hands of the Nazis, fled the country. A few went to Palestine, while others sought refuge in the United States, Portugal, and elsewhere. More than five hundred merchants from Antwerp regrouped in England. In an attempt to save as much of the existing diamond stocks as possible from the Germans, they transferred the diamonds to England as well. By agreement with the British-

Opposite: A "sight" from the London-based CSO consigned to a major Antwerp diamond merchant. *Photo Michel Plassart, Paris.*

ish government, an organization known as the Correspondence Office for the Diamond Industry (COFDI) was set up to register the diamonds and keep them for the duration of the war. Thanks to the COFDI, which was founded by Camille Huysmans, mayor of Antwerp, along with two eminent Antwerp merchants, Romi Goldmuntz and Herman Schamisso, large quantities of diamonds were returned to their owners after the city was liberated.

Thus the Antwerp industry got off to a promising start after the war. On April 1, 1945, only 3,480 people were employed in the various sectors of the diamond industry, but by December of that year the number had risen to 11,000. Today there are about 2,000 employers, 200 cutting establishments, 50 cleaving workshops, and a dozen polishing centers in Antwerp. The numbers employed vary between about 10,000 and 16,000 people: as a luxury trade, the diamond business has always been strongly affected by general economic conditions, and employment fluctuates accordingly.

The "Diamond City." A few minutes from the main railway station in Antwerp is the diamond center, a compact group of buildings occupying an area of 24,000 square yards (20,000 sq m) and bounded on one side by Pelikaan-

The Beurs voor Diamanthandel, the most important of Antwerp's four diamond exchanges. *Photo Guy Philippart de Foy, Brussels.*

straat (the street was given its rather unusual name because the city's splendid zoological park is nearby). Within these buildings are the four Antwerp diamond exchanges, four large and teeming halls, all with the north-facing windows that are essential for the accurate examination of diamonds in natural light. The very nature of the trade encloses the world of diamonds in an aura of secrecy. No one outside the profession is admitted to these halls, and it is not easy to become a member of an exchange. Each is a closed corporate society governed by its own laws. Members have a deep sense of allegiance to the society, and customs and traditions are strictly observed. Prospective members must provide solid proof of many years of successful and irreproachable business activity, and each candidate must be proposed by several members of the corporation. Once admitted, members answer only to their peers. Disputes are never taken to the civil courts, for each exchange has its own tribunal whose decisions are final. The penalty for refusing to abide by these decisions is permanent exclusion from the profession throughout the world. Total integrity of conduct is assumed. If a dealer should make the mistake (more common than one might suppose) of accidentally dropping or leaving on a table one of the paper envelopes used by all diamond dealers to carry their stones, he can be quite certain of getting it back. Each exchange has a board where mislaid envelopes are pinned, together with a detailed description of their contents, so that they may be reclaimed by their rightful owners.

These feverishly bustling halls are a spectacular sight: dealers, businessmen, brokers, jewelers, and other experts are all assembled to pursue the business that has brought them here. Some display blunt determination, some show artful cunning, and some manage to combine both approaches. It is impossible to describe all the activities that go on at one time. A wholesaler who has come to buy gemstones for resale to jewelers may encounter a local craftsman in search of a few rough stones to keep his workshop going. Or there may be a broker who is looking for just four or five stones of a certain type because he knows a dealer in one of the other exchanges who needs them urgently enough to buy them a few hours later for a higher price. There is a continuous hurly-burly of buying and selling of both rough and cut stones, wholesale and retail.

As explained in an earlier chapter, dealing in cut stones is limited by the strictly defined criteria for their evaluation. The same is not true, however, of uncut stones. The uncertainties involved in estimating the potential of a

rough stone can sometimes lead to heated arguments. This is where professional expertise is indispensable, and a dealer's personal judgment and experience can help him make the most profitable deals. Nevertheless, everybody likes a little gamble, and there is always an element of risk.

The most important business is usually transacted in the private offices of prestigious dealers, which are distributed on various floors of the building and not among the noisy crowds in the halls. The modern demand for efficiency has hardly altered the quaint traditions of the exchanges. Though almost every European language is spoken here, all transactions are still concluded with a firm handshake and the traditional Yiddish greeting *Mazel und broche* ("Luck and prosperity"). There is no need for signatures—these three words are enough to seal the contract.

The Diamond High Council. The "Diamond City" contains more than 500 commercial houses with more than 2,500 people involved in buying and selling. In addition, there are about 10,000 people working in various private or public administrative services. The major banks play a part in this dynamic world, as do insurance companies and specialized firms that provide and maintain machinery and materials. There is one central body, the Hoge Raad voor Diamant (Diamond High Council), or HRD, which makes certain the "Diamond City" is running smoothly and looks after the

interests of the Antwerp industry as a whole. Its administrative council is made up of representatives from the exchanges, the professional associations, and the unions. A department called the Diamond Office supervises the import and export of diamonds and processes the relevant paperwork on behalf of the interested parties. The recently opened Certificates Department, which is supported by the University of Antwerp, evaluates the diamonds submitted to it and issues certificates of attestation with precise descriptions of the characteristics of each stone. Finally, the Scientific and Technical Research Department conducts a continual study of tools and materials, calling on the experience of practical craftsmen and using the most advanced scientific techniques to improve production processes.

Amsterdam

When the South African mines were discovered, Holland's diamond industry, like Antwerp's, was suffering a high rate of unemployment. But thanks to the many investments that had been made in the 1840's, when the future had looked more secure, the Dutch industry had certain technical and commercial advantages that gave it an underlying strength. It was not merely through good fortune that the first rough diamonds from South Africa were brought to Amsterdam for cutting—some of the Dutch factories were the most modern in Europe. Things soon took a turn for the better, and by 1871 there was a feeling of great opti-

Below: Cullinan II (317.4 carats), a cushion-shaped diamond with 66 facets, mounted on the band of the British Imperial State Crown, on display in the Tower of London. *By permission of HMSO, London.*

Below right: The tools that the Asscher brothers made especially to cleave the Cullinan. *Photo Guy Philippart de Foy, Brussels.*

Replica of the Cullinan rough (3,106 carats) and of the nine principal diamonds cut from it. *De Beers Archives.*

mism in the diamond community. Numerous stories, not all of them fictitious, were told about the opulent existence enjoyed by diamond dealers and workers. There were 1,200 diamond workers in Amsterdam, but there was work for at least 2,000. Wages reached the dizzy height of 200 florins a week, and some skilled craftsmen could earn up to five times that, achieving a standard of living that has never been surpassed, even today. Diamond workers left their crumbling homes in the Jewish quarter for fine new houses, and private boxes were permanently reserved for them at the opera and the theater. The "diamond fever" that gripped the little town of Kimberley, thousands of miles away, spread through Europe, and every sector of Amsterdam's economy benefited from the booming diamond industry.

With their economic strength restored, workers and employers alike were quick to form organizations to protect their new affluence. The workers were the first to act, and in 1894 the Algemene Nederlandse Diamantbewerkersbond (Amalgamated Union of Dutch Diamond Workers) replaced the eleven associations then in existence. Two years later it was the employers' turn—they formed the Amsterdam Juweliersvereniging (General Association of Jewelers: the word "jewelers" was used in a broader sense than we are accustomed to and included managerial staff in the diamond industry).

The Cullinan, the Largest Diamond in the World. It was generally acknowledged that the best Amsterdam cutting shops were second to none. In 1903, when De Beers decided to cut the Excelsior, which had been found in the Jagersfontein mine ten years earlier and was the largest diamond known at that time (925.2 carats), they sent it to the Asscher workshops in Amsterdam. This confirmed the reputation of the Asscher brothers as the finest cutters in the world, and four years later they were chosen by King Edward VII of England to cut the Cullinan diamond, which had been presented to him by the government of the Transvaal as a token of allegiance on his birthday.

The Cullinan was discovered by an African worker at the Premier mine near Pretoria on January 26, 1905, at five o'clock in the evening. It was, and is, the largest diamond ever found, weighing 3,106 carats in the rough and measuring 4 inches long, 2 inches wide, and 2.5 inches high (10 × 5 × 6 cm). It was named after Sir Thomas Cullinan, who had discovered the Premier and was the president of the company operating the mine. The stone did not have the appearance of an octahedral crystal and displayed a natural cleavage plane on its largest face. It therefore appeared to be a fragment of an even bigger stone. Many theories have been advanced concerning this "greater Cullinan," and people of a romantic disposition still cherish the hope that the missing part of the stone will someday be discovered.

The diamond was acquired by the Transvaal government at the instigation of Prime Minister Louis Botha for $750,000. Amid a show of elaborate security precautions, a box supposedly containing the stone was dispatched to London. The box, however, was empty. The Cullinan in fact traveled by registered parcel post with a 3-shilling stamp. It arrived safely, and the Asscher brothers were summoned to London for a private audience with the king to discuss the enormous responsibilities they would assume as cutters of the stone. Edward at first wanted to keep the diamond uncut, but the Asscher brothers persuaded him that such a huge "rock" had nothing to commend it apart from its enormous size, and they pointed out that certain impurities could be removed by cutting. He was quite easily convinced, and the stone was sent to Amsterdam. A ruse was again adopted for safety's sake—the Royal Navy

Cullinan I (530.2 carats), a pear-shaped diamond with 74 facets, mounted on the British Imperial Scepter. The largest cut diamond in the world, it is on permanent display at the Tower of London. *By permission of HMSO, London.*

day, such as polariscopes, was available at that time. It took several days to make the tiny V-shaped incision for the cleaving blade, and on February 10, 1908, all was ready at last. Joseph Asscher placed the steel blade in the cleft and tapped it firmly, as the rules dictated. The cleaving blade promptly broke while the diamond remained intact. Two more attempts were equally fruitless, but finally the diamond split perfectly in two, exactly as planned.

Subsequently the two large pieces were cleaved and fashioned into nine large jewels and ninety-six smaller brilliants, leaving fragments totaling 9.5 carats. The nine principal gems, now part of the British crown jewels, are as follows:

Cullinan I (530.2 carats), also known as the Great Star of Africa, is a pear-shaped stone with seventy-four facets. The largest cut diamond in the world, it is mounted in the royal scepter and is on permanent display among the British crown jewels in the Tower of London.

Cullinan II (317.4 carats), also known as the Lesser Star of Africa, is a cushion-shaped stone with sixty-six facets. It is set in the band of the Imperial State Crown and may also be seen among the crown jewels in the Tower of London.

Cullinan III (94.4 carats), a pear-shaped stone, was originally mounted in the finial of the crown of Queen Mary. It is now set in a brooch together with Cullinan IV.

Cullinan IV (63.6 carats), a cushion-shaped stone, was also set in Queen Mary's crown before being mounted in the brooch, which is sometimes worn by the reigning monarch.

Cullinan V (18.8 carats) is heart-shaped; *Cullinan VI* (11.5 carats) is marquise-cut, as is *Cullinan VII* (8.8 carats). *Cullinan VIII* (6.8 carats) is oval, and *Cullinan IX* (4.39 carats) is a pear-shaped stone. All these stones are occasionally worn by Elizabeth II, particularly the beautiful marquise, Cullinan VI, which now appears as a drop in an emerald-and-diamond necklace.

Decline but Not Disappearance. The Cullinan was cut during Amsterdam's great days. The industry still continues there, but it is much less important nowadays. For some unexplained reason, Amsterdam failed to exploit the advantage it enjoyed as a result of Dutch neutrality during the First World War, and by 1921 seven thousand of the nine thousand workers in the Union of Dutch Diamond Workers were unemployed. Antwerp was the magnet that attracted not only Dutch diamond workers but also dealers, who found a more congenial environment and a more favorable tax situation there. A slump in the market for uncut stones accelerated the workers' exodus,

provided a powerful escort for an empty box that was taken across the North Sea while Abraham Asscher, with the diamond in his pocket, traveled to Holland incognito by train and night ferry.

In Amsterdam, in the Asscher brothers' Tolstraat workshops, the stone was studied for several months. Because of its extraordinary dimensions, the usual tools could not be used, and new ones had to be specially made. Since the Cullinan was to be cleaved, the tensions that are present in all crystals had to be calculated with absolute precision to minimize the risk of ruining the stone at the moment of cleavage. Of course, none of the sophisticated equipment used in the diamond industry to-

Cutting factories in Israel. Left: Bruting. Center: Rough diamonds mounted on dops, ready for bruting. Below and right: Faceting. The craftsman in the blue shirt is using an automatic machine, recently invented. *Photos Guy Philippart de Foy, Brussels.*

and the Depression hit Amsterdam even harder than its neighbor and rival, Antwerp. Finally, the German occupation during the Second World War delivered a nearly fatal blow to the Dutch diamond industry. Recovery was slow and painful. In 1950 the association of manufacturers had only forty members, and the number continued to dwindle. Only the old and soundly established firms are still prospering. Where thousands once worked, there are only a few hundred today.

Israel

Traveling from the exchange at Antwerp to that at Tel Aviv is likely to induce mild culture shock, even though one is likely to meet in Tel Aviv a number of people seen in Europe only a few days before. The atmosphere here is somewhat more feverish, more intense than in Antwerp. It would be difficult to imagine two institutions that evolved more differently. Antwerp has a thousand years of experience behind it, but the Tel Aviv exchange came into being only shortly after the Second World War, along with the state of Israel itself, which at that time was surrounded by hostile Arab armies. Israel had opened its doors to thousands of refugees, survivors of the holocaust in Europe who wanted only to return to the land of their ancestors. New immigrants were arriving every day, and provisions had to be made for them quickly. Improvisation was the order of the day.

It was in these circumstances that the idea

of building up a diamond industry in the country was conceived. Admittedly, there was already some foundation to build on: a diamond industry of a kind had been set up during the war, and although organized only on a temporary basis, it had flourished. Veterans of the Antwerp and Amsterdam industries who had come to Palestine to escape the threat of the Nazis had set up the first workshop in an abandoned stable on the outskirts of Tel Aviv. They put their maximum effort into their work, trained young craftsmen in the trade, and invited other diamond merchants to join their enterprise.

This new local industry, if that is the right word to describe the modest workshops of Tel Aviv, was founded on two novel concepts. The first was the introduction of a production line. Instead of one craftsman being responsible for one stone from start to finish, which was the general practice at the time, the work was divided into six separate operations, with one man in charge of each. As a result of this division of labor, the period of apprenticeship was considerably shortened, and a man could begin earning his living as a qualified craftsman after only a few months' training. That benefited the employers as well as the workers. The second new idea introduced in Israel was also totally alien to the profession at that time. To motivate the workers, it was decided that each employee would be paid on a "piecework" basis. To this day, the Israeli diamond industry is the only one in the world that operates on the piecework system.

These innovations made it possible for workers to earn money quickly, and an efficient work force was soon built up. Admittedly, the division of labor led initially to a decline in quality, but that hardly hindered the continuing development or the considerable profitability of the industry, since Palestine was practically the only cutting center for small diamonds during the Second World War. However, that situation lasted only as long as the war itself, for after 1945 Antwerp resumed its place as world leader. The Israeli industry suffered a series of setbacks, notably the blocking of its supplies of rough diamonds on two occasions by the CSO in London.

A Simple Decision. Despite these problems, the decision the Israeli authorities were faced with—whether it would be profitable to support a diamond industry—was a simple one. Diamond manufacturing had a number of clear advantages over most other forms of economic activity. First, there were many members of the profession in the country, skilled craftsmen and dealers who knew the basics of the trade and were qualified to deal with the various technical and commercial problems. In addition, the installation of a cutting shop presented no great problems. Any house or apartment would do, and the equipment required was not only less expensive than that used in most other industries, it was also light and could be easily transported from one location

A dealer examines a large batch of stones at the Ramat Gan exchange, near Tel Aviv. *Photo Jacques Legrand.*

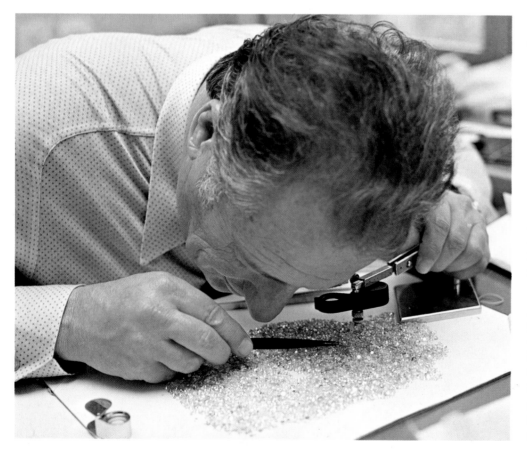

to another. For a country suffering grave shortages of energy and raw materials, the diamond industry offered still another advantage: cutting shops require very little energy and—a crucial point at the time—no water. Nor was transportation a problem. The raw materials necessary to keep a cutting shop functioning for a month can be carried in a cigar box, and the finished product can be transported just as easily. Moreover, the Jews had for centuries occupied a prominent place in the international diamond world, a position that gave them considerable commercial advantages. There was good reason to assume that in both price and quality, the Israeli product would stand comparison with that of other centers of production.

Taking all these factors into consideration, the Israeli government decided to provide generous support to this sector of the economy, and began by exempting it from the complex tangle of formalities then obligatory for all commercial and industrial enterprises. Thus the diamond industry found itself in an ideal situation—it enjoyed all the benefits of a liberal economy while remaining sheltered by a strictly controlled system. The banks were authorized to advance the necessary financial support to the businesses being created and agreed to accept actual diamonds, either cut or rough, as security for loans. In London, the birth of the Israeli industry was closely watched by the Diamond Trading Company (the "Syndicate," as it is called in the trade), which offered both advice and assistance.

An Exporting Industry. When the Isreali industry was established, there was no domestic market for Israeli diamonds. At that time, the regulations controlling the allocation of foreign currency for the purchase of rough stones required that all imported stones be cut in the country and reexported. A state controller, appointed by the minister for trade and industry, registered all imports and exports and kept checks on the amount of currency involved in each transaction. Between 1949 and 1977 the export of gemstones increased from 75,670 carats to 3,555,620 carats—in other words, by a factor of 47. In terms of value, the increase was from $5,118,000 to $1,002,507,335—a factor of 195.

Until the early 1960's, the rough stones allocated by the Diamond Trading Company of London satisfied only a fraction of the Israelis' needs. Forced to seek alternative sources of supply, they turned to other clients of the London "Syndicate" in Belgium for "secondhand" supplies and also to so-called outside sources in other diamond centers—that is, suppliers who dealt directly with the independent pro-

At the Ramat Gan exchange
business is conducted
even on the staircases.
Far right: Despite all the
bustle, the smallest stones are
still scrutinized with the
greatest care.

Below: The exchange
buildings at Ramat Gan.
*Photos Guy Philippart
de Foy, Brussels.*

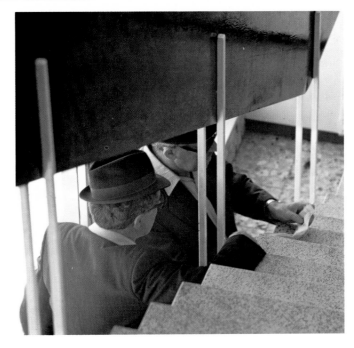

ducers in Africa or South America.

In spite of difficulties with supplies, by 1961 the Israeli industry had become the world's leading producer of melee, very small brilliants cut from equivalent rough stones, usually round and well shaped and weighing from about a quarter of a carat to a carat. Quality improved markedly as the industry became more flexible and better able to adapt to fluctuating market conditions. Since the general standard of living in Israel was lower than that in Europe, wages and overheads were also lower. These factors, plus an unusually narrow profit margin, enabled the Israeli industry to take its place among the major world markets.

Unlike the other countries, Israel had a number of professional institutions right from the beginning. The major one was the Diamond Manufacturers' Association, which represented the interests of the manufacturers in all negotiations with the authorities, the labor unions, and the Diamond Trading Company. The Diamond Exchange was created to provide the official framework within which all business transactions were conducted.

Decisive Changes. The year 1961 was a significant one in the development of the Israeli diamond industry. In that year it came of age, so to speak—its importance was officially acknowledged by the Diamond Trading Company of London. Reviewing the current state of the market, the CSO decided to allocate the bulk of the available melee to Israel. In addition to manufacturers already on its list and receiving supplies, the DTC undertook to supply certain dealers who in turn would supply uncut stones to manufacturers receiving no allocation, or an insufficient one, from the DTC. So, while the Diamond Trading Company re-

mained the sole distributor, these dealers took on the role of retailers.

Another milestone was the opening of the new Diamond Exchange in 1968. Located in the suburban center of Ramat Gan, northeast of Tel Aviv, this modern, 28-story building put the business of diamond trading in a new perspective. In addition to the halls where the actual transactions take place, the manufacturers and dealers have every necessary facility at hand; they can even dispatch and receive merchandise without leaving the building. Besides the more than five hundred Israeli and foreign companies that have their offices here, four specialist banks, the headquarters of the Diamond Manufacturers' Association, and the George F. Prins Club are all located in this center.

When the Diamond Exchange building opened, new cutting shops sprang up nearby and others moved into the neighborhood from central Tel Aviv. As business increased, the building soon became too small, and a second building, containing eight hundred offices, was opened in 1980. There is yet a third building for auxiliary services. In 1975 a second exchange, called the Etgar, was opened in the Ramat Gan area by a group of young manufacturers and dealers.

There are no precise figures, but it was estimated in 1977 that about fourteen thousand people were employed in about eight hundred workshops or factories. As noted above, the exports for that year exceeded $1 billion, representing 32.5 percent of Israel's total exports.

The Israel Diamond Institute, founded in the same year as the Diamond Exchange, provides a public relations service and includes various departments devoted to technical research and development and professional training. It sponsors a research laboratory in Haifa, which operates in conjunction with an assaying and testing laboratory in Ramat Gan; recent work there led to the development of automatic cutting machines.

In 1976 an institute for the study of gems was created. There is so much going on in the profession that two independent periodicals, *Yahalom* (in Hebrew) and *Israel Diamonds* (in English) are published bimonthly. As one of the principal resources of the Israeli economy, the diamond industry enjoys total government support, and although there are occasional outbreaks of opposition to its privileged position, there appears to be no reason for a change of policy.

Bombay and Surat

The Bombay exchange, third in importance after Antwerp and Tel Aviv, occupies an enviable position today. This is not because of the quantity of diamonds mined in India, which is minimal. Bombay's success stems from the fact that it has countless cutting shops, which came into being after the Second World War. Most of the work done in these shops involves stones that are too small or impure to be worth cutting in Europe or America, where the cost of fashioning would be likely to exceed the value of the rough stones. India was well equipped to meet the sudden demand for these small stones, since its cutting shops had never closed down and qualified craftsmen were therefore available. In view of the comparatively small capital investment and simple infrastructure of the diamond industry, and the fact that Bombay is only twelve flying hours from Antwerp and London, it is not hard to understand how the Bombay exchange, whose annual exports approach 500 million rupees

One of the countless cutting shops that are responsible for the relative prosperity of Surat. Situated on the Gulf of Cambay, in a region that has a long association with the diamond trade, Surat is about 180 miles (300 km) from Bombay. Nearly 120,000 of its inhabitants make their living from diamond cutting or trading. *Photo Guy Philippart de Foy, Brussels.*

Cutting techniques in India are no different from those in Europe: a cutter checks the accuracy of his or her work with the same care in both continents. Only the faces are different. *Photo Guy Philippart de Foy, Brussels.*

Children who are too young to work are adept at recovering stones dropped in the street. They scratch about busily in the crowded alleys of Surat, where the diamond trade is a purely local affair. *Photo Guy Philippart de Foy, Brussels.*

Animated discussions take place as diamonds change hands. At right, the scene in a Surat apartment. *Photo Guy Philippart de Foy, Brussels.*

(about $62.5 million), gained its current importance.

The exchange is in the center of the city and houses the offices of many of the chief dealers. Some of them are CSO-approved and receive their stones directly from London. In addition, the Bombay workshops receive masses of small stones from other parts of the world, and there is constant traffic between Bombay and the world's main diamond centers. The stones are sorted in the grinding shops, most of which are located in the center of the city. The cutting shops themselves are spread out over a broader area.

Many of the most important establishments are in the port of Surat, about 180 miles (300 km) north of Bombay on the Gulf of Cambay. Though it is a relatively modern city, Surat, founded in 1512, has long been linked with diamonds. The English established their first trading posts there in 1614, but the city's commercial prosperity suffered somewhat when the East India Company made Bombay its chief entrepôt in northwestern India.

Today Surat is a colorful, active place. Amid a constant ringing of bells and tooting of horns, thousands of bicycles and tricycles compete with yoked oxen and a few cars for passage through the narrow streets. One of the most picturesque streets is given over to a true "market." The ground floors of all the houses open directly onto the sidewalk and the numerous dealers sit cross-legged on the ground with their little scales, trying to tempt passersby with their diamonds. Some of these merchants have no shop of their own and use the street itself for all their dealings. In this crowded and lively atmosphere, an occasional

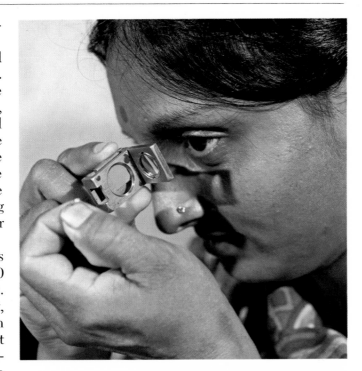

Diamond cutting in Surat is a domestic industry, usually family-based. An experienced older woman dispenses the work and supervises the younger workers. *Photo Guy Philippart de Foy, Brussels.*

The kind of house in Surat that often contains a cutting shop. *Photo Guy Philippart de Foy, Brussels.*

scuffle breaks out, and one of the dealers may lose a few stones from his precious paper packet. Then a horde of children, experts at recovering lost stones, scramble about picking them up and promptly offer to return them to their owner—for a price.

This is purely a local market; there are no foreigners involved. Important transactions take place only in Bombay, which feeds Surat its considerable supply of rough stones—enough to provide work for about 120,000 of the 400,000 inhabitants. There is a little cutting shop concealed behind a bead curtain in nearly every dwelling, for the local industry consists of family-run businesses. Work usually goes on in the two front rooms downstairs, with the remainder of the house reserved for living quar-

ters. There are seldom more than a dozen people in each workshop, and most of them are adolescents, boys and girls averaging about fifteen years of age. An experienced woman is in charge, distributing the work and supervising its progress. Groups of four or five sit on the floor or on rush mats around the wheel, while, in another part of the room, a younger boy may be learning how to judge rough stones. The wheels are driven by belts powered by an electric motor in the middle of the room, making a racket like that heard in the old workshops of Europe.

Only faceting and polishing are done in Surat. For a dollar or two these craftsmen and craftswomen can cut sixteen, thirty-two, or even fifty-eight facets on a diamond no larger than

Two New York exchanges—
one exclusively for diamonds,
the other for jewelry—are on
47th Street, in the heart
of Manhattan, not far from
Rockefeller Center.
Photo Jacques Legrand.

the head of a pin (to the eventual detriment of their eyesight). Basically, their techniques conform to European principles. Indian diamond cutters check their work the same way Europeans do, by examining the stones with a lens and deciding exactly what they must do to achieve the best result. Times have changed, but here as elsewhere ancient traditions have survived for centuries, through good and bad times alike.

Other Exchanges and Cutting Centers
Compared with the Low Countries, New York is quite new as a diamond-cutting center. It has some characteristics, however, that add to its importance in the diamond industry as a whole.

The cutting industry in New York was tiny before the First World War. When the war broke out, a number of cutters, escaping the advancing German armies, emigrated to New York and established cutting factories there.

The industry's growth was accelerated in the late 1930's, when, with the onset of the Second World War, many more cutters fled the Low Countries and came to New York.

With smaller stones, labor is a much more important cost factor than it is with larger ones. It soon became obvious, therefore, that the high cost of labor in the New York area made the fashioning of small diamonds uneconomical there. For many years the American cutting industry was protected by a 10 percent duty on polished stones, whereas there was no duty on rough. The dividing line between those stones considered economical for cutting and those considered uneconomical varies with the quality of the rough, but generally stones under five-eighths or one-half carat were considered too small to be profitable. Attracted by lower labor costs and a government eager to attract new business by reducing initial taxation, a number of manufacturers established cutting factories on the island of Puerto Rico, where smaller stones could be cut more profitably.

Cutting in New York City is confined largely to high-quality stones that, when cut, weigh a carat or more. The value of such stones is great enough to absorb the higher labor costs associated with New York. Over the years, New York has become the cutting center for a significant proportion of the world's large, fine diamonds. Since about 1970, European buyers have been flocking to New York to purchase high-quality diamonds of a carat and over. Thus, among the world's gem markets, New York has assumed a significance beyond the

In addition to Antwerp
and Amsterdam, Idar-
Oberstein in Germany and
Saint-Claude in the French
Jura are among the few
diamond-cutting centers in
Europe. Right: The Idar-
Oberstein diamond exchange
building provides a contrast
to the old-fashioned,
traditional houses around it.
Saint-Claude, a highly
reputed diamond center at the
beginning of the twentieth
century, still has a few cutting
factories and shops scattered
about the valley. The picture
at far right shows one of these
shops. *Photos Guy Phillipart
de Foy, Brussels.*

A balance used at the beginning of the twentieth century for weighing diamonds, now a museum piece. *Photo Guy Philippart de Foy, Brussels.*

Fashioning techniques in Saint-Claude are the same as elsewhere, and "setters," or vestellers, there are no less skilled than their colleagues in Antwerp or Tel Aviv. *Photos Guy Philippart de Foy, Brussels.*

number of cutters employed there.

The industry in New York City is concentrated in midtown Manhattan. A long block on West 47th Street between Fifth Avenue and the Avenue of the Americas, near Rockefeller Center, is lined with multistoried buildings that house many small cutting firms and a few slightly larger ones. In terms of the number of cutting benches and the number of diamonds cut, the industry is tiny. But in terms of value, New York's output is very significant.

There are two large organizations on 47th Street, the Diamond Dealers Club (DDC) and the Diamond Trading Association (DTA).

A considerable percentage of the diamonds cut in New York is sold overseas, particularly in Europe and the Far East, where the demand for large, high-quality stones is great.

London has no tradition of a diamond-cutting industry comparable with that of Antwerp, or of Amsterdam in former times. The "cottage-industry" organization that even today is somewhat characteristic of Antwerp and other centers hardly exists in England, and that is one reason that costs tend to be high. The only significant cutting and polishing establishment remaining today is that of A. Monnickendam Ltd. in Brighton, which was founded in 1912 by a family previously in business in Amsterdam.

England's diamond industry enjoyed a brief moment of glory during the Second World War, when diamond workers from the Low Countries, in flight from the Nazis, arrived in large numbers and established sizable diamond-cutting factories in various Midlands towns such as Stafford. Their relatively high

wages and lively behavior earned them the same kind of reputation as their predecessors in the days of the "Antwerp Mondays." With an ample supply of rough stones from South Africa, England was for a while the main supplier of polished gem diamonds in the free western world. After the war, most of the émigrés naturally returned to their native cities, but a number remained to become pillars of the present diamond establishment.

The London Diamond Bourse was scheduled to move into a new building in the jewelry district of Hatton Garden in 1979. Though it cannot be compared with the exchanges of Antwerp or Tel Aviv, it is a lively place with a highly cosmopolitan membership, where colored stones and jewelry may be bought and sold, and individuals engage in a remarkable variety of deals. The Diamond Club, also in Hatton Garden, is a much quieter and more obviously "respectable" institution; a greater proportion of its members are dealers in rough. Today its grand premises occasionally have an almost tomblike atmosphere. The London market is small and shrinking. In the past few years the number of brokers has dwindled to a mere handful, and it is hard to believe that even the few that remain can make a very good living.

Of the other diamond exchanges in the world today, Johannesburg occupies a unique position in that it receives its supply directly from the producers, albeit within the approved system of the CSO. The exchange at Idar-Oberstein, little known outside Germany, derives its importance from the size of the retail market in that wealthy country. West Germany, with 7 percent of world trade in 1975, is in fact the third largest consumer of diamond jewelry, after the United States (52 percent) and Japan (22 percent). But Idar-Oberstein is also one of the few European cutting centers with a long tradition, going back more than 150 years. It has always been primarily associated with the cutting of colored stones, which has become a local specialty. In this and other respects, Idar-Oberstein is similar to the French cutting center of Saint-Claude, in the Jura. Both are small towns in a mountainous region, and both have a cozy, family atmosphere. In the late nineteenth and early twentieth centuries, there was a thriving industry in Saint-Claude, but the slump that began in 1929 destroyed most of the little family businesses. A few years ago a new and very up-to-date business was established, and this has put new life into a tradition on the verge of extinction. An annual exhibition of diamonds and the diamond trade in Saint-Claude attracts between 25,000 and 30,000 visitors during the three summer months it is open.

Investment in Diamonds and Diamond Certificates

After 1960, when the dollar ceased to be a symbol of monetary stability, and the inflation from which the world was already suffering was aggravated by the energy crisis, some people felt that diamonds represented the investment most likely to retain its real value. Although the media presented this as a new development, it was nothing of the sort. For centuries capital has been invested in diamonds and has thereby been kept safe during crisis situations, and untold numbers of people, after fleeing peril, have been able to reestablish their lives without the wherewithal provided by the sale or barter of diamonds held for emergency. As one of the most easily portable forms of wealth, diamonds have been the salvation of many who would otherwise have been ruined.

Apart from the special value of diamonds in such desperate and dramatic circumstances, a comparison between the value of money and the value of diamonds over recent years offers some weighty support for the arguments of those who advocate investing in diamonds today. The value of diamonds in real terms has not only been maintained, it has increased considerably. In fact, over the past fifty years, diamonds have generally been a much better investment even than gold. Though the recent rash of speculation in precious metals has brought about spectacular increases in the price of gold, there is little likelihood that prices will remain at such high levels for very long. The price of diamonds, on the other hand, has risen steadily and predictably, with almost no fluctuation. This impressive record is due largely to the monopolistic control of the world diamond market, the advantages of which have been explained in an earlier chapter. A clever though conservative pricing policy constantly enforced from the top has enabled the diamond market to survive the various crises of the last half-century without much difficulty.

Traditionally, the diamond business has been based on personal evaluation by jewelers of the criteria known as the "four C's": carats (weight), clarity, color, and cut. Because dialogue and mutual agreement between supplier and client is central to such a system, it is essential that there be absolute trust between the parties to any transaction. As the diamond trade expanded, however, and more members of the lay public became involved in diamond buying and investment, confidence in the old relationships began to break down. Laymen found it difficult to understand how the price of a precious stone could be the subject of long debates between vendor and purchaser, or why the value should depend entirely on the subjective opinion of a single individual, how-

Examining a diamond in the HRD laboratories in Antwerp under 10× magnification. The degree of clarity is determined, in accordance with criteria agreed on by professional associations the world over, by analyzing the size and position of inclusions. *Photo Michel Plassart, Paris.*

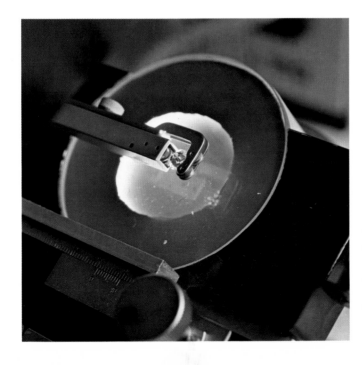

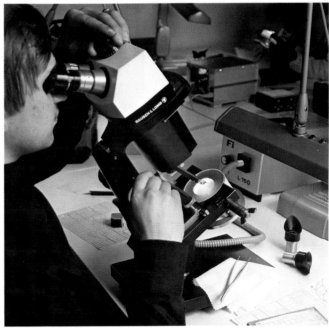

ever capable. There was no official classification, as there was for gold, and each diamond dealer, each jeweler, seemed to have his own standards for judgment.

The Birth of Certificates

In 1931, the Gemological Institute of America (GIA) was established in Los Angeles to educate jewelers, through night classes and correspondence courses, in the evaluation of gemstones in general, and to provide guidance with regard to the wholesale prices of precious stones. Prices, however, are linked to grading, and so the GIA, of necessity, established its own system of grading diamonds and other precious stones.

In the years following the Second World War, as New York became an increasingly important center for the cutting of large diamonds, and as world-wide demand for these stones grew, more and more jewelers consulted the GIA on the value of the stones offered to them for sale. In the early 1950's, to meet the burgeoning need for its services, the GIA established its first grading laboratory in New York to analyze individual stones and to issue reports on their value. These reports, known as certificates, revolutionized the international diamond trade. Shipping diamonds, even by registered mail, has always been a risky business, and dealers were loath to send diamonds overseas any more often than was absolutely necessary. When diamonds were analyzed in a GIA laboratory, merchants could send the certificates instead of the actual stones, and diamonds could be bought overseas sight unseen.

The demand for diamond certificates grew rapidly as their availability was bruited about. The GIA grading system became well known in the diamond industry and, eventually, to the consuming public. When the demand for the GIA's grading services outgrew the ability of its laboratories to supply enough certificates, as well as to provide similar services in Europe and Asia, other laboratories proliferated. Many of these were not only privately owned but under the same ownership as diamond sales companies. There was no certainty, therefore, that they were grading diamonds impartially. In Europe the situation became particularly aggravating and serious.

Action by the CIBJO

In 1975 it was decided that a systematic study of the certificates in current circulation should be initiated. The International Confederation of Jewelry, Silverware, Diamonds, Pearls, and Precious Stones (Confédération Internationale de la Bijouterie, Joaillerie, Orfèvrerie, des diamants, perles, et pierres pré-

cieuses, or CIBJO), together with the two other international professional diamond organizations, the World Federation of Diamond Bourses (WFDB) and the International Diamond Manufacturers' Association (IDMA), undertook the task of bringing standardization and harmony to the business. In May, 1975, representatives of the three organizations started developing a set of objective, universal standards to be used throughout the world. They analyzed the methods of the most important laboratories, and, based on experience and the results of research done by the GIA in the United States and the HRD (Hoge Raad voor Diamant, or Diamond High Council) in Antwerp, they began to redefine the "four C's" with the greatest possible precision and to establish standard methods of application.

It was agreed that weight should continue to be expressed as it always has been, in carats (1 carat = .2 grams), up to two decimal places. An international nomenclature for color and clarity was established. Master Diamonds to be used for comparison in color grading were chosen by several experts, who devoted more than two years to the selection process. Their results were submitted to the GIA for testing. The highest color grade on the international scale is exceptional white +, which corresponds to the GIA's grade D. (A, B, and C were omitted from the GIA scale to avoid confusion with another system, which used AAAAA as its highest designation, then AAAA, and so on through B and C.) Clarity grading is determined by the size of inclusions and their position within the diamond.

The rules adopted for grading cut deliberately state that, in the case of round brilliants at least, a good cut, or "make," cannot be defined merely by measurement of the angles. Overall proportions and specific visual qualities—brilliance and dispersion—must also be taken into account, for maximum effect is obtained only by a combination of these different elements. Because every stone is unique, there can be no hard-and-fast rules, and custom and fashion must be considered as well. For the round brilliant, for example, the ideal proportion of the table was considered by Tolkowsky to be 53 percent. Because of recent preferences, however, the table in many cases is now extended to 56 or even 60 percent or more, and, provided other proportions are correct, the cut is still regarded as good.

The standards established by the CIBJO, WFDB, and IDMA are not yet universal, but it is hoped that they will be adopted worldwide in the near future. CIBJO laboratories are already in operation in Great Britain, Italy, Spain, Switzerland, and West Germany. In France there is a laboratory that operates as a

Examining a diamond in the HRD laboratories in Antwerp with a ProportionScope, an "optical comparator" patented by the GIA in 1967. It analyzes the proportions of the modern round brilliant (also of certain fancy cuts) and can accommodate stones from .18 to more than 8 carats. A system of lenses and adjustable mirrors projects a magnified image of the stone onto a glass screen, which is marked with scales indicating the correct proportions. With this instrument, comparison between the proportions of the diamond being examined and the ideal proportions marked on the scale can be made very quickly and precisely. *Photo Michel Plassart, Paris.*

public service, since it is dependent on a department of the Ministry of Agriculture. Founded more than fifty years ago and managed by the Paris Chamber of Commerce, it was the first official body in the world to issue certificates. Among the other laboratories of established international repute are those of the GIA in New York and Los Angeles and of the HRD in Antwerp. So far, only stones of 1 carat or more have been accepted for grading by these laboratories. Facsimiles of their certificates are shown in the appendix, on pages 282–83. Besides these institutions, firms claiming to offer similar services have sprung up like mushrooms after rain. Most should be approached with caution, since a number of them are not to be trusted. Some of these laboratories are run by people unknown to the profession, base their business on advertising, and offer no reliable guarantees.

Choosing a Jeweler
Buying a diamond is a venture that should

naturally be undertaken carefully, and the customer's first and wisest precaution should be to choose a good, reliable jeweler in whom he can put his trust. The old saying is still true: "If you know nothing at all about jewelry, at least know your jeweler." Choose a well-established firm with an irreproachable record; that is the best possible guarantee.

Investment in diamonds is growing steadily, but it is by no means so common a practice as is widely believed—it involves only 10–15 percent of world diamond sales. For a long time to come, the vast majority of diamonds will continue to be bought purely for pleasure, even if future financial considerations are not entirely absent from the purchaser's mind. It must be admitted that the idea of buying diamonds as an investment clashes with the emotional value traditionally attached to the king of precious stones, and when all is said and done, the emotional appeal of the diamond is still the strongest factor. And that is as it should be.

IV

From Jewelry
to Industry

The Diamond in Jewelry

Strange as it may seem, man apparently thought of decorating himself before he ever thought of wearing clothes. He borrowed from nature various charms that, when hung about his body, seemed to have the double effect of warding off evil forces while increasing his own powers. The first such ornament that could be called a piece of jewelry was probably a simple but beautiful iridescent seashell suspended from a thin strip of leather. Leather was later replaced by copper, and shells were replaced by stones picked up from the ground. Eventually, man learned how to retrieve the stones from the earth itself. At first, of course, he had no means of polishing these stones to bring out all their potential luster, but a few thousand years ago a day came when true jewelry was born. Because gemstones were rare, for a long time they remained the prerogative of chiefs and leaders. As late as the seventeenth century, all diamonds of 10 carats or more found in the mines of Golconda belonged by right to the nizam of Hyderabad.

Man was quick in finding ways to fashion most precious stones, but one stone—the king of gems, the diamond—resisted all his efforts for centuries. In its natural state, the diamond often has a somewhat dull or opaque appearance. There is no indication of the qualities that gave one of the most famous diamonds the name "Mountain of Light." For hundreds of years, diamonds were simply cleaved and the faces polished—but not cut. Yet this step alone represented considerable progress, and the delicate beauty of many Indian gems bears witness to the admirable results that ancient jewelers could achieve with simple techniques.

As soon as cutting was invented, things started to change very quickly. Until then, the diamond had played only a modest part in the making of jewelry. Suddenly it was transformed into the unchallenged star among jewels. From that time on, the diamond held its undisputed place, and the fact that it remained the rarest of precious stones led kings and princes to take a special delight in displaying it. The costume of the Mughal emperor Jahangir (1569–1627), as described by the English ambassador, Sir Thomas Rowe, was lavishly adorned with jewels, particularly diamonds. On his head the emperor wore a rich turban decorated with a spray of long, slim feathers with an unmounted ruby "as big as a nut" on one side, a diamond the same size on the other, and a much larger emerald, in the shape of a stag, in the center. Pearls, rubies, and diamonds embellished his sash, and his bracelets were studded with diamonds.

A Passion Shared:
The Mughal Emperor and the Sun King

Two sovereigns, almost exact contemporaries, left an idelible mark on the century they

Antoine Coypel: Louis XIV receiving the special envoy of Persia, Muhammad Riza Beg, in the great gallery of Versailles on February 19, 1715. Musée historiqué, Château de Versailles. *Photo Lauros-Giraudon, Paris.*

Below: "Perles Mancini," one of the two earclips given to Marie Mancini by Louis XIV. 17th century. *Photo Cooper Bridgeman Library, London.*

A superb engraved diamond surrounded by rubies and set in green jade, part of a bracelet that was worn on the upper arm. It is thought that the bracelet originally belonged to Mumtaz-i-Mahal, wife of Shah Jahan. Early 18th century. This unique piece had a pendant that was bought by Cartier in 1960 and later given to the actress Elizabeth Taylor by her husband, Richard Burton. Collection M. G. Mehta, Bombay. *Photo Guy Philippart de Foy, Brussels.*

dominated: Aurangzeb, the inflexible grandson of Jahangir, who ruled the Mughal Empire in India from 1658 to 1707, and Louis XIV of France, *le roi soleil,* who held absolute power from the death of Cardinal Mazarin in 1661 until his own death in 1715. It might seem at first that the two monarchs had nothing in common. But besides the great influence they wielded, they shared a liking for ostentatious entertainments and a passion for gems and jewelry. Jean-Baptiste Tavernier, who was allowed to see the treasures of the Mughal emperor, left an awestruck description of them. And Tavernier was not only the first European to be granted this unusual privilege, he was also the chief supplier of precious stones to the king of France.

From whom did the Sun King acquire his unquenchable passion for precious stones? Was it from his mother, Queen Anne of Austria, or from his godfather, Cardinal Mazarin? No other Christian monarch, before or since, has indulged in such ostentatious display, such courtly magnificence. In his reign, wrote the historian Bernard Morel, "the diamonds and precious stones belonging to the French crown became worthy of Versailles."

Louis XIV's queen, Maria Theresa of Austria, did not share his extravagant tastes. A comparatively retiring figure, she did not care for luxurious self-indulgence and contributed nothing to the growth of the royal collection. Nor did she make much use of the treasures it contained. Her indifference allowed the king to have the crown jewels mounted in sword hilts, in belt buckles, and as studs and buttons.

Not a year passed in which the king did not increase his collection of precious stones. From Tavernier he bought 44 large diamonds, among them the famous Blue diamond weighing 112 carats, as well as 1,122 smaller stones. From Marie of Lorraine he acquired the diamonds of the House of Guise, among them one stone of 33 carats. From the traveler Bazu, who like Tavernier had visited India, he bought 15 large diamonds, including one of 42 carats, 131 smaller diamonds, a quantity of fine pearls, and other jewels. Lesser rulers whose respect he wished to cultivate, generals and courtiers whom he wished to favor, domestic servants, and above all his mistresses—all were showered with jewels. Records of these political presents were kept by the finance minister, Colbert, who deplored such lavish expenditure. "I have let myself be damned because of that man," he cried on his deathbed.

Vestments to Adorn the Sun

The king's jewels were listed in an inventory drawn up in 1691. Actually, the word "inventory" does not fully convey the substance of what was more like a catalogue, and quite a thick one at that. As Saint-Simon said, the person of the king "crackled with diamonds." In his hat he wore the Sancy, in his cravat the Blue diamond and the Great sapphire, which weighed 132 carats. The necklace he wore contained 45 diamonds, many of which were the famous Mazarin diamonds. Besides those jewels, there were 123 studs, each with one large diamond; 149 rosettes with a single stone each; 151 *boutonnières* with five diamonds each; and 19 floral sprays with three large diamonds in each one. His coat was ornamented with 48 single-diamond clasps and 48 *boutonnières* with five diamonds each. And that was not all. There were also the badges and the cross of the Order of Saint-Esprit. There was a *crochet* (a jeweled hat or hair ornament) with seven huge diamonds, one of them weighing 42 carats. There were sashes, garters, shoe buckles, and swords—all adorned with precious stones. Every article the king wore was bedecked with jewels. Even if Louis XIV had not chosen the daystar as his emblem, his appearance alone might have led his contemporaries to name him the "Sun King." When he appeared in all his glory among the lights of the palace of Versailles, the constellations of diamonds that adorned him flashed with incomparable brilliance.

Among the stones actually bought by Louis

XIV, there were 109 diamonds of more than 10 carats each and 273 that weighed between 4 and 10 carats. These were the jewels of the state collection alone. The king himself, his brother, and the royal children all had their own personal collections.

By the end of the seventeenth century great progress had been made in the art of cutting diamonds. Besides the old table cut of late medieval and Renaissance times, a variety of other cuts were now possible, among them the rose cut and the fifty-eight-facet brilliant cut. It was only a short time earlier that the role of the diamond in jewelry had reached the eminent position it has maintained ever since. Previously, the diamond had usually played only a supporting part in relation to the colored stones, which were more highly favored. By the time of Louis XIV it had claimed its place in the center of the stage. The intangible beauty

Pierre Mignard: Portrait of Maria Theresa, queen of France, in state dress. Details from the dress and hat. Prado Museum, Madrid. *Photo Telarci-Giraudon, Paris.*

The famous Aigrette of Charles the Bold, with rubies, pearls, and diamonds that were described as *pointes facettées*. Painting on parchment, about 1480. Historisches Museum, Basel. *Photo Maurice Barbey, Historisches Museum.*

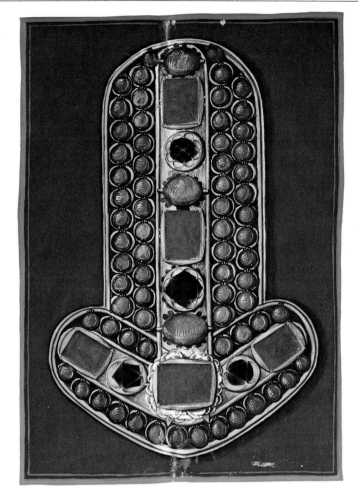

princesses or commoners, were expressly forbidden to wear them by order of Saint Louis (1214–70). Moreover, the trade of the jeweler or gem setter was not recognized by the guilds. It was regarded as only a modest adjunct to the goldsmith's craft, and goldsmiths worked mainly on religious objects and royal crowns—in other words, for church and king, as the goldsmiths' motto, *In sacra inque coronas*, implied. In the eyes of Saint Louis, the only woman worthy of wearing diamonds was the Holy Virgin herself.

The first woman in France to violate the established sumptuary laws was Agnès Sorel (ca. 1422–50). She was not a princess; she was not even a lady of aristocratic lineage. She sprang from the ranks of the minor, provincial nobility. What raised her from this humble station was the love of the king. Charles VII fell under her spell, and because Agnès adored jewels, the rules were disregarded. The royal favorite wore jewels—diamonds and other precious stones—in profusion. The ships of the wealthy merchant Jacques Coeur were employed to satisfy the desires of the beautiful Agnès and, at the same time, to lift the jeweler's trade from its subordinate status and establish it as a distinguished craft in its own right.

One of the first instances of diamonds being used in jewelry in the West is recorded in an inventory of the personal possessions of King Charles V ("the Wise") of France, which was drawn up in 1379, a year before the king's death. It naturally refers to jewelry made somewhat earlier. Among the items listed is a gold scepter ornamented with "*troys ballaiz* [three balas rubies or spinels], *troys saphirs*, *troys troches* [clusters of four pearls]." The latter consisted of four large pearls with "*ung diamant*" in the center. The document goes on to state that the order for the scepter had been given not long before to one Simon de Dammartin, who, in 1352, had made for the queen (probably Jeanne d'Auvergne, second wife of John the Good, who reigned from 1350 to 1364) a gold brooch consisting of twenty-five clusters of four pearls with a diamond in the

of its fire and brilliance had captured the full attention of the audience. But here it is necessary to take a step backward in history.

Agnès Sorel: Women Adopt the Diamond

According to tradition, it was Charles the Bold (1433–77), the proud and valiant master of the court of Burgundy, who made the first major contribution toward establishing the prestige of the diamond. Tradition, however, frequently disregards facts. It is certain, for example, that diamonds had been known in Europe for several hundred years before the time of Charles the Bold, although they were extremely rare and very few people ever had the opportunity to acquire any. Diamonds were reserved for kings alone, and women, whether

Charles the Bold presiding over the parlement of Burgundy. French school, 15th century. Musée historique, Château de Versailles. *Photo Giraudon, Paris.*

A lapidary's shop in the Middle Ages. Miniature from the *Lapidaire* of Jean de Mandeville (1300–72). French manuscript, 15th century. Bibliothèque Nationale, Paris. *Photo Bibliothèque Nationale.*

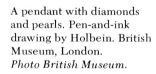

A pendant with diamonds and pearls. Pen-and-ink drawing by Holbein. British Museum, London. *Photo British Museum.*

center. But that was for a queen, and it is not hard to understand why the beautiful Agnès Sorel caused a near revolution less than a century later with the audacity of her luxurious dress. However, while the followers of the queen might criticize the king's mistress, they were perfectly willing to follow the fashion she had set. Only the rarity and the cost of jewelry now prevented aristocratic ladies and the wives of the wealthy bourgeoisie from aping the royal mistress more closely.

The Treasure of Charles the Bold

The fashion in rich jewelry that had been established in the fourteenth century continued into the fifteenth, reaching its apogee in the work of the goldsmiths of the court of the dukes of Burgundy, Jean Vilain, Jean Mainfroy, Guillaume van Vlueten, and Gérard Loyet. The story of Lodewijk van Berckem of Bruges, who was asked to cut, "according to his capacity," three large diamonds for Charles the Bold, has been mentioned in an earlier chapter. What were these three stones? Since the chronicler Philippe de Commynes described the pillage of the treasures of Burgundy by Swiss mercenaries after the battle of Grandson (1476), many extravagant theories have been advanced to explain this assignment. It does not matter that some historians believe that the famous treasure was lost at another time. In the present context we are interested only in the jewelry that was worn by the duke or that at one time or another formed part of the Bur-

gundy treasures. This included:

—The "largest diamond in all Christendom," which can probably be identified as the famous pale yellow Florentine diamond, not (as is sometimes said) the Sancy.

—A dress sword set with diamonds, which was sold in Zurich in 1492 and subsequently disappeared.

—The Order of the Garter in gold enriched with diamonds.

—A gold ring with the letter N outlined in diamonds and the letters CHI (an abbreviation of the name of Jesus Christ) on the inside. This apparently belonged to Mary, daughter of Charles the Bold, who married the future Holy Roman Emperor Maximilian.

—An enameled gold brooch, fashioned in relief, that was regarded as the most beautiful example of this popular type of jewelry then in existence. A cabochon ruby surmounted by a triangular diamond was set between the heads of two angels surrounded by a delicate garland.

—The duke's ceremonial headdress, a tall, round, velvet hat ornamented with a badge known as the Aigrette, or Feather Jewel. This was probably a gift from the duke's cousin, King Edward IV of England, presented at the same time as the Order of the Garter. The Feather Jewel comprised gold openwork set with seventy pearls, three very large pearls, five balas rubies, and four diamonds. It was surmounted by the famous piece known as the Three Brethren, described in an inventory of 1603 as "a fayre Flower with 3 great ballaces in the myddest a great pointed dyamonde, and 3 great perles fixed, with a fayre great perle pendant." It was acquired by the Fuggers and resold to Emperor Maximilian, who in turn bequeathed it to his son, Emperor Charles V. At Charles V's abdication, it passed to his brother and successor, Emperor Ferdinand. The Feather Jewel was sold by the Fuggers to King Henry VIII of England and remained in the royal collection until the civil war, when it was smuggled out of the country by Henrietta Maria, wife of Charles I, without the king's knowledge, and broken up a short time later. All trace of it has vanished, and in fact not one piece of jewelry from the court of Burgundy is known to have survived to this day. Our knowledge of it comes only through written evidence and from miniature paintings on vellum, dating from the 1500's.

Artists and Goldsmiths in the Renaissance

Until the end of the Middle Ages, the precious objects in royal treasuries served primarily symbolic and political purposes. They symbolized the notion of divine right attached to hereditary rulers and served as a concrete rep-

A Renaissance ring with a superb pyramid-shaped diamond at the center and three diamond points on each side in pyramidal mounts. Musée de Cluny, Paris. *Photo Luc Joubert, Paris.*

resentation of a monarch's financial power. Indeed, they could be used as security for loans to raise armies and fight wars. Obviously, therefore, the costly jewels in the royal treasuries were not intended for everyday wear. They were worn only on grand diplomatic or political occasions. To some extent this tradition still prevails—the queen of England wears the crown jewels when opening a new parliament but not when attending a race meeting— but the Renaissance brought with it new attitudes and new customs. A spirit of *joie de vivre* spread throughout most of Europe. People experienced a new delight in earthly pleasures, among them the pleasure of wearing rich personal ornaments. As it happened, this interest in wearing jewelry coincided with the growing availability of diamonds. It became possible, at least for people of high birth, to cover themselves with precious stones. They began choosing their jewels to match their clothing, and from that time on, fashions in clothes and jewelry evolved as one.

It is fashion that must bear the blame for the disappearance of the majority of the rich and elegant jewels of the Renaissance. As the years went by and fashions changed, old pieces of jewelry were broken up, and the stones were recut according to prevailing styles. Only a few Renaissance pieces still remain in European museums and in one or two private collections. They are characterized by striking color combinations and by a markedly individual use of different techniques and materials. Besides these survivals, artists of the period have left numerous paintings that give evidence of the imagination and inventiveness of the Renaissance jewelers. By this time, the craft of the goldsmith-jeweler carried considerable prestige, and many a painter, sculptor, and architect had reason to be thankful for the years he had spent as a young man working in a goldsmith's workshop. This well-known custom was most common in Italy, where the sculptor Donatello, the painters Botticelli and Ghirlandaio, and the architect Brunelleschi are among the most notable examples of artists who were apprenticed to jewelers, but it existed in other countries as well. Among those who gained early experience in the goldsmith's

Far left: The Lyte Jewel, a gold enameled pendant with 25 table-cut diamonds (nine are mounted on the obverse of the monogram) and four rose-cut diamonds, with a portrait of James I by Nicholas Hilliard. About 1600–10. British Museum, London. *Photo British Museum.*

Left: Portrait of Henri III of France (1574–89). Musée historique, Château de Versailles. *Photo Hubert Josse, Paris.*

Below: Allegorical figures with diamonds. Painting by Hans Muelich from the *Livre des joyaux de la duchesse Anne*, 1560. Bayerische Staatsbibliothek, Munich. *Photo Bayerische Staatsbibliothek.*

Dame à sa toilette, School of Fontainebleau, second half of the 16th century. Musée des Beaux-Arts, Dijon. *Photo Giraudon, Paris.*

Two portraits showing the growing importance of the diamond in jewelry for women in the early 17th century. Right: Archduchess Isabella of Austria, regent of the Netherlands from 1599 to 1633. Flemish School. Rijksmuseum, Amsterdam. Far right: Louise Marguerite de Lorraine, princesse de Conti (1574–1631). French School. Musée Condé, Chantilly. *Photos Rijksmuseum (right); Hubert Josse, Paris.*

trade were Hans Muelich in Bavaria; Albrecht Dürer (the son of a goldsmith) in Nuremberg; Hans Holbein, who became court painter to Henry VIII of England; Étienne Delaune in Strasbourg; and Jacques Androuet de Cerceau, architect to the king of France.

Catherine de' Medici was so fascinated by jewelry that she liked to design it herself. Catherine, of course, came from Florence, the city that led in the revival of the arts at the end of the Middle Ages. She was also a member of the great banking family whose influence spread far beyond Florence—the Medici had branches and agents in places as widespread as London, Bruges, Avignon, and Milan. Under their benevolent patronage, the goldsmiths' guild in Florence flourished as never before. Cosimo I (1519–74), the first duke of the younger branch of the Medici family, went so far as to order the eviction of all "lowly trades" from the shops on the Ponte Vecchio, which were thenceforth to be reserved exclusively for goldsmiths, silversmiths, and jewelers. Florence was not the only great commercial city with an interest in precious stones. Venice also exercised great international influence, had links with Germany and the Netherlands, and, most notably, was the main source of precious stones arriving from the East.

After the Medici, the most generous patron of the jeweler's trade was undoubtedly François I, who reigned from 1515 to 1547 and regained for France her prominent place in the world of jewelry. His most remarkable and—

Marc Gheeraerts: Portrait of Elizabeth I of England (1558–1603). National Maritime Museum, Greenwich. *Photo Hubert Josse, Paris.*

for posterity—most beneficial act was to transform his personal collection of jewels into an inalienable asset of the state. Included in this splendid collection were a large necklace with eleven diamonds (mentioned in an earlier chapter) and two diamond brooches, one containing a large stone called the Poincte de Bretagne, the other a large, square, table-cut stone with a high crown.

Renaissance Jewelry

Renaissance jewelry varied so much in form and design that it is impossible to classify. It is not even possible to identify a particular style with a particular country, since good artists frequently traveled from place to place, and as a result their styles became international. Among the most prized types of jewelry of the period were *enseignes* and pendants. An *enseigne* is a type of badge meant to be worn in a hat, and its design was controlled by the sumptuary laws of each court. Some were very beautiful, like the badge that Louis XI (who reigned from 1461 to 1483) had made for the Order of Saint Michael. It was described in an inventory of 1561 as "a large gold *enseigne* depicting the figure of Saint Michael, decorated with diamonds, who is fighting a

devil fashioned of mother-of-pearl and embellished with turquoises and rubies." The *enseigne* traditionally symbolized the wearer's loyalty to a particular family, clan, or group, but during the Renaissance its purpose gradually changed. It became a means of individual self-assertion and provided an opportunity to flaunt one's originality. It was usually worn accompanied by emblems, mottoes, or other personal symbols. Hats were also often ornamented with bands on which gold- or silver-mounted studs of diamond, pearl, or colored stones were sewn.

However, the most common piece of jewelry was still the pendant, which became the central element of the heavy chains customarily worn in the Middle Ages and was in fact a direct continuation of medieval fashion in jewelry. With the pendant, jewelry designers let their imaginations soar, using a wide range of allegorical, religious, mythological, natural, and other themes. Little by little, diamonds came to figure more largely in pendants. From about the end of the sixteenth century they became not only an essential element of the composition, but the very raison d'être of the finest pieces of jewelry. It was idle for the poet Ronsard to write:

Opposite: A pendant in enameled gold, set with table-cut and rose-cut diamonds with a point-cut stone at the center. About 1600. Probably made in Munich. Residenz Schatzkammer, Munich. *Photo Residenz Schatzkammer.*

De quoi te sert mainte Agathe gravée,
Maint beau Ruby, maint riche Diamante?
Ta beauté seule est ton seul ornement.

("What need have you for so much carved agate,

So many fine rubies, so many rich diamonds?

Your beauty alone is ornament enough.")

Such idealistic sentiments meant little to those who could afford precious stones. In the portraits of the period, monarchs and princes, lords and ladies, all appear adorned like shrines. For example, the many portraits of Queen Elizabeth I in all her finery show her weighed down with brilliant diamonds, pearls, and other jewels.

Pendant earrings were worn chiefly by men, but in a fairly discreet manner. The fashion did not last very long. Pendants on ribbons or chains were much more common. Belts and belt buckles were adorned with precious stones and often ornamented with small diamonds. The first watches appeared in this period, attached to ribbons or chains and hung from the belt. Watch cases were among the finest examples of the jeweler's art, with diamonds and precious stones set in gold and enamel, a style carried over from the Middle Ages that remained popular during the Renaissance. More common than watches, of course, were rings, which were sometimes worn on every finger. Jewelers found new ways to show off precious stones to the best advantage, and mounts and settings gradually became finer, allowing the stones themselves to be displayed in their full brilliance. It was in finger rings above all that the diamond predominated, soon gaining preference over all other stones.

The history of rings and bracelets illustrates how the wearing of jewelry was influenced by fashion in clothes and vice versa. Before the seventeenth century, bracelets were seldom worn because sleeves, which often had lace cuffs, completely covered the wrist and frequently extended over part of the hand. The painting of the Fontainebleau school called *Dame à sa toilette,* now in the Musée des Beaux-Arts in Dijon, appears misleading in this respect, since this famous representation of a female nude shows the subject wearing bracelets on both arms. This is, of course, neither a genre painting nor a portrait—not even an idealized one. Whether or not it was painted from life, it is essentially the painter's image, the artist's dream, representing some traditional figure such as Vanitas reinterpreted in the spirit of the time. In their nudes, the artists of the Fontainebleau school discarded the moralism of the previous century and conveyed a new message—that jewels are part of the equipment of the game of love. They were concerned with displaying jewelry to its finest advantage, offset by a triumphant nudity.

Some women, however, especially in England, were unable to resist the allure of bracelets, and their preference gave rise to the fashion for slit sleeves, which allowed such jewelry to be glimpsed on the wrist. Gloves were treated in the same way to reveal the many

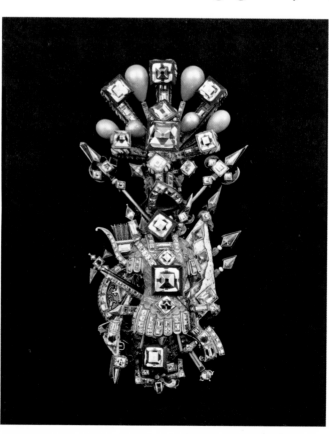

Far left: A clasp in the form of a trophy, in gold, enamels, pearls, and diamonds. Augsburg, 1603. This is the work of the goldsmith Hans Georg Beuerl and was made for the elector Maximilian I of Bavaria. Residenz Schatzkammer, Munich. *Photo Residenz Schatzkammer.*

Clusters of pearls and brilliants. Detail from an anonymous portrait of Countess Marie-Elizabeth Cavriani, 1648. Château national de Nelahozeves. *Photo Ladislav Neubert-Dilia, Prague.*

Opposite, top: A bow for
a state dress set entirely with
diamonds, 16 inches (20 cm)
wide. Early 18th century.
Grünes Gewölbe, Dresden. A
bow designed by Pouget from
his *Pierres Précieuses*, 1762.
Bibliothèque Nationale, Paris.
Photo Hubert Josse, Paris.
Center: Bouquet of brilliant-
cut diamonds and emeralds.
Russia, about 1760. Diamond
Collection of the Soviet
Union, Moscow. *Photo APN,
Paris.* Hat badge in gilded
silver with diamonds, some
rose-cut. Johann Staff, 1765.
Residenz Schatzkammer,
Munich. *Photo Residenz
Schatzkammer.* A *coulant*
from an emblem of the Order
of the Golden Fleece
comprising an oval diamond
of about 50 carats surrounded
by small brilliants.
About 1750. Residenz
Schatzkammer, Munich.
Photo Residenz Schatzkammer.

rings decorating the fingers. English jewelry in the early seventeenth century reached a high standard, surpassing French jewelry, which underwent a temporary decline in the aftermath of the enervating Wars of Religion.

The Seventeenth Century: Pomp and Puritanism

This situation was soon reversed. The rise of Puritanism in England created a climate unsympathetic to ostentatious luxury, while in France, jewelers and goldsmiths began making up for lost time. They were soon producing the most influential models for jewelers throughout Europe. Cardinal Mazarin seems to have played an important part in this revival. By encouraging the jeweler's and diamond cutter's trades, and by his own personal taste for jewelry—he acquired for himself eighteen of the most beautiful diamonds of the time, including the Sancy (53.75 carats), the Mirror of Portugal (25.37 carats), and the Great Mazarin (21 carats)—the cardinal-minister paved the way for the extravagance of the reign of Louis XIV. By the mid-seventeenth century the fashion was for bow-shaped jewels with designs in rose-cut diamonds. The bow, which soon figured largely in all royal courts, was the creation of the famous jeweler Gilles Legaré. It was seen in the form of brooches, pendants, and necklaces. Women often wore a black velvet ribbon around the neck, with miniature diamond-studded portrait cases attached to the ribbon. Coiffures of the time left the ears ex-

posed, so that pendant earrings could be worn. At first these were of modest proportions, but eventually they evolved into comparatively large and complex ornaments of diamonds and precious stones, acquiring the name *girandoles* after the crystal chandeliers that hung in the palace of Versailles. (*Girandoles* have three pendant diamonds, turning and flashing independently.) Each royal court wanted to outdo its rivals in luxury, and jewelers devised ever more extravagant designs.

At the very end of the seventeenth century, Johann Melchior Dinglinger, who was in the service of Augustus the Strong, elector of Saxony and king of Poland, turned away from the fashions dictated by Paris. His creative originality was so impressive that some people compared him to Benvenuto Cellini. If not quite the legitimate artistic successor to the great Florentine goldsmith, he might well be regarded as the forerunner of Peter Carl Fabergé, whose St. Petersburg workshop stood at the forefront of the jewelry profession in the last quarter of the nineteenth century. Some of Dinglinger's most dazzling creations can be seen in the Grünes Gewölbe in Dresden.

The "Brilliant Century"

Perhaps more than any other time, the eighteenth century was the age of jewelry. It was an age that delighted in light, and precious stones—diamonds above all—flashed and sparkled in the light of myriad candles in the chambers of the royal palaces. Wealth and

Opposite, bottom: Watch
and chatelaine belonging to
Queen Caroline-Mathilde.
J. F. Fistaine, 1767. Royal
Collection, Rosenborg Castle,
Copenhagen. *Photo Claus
Hansmann, Munich.* The star
of the Order of Saint-Esprit
presented to a member of the
Bourbon-Parme family
by Louis XV, composed of
brilliants and one ruby.
About 1765. Musée du Louvre.
Paris. *Photo Musées
nationaux, Paris.* Order of the
Golden Fleece in pink and
white diamonds. Made for the
elector Maximilian III Joseph
of Bavaria by Johann Staff.
Residenz Schatzkammer,
Munich. *Photo Residenz
Schatzkammer.*

Left: Michel Ollivier:
Fête given in 1766 by the
prince de Conti for the
prince of Brunswick in the
Bois de Cassan, 1777.
Musée historique, Château
de Versailles.
Photo Hubert Josse, Paris.

Opposite: Marie-Christine de Bourbon, queen of Spain. Detail from a painting by Vincent Lopez, about 1830. Prado Museum, Madrid. *Photo Giraudon, Paris.*

power were expressed in costume, and jewelry, as always, marched side by side with fashion. A complete parure (set of matching jewelry) for women included an aigrette for the hair and *girandoles* for the ears, as well as ring, brooch, necklace, and bracelet. For men there were diamond coat buttons and shoe buckles worth a fortune: some pairs of buckles incorporated more than a hundred diamonds. Diamonds appeared on sword hilts, chivalric emblems, snuffboxes, watches, and medallions. Frederick Augustus II of Saxony wore as a pendant an extraordinary almond-shaped apple-green diamond weighing 41 carats and known as the Dresden Green. The Order of the Golden Fleece worn by the sovereign of Bavaria bore a famous 35.56-carat blue diamond, known as the Wittelsbach Blue, at the center. The grand duke of Tuscany had the famous Florentine diamond (137 carats) mounted in a hatpin. These were only the most famous

stones. There were of course many other jewels, but most were later dismantled so that the stones could be recut and remounted in settings that conformed to current fashions. Aside from museum displays of the surviving pieces, the most fruitful sources of information about the jewels of the eighteenth century are the paintings and drawings by artists of the period.

Of all the brilliant European courts in the second half of the eighteenth century, for sheer opulence the court of Catherine the Great of Russia outshone all others. For her coronation in 1762, Catherine ordered a magnificent crown from Jérémie Posier, a French jeweler based in St. Petersburg. The crown was not completed in time, but it was worn by Catherine's successors and is today one of the most astounding pieces in the diamond collection of the Soviet Union.

Unlike Catherine the Great, Marie Antoinette preferred to wear more simple jewelry, diamonds mounted on pins or clips and placed as if at random in her hair or scattered discreetly on her clothes. The famous Queen's Necklace, designed by the royal jewelers Boehmer and Bassanger, was offered at the price of 1.6 million francs, but Marie Antoinette is said to have rejected it, claiming that "France had greater need of a ship than a diamond necklace." Even in the unlikely event that the statement is not wholly apocryphal, the queen might have had other reasons for rejecting the necklace, which had originally been ordered by Louis XV for Madame du Barry. Marie Antoinette would not have cared for such a great breastplate, as it would have hidden the beautiful neckline of which she was so proud.

The Nineteenth Century
The French Revolution did more than

The crown presented to the empress Josephine by Napoleon I. Collection Van Cleef et Arpels, Paris. *Photo Hubert Josse, Paris.*

Napoleon's sisters, Caroline, Pauline, and Elizabeth Bonaparte, with Hortense Beauharnais (extreme right), at the emperor's coronation in Notre-Dame, Paris, December 2, 1804. Detail from the painting by Jacques Louis David, 1806–07. Musée du Louvre, Paris. *Photo Hubert Josse, Paris.*

René Lalique:
Bracelet in gold, enamels,
and diamonds, 1900.

break up the social structure in France; it disrupted the equilibrium of all of Europe and set the world on new paths. During the period of the Directoire, jewelry remained rather plain, largely gold, seed pearls, and enamel, with very few colored stones and almost no diamonds—distinctly undemocratic stones. Opulence returned with the establishment of the Empire, when newly exalted dignitaries sought to emphasize the importance of their imperial offices. Heavy brocades and embroidered satins replaced the ethereal, romantic muslins of the Directoire and the Consulate, and people brought out their long-hidden diamonds, whose brilliance enhanced court festivities. The new note was emphatically struck on the day of

Napoleon's coronation. A dazzling image of this event was bequeathed to posterity by the court painter, Jacques Louis David. His painting of the coronation is a rich harmony of sparkling diadems, bandeaux, necklaces, and bracelets blended with the soft folds of satin dresses and the gleam of splendid uniforms.

It was at this time that purely decorative jewelry began to compete with parures of precious stones, and the distinction was born between *bijouterie*—lesser jewels, imitations, paste, and costume jewelry—and *joiallerie*—jewelry set with precious gems. The restrained taste of the July Monarchy tended to favor the *petit bijou,* and this, together with the advent of new manufacturing methods, eventually put

Paul and Henri Vever:
Sylvie, pendant in enamel,
rubies, and brilliants, 1900.
Musée des Arts Décoratifs,
Paris. *Photo Luc Joubert,
Paris.*

A. E. Marty: *L'Adieu dans la
nuit.* A Paquin evening dress
in brocaded satin, with tulle
mantlet embroidered with
diamonds and paste. From
"La Gazette du bon ton,"
1913. Bibliothèque des Arts
Décoratifs, Paris.
Photo Hubert Josse, Paris.

Salvador Dali: *The Eye of Time*. Watch with diamonds, cabochon ruby, and enamel. Owen Cheatham Foundation, New York. *Photo Robert Descharnes, Paris.*

the more modest types of jewelry within reach of an ever-widening clientele. An era of democratization was dawning. But the great French jewelers continued to lead the world in fashion.

Nineteenth-century taste was exceedingly eclectic. The antique styles favored in the Neoclassical period soon gave way to more naturalistic ones. There was a profuse blooming of jeweled "bouquets," which sought to imitate flowers with the utmost fidelity. Motifs based on Gothic or Renaissance architecture aroused equal enthusiasm, and for a time imitations of ancient Egyptian jewelry were popular. Sentimental jewelry made its appearance: lockets were designed to hold a portrait or a lock of hair of a loved one.

The establishment of the South African diamond mines in 1870 caused an upheaval in the jewelry industry by suddenly placing diamonds within reach of almost everyone. Gems became not only more abundant, they were larger and more beautiful as well. Mounts and settings tended to become increasingly light and inconspicuous, allowing the stones themselves to dominate. Diamonds that would previously have been set in silver were now generally mounted in gold or platinum. At the same time, the art of cutting precious stones reached its greatest development. Within a few decades such perfection of finish and such geometric accuracy had been attained that stones appeared not only magnified but quite beautiful enough on their own to need no other ornament. To the classic cuts—brilliant, marquise, pear, oval, and emerald—were added new fancy cuts—heart, triangle, baguette, and trapezium—which permitted all manner of combinations, however strange or whimsical.

After the humdrum, "petit-bourgeois" cli-

mate of the Second Empire in France, a new burst of creative energy emerged around the turn of the century. The true richness of Art Nouveau design (as it was called) has only recently received general appreciation—it was considered decadent by its contemporary critics. However, aesthetes, artists, and others enthusiastically embraced the creations of Lalique, Fouquet, and Vever in Paris and of Tiffany in New York. Motifs based on plants (vines, flowers) and animals (dragonflies, butterflies, multicolored birds), made with translucent and *plique-à-jour* enamels, colored stones, and diamonds, appeared in shimmering profusion. Women, flowers, and snakes were constantly recurring themes. Never before had fashion sprung upon the world a style so totally new, bearing little resemblance to anything that had gone before or, for that matter, anything that has been done since.

The riot of arabesques, flowing lines, and brilliant light effects that was Art Nouveau was in direct contrast to the style known as Art Deco, which appeared in the mid-1920's. Gentle, plantlike curves were replaced by hard-edged geometric patterns inspired by the cubist movement in art. But no matter how styles, fashion, or techniques might change, the diamond was by this time firmly established in the jeweler's repertoire all over the world.

What of today? Is it still possible to speak in terms of style or fashion? The answer is far from obvious. Individuals follow their own inclinations, without conforming to some universal style: in the modern world there is not enough uniformity of taste for such a style to develop. Some may feel that this diversity is a regrettable development, but surely the essential thing is that designs should be beautiful. And beautiful they are. Many contemporary artists, including Salvador Dali, Georges Braque, and Giorgio de Chirico, have revived the great tradition of the artist-jewelers of the Renaissance by producing glorious ornamental objects that attest to the genius of their makers. At the same time, the world has become more democratic: fashion is no longer dictated by the aristocracy, nor are diamonds the sole prerogative of the wealthy elite. It is now possible to cut fifty-eight facets on stones so small that five hundred of them may weigh less than a gram. Thus, in spite of the high price of diamonds, there are few people in western society so poor that they cannot, at some point in their lives, afford at least one piece of jewelry that contains one or more diamonds. Colored stones have not lost their attraction—they still have many admirers—but the diamond remains unique. For it is through the diamond that jewelry has found its true spirit and achieved its most exquisite effects.

Modern Jewelry

Until the Renaissance, the goldsmith's craft was devoted not only to making jewelry and setting precious stones, but, more importantly, to making large ceremonial and religious objects. With the expansion of the business in gems and the ensuing development of jewelry and costume, however, the crafts diversified. The term *joaillier* (jeweler) first appeared in France during the fifteenth century. Much later, a further distinction arose between the *joaillier* and the *bijoutier*. The output of the latter consisted entirely of pieces to be worn as personal ornaments, made of precious or nonprecious materials. The *joaillier* was concerned with precious stones exclusively, creating compositions in which the metal, however precious in itself, performed only a supporting role. Whatever the cost of the setting in time or materials, it is always subordinate to the design and decorative effect that the *joaillier* seeks to create with the gems themselves. In this respect the work of the jeweler can be compared with that of the painter. The cutter who fashions the stones is the craftsman who releases their hidden beauty, and the jeweler is naturally dependent on him to some degree,

but this dependence should not be exaggerated. The jeweler accomplishes his aim—to display the stones in the way that will best reveal their intrinsic splendor—through compositions that he alone truly understands. As head of the overall operation, he recruits many assistants—designers, cutters, engravers, and so on—and, unlike the goldsmith or the *bijoutier*, he requires the services of craftsmen who perform the actual setting of the stones in their mounts. The setters, who work closely with him, are his most important assistants, and their effect on the final result is decisive.

Despite the novelties introduced by changing fashions, many aspects of the jeweler's work have remained virtually unchanged for centuries, and some techniques still in use today have been used since time immemorial. One example is the *cire perdue* ("lost wax") method of casting, in which a wax coating is applied to a model, clay packed around it, the wax melted out, and molten metal poured into the clay mold. This technique was known to the ancient Greeks and to the Chibcha Indians of pre-Columbian America, and a similar process was used by the bronze sculptors of the old African kingdom of Benin.

Still, it is only in recent times that jewelry has achieved its full splendor. Although some stones owe much of their effect to their natural coloration, the beauty of a diamond is largely dependent on how skillfully it is cut. Moreover, there are special problems involved in the use of diamonds in jewelry that do not occur with other precious stones.

The first decision to be made concerns the nature of the piece of jewelry to be created. Should the emphasis be on the diamond alone, or should the diamond be set among other rare stones, emphasizing their beauty without sacrificing its own preeminence? The decision depends on the skill and experience of the jeweler. The diamond may even be relegated to a secondary role, with the modest purpose of highlighting a design in precious metal. Subtle nuances must be considered, and such decisions are seldom clear-cut.

The second factor that must be taken into account is economics. The design of a piece of jewelry does not depend solely on the whim of the craftsman. Its likely selling price and the

A jeweler's tools. Clockwise from top left: brush, lens, fret saw, setter's haft coated with wax, pliers, hammer and set of countersinks, small hand vise (bottom right) with bar of wax, selection of gravers and small nails, files. *Photo Michel Plassart, Paris.*

Alessandro Fei:
A goldsmith's workshop,
16th century. Studiolo,
Palazzo Vecchio, Florence.
Photo Scala, Florence.

Plaster cast of a brooch set with gems. Before photography was invented, these casts were made as records of jewelry designs. *Photo Guy Philippart de Foy, Brussels.*

Parts of a ring set with a cabochon sapphire surrounded by diamonds: the initial design on tracing paper, the setting ready for the stones, and the stones themselves temporarily mounted in wax. *Photo Guy Philippart de Foy, Brussels.*

question of customer demand must also be considered. Making a solitaire (a ring with a single diamond), which is nowadays the customary symbol of a marriage engagement in many countries, is a rather frustrating task for the jeweler—so many thousands of these rings have been made that there really is no longer any opportunity for originality. Nevertheless, in the past some of the most beautiful jewelry was created to fulfill specific demands of individual clients (although, admittedly, in many cases the beauty of the finished piece was a greater consideration than the price). Pierre de Montarsy, jeweler to Louis XIV; Arnold Lulls, who worked for Anne of Denmark; J. M. Dinglinger, who was in the service of Augustus the Strong; Rondé and Jacquemin, jewelers to Louis XV; Bapst, Marie Antoinette's jeweler; Fabergé and Castellani, the masters of the nineteenth century—all these artists, notwithstanding their great fame, were to some degree subject to the same constraints as today's craftsmen.

There are several other factors, impossible to ignore, that influence the jeweler's profession, such as social and cultural values and changing fashions. Like all other forms of art, jewelry design cannot be separated from its historical context, from the type of society in which it is produced and which it therefore reflects. Changes occur here as rapidly as they do in all other decorative arts. But although the jeweler is in business in order to satisfy a specific current demand, he cannot forget that he is making objects that will last virtually forever. The products of his creativity will not be confined to the era that gave them birth, but may appeal to generations of admirers in an unknown future.

Some Aspects of Modern Jewelry

The principal development in the world of jewelry since the end of the Second World War has been the growth of the market for fine jewels. The time has long passed when jewelry was the exclusive property of the rich. Two examples serve to illustrate this development—first, the popularization of the solitaire, and second, the marked success of composite pieces, in which diamonds are mixed with carefully selected colored stones. The recent history of the solitaire is particularly instructive because it gives an insight into the complex workings of the international diamond market. Since the mid-1960's the solitaire has been in extraordinarily high demand, yet its share of total diamond jewelry sales in that period has actually declined, from 45 percent in 1967 to 35 percent in 1975. The contradiction here is more apparent than real: what these figures actually illustrate is the remarkable world-wide success of the commercial strategy of the Central Selling Organization. The world market has been expanding at such a great rate that the proportionately lower figures for the solitaire are largely a reflection of the rapidly rising sales of other types of jewelry. Meanwhile, the growing number of people who wish to own a diamond ring for a relatively modest financial outlay has put great pressure on the market, leading to the use of stones that are not only smaller but also inferior in quality. Not so long ago, a diamond solitaire nearly always weighed about 1 carat. Now, however, stones weighing no more than one-tenth of a carat, and often with distinctly imperfect clarity as well, are widely used.

Another characteristic of the modern jewelry market is the emergence of a new class of customers. These are generally young, dynamic people with no particular desire to be ostentatious but eager to take advantage of improved economic circumstances. Rejecting traditional jewelry, they have seen the appeal of imaginative ornaments in which the most up-to-date manufacturing techniques have been used to produce jewelry that is relatively inexpensive but undeniably fascinating. In response to public demand, "design centers" have been established in many places. Without pretending to compete with the great names of international jewelry, these are aimed at fulfilling local needs. The growth of such centers has brought about an unprecedented proliferation of styles.

Finally, the general public has never shown so much interest in jewelry as it does today.

The work of the setter. Left: Sharpening a burin. Right: The actual setting. *Photos Guy Philippart de Foy, Brussels.*

Below: Mounts arranged in clusters, made by the *cire perdue* method. Bottom: Soldering a platinum ring that is laid out on a jeweler's *perruque*. *Photos Guy Philippart de Foy, Brussels.*

Market research has established conclusively that jewelry is now regarded as the ideal type of gift. In addition, exhibitions and competitions like the Prix de la Ville de Genève and the Diamonds International Award (founded in the United States in 1953 at the initiation of De Beers and subsequently opened to worldwide competition) have undoubtedly contributed to the growing interest in creative jewelry. It would be wrong to dismiss this passion for jewels as merely a defensive reaction to the depredations of inflation or the unpredictability of the stock market. The process of adaptation and transformation has made today's jewelry fresher and livelier than ever. Hardly a day goes by without the birth of a new model, whether it is a small, modestly priced brooch or an opulent piece that costs a fortune.

How is the jewelry profession organized, and what are the links between the different branches of the trade that together create a piece of jewelry? The producers of jewelry can be broadly divided into three categories. First, and somewhat divorced from the rest of the trade, are those creative artists who work alone or in very small groups producing individual pieces, stamped with their own individual style, which are sold directly to a necessarily limited clientele. Second, there are the designers who work for the large jewelry houses. These people may be self-employed, with their own workshops, or they may work for the firm full-time. Finally, there are the firms engaged in large-scale mass production. All three may have characteristics in common, and each may be connected in some way with the others.

The individual artist, for example, may well use a partially finished industrially produced piece as the basis of his own creation; a manufacturer may call on the services of a good jeweler before he sets his production line in motion. However, accomplished jewelers—craftsmen capable of making a piece of jewelry from start to finish—can be found in the first two categories only. Firms engaged in mass production depend on mechanization and division of labor; their workers are skilled in only one part of the manufacturing process.

Gold or Platinum?

The basis of most gemstone jewelry is a precious metal. At one time silver was highly regarded for this purpose, but it is much less popular today. From the earliest times to the present, gold has held the first place among metals. Its many remarkable qualities, including its malleability and resistance to oxidation and tarnishing, have driven men to seek it passionately. Wars have been started for gold, and great expeditions have been undertaken in pursuit of it. The search for gold has led to the discovery of continents; the possession of gold has allowed mighty civilizations to flourish. The earnest efforts of some economists to dissuade modern societies from using it as the basis of their monetary systems have not prevented speculation in gold, and the consequent leaps in price cause dismay in the jewelry industry. To the jeweler, gold is not money in the bank, it is a basic raw material, like leather for the shoemaker or bricks for the builder. The jewelry trade desires only stable

A floral bouquet in brilliants. Made by Hans Stern, Rio de Janeiro.

Right: Diamond pendant, Zale Corporation, Dallas, Texas. *Photo Michel Plassart, Paris.*

Setting the stones by hand, detailed work that is very tiring for the eyes. In some workshops, globes filled with blue liquid are placed between the light source and the workbench to give a more soothing light. *Photo Guy Philippart de Foy, Brussels.*

prices and regular supplies.

As a setting for gemstones, gold is normally preferred with its natural color unaltered, even when another metal is introduced to increase its hardness. Some alloys, however, are deliberately given various tints, such as red, green, or blue, and in recent years white gold has been used increasingly, especially in rings, as an interesting and less expensive substitute for platinum. The use of gold is governed by strict standards, and the purity of the gold that is used in jewelry is measured in karats. (The term "karat" here has no connection with the unit of weight used for diamonds and other precious stones.) Twenty-four-karat gold is 100 percent pure gold, 18-karat gold is 75 percent pure, 14-karat is 58 percent pure, and so on.

For diamond jewelers today, gold has been to some extent superseded by platinum. The color of platinum harmonizes more effectively with diamonds and appears to accentuate the brilliance of the stone to a greater degree. The use of platinum in jewelry is a comparatively recent development—the metal was virtually unknown until the Spanish conquest of South America in the sixteenth century, and for some time after that it was held in comparatively low regard. Its qualities could not be effectively exploited until new techniques were invented to refine and work it. Today it is more costly than gold. It is hard yet malleable, and it is highly resistant to chemical action and oxidation. Its color never varies, and it can take—and retain—a high polish. These qualities make it virtually the perfect complement for diamonds. A small proportion of another metal is usually added to give extra strength without detracting from any of platinum's desirable properties. A hundred years ago brilliant-cut diamonds would have been mounted in silver, which was heavy in appearance and soon tarnished. Today the use of platinum makes much lighter and more durable settings possible. Moreover, the separate elements of a piece of jewelry can be joined by links that are extraordinarily fine and supple yet strong enough to withstand any reasonable test. Thanks to platinum, precious stones can be arranged in a fine mosaic whose supporting framework is barely visible. It was platinum, too, that in the 1930's encouraged the revival of the fashion (known also in the eighteenth and nineteenth centuries) for jewelry that can be taken apart and reassembled in different forms for different occasions—for example, a necklace that can be converted into a bracelet and clips.

Other metals related to platinum are also used in jewelry making. Palladium, for example, possesses most of the characteristics of platinum. But palladium is seldom used by itself because it has never been officially recognized as a precious metal, and there is no hallmark to guarantee its authenticity. It is chiefly employed in making white gold. Iridium, harder and rarer than platinum, is sometimes mixed with platinum in very small proportions to give it greater strength and hardness. Because of its brilliance and reflective qualities, rhodium is sometimes used as

Among other peculiarities, jeweler's workshops have a grid on the floor that allows any scraps of gold or precious powder dropped accidentally to be recovered at the end of the day. Right: One of the last steps in making a piece of jewelry—in this picture a splendid ruby-and-diamond necklace—is to place it on a bust so that its balance and "fall" may be checked. *Photos Guy Philippart de Foy, Brussels.*

a very thin protective coating on platinum and on white gold. It does not tarnish, and it gives exceptional brilliance and—more importantly—greater durability to the jewel. As rhodium is rarer and more expensive than the precious metals it is used to protect, its use is generally limited to this cosmetic application.

The Birth of a Piece of Jewelry

In his capacity as master craftsman, the jeweler calls on the services of many collaborators. First among them is the diamond cutter, from whom he obtains the particular stones he requires. The cutter himself adapts his wares to prevailing market conditions and to satisfy the needs and ideas of the jeweler. As far as diamonds are concerned, the options are much fewer than they are with other precious stones, but the jeweler must still take into account various factors that restrict his field of action. Above all, he must be aware of the type of customer and the maximum price level he is aiming at. Once these have been established, he begins to look for the type of stones he needs. This may not be as simple as it seems. For a

particularly fine piece of jewelry, it may take years to find all the necessary stones. Even something as apparently straightforward as a diamond necklace may require many months of preparation. The jeweler must select his stones one by one, carefully matching them according to their size, cut, color, and optical properties, in order to make the finished necklace a perfect and unique piece. Alternatively, if a jeweler acquires an exceptional stone, it may be the starting point for a design in which it will be the central element.

The jeweler himself may also be the designer, but the growing complexity of the trade makes this less likely today. Large firms generally have special workshops for designers and *modelistes*. It is not essential for a designer to be a trained jeweler, although some knowledge of precious metals is necessary. If the intention is to produce readily marketable jewelry, the designer should have a thorough knowledge of production techniques. Plenty of painters and sculptors have tried their hands at the business but failed to produce "viable" jewelry because of their ignorance of the nature of the materials or the methods of work. On the other hand, to be an accomplished jeweler, it is not enough just to know all the tricks and pitfalls of the craft and to be able to make a piece of jewelry entirely unaided. The spark of inspiration is also necessary. Creativity follows no ordered path, but any route is a good one if it leads to a happy result.

A fine piece of jewelry bears the stamp of

Necklace in gold and diamonds. The band around the neck is formed from two bracelets, adjustable by an ingenious system of clasps, and the attached pendant is a cognac-colored diamond of 107 carats surrounded by brilliants. The ring, navette-shaped, has a matching diamond of 16.04 carats surrounded by brilliants. Boucheron, Paris. *Photo Michel Plassart, Paris.*

the jeweler's own style and personality; but it also represents the successful solution of practical problems in the course of perhaps hundreds of hours of work. Once the design has been decided, it is up to the designer to convey his ideas with clarity and precision, so that the craftsmen who are to execute them understand exactly what he wants. At this stage drawings are not enough, and a model of the piece is made in wax. The model must be made with the greatest care to give an accurate, three-dimensional impression of the piece as it will look when finished. Imitation stones are normally used in the wax model. The next stage is the casting of the metal—the support or setting for the gems. Thanks to technical advances made in the past fifty years, it is now possible to produce jewelry of extraordinary lightness and flexibility, so that in some pieces the stones can be made to appear as though they have no mounts at all. Precision of that degree cannot be achieved without a preliminary "trial run." The fall and balance of the necklace are minutely checked by placing it on a wooden bust. Every adjustment, no matter how tiny, is important to ensure that the balance is right. The life of the piece as well as the way it will behave when worn are at stake here, and an experienced eye is essential.

Meanwhile, the setting is prepared for receiving the stone. There are many types of settings, each designed to display the stones to their best advantage in a particular way. First, holes are made in the appropriate places with a fine saw. Then the most delicate operation of all, the minutely detailed work of the setter, can begin. Each stone is put by hand in its proper place and then permanently fixed in position. This extremely delicate work is very tiring for the eyes, and it was formerly done under the soothing bluish light of huge glass globes filled with a colored liquid (nitric acid that has been in contact with copper). If he is quick and capable, a setter can place up to eighty stones in position in one day, but a necklace may contain several hundred gems, as well as a thousand or more welded joints in the metalwork. Statistics like these give no idea of the painstaking quality of the work, but they do at least provide an indication of the precision required in assembling such a delicate object, in which each operation demands an almost microscopic attention to detail.

The piece of jewelry is now complete, except for the finishing touches. For this final process, soft leather and mechanical brushes with special polishing fibers are used; sometimes electrolytic processes are employed to apply the perfect finish. After the master jeweler has given it a final loving check, his beautiful offspring is ready to go out into the world.

Paris, the Jewelry Capital

Backed by a tradition more than two hundred years old, Paris today is still a center for jewelry of the highest quality. In many ways the jewelry tradition can be compared with that of Parisian *haute couture*. Paris remains one of those cities in which, despite all the problems of a world in constant and rapid change, it is still possible to assemble and unite in a common endeavor all the branches of a trade indispensable to the creation of that unique object that is a piece of jewelry. Jewelry making is an artistic discipline in which a single individual, no matter how talented or

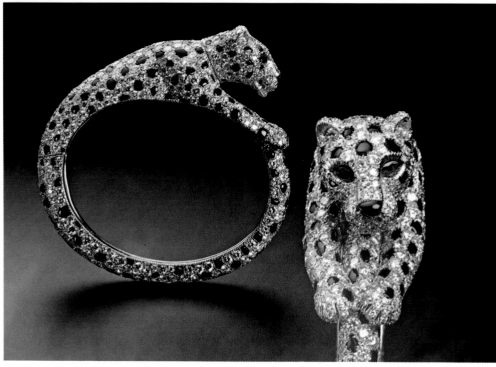

Right: Collar of diamonds and sapphires mounted in gold. It contains eight faceted oval sapphires of about 76 carats and one faceted oval sapphire of about 46 carats, as well as eighteen pear-shaped diamonds of 8.4 carats, five navette diamonds of 18.12 carats, and 265 brilliants of 42 carats. Creation Van Cleef et Arpels, Paris.
Far right: Platinum necklace made with 202 diamonds weighing a total of 181.99 carats. The 109 pear-shaped diamonds (16 of which are graded flawless) and 93 marquise diamonds were all cut by the firm of Harry Winston in New York, where the necklace was designed and mounted in 1979.

Right: Necklace of round, navette, and pear-shaped diamonds mounted in platinum. The largest pear-shaped diamond weighs 14.24 carats. Creation Chaumet, Paris. Far right: Necklace and earrings of fine Burma rubies and diamonds, part of a set comprising necklace, earrings, bracelet, and a ring. The complete set contains 75 carats of rubies and 105 carats of diamonds. Creation Garrard, London.

Opposite bottom: A "panther" bracelet of brilliants and onyx mounted in platinum. The eyes are emeralds. Made in 1920, the piece contains about 2,000 stones. Cartier, Paris.
Photo Michel Plassart, Paris.

gifted, cannot alone create out of nothing the almost timeless beauty of a jewel. There are many stages between the original design and the finished piece, and many skillful and industrious people must play their parts in conquering the thousand and one difficulties of a craft whose supreme achievement is to make those very difficulties invisible. Each of the 250-odd jewelry workers in Paris, the elite of the profession, is at some time or other an essential link in the manufacturing process. Whatever the quality of the work produced in other countries, the creations of the Paris jewelers remain incomparable. No other city can boast of having so many great jewelers, and firms with more than a century of experience assure the continuing renown of Paris as the jewelry capital of the world.

Synthetic and Industrial Diamonds

Since the experiments done by Antoine Lavoisier and the British scientist Smithson Tennant some two hundred years ago, it has been known that the diamond consists of nothing more than pure carbon. The idea that something so rare and costly can be composed of a substance so common and cheap has always been intriguing, and through the years many people have, understandably, been tempted to try to make diamonds in the laboratory. In fact, the history of the attempts to synthesize diamonds is no less interesting (though shorter) than the history of the natural diamond, and has an equal share of frustration and failure.

Diamond is a rare mineral in its natural state, and it is extremely difficult to manufacture industrially. We have seen that diamond conforms to the cubic system of crystallization, that each atom of carbon it contains has very strong covalent links with its neighbors, and that there is no such thing as a "molecule" of diamond, unless one considers the crystal itself a giant molecule. This peculiarity explains the extraordinary properties of diamond, such as its hardness and its high refractive index.

Graphite, the other crystalline form of carbon, has a different structure from diamond. Graphite consists of flat hexagonal rings arranged in layers or planes, with very weak bonds between them. The weakness of these bonds accounts for the lower density of graphite compared with diamond, and for its lubricating properties—the layers "slip" against each other.

Synthetic Diamonds

Synthesizing diamond amounts to transforming graphite, or carbon crystallized according to the hexagonal system, into diamond, or carbon crystallized according to the cubic system—in other words, producing a more compact atomic structure. The operation requires very high pressures and very high temperatures. Stated this way, it seems simple, and in principle it is. In practice, however, the process is extremely difficult.

Numerous attempts to synthesize diamond were made for 150 years or so without any real success. The Scotsman James Ballantyne Hannay thought he had succeeded in 1878, and so did the Frenchman Henri Moissan in 1904. Current knowledge, however, sheds doubt on their achievements. They were certainly able to manufacture a crystalline substance that was capable of cutting glass, but that quality alone is not enough to identify a substance as diamond. (X-ray examination, which would have provided a more accurate analysis, was, of course, unknown at that time.)

Not surprisingly, there was a certain amount of chicanery on the part of some experimenters. A Frenchman named Henri Lemoine embarked on a series of experiments in Paris in 1905 and managed to obtain financial support from Sir Julius Wernher, a life governor of De Beers, for the "secret process" he claimed to have invented. Lemoine conducted a fake experiment in Sir Julius's presence and regularly sent him good-looking crystals that he said he had produced in his laboratory. Eventually, Sir Julius observed that Lemoine's "synthetic" diamonds were indistinguishable from natural diamonds produced at the Jagersfontein mine in South Africa. Confronted with the evidence, Lemoine had little choice but to admit his fraud. He was subsequently tried and sentenced to six years in prison.

Genuine progress was made at last by the American physicist and Nobel Prize winner P. W. Bridgman, who, over a period of about

A natural diamond crystal of gem quality with some synthetic diamonds. The latter are about .5 mm in height and weigh about .0017 carats each. The natural diamond weighs .18 carats and is 3.6 mm high.
Photo Michel Plassart, Paris.

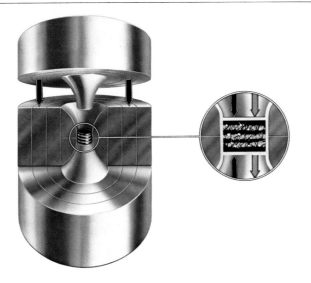

Manufacturing synthetic diamond. The black arrows indicate pressure exerted on the central chamber, and the red arrows the passage of electric current, which provides the requisite heat. *Keith Harmer, The Old Priest House, London.*

forty years, conducted pioneering research into high-pressure conditions. With the cooperation of three private companies, he set up a research program in 1941 with the objective of synthesizing diamond.

Work was interrupted by the Second World War, but afterward it was taken up again independently by Norton International, Inc., and by the General Electric Company. In 1955 General Electric announced that its research had been successful, but its triumph was considerably diluted a few days later when a Swedish firm, Allman Svenska Elektriska Aktiebolaget (ASEA), announced that it had been conducting similar research since 1930 and had in fact succeeded in manufacturing diamonds in February, 1953, two years earlier than General Electric. The Swedish team, led by B. von Platen, had assumed that they were the only ones working on the problem, and they had preferred to keep their results secret. They were interested in manufacturing gemstones, and they had not considered that the creation of very small diamond crystals, the largest hardly exceeding one-twentieth of an inch (1 mm), could be regarded as the successful culmination of their program.

How had the Swedish and the American scientists succeeded in performing this operation when the necessary pressure (more than 60,000 atmospheres) far exceeded the capacity of the strongest materials known at the time and, moreover, correspondingly high temperatures (around 2,500° F, or 1,400° C) were required?

For the Americans, the process was made possible by an ingenious apparatus known today as the Belt, which was perfected by research scientists at General Electric. The Belt owes its success to the fact that, at the moment when the highest pressures occur, all the mechanical parts are interdependent and mutually supportive.

In this system, any excessive tension that may be created at a given point is immediately redistributed among neighboring parts and is thus reduced to tolerable levels. A tungsten carbide ring contains at its center a short tube of pyrophyllite (a natural stone that somewhat resembles talc) filled with alternating discs of graphite and a nickel, cobalt, or iron catalyst. Two pistons in the shape of truncated cones are driven into the tube from opposite ends, sealing it completely. Finally, enormous pressure is exerted by a hydraulic press while, at the same time, the temperature is being raised by an electric current passing through the central cell.

The system used in Sweden differed slightly from the one developed at General Electric. In the Swedish system the necessary pressure was achieved with six inward-pointing pyramids, their truncated points forming a central, circular chamber. This apparatus permitted larger volumes to be worked, but it had the corresponding drawback of being rather complex to operate.

Whatever the technical details, it was clearly established that synthetic diamonds could be produced, and in 1958 De Beers announced its own success in this field. Since then, successful experiments have evolved into commercial production throughout the world. Today no less than 110 million carats are manufactured by De Beers in Ireland, South Africa, and (following an agreement with ASEA in 1967) Sweden; by General Electric in the United States; by the Soviet Union (in Kiev); by Japan; and, in smaller quantities, by a number of other countries. Various new production processes have been developed.

Synthetic crystals are generally very small, seldom exceeding 20 mesh (.8 mm). Bonded in synthetic agglomerates, they have numerous uses in industry, where the supply of natural diamonds has long been insufficient to meet demand.

Once the manufacture of small diamond crystals had been proven possible, researchers naturally turned their attention to the manufacture of diamonds suitable for jewelry, which meant making larger crystals. That was, of course, the aim of the earliest pioneers in synthetic diamonds, but it was not until 1970 that the laboratories of General Electric succeeded in producing a few stones of very fine quality, weighing as much as 1 carat each. The finest of them were judged equal to natural white rough of excellent clarity, and they responded quite normally when subjected to various cutting tests. These early synthetic gem diamonds are now on display at the Smithsonian Institution, in Washington, D.C.

The successful General Electric experiments proved that commercial production of syn-

The diamond window in the Pioneer spacecraft launched in August, 1978, to study the planet Venus. Diamond was chosen for the window, through which readings were taken by instruments, because it was the material most likely to withstand the high pressures and temperatures anticipated. The original rough weighed 205 carats; it was cut in the Netherlands by the firm of Drukker and weighed 13.5 carats when finished. *Photo NASA.*

Polishing contact lenses. *De Beers Archives, Industrial Diamond Division.*

thetic gem diamonds was no easy matter: it is necessary to maintain extremely high pressures and temperatures for more than fifty hours at a time. The choice of catalyst is also vital. The cost of making a synthetic diamond far exceeds the cost of producing a natural stone of equivalent size and quality, and for the time being at least, the natural gem diamond is in no serious danger of competition from its synthetic rival.

Industrial Diamonds and Their Uses

The discovery of many industrial uses for diamonds during the Second World War was a powerful incentive to the laboratories seeking to synthesize diamonds, especially since none of the major industrialized countries, except for the Soviet Union, is a producer of natural diamonds. They depend largely on developing nations, in which volatile political

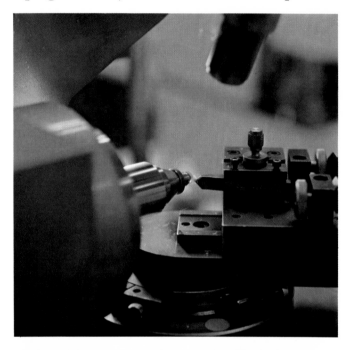

Cutting a geode with a diamond-edged saw. *De Beers Archives, Industrial Diamonds Division.*

conditions may be a threat to supplies.

In the past twenty or thirty years total worldwide production of all types and qualities of diamonds (including synthetic diamonds) has reached an average of about 140 million carats a year. This may seem at first to be an enormous quantity, but less than 4 percent of the annual production is still in existence a year later. All industrial diamonds, whether natural or synthetic, "wear out" in a comparatively short time, and gem-quality rough loses about half its weight during cutting and polishing. Of all the gem diamonds produced each year, little more than 5 million carats remain to make their way into the display windows of jewelry shops.

The tremendous importance that the diamond has acquired in industry—diamond-edged saws, for example, are now widely available in hardware stores—is due chiefly to its unique hardness. On the comparative scale of hardness established by Mohs, the diamond is rated 10, at the top of the scale, while talc is rated 1, at the bottom. But the Mohs scale is somewhat deceptive because it is arbitrary: there is no exact ratio between the categories, and in fact the difference between corundum, rated 9, and diamond is much greater than the difference between talc and corundum.

In 1940 Chauncy G. Peters and Frederick Knoop perfected a method of testing hardness by indentation. According to their system, talc was rated at 32, green carbide of silicon at 2130, and diamond at between 5500 and 6950. In addition, as Dr. Eileen M. Wilks has demonstrated, diamond varies in hardness, not only between different stones, but also in different parts of the same stone, and the variation may be as much as 10:1.

Industrial diamonds are generally available in three broad categories. The first and by far the largest comprises crushing boart (natural diamond of poor quality, found mostly in Zaïre), which is crushed and graded to make fine diamond grit or powder. Tiny metal-clad synthetic crystals are also included in this category. To obtain these crystals, the diamond is given a fine metal coating before being bonded in resin. The second category comprises very small stones (.005–.5 carats) of regular shape, which are used primarily in rock and masonry drilling bits, and in trimming or grinding tools that are set with multiple diamonds. Finally, larger stones (up to 10 carats) and those with specialized shapes make up the third category. They are used in single-point abrasive tools of various kinds, in diamond wire-drawing dies, and for many other applications. In this area, synthetic agglomerates are being used in increasing quantities.

The first major problem that had to be over-

A close-up view of the industrial diamond crystals set in a drill head. *Photo Guy Philippart de Foy, Brussels.*

Polishing samples of resin-bonded kimberlite with diamond powder. *De Beers Archives, Industrial Diamonds Divison.*

come in using diamonds in industrial equipment was finding an effective way to fix the diamonds or diamond powder in the tool. The diamond must be set firmly enough to withstand the stress it will have to endure. At first brazing, clamping, and casting methods were used. These have now been replaced by the use of sintered metal powder to affix larger diamonds and, in grinding wheels for example, sintered metal powder and resin. When a single layer of very small diamonds is required, the stones are fixed on a metal base by electrodeposition. In apparatus that is not subjected to great stress, such as the stylus of a record player, direct adhesion between diamond and metal is possible.

The diamond's uses in industry are so numerous that it would be impossible to list them all here. Some of the more spectacular applications are well known; others are not. One of the most ancient uses of the diamond is for cutting and engraving glass and precious stones. Everyone who has framed a picture or replaced a broken window is familiar with the glazier's diamond. Rather less well known, though following logically enough from the glazier's work, is the vital role the diamond plays today in the manufacture of optical lenses. Equally important is its use in machining the more delicate parts of internal-combustion engines, such as pistons and valves. The diamond-tipped tools designed for this kind of work produce an extremely precise finish, with variations that can be measured in a few tens of microns only. Moreover, thanks to the diamond's high thermal conductivity, diamond-tipped tools reduce heating and consequently minimize the distortions that overheating can cause.

The diamond has also become indispensable in the electronics industry. For example, the extraordinary precision obtained with diamond wire-drawing dies has made possible the manufacture of extremely fine (.05-mm and even thinner) but perfectly regular conducting wires. Making the diamond die itself is an extremely delicate operation. The wire must pass through a conically shaped hole in the die, the narrowest part of which corresponds to the desired diameter of the wire. The angles of each zone of the cone—entrance, approach, reduction zone, and drawing duct—are precisely calculated so that each zone reduces the wire with equal accuracy. Formerly, the hole was drilled with needles of varying sizes, coated with diamond powder and revolving at high speed, but it could take several days to make a die by that method. More refined techniques have since been introduced, including ultrasonics and, more recently, laser beams, which complete the job in just a few seconds.

From Inner Earth to Outer Space
Of all the industrial processes in which

diamond is employed, the most revolutionary effects have been achieved in rock drilling and core cutting. The distressing din of the percussion drill is familiar to everyone, but since the introduction of diamond-set bits percussion drilling is rapidly becoming unnecessary. Drilling can be done in the middle of the night on a residential street without disturbing anyone's sleep.

Diamond drills are not only quieter, they are also a great deal quicker than percussion drills. When a runway at Orly airport, in Paris, had to be reinforced with prestressed steel bars in order to accommodate the new generation of heavier airliners, the task of drilling the concrete for the reinforcing bars was completed by diamond-set drilling machines in such a short time that there was no serious disruption of air traffic.

The use of diamond in drilling is not new. It goes back more than a hundred years, to the boring of the Mount Cenis tunnel through the Alps in the 1860's. Brazilian carbonados, one of the toughest forms of industrial diamonds, were hand-set in the drill bits, and the drills were powered by steam engines. Techniques have of course changed since then; today, rotating diamond-set heads are used, with fluid circulating to carry the debris away from the drilled cavity.

Diamond-edged saws cutting a 15-ton stone block in sections. Work proceeds at between .4 inches and 3 feet (10 cm–1 m) an hour, depending on the type of stone. *De Beers Archives, Industrial Diamonds Division.*

The diamond has countless applications in engineering and construction, where it has made possible methods that are both faster and cheaper. For example, when pouring concrete, the normal method in the past was to make drainage holes in advance, which required costly and complicated grooves and linings. With a diamond-set bit, however, concrete can be drilled without difficulty. This process is not only much simpler, but has the added advantage of permitting greater precision.

Even more spectacular is the advance in drilling bore holes since the introduction of diamond-set coring bits. For centuries man has tried to sink holes into the earth, particularly in the search for water. Generations of prospectors have gradually improved the methods used, but by far the most startling advance was made when bits were fitted with diamonds. Power increased tenfold, with consequent savings in time and money. The best example is the boring of oil wells, in which extraordinary savings have been achieved when drilling through very hard rocks.

Of course, diamond drills are expensive. A diamond crown 12 inches (30 cm) in diameter containing some 1,200 carats of diamonds costs about $27,000. But it lasts for nearly two hundred hours, whereas a metal bit wears out after about thirty hours. Since the diamond drill advances at about twice the rate of more conventional drills, and since changing the bit on a rock drill takes about eighteen hours, it is obvious that the initial investment is well worthwhile. The savings for a 3,300-foot (1,000-m) bore hole amount to nearly $1 million, or two weeks' work.

The most exalted use that man has so far found for the king of precious stones makes a fitting conclusion to this book. Because of its exceptional hardness and extraordinary optical properties, a diamond was chosen as the material for a small porthole in the Pioneer spacecraft launched toward Venus in August, 1978. Behind the sheltering pane, measuring instruments functioned in total security. This was no industrial stone. A faultless gem of perfect clarity, it was chosen from among thousands of others, and it was cut in a manner that gave it maximum strength combined with maximum visibility. The actual cutting, based on minute calculations, was done with breathtaking precision and took several months to complete. Tests proved that no other material, either natural or synthetic, would have performed as successfully.

This latest exciting application of one of nature's most perfect creations may justify, even to skeptics, the strange fascination that the diamond has exercised for so long over the minds of men.

Appendix

Scale of Colors	Weight in Carats	Scale of Clarity		
		FL/IF	VVS₁	S/2
exceptional white or River	.25	45	35	20
	.50	160	115	60
	1.00	1,000	700	300
	2.00	3,000	2,000	900
rare white + or Top Wesselton	.25	40	30	15
	.50	145	100	50
	1.00	900	600	275
	2.00	2,600	1,700	800
rare white or Top Wesselton	.25	35	27	15
	.50	110	85	45
	1.00	650	500	300
	2.00	1,800	1,400	700
white or Wesselton	.25	27	24	13
	.50	90	80	45
	1.00	500	450	250
	2.00	1,400	1,250	650
slightly tinted white or Top Crystal	.25	21	19	10
	.50	70	65	35
	1.00	380	340	170
	2.00	1,100	1,000	500
tinted white or Crystal	.25	15	14	8
	.50	50	48	25
	1.00	260	250	130
	2.00	750	725	360

Above: Table of price variations depending on color and clarity of diamonds of four different weights, assuming identical quality of cut. The figure 1,000 corresponds to a 1-carat brilliant of color E, which is classed as flawless under a 10× lens. A price reduction of about 20 percent must be taken into account for stones weighing between .99 and .97 carats, as well as those in which the 1-carat figure has been achieved by contrived cutting.

Variation in the diameter of round brilliants according to weight, each diamond assumed to be of correct proportions. Actual size.

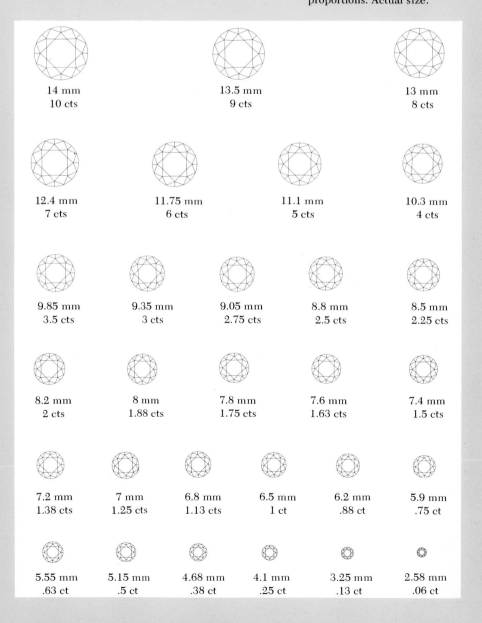

14 mm
10 cts

13.5 mm
9 cts

13 mm
8 cts

12.4 mm
7 cts

11.75 mm
6 cts

11.1 mm
5 cts

10.3 mm
4 cts

9.85 mm
3.5 cts

9.35 mm
3 cts

9.05 mm
2.75 cts

8.8 mm
2.5 cts

8.5 mm
2.25 cts

8.2 mm
2 cts

8 mm
1.88 cts

7.8 mm
1.75 cts

7.6 mm
1.63 cts

7.4 mm
1.5 cts

7.2 mm
1.38 cts

7 mm
1.25 cts

6.8 mm
1.13 cts

6.5 mm
1 ct

6.2 mm
.88 ct

5.9 mm
.75 ct

5.55 mm
.63 ct

5.15 mm
.5 ct

4.68 mm
.38 ct

4.1 mm
.25 ct

3.25 mm
.13 ct

2.58 mm
.06 ct

Examples of certificates issued by laboratories of the GIA, CIBJO, HRD, and the Paris Chambre de Commerce et d'Industrie.

Gemological Institute of America
GEM TRADE LABORATORY
Scientific Identification of Gemstones and Pearls

Diamond Report
No. NY120807
3/2/77

In the opinion of the Laboratory, the following are the characteristics of the stone, or stones, described on the attached report as based on measurements and also on observations made through the Gemolite (10X binocular darkfield magnification) and in the DiamondLite, utilizing master comparison stones. Mounted stones graded only to the extent that mounting permits examination.

(Red symbols denote internal characteristics; green, external. Symbols indicate nature and position of characteristics, not necessarily their size. Where applicable, setting prongs are shown by black symbols.)

SHAPE AND CUT	round brilliant
Measurements	approx. 6.45 - 6.59 X 4.15 mm
Weight	1.08 carats

PROPORTIONS

Depth Percentage	62.9% - 64.3%
Table Diameter Percentage	61%
Girdle Thickness	medium to slightly thick, faceted
Culet Size	medium

FINISH

Polish	good
Symmetry	good
CLARITY GRADE	Internally Flawless
COLOR GRADE	E
Ultraviolet fluorescence	none

COMMENTS:

Minor details of polish not shown.

GEM TRADE LABORATORY
Gemological Institute of America

By _____

GIA CLARITY-GRADING SCALE

Flawless | VVS₁ | VVS₂ | VS₁ | VS₂ | SI₁ | SI₂ | I₁ | I₂ | I₃
I.F.
Imperfect

GIA COLOR-GRADING SCALE

D E F G H I J K L M N O P Q R S T U V W X Y Z
Colorless | Near Colorless | Faint Yellow | Very Light Yellow | Light Yellow | Fancy Yellow

(Copyright 1975, GIA)

CIBJO

LSI
LABORATORIO SCIENTIFICO NAZIONALE
CONFEDORAFI – ITALIA
Ufficialmente riconosciuto dalla CIBJO il 27/4/1978

CIBJO

CONFEDERAZIONE INTERNAZIONALE DELLA OREFICERIA, GIOIELLERIA, ARGENTERIA, DIAMANTI, PERLE E PIETRE	CONFEDERATION INTERNATIONALE DE LA BIJOUTERIE, JOAILLERIE, ORFEVRERIE, DES DIAMANTS, PERLES ET PIERRES	INTERNATIONAL CONFEDERATION OF JEWELLERY, SILVERWARE, DIAMONDS, PEARLS AND STONES

Diamond Report
Diamante: referto di analisi Nr. I – **00000**

Carat weight/peso in carati:

Colour grade/grado di colore:

Purity grade/grado di purezza:

Shape and cut/forma e taglio: SPECIMEN

Measurements/misure: mm

Proportions/proporzioni: Height/altezza   %   tavola   %

Symmetry/simmetria:
Finish/finitura:
Polish/politura:

Girdle/cintura:

UV-Fluoresence/fluorescenza:

Comments/osservazioni:

This diamond report is based on the Rules of application decided upon by CIBJO up to 1978, in particular on grading with the ten-power aplanatic and achromatic lens and on colour comparison with the CIBJO master diamonds.
The diamond has been tested independently in an absolutely objective way by at least two experts according to the present knowledge in the field of diamond grading.
The report does not make any statement with respect to the monetary value of the diamond. Only the original report with signature and embossed stamp is a valid identification document. Misuse of this document will be prosecuted.

Questo referto sul diamante è basato sulle Regole di applicazione approvate dalla CIBJO nel 1978, in particolare la classificazione è eseguita con lente a 10x aplanetica e acromatica e per confronto di colore con i diamanti campione CIBJO.

Il diamante è stato analizzato in modo assolutamente obiettivo da almeno due esperti in osservanza alla attuali conoscenze nel campo della classificazione del diamante.
Questo referto esclude e non costituisce alcuna dichiarazione in riferimento al valore del diamante preso in esame.
Soltanto il referto originale con la firma e il timbro a secco è valido documento di identificazione. Incorretto uso del documento stesso sarà perseguito.

LSI
Laboratorio Scientifico Nazionale

Data

Firma

LSI – Via Ugo Foscolo, 4 – 20121 Milano – Tel. (02) 871.492

certificate no.   014404

This certificate is established in conformity with the "International Rules for Grading Polished Diamonds", approved by the World Federation of Diamond Bourses and the International Diamond Manufacturers Association at the May 1978 Congress.

The stone in accordance with the above mentioned number has been identified as a natural gem diamond and has the following description :

shape	brilliant
weight	1,33 ct
clarity grade	loupe-clean
colour grade	rare white + (F)
fluorescence	slight
measurements	7,10-7,19mm x 4,32mm
proportions	good
girdle	medium, 3%
culet	pointed
table diam.	64%
cr. height	12%
pav. depth	46%
finish grade	very good
comments	

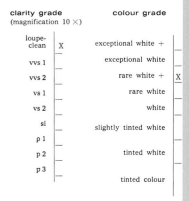

clarity grade (magnification 10 ×)		colour grade	
loupe-clean	X	exceptional white +	
vvs 1		exceptional white	
vvs 2		rare white +	X
vs 1		rare white	
vs 2		white	
si		slightly tinted white	
p 1			
p 2		tinted white	
p 3			
		tinted colour	

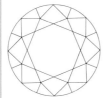 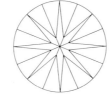

proportions		finish grade	
very good		very good	X
good	X	good	
unusual		medium	
		poor	

antwerpen,   6/11/1978

gemmologists

identification marks :

Red symbols refer to internal and green symbols to external characteristics. The symbols do not usually reflect the actual size of the characteristics.
The characteristics have been indicated in order to clarify the description and/or for further identification.

The characteristics of the above mentioned diamond have been established by scientific measurements and observations, carried out in the laboratory of the Diamond High Council.

Attestation de garantie concernant un diamant

La pierre facettée contenue dans le sachet transparent scellé au timbre du Service Public du Contrôle des diamants, perles fines, pierres précieuses, de la Chambre de Commerce et d'Industrie de Paris, sous le numéro 71.414 réf. 069988 est un diamant présentant les caractéristiques suivantes :

CARACTÉRISTIQUES DE TAILLE :

forme	Ronde
type de taille	Brillant
diamètre de la pierre	7,34 à 7,45 mm
épaisseur de la pierre	4,17 mm
diamètre de la table	4,4 à 4,8 mm
hauteur de la couronne	0,8 mm
hauteur de la culasse	3,3 mm
rondiste épaisseur	Mince
nature	Facetté
colette	Petite
symétrie	Bonne
poli	Bon

POIDS : 1 carat 36
(un carat trente six centièmes)

GRADATION DE COULEUR Blanc Extra (G)
Fluorescence : Très faible

PURETÉ : Pur à la loupe de grossissement dix fois

REMARQUES :

Paris, le   21 Février 1979

Directeur du Service Public du Contrôle des Diamants,
Inspecteur agréé du Service de la Répression des Fraudes et du Contrôle de la Qualité.

N° 044111

ÉCHELLE DE PURETÉ

X	Pur à la loupe de grossissement 10 × (Internally flawless)	
	VVS1	Pur à la loupe de grossissement 3×
	VVS2	
	VS1	
	VS2	présence d'inclusion(s)
	SI	
	P1	
	P2	
	P3	

ÉCHELLE DE COULEUR

Normes internationales*		G.I.A.**
	Blanc exceptionnel + *i* Exceptional white +	D
	Blanc exceptionnel / Exceptional white	E
	Blanc extra + / Rare white +	F
X	Blanc extra / Rare white	G
	Blanc / White	H
	Blanc nuancé / Slightly tinted white	I - J
	Légèrement teinté / Tinted white	K - L
	Teinté / Tinted colour	M à Z
	Diamant de couleur particulière Fancy diamond	

* les définitions ci-dessus et leur correspondance avec G.I.A. ont été approuvées le 9 mars 1977 par la Confédération Internationale de la Bijouterie, Joaillerie, Orfèvrerie (C.I.B.J.O.), par le Conseil Supérieur Belge des Diamants, par l'Association Internationale des Tailleurs de Diamants (I.D.M.A.) et la Fédération Mondiale des Bourses de Diamants (W.F.D.B.).
** Gemological Institute of America

Index

Italic numbers refer to illustrations.

A

Abaeté, 54, 176
Abdul Hamid II, *52, 53*
absorption spectra, 195–96, *196*
adamas, 12, *13–16*, 18
Affaitati family, 32
Agastimata, 20
Aigrette of Charles the Bold, *255*, 256
Aikhal pipe, 184
Albert V, Duke of Bavaria, 205
Alderson, William, 70–71
Aleppo, 28–29
Alexander Bay, 84, 113
Alexander the Great, 16, 17
Alexandria, 24, 28, 31
Algemene
    Diamantbewerkersbond
    van België (Amalgamated
    Union of Belgian
    Diamond Workers), 232
Algemene Nederlandse
    Diamantbewerkersbond
    (Amalgamated Union of
    Dutch Diamond Workers),
    237
alluvial deposits, 27, 90, 113,
    135, 137, 155–56, *155,
    157*, 175. *See also* beach
    mining
Alto Paraguai, 173, 174, 175,
    176
Amsterdam, 33, 36–38, 64–65,
    82, 236–37, 238–39
Amsterdam
    Juwelliersvereniging
    (General Association of
    Jewelers of Amsterdam),
    237
Anglo-American Corporation,
    83, 99, 125
Angola, 137–40
Anglus, Wilhelmus, 38
angstrom, 193
Annex Kleinzee mine, 100,
    101, 113, 114
Antwerp, 30–36, *34, 35*, 36, 65,
    131, 232–36, 238, 239
"Antwerp Mondays," 232
Antwerpse
    Diamantbewerkersbond
    (ADB), 232
Arcet, Jean d', 192
Arfe, Juan de, 209
Art Deco jewelry, 267
Artha-Sastra (Kautilya), 13, 14
Art Nouveau jewelry, 267
Asscher brothers, 236, 237,
    238
Astronomica (Manilius), 14
Atherstone, W. Guybon, 68
Augsberg, 31, 32
Augustus ("the Strong" of
    Poland), 212
Aurangzeb, 180, 252, 253
Australia, 186
Averani, 192

B

Bafi river, 142, 143, 144
Bagagem river deposits,
    55
Bagbe river, 143, 144
Bahia, 55, 61, 64, 65
Ball, Sydney, 129
Bamian valley, 23
Bancroft, Austin, 125
Bandelkhand, 23
Banjermasin, 37, 182
Bapst (jeweler), 270
Barkly, 70
Barnato, Barney, 77–81, 82
Batuobiya field, 185
beach mining, 114, 116–17
Bécéka (Compagnie du
    Chemin de Fer du Bas-
    Congo au Katanga),
    132–33
Beetz, B. F. Werner, 138
Belgian Union of Christian
    Diamond Workers, 233
Bellsbank, 99
Belo Horizonte, 177, 178
Berberati, 186
Berquen, Robert de, 30
Beuerl, Hans Georg, 260
Beurs voor Diamanthandel
    (Diamond Trading
    Bourse), 233
Bible, references to diamonds
    in, 12, *12, 13*
"Big Hole" (Kimberley), *66,
    72, 74, 75, 78–79*
bijouterie, 266, 268
birefringence, 197
Birim valley, 186
Bisnager market, 32
"black" diamonds, 15, 22
block-caving, 110–11
blue ground, 74, 89, 107
Bo, 146, 148, 152
boart, 197, 278
Boehmer and Bassanger,
    264
Boer War, 81–82
Boetius, *see* De Boot,
    Anselmus
Boise, C. W., 131
Bombay, 242–45
Book of Marvels (Marco Polo),
    17, 18, *18*, 39
Borneo, 37, 182–84
Botha, Louis, 237
Botswana, 85, 94, 99, 100, 101,
    102, 104, 108, 113
Boucheron (jeweler), 274
bow, 262, *263*
Boyle, Robert, 192, 195
Bragg, William Henry, 193
Braque, Georges, 267
Braun, Johannes, 13
Brazil, 54–65, *172–79*
breccia, 89
Breitmeyer (dealer), 82
Bretschneider brothers, 62
Bridgman, P. W., 276

Brihatsamhita (Varahamihira),
    14
"brilliance," 201–02, 220,
    220
Britmond (British-Zaïre
    Distribution Ltd.), 132,
    136
Bruges, 29–30
Brussels, 36
bruting, 199, *200, 216*, 218
Buddhabhatta, 14, 15, 20, 28
Buffels river, 113, 114
Buffon, Georges, 91
bukebuke, 132
bulla, 162
Bultfontein mine, 71, 72, 81,
    99, 101, 108, 110
Bureau de Recherches
    Géologiques et Minières
    (BRGM), 98
Bushimaie river, 132, 134
Buttgenbach, Henri, 130

C

caldeirões, 56, 74
Calonda formation, 140
Cambay, gulf of, 22–23, 28,
    242
Campine, 233
Cape Town, *67, 68*, 70
carat, unit of weight, 248
carbonado, 55
Caroní river, 160–61
Cartier (jeweler), 253, 275
cascalho, 56, *56*, 59, 178
Castellani (jeweler), 270
caste system, 20, 21, 23
Catherine the Great, 47, *47,
    48*, 264
Cellini, Benvenuto, 16, 199,
    202
Central African Republic, 186
Central Selling Organization
    (CSO), 150, 188–89, 270
chambering, *108*, 110
Chandragupta Maurya, 13, 16
Chapada Diamantina deposits,
    55
Charles the Bold, 30, 31, 203,
    205, 210, 255–56
Charles V (France), 40, 255
Charles V (Holy Roman
    Empire), 31, 256
Charles VII (France), 255
Charles X (France), 51
Chatrian, Nicolas, 40, 56, 58
Chaumet (jeweler), 275
Chicapa river, 140
China, 18, 25–26, 186
Chirico, Giorgio de, 267
Chiumbe river, 139
Chopra, Iqbal Chand, 126
Cincorá deposits, 61
Ciudad Bolívar, 160, 161
claims, 70, 74, 77, *85*
Clarisse family, 36
cleaving, 198, 200, 215, 216,
    217
Coleroon river, 52

Colesberg, 68, 72, 75
Commynes, Philippe de,
    256
Compagnie Française des
    Mines de Diamants, 80
Companhia de Pesquisas
    Mineiras de Angola
    (PEMA), 137, 138
Condiama (Consorcio Mineiro
    de Diamantes), 137
Confédération Internationale
    de la Bijouterie, Joaillerie,
    Orfèvrerie (CIBJO),
    248–49
Consolidated African
    Selection Trust (CAST),
    144
Consolidated Diamond Mines
    (CDM), 83, 99, 100, 101,
    105, 106, 113, 114, 117,
    120, 123
Corneilsa, 71
Coromandel, 55, 176 (Brazil);
    37 (India)
Correspondence Office for the
    Diamond Industry
    (COFDI), 233–34, 240,
    241, 243
Coster (cutter), 55
Crookes, William, 195
Crystal Palace, 46, *46*
Cuddapah deposit, 32
Cuiabá, 176
Cullinan, Thomas, 237
cut(s)
    American ideal, 213
    baguette, *218, 219*
    Baroque, 203, 211, 213
    brilliant, 203, 205, *206*,
        210–20, *212–13, 216–17,
        219*, 254
    diamond rosette, 206, *206*
    emerald, *218*, 220
    Gothic point, 203
    lasque, 209
    marquise, *218, 219*, 220
    mirror, 207, 209
    Mughal, *21, 203*, 210
    Peruzzi, 203, 212, 213
    point, 203, 205
    Regent, 203, 212, 213
    rose, 209–10, *209, 211*,
        254
    Sancy, 210
    Scan.D.N., 213
    scissor, 210, *211*
    single, 207
    Swiss, 207
    table, 203, 206–07, 209, *209,
        211*
    Tolkowsky, 213
cutting, 25, 29, 30, 33, 34, 38,
    64–65, 194, 198–222, 254,
    267
cutting centers, 232–46
Cuyuní river, 160

Dali, Salvador, 267
Dammartin, Simon de, 255
Daubrée, Auguste, 196
De Beer family, *69, 71*
De Beers Consolidated Mines
    Ltd., 80–81, 82, 83, 84, 85,
    99, 101–03, 106, 109, 110,
    120, 137, 144, 150, 186,
    188, 276, 277
De Beers mine, 68, 71, 72–76,
    99, 101, 108, 120, 231
De Beers Mining Company,
    81
De Boot, Anselmus, 14, 200
Debret, J.-B., 54, 62
Debye (physicist), 193
De Groote family, 36
Delaune, Étienne, 258
Delhi, 23, 180
Diamang (Companhia de
    Diamantes de Angola),
    137, 139
Diamant Boart, 134
Diamant, Le (Jacobs and
    Chatrian), 56, 58, 59
Diamanten-Regie, 82
Diamantina, 54, 58, 59, *60*, 63,
    175, *176*, 177–78
Diamantslijperij Maatschappij,
    65
diamond certificates, 248,
    282–83
Diamond Club, 233
Diamond Corporation of Sierra
    Leone (DCSL), 150, 152,
    154
Diamond Corporation of West
    Africa (DCWA), 153, 155,
    156, 188
Diamond Design (Tolkowsky),
    213
diamond exchanges, 232–46.
    See also marketing of
    diamonds
"diamond fever," 161–68
Diamond High Council, 236
diamond mines, world
    production, 187
Diamond Office, 236
Diamond Producers'
    Association (DPA), 84
Diamond Purchasing and
    Trading Company, 188,
    189
Diamond Research
    Laboratory, 122
Diamond Syndicate, *see*
    Diamond Trading
    Company
Diamond Trading Bourse, 233,
    234
Diamond Trading Company
    ("the Syndicate"), 82, 83,
    84, 150, 240, 241
Diamonds, criteria of value,
    14–18, 20–22
diamonds, famous
    Brunswick, 231
    Condé, *230*
    Cullinan, 82, 100, 231,

D

Daaldinsk pipe, 185

237–39, *236, 238*
Darya-i-Nur, 41, 231
Dresden, 55
Dresden Green, *212,* 213,
231, 264
Elizabeth II, 231
El Libertador, 161
Estrela do Sul, 55
Eureka, 68
Fiftieth Anniversary of
Aeroflot, 186
Florentine, 264
Great Blue, 41, 43, 51–52,
253. *See also* Hope
Great Mazarin, 262
Great Mughal, *41*
Great Table, *41*
Hope, 51–54, *51,* 211, 230,
231
Idol's Eye, 230, 231
Koh-i-Noor, 43–44, *44,* 46,
180
Light of the Eye, 41
Mirror of Portugal, 262
Nur-ul-Ain, 41
Orlov, 46–48, *47,* 180
Poincte de Bretagne, 256
Premier Rose, 123, 231
President Vargas, 176
Red Cross, 231
Regent, 48–51, *49, 50,* 180,
199
Sancy, *50,* 253, 262
Sea of Light, *see* Darya-i-
Nur
Shah, 180
Star of Sierra Leone, *149,*
155
Star of South Africa, 69
Star of the South, 55
Star of Yakutsk, 186
Three Brethren, 203, 205,
205, 210, 256
Tiffany, 231, *231*
Tri-sakti, 184
Wittlesbach Blue, 230, 231,
264
diamonds, geology of, 88–92
Brazil, 56
southern Africa, 93–94,
101–02, 103–04, 113–14,
117–21
South America, 159, 172–73,
177
U.S.S.R., 185
See also alluvial deposits;
kimberlite
Diamonds International
Award, 271
diamonds, physical properties,
192–96
clarity, 221–22, *244–45,*
226
color, 20, 22, 195–96,
226–31
conductivity, 194
cubic structure, 193, 202
density, 194
forms, 14, 20
hardness, 193–94, 218
luminescence, 122–23
optical properties, 194–95
specific weight, 18, 20
"wettability," 121
diamonds, as talismans, 39, 40
diamonds, as investments,
247–49
diggers' race, 83
Diggers' Republic, 70
Diminco (National Diamond
Mining Company), *145,*
154
Dinglinger, Johann, 252, 262,
270

dop, 183–84, *201*
doublet, 197
Doyle, Donald, 138
dry diggings, 72, 74
dredging
Brazil, *177, 178,* 179, *179*
Venezuela, 169–71, *170,*
171
Dreyers Pan mine, 100, 101,
113
drills, diamond, 279–80
Duarte family, 32
Duflos (jeweler), 50
Du Jon family, 34, 36
Dunkelsbuhler, A., 82, 83
Duplooy, Cornelius, 71
Dürer, Albrecht, 31
Dutch East India Trading
Company, 36–38
Du Toit, G. J., 125
Dutoitspan mine, 71, 72, 81,
99, 101, 108, 109

E
Edward VII (England), 237
electrical prospecting
methods, 96–97
Elizabeth I (England), 237,
259, 260
Ellore deposits, 28, 32, 38
El Polaco mine, 161
enseignes, 259
Epiphanius, 16
Etgar exchange, 241
Ethiopia, 28
Eudoxus of Cyzicus, 27
Eugénie (empress), 51
Evelyn, John, 223

F
Fabergé, Peter Carl, 262, 270
faceting, 200, *200, 217,* 218,
219
factories, 64–65
false diamonds, 30. *See also*
synthetic diamonds
Fath Ali Shah, *181*
feitores, 62
Fincham, Alister, 101
Finsch mine, 85, 99, *100,* 101,
102, 104, 105, 106, 107,
117, 120, 122
"fire," 201, 210
Fistaine, J. F., 262
float-and-sink method, 121
Florence, 258
fluorescence, 195, *197*
foiling, 201–02
Fonseca Lobo, Bernardino da,
54
foot rocking screen, 155–56
Forminière, La, 92, 127–32,
134, 136, 137
Fortuna N.V. Society, 233
Fouquet (jeweler), 267
Fourchoudt family, 34, 36
Fourment, Helen, 36
Francis I (Holy Roman
Empire), 51, 192
Francistown, 101, 104
François I (France), 33, 40,
207, 258
Frankfurt-on-Main, 33, 36
Frederick Augustus II, 264
Freetown, 142, 145, 148
Freire de Andrade, C., 138–39
Fugger, Jacob, *30,* 31, 256

G
Gama, Vasco da, 30, 32, 33
Ganges plain, 22

Gani Coulour mines, 26, 28,
43
Garden of Health (Saint
Hildegarde), 40
garimpeiros, 61, 173–74, *174,*
175, 176, 177–78
Garrard (jeweler), 275
Gemological Institute of
America, 248
geochemical prospecting
methods, 97–98
George F. Prins Club, 241
Ghana, 92, 93, 186
girandoles, 262, 264
girdling, 199, 218
Goa, 26, 31–32, 63, 64
Goes, Peter, 33
Golconda, 32, *32,* 38, 121, 180,
252
gold, 271–72
Goldmuntz, Romi, 234
Gorceix, M., 58
gorgulho, 56, 58, 178
Gori hills, 143, 144
grabens, 140
Grão Moghol deposits, 54–55
grease belts, 121–22
Great Lakes region, 91
Greece, 18
grinding, 199–200
Griqualand West Company,
81
Guaniamo, 159, 161–69, *161,*
162, 166–67, 168, 169
Guicciardini, Ludovico, 33
Guild of Diamond Cutters, 33,
34, 36, 38
Guillebert of Metz, 33
Guinea, 93, 149, 186
gupiaras, 56

H
Hannay, James Ballantyne,
196, 276
Harris, David, 77
Hase, Daniel de, 211
Haüy, René-Just, 194, 195
Hendrickx family, 36
Henri III (France), 257
Henry IV (England), 40, *40*
Henry VIII (England), 256
Hesiod, 12–13
high-level deposits, 56
Hilliard, Nicholas, 257
Hindu Kush, 23
Histoire des Minéraux
(Buffon), 91
Hoge Raad voor Diamant
(HRD), 236, *247, 249*
Hond, Louis, 69
Hope, Henry Philip, 52, 53
Hopetown, 68, 69
Hormuz, 28–29, *29*
Horto, Garcia ab, 16, 26, 27
Huggins (physicist), 193
Hull (physicist), 193
Hunan province, 186
Hunt, George, 126
Huysmans, Camille, 234
Hyderabad, 32, 252

I
Idar-Oberstein, *245,* 246
illegal diamond trade, 145–49,
152
inclusions, 196, 214, 221–23,
221, 222, 223, 226
India, 24, 26–28, 32, 37, 39,
43–44, 181–82
industry, diamonds in, 278–80
International Diamond

Manufacturers'
Association (IDMA), 248
Isabella of Austria, *258*
Isidore of Seville, 25
Israel, 239–42
Israel Diamond Institute, 241
Ivory Coast, 186

J
Jackson, Richard, 71–72
Jacobs, Henri, 40, 56, 58
Jacquemin (jeweler), 270
Jagersfontein mine, 70, 81, 82,
99, 100, 102, 111, 237
Jahangir, 180, 252
James I (England), 257
Janot, Narcisse, 92, 129–30
Jaurchund (merchant), 48
Jeffries, David, 64, 212
Jehan à la Barbe (Sir John
Mandeville), 12, 202, 256
Jensen, E., 233
Jequitinhonha river, 55, 56,
58, 177, 178
jeweler, how to choose, 249
jewelry
crafting of, 273–75
history, 252–70
Johannesburg, 82, 84, 246
joaillerie, 266, 268
Jonathon, Leaboa, 102
joplin jig, 132
Jwaneng pipe, 94, 99, 100,
101, 102, *103,* 104, 107

K
Kalahari desert, 66, 94
Kalimantan, 182
Kalinga, 22
Kanshi river, 134
Kaplan, Lazare, *214*
Kasai, 127, 128–31, 137
Kathiawar, 20, 23
Katsha river, 134, *135*
Kautilya, 13
Kenema, *142,* 143–50, *151,*
152, 153, 156
Khojeh, 46, 47
Kimberley, *66, 70, 71,* 72–73,
81, 82, *83,* 99, 105, 108
mines, 74, 77, 78–79, 80, 100
Kimberley Central, 80, 81
kimberlites, 85, 88, 89–90, *89,*
91, *91,* 92, 95, 97–98,
106–07, 108, 110, 113,
120, 121, 143, 223
Kinshasa, 136
Kisumbe, 125
Kleinzee, 105, 113
Klip Drift, 70
Knoop, Frederick, 278
Koffiefontein mine, 70, 99,
100, *101,* 102, 104, 105,
106, 107, *107,* 110, *117,*
120
Koidu field, 155
Koingnaas mine, 99, *100,* 101,
102, 104, 113, 114, 120
Kollur mines, 26, *42,* 180
Kolmanskop mine, *124*
Komkommer, A., 132
Koraalberg, 34
Kotto basin, 186
Kovalenok, Vladimir, 94
Krestovoz-Dvichensk, 184
Krishna river, 48

L
Laborde, Léon de, 209
Laet, Ioannis de, 28
laghu, 20

Lahore, 44, 46
Lalique, René, 266, 267
Lamont, Gavin, 101, 102
Lancsweert, Prosper, 130
Langhoogte mine, 101
Lapidaire (Jean de
Mandville), 12
Laue, Max von, 193
Lavoisier, Antoine, 192
lavras, 56
Lavrinha, 178
Law, John, 48
Lebanese diamond trade, 148,
153, 157
Legaré, Gilles, 262
Leme do Prado, Sebastino,
54
Lemoine, Henri, 276
Lena river, 185
Leopold II (Belgium), 127–28
Leroy, George, 171, *171*
Lesotho, 99, 100, 102, 104,
113
Letlhakane mine, 85, 99, 100,
101, 104, 120, 123
Letseng-la-Terai mine, 100,
102, 103, 104, 107, 117,
118–19, 120
Liang dynasty, 16
Lichtenburg, 83, 85
Liers, 36
Lie Tseu, 25
Lisbon, 29, 30–31
*Livre des joyaux de la
duchesse Anne,* 205, 209,
257
Livre des symples medichines,
39
London, 38, 82, 83, 150, 240,
241
Longatshimo river, 131
Lost-wax casting, 268, *271*
Louis IX (France), 255
Louis XI (France), 259
Louis XIV (France), 41, 52, 53,
210, 253–54, 270
Louis XV (France), *48,* 50,
270
Louis XVI (France), 35, 50,
52
Louis XVIII (France), 50
low-level deposits, 56
Loyet, Gérard, 256
Luachimo river, 139
Luana formation, 139–40
Luana river, 138
Lucapa, 140
Lucapa theory, 139–40, *140*
Lüderitz, 113, 124
Luebo river, 129
Luembe river, 137, 138, 140
Luena, 137
Lulua, 132
Lulls, Arnold, 270
Lunda, 137–41, *139*
Lyte Jewel, 257

M
Mabuki, 125
Macenta, 186
macles, 194, *195*
Macquer, Pierre, 192
Madras, 46
magnetic force, 18, 20, 22
magnetic prospecting, 96
magnetite, 22
Mahmud of Ghazni, 23, *24*
Mainfroy, Jean, 256
Majhgawan Diamond Mines,
181
"make," 201
Malabar, 24, 28
Malaysia, 182

Malines, 36
Malo river, 144
Maludi, 138, 140
Maludi Caquece, 138, 140
manchaoes, 174
Mandanga, 59
Mandeville, Jean de, *see* Jehan à la Barbe
Maniema, 128, 130
Manilius, 14
Maria Leszczynska, 50
Maria Luisa (Spain), 52
Maria Theresa (France), 253, *254*
Marie Antoinette, 264
Marie-Christine de Bourbon, *264*
Marie Louise (empress), 51
Marinhos river, 54
marketing of diamonds, 63–64, 75, 82–85, 188–89. *See also* diamond exchanges
Martapura, 182, 183
Marty, A. E., 266
Mato Grosso, 55, 174–76, *175*
Mawe, John, 56, 58, 59, 199, 200
Maximilian I (Holy Roman Empire), 31, 256
Maximilian II (Holy Roman Empire), 262
Mazarin, Cardinal, 209–10, 253, 262
Mbuji-Mayi mine, 127, *129*, *131*, 132–36, *133*, *134*, *135*
McLean, Edward B., 53
Medici, Catherine de', *40*, 41, 258
Medici family, 258
melee, 241
Merensky, Hans, 84, 113
Minas Gerais, 54–56, *172*, 173, 174, 176–77
mine development, 102–06
mining methods, 26–28, 58–59, 74–75. *See also* alluvial deposits; open-pit mining; underground mining
"Mining Triangle," 176–77
Mirnyi field, 186
Mir pipe, 185
Misk, Alexander, 178
Moa river, 144
Molenhuur, 65
Mohs, Friedrich, 193
Mohun, Richard, 129
Moissan, Henri, 196, 276
Monnickendam, A., 246
Monrovia, 148–50, 152
Montarsy, Pierre de, 270
Morveau, Guyton de, 194
Motloutse river, 101
Muelich, Hans, *204*, *205*, *209*, *211*, *257*
Mughal empire, diamond jewelry in, 252–53
Mulamba, 128
Murfreesboro, 186
Mwadui mine, 85, 101, 125–26

N
Nadir Shah, 180
Namaqualand, 84, 100, *100*, 104, 113, *113*, 120
Namibia, 99, 113
Nandial deposit, 32
Nan tchou i Wu ki (Wang Chen), 26
Napoleon I, 50–51
Napoleon III, 51

Natural History (Pliny the Elder), 13, 18, 28
Newton, Isaac, 194
New South Wales, 186
New York, 245, *245*
Nileshwar, 24
Nimini hills, 143, 144
Nouveau Traitté des Pierres Precieuses (Berquen), 30
Nullagine, 186
Nuremberg, 31, 32
Nzega, 125

O
Observations on the Art and Craft of Diamond Working (Jensen), *233*
octavo, 59
Oliveira, João Fernandès, 59–60
Olivieira, Francisco Fernandès, 59, 62
Oliver, R. B., 129
open-bench mining, 111–13
open-pit mining, 106–08
Oppenheimer, Ernest, 83, 84, *84*, 99, 113, 188
Oppenheimer, Harry, 68, 102
Oppenheimer, Philip, 150
Orange river, 67, 68, 69, 100, 102, 105, 113, 114
Oranjemund, 105, 114–17, *114*, *115*, *116*, 124
Orapa mine, 85, 94, 99, 100, 101, 104, 105, 108, 120
Order of the Garter, 256
Order of the Golden Fleece, 52, 262
ore, processing, 117–23
Orinoco river, 158, 160
Orlov, Grigori, 47, *47*, 48

P
pagoda (coin), 20
palladium, 272
Pamali pipe, 182
Panna, 23, 180, 181, 182
pans, 71, 121
Paragua river, 160–71
Paraná river, 173, 174, 176
Paranaíba river, 176
Paranatiga, 176
Paris, 274–75
Parker, Stafford, 70
Parsons, Charles, 196
Partial mine, 48, 180
Peacock throne, 44, *44*
Pedro I (Brazil), 63
pendants, 259, *261*
"Perles Mancini," *253*
Perm, 184
Persian gulf, 24, 25, *29*
Peruzzi, Vincenzo, 212
Peters, Chauncy, 278
Philippe d'Orleáns, 48
photogeology, 95–96
pipes, 89
Pirkheimer, Willibald, 31
Pitau (jeweler), 52
Pitt, Thomas, 48, 50
Platen, B. von, 196, 277
platinum, 272
Pliny the Elder, 13, 14, 15, 18, 25, 28, 39
Pogge falls, 129, 131
polishing, 200–01
Pollett, J. D., 142, 143
Polo, Marco, 17, 39
Portugal, diamond policy, 61–62

Posier, Jérémie, 264
pots, 141, 178
Pouget (jeweler), 262
Precious Stones and Gems (Streeter), 48
Premier mine, 72, 82, 99, 100, 111, *111*, 112, 120, 123, *124*, 237
Pret family, 36
Pretoria, 72, 82
Pretorius, Andries, 67
prices, 281
ProportionScope, *249*
prospecting methods, 92–95, *94*, *95*, *96*, *97*, *98*; modern technologies, 95–98

Q
Quebrade Grande, 162–69

R
Raolconda mine, 26
Rabelais, François, 18
Ramat Gan exchange, 240, 241–42, *241*
Ranjit Singh, 46
Ratnapariska (Buddhabhatta), 14, *14*, 23
Ratna-Sastra, 14
Rawsthorne, Fleetwood, 72
Real, F., 140
recovery, 122–23
refractive index, 194–95
Renaissance jewelry, 256–60
Reuning, Ernest, 113
Rhodes, Cecil, 75–77, 80–82
rhodium, 273
Riberão do Inferno, 56, 58, 59
rocking screen, 132
Rodriguez d'Evora, Simon, 32, 34, 36
Rome, ancient, 14–16, 25
Rondé (jeweler), 270
Roraima, 159, 160, *161*
rubbing, 199
Rubens, Peter Paul, 36
Rudd, Charles Dunell, 75–76
run theory, 138–39
Russalmaz, 186
Ryan-Guggenheim group, 128

S
Saint-Claude, *245*, 246
Sambalpur deposits, 28, 180
Santa Elena, 160, 161, 169, 173
Santos Champlon, Alberto dos, 140
Saremci, 186
sawing, 198, *215*, 216, 218
scaife, *198*, 200, *217*, 218
Schamisso, Herman, 234
Scherrer (physicist), 193
Schwabel, Ernest, 101
Schwartz, Matthew, *30*
scintillometry, 96
Scott, Jack, 102
scrubbers, 120
security, in mining operations, 123–24
Senga-Senga, 135–36, *135*
separation methods, 120–21
Serro, 59
Serro do Frio, 54
Sewa river, 143, *143*, 144, 152, 155, *155*, *156*, *157*
Shah Jahan, *45*, 253
Shaler, Millard, 129–30
Shantung, 186
Sibeka, 178
Siberia, 184
siderite, 22

Siebenberg, Maurice, *161*
Sierra Leone, 93, 142–58
Sierra Leone Selection Trust (SLST), 144, 145, 146, 150, 154
"sight," 232, *235*
Silva, Chica da, 59–60, 61, 176, 177
Six Voyages (Tavernier), 29, *41*, 53
Smithsonian Institution, 53, 277
Société Minière de Bakwanga (MIBA), 134
solitaires, 270
Sopa, *173*, 178
Sopa (conglomerate), 173, 178
Sorel, Agnès, 39, 255, 256
Soumelpur, 26, 28
South Africa, 113
spinel, 22
Sri Lanka, 28
Staff, Johann, 262
State Alluvial Diggings, 99–100, 113
Steel, Donald, 137
Stern, Hans, 272
"stone of reconciliation," 22
Strasser, Joseph, 197
Streeter, Edwin, 48
Surat, 243–45
surucas, 171
Swartruggens mine, 99
synthetic diamonds, 196–97, 276–78, *276*, *277*

T
takungan, 183, *183*
Tamerlane, 44
Tanganyika Diamond and Gold Development Company (Tank Diamonds), 125
tangguk, *182*, 183
Tanzania, 85, 94, 101, 125–26
Taube, Frank, 169–71
Tavernier, Jean-Baptiste, 20, 26, 27, 28, 29, 41, *41*, 43, 51, 52, 53, 182, 200, 223, 253
Taylor, Elizabeth, 253
Tejucana mine, 178
Tejucana Mining Company, 177
Tejuco deposits, 54, 61
Tel Aviv, 239–41
Tennant, Smithson, 192
Thousand and One Nights, 17
Tiffany (jeweler), 267
tinting, 201–02
Tolkowsky, Marcel, 210, 213
Tongo, 144, 146, 154
tools, jewelers', 268
Tortiya deposits, 186
trading, in antiquity, 22–26, 28, 42
Tragoni (scientist), 192
Treatise on Diamonds and Pearls (Jeffries), 64
Treatise on Diamonds and Precious Stones (Mawe), *200*
Treskow (banker), 50
trommel, *129*, *179*
Tshikapa, 127, 130–32, 136, 137
Tweepad mine, 100, 101
twinning, 194

U
Udatchnaya pipe, 185
Umpung, 182, *182*, *183*

underground mining, 108–12, *108*, *109*, *110*, *111*, *112*
United States, 186
United States Bureau of Mines, 187
Ural mountains, 184
U.S.S.R., 184–86

V
Vaal river, 67, 69, 70, 71, 113, 131
Valley of Diamonds, 16–17, *17*, *18*, *19*
Van Berckem, Lodewijk, 30, 206, 256
Van Cleef and Arpels, 275
Van Coolen family, 36
Vanlerberghem (banker), 50
Van Linschoten, Jan Huyghen, 32
Van Niekerk, Schalk, 68, 69
Van Riebeeck, Jan, 66
Van Vlueten, Guillaume, 256
Van Wyck family, 70, 71
Varahamihira, 14, 20, 28
Veatch, A. C., 138
Venezuela, 159–71
Venice, 28–29, 31, 36
Vereniging voor Vrije Diamanthandel (Association for Free Diamond Trade), 233
Vermaet, Willem, 33
Vever, Henri and Paul, 266, 267
Victoria (England), 46
Vilain, Jean, 256
virada technique, 176
Voorsanger (cutter), 46

W
Wade, E. F., 213
Wairagargh, 180
Walgrave, Jan, 30
Wallis family, 34, 36
Wang Chen, 25
Welser family, 31
Wernher, Julius, 276
Wessel, Petrus, 72
Wesselton mine, 72, 81, 99, 101, 108, 110
Wilks, Eileen, 278
Williams, Gardner, 110
Williamson, John, 85, 101, 125–26, *126*
Williamson mine, 106, 125–26, *126*
Winston, Harry, 155, 176, 275
Wodehouse, Philip, 69
World Federation of Diamond Bourses (WFDB), 248

X
Ximenes family, 32, *36*
x-ray sorting, 122–23

Y
Yakutsk fields, 98, 184, 185
yellow ground, 75, 89
Yengema, 43–44, 142–46, 148, 149, 154
Yenisey river, 185
Young, George S., 131, 132

Z
Zaïre, 92, *94*, *95*, *97*, 127–36

Bibliography

Part I

Anonymous, *Inventaire des diamons* [de la Couronne de France]. Paris, 1791.

Bapst, Germain, *Histoire des joyaux de la Couronne de France*. Paris, 1889.

Bauer, Max, *Edelsteinkunde*. Leipzig, 1896.

Berquen, Robert de, *Les Merveilles des Indes orientales et occidentales. . . .* Paris, 1661.

Chilvers, Hedley A., *The Story of De Beers*. London, 1939.

Copeland, Lawrence L., *Diamonds . . . Famous, Notable and Unique*, rev. ed. Los Angeles, 1974.

De Beers Consolidated Mines Ltd., *Notable Diamonds of the World*. U.S.A., 1972.

Doughty, Oswald, *Early Diamond Days*. London, 1963.

Finot, Louis, *Les Lapidaires indiens*. Paris, 1896.

Francis, K. H., "The Mechanism of the Magnetic Doors in Rabelais." *French Studies* 13, Oxford, 1959.

Gael, Robert A., *The Diamond Dictionary*, 2nd ed. Los Angeles, 1977.

Giard, Maurice E., "Les Diamants célèbres." *La France horlogère*, Besançon, 1976–1979.

Guicciardini, Ludovico, *Descrittione di tutti i Paesi Bassi*. Antwerp, 1581.

Guillebert de Metz, *Description de Paris*. Paris, 1407.

Hatem, Simone, *L'Empire des perles et des pierres précieuses*. Paris, 1956.

Jacobs, Henri, and Chatrian, Nicolas, *Le Diamant*. Paris, 1880 and 1884.

Laet, Ioannis de, *De Gemmis et Lapidibus*. Lugduni Batavorum, 1647.

Laufer, B., *The Diamond A Study in Chinese and Hellenistic Folklore*. Chicago, 1915.

Lenzen, Godehard, *Produktions und Handelsgeschichte des Diamanten*. Berlin, 1966.

Linschoten, Jan Huygen, *Navigatio ac itinerarium in Orientalem . . . .* La Haye, 1599.

Mawe, John, *Travels in the Interior of Brazil*. London, 1816.

Meen, V. B., and Tushingham, A. D., *Crown Jewels of Iran*. Toronto, 1968.

Michielsen, Albert, *De Diamanteconomie*. Antwerp, 1955.

———, *Overeenkomst: De sterkte der Diamanteconomie*. Antwerp, 1963.

Møller, Jørgen, "The Entrancing World of the Diamond." Copenhagen, unpublished.

Pliny the Elder, *Naturalis Historia*.

Santos, Joaquin Felicios dos, *Memorias do Districto diamantino da Comarca do Serro Frio, Provincia de Minas Geraes*. Rio de Janeiro, n.d.

Schlugleit, D., *Geschiedenis van het Antwerpsche Diamantslijpersambacht (1582–1797)*. Antwerp, 1935.

Shipley, Robert M., *Famous Diamonds of the World*, 6th ed. Los Angeles, 1955.

Streeter, Edwin W., *The Great Diamonds of the World*. London, 1882.

Tavernier, Jean-Baptiste, *Les Six Voyages de J.-B. Tavernier en Turquie, en Perse et aux Indes . . . .* Paris, 1676.

Tillander, Herbert, *The "Hope" Diamond and Its Lineage*. Helsinki, 1975.

Twining, Lord, *A History of the Crown Jewels of Europe*. London, 1960.

Walgrave, Jan, *The History of Diamonds in Antwerp*. Antwerp, 1973.

Williams, Alpheus F., *The Genesis of the Diamond*. London, 1932.

Williams, Gardner F., *The Diamond Mines of South Africa*. London, 1902.

Part II

Adamson, R. J., "Some Account of Diamond-winning Practices in Southern Africa." *Journal of S.A.I.M.M.*, Johannesburg, August 1959.

Anglo-American Corporation of South Africa Ltd. (Public Relations Department), Annual Reports of De Beers Consolidated Mines Ltd., 1962–1978. Johannesburg.

Bardet, M. G., "Géologie du diamant." *Mémoires du B.R.G.M.*, Paris, 1973–1976.

Beetz, B. F. W., "Preliminary and Final Report on the Angola and Belgian Congo Diamond Fields." Unpublished.

Cleasby, J. V., Wright, H. J., and Davies, M. T., "Mining Practice in the Kimberley Division of De Beers Consolidated Mines Ltd." *Journal of S.A.I.M.M.*, Johannesburg, December 1975.

Colvin, E., and Simpson, H. S., "Treatment and Recovery Practice at Kimberley Mines of De Beers Consolidated Mines Ltd." *Journal of S.A.I.M.M.*, Johannesburg, May 1960.

Cornet, J., *Les Dislocations du bassin du Congo. I: Le graben de l'Upemba; II: La faille de la chute Wolf*. Ann. S.G.B., vols. 32 (1905) and 34 (1907).

Cuypers, Louis, *Forminière 1906–1956*. Brussels, 1956.

Delville, R., "Rapports de prospection, 1950–1958." Unpublished.

Du Toit, Gay J., "History of Williamson Mine." Mbabane, Swaziland, unpublished.

Freire de Andrade, "Diamond Deposits in Lunda." *Publ. Cult. Diamang* 17, 1953.

———, "Subsidios para o conhecimento da geologia dos jazigos diamantiferos do Nordeste da Lunda." Unpublished.

Gallagher, W. S., and Loftus, W. K. B., "Block-caving Practice at De Beers Consolidated Mines Ltd." *Journal of S.A.I.M.M.*, Johannesburg, April 1960.

Hanks, R., "Boulder Bouncing at C.D.M." *Optima*, vol. 24, Johannesburg, 1974.

Jorgensen, A., "The Premier—Diamond Cornucopia with a Double Bottom." *Optima*, vol. 24, Johannesburg, 1974.

Lampietti, F. M. J., and Sutherland, D., "Prospecting for Diamonds—Some Current Aspects." *Mining Magazine*, August 1978.

Linari-Linholm, A. A., *Occurrence, Mining and Recovery of Diamonds*. De Beers Consolidated Mines Ltd., 1973.

Loftus, W. K. D., Stucke, H. J., and Rankin, D., "Mining and Treatment-plant Practice at the Finsch Mine, De Beers Consolidated Mines Ltd." *Journal of S.A.I.M.M.*, Johannesburg, March 1969.

Polinard, "Les gisements de diamants du bassin du Kasaï au Congo belge et en Angola." *I.R.C.B.*, vol. 7.

Rauw, H. de, *Les Gisements diamantifères du Kasaï*. Congrès Sc. Intern., Liège, 1922.

Reis, E., *Os Grandes Diamantes Brasileiros*. Rio de Janeiro, 1959.

Van Der Laan, H. L., *The Sierra Leone Diamonds: An Economic Study Covering the Years 1952–1961*. Oxford, 1965.

Veatch, A. C., *Evolution of the Congo Basin*. Geol. Soc. Amer., Mem. 3.

Williams, E. L., "Diamond Harvest of the Namib Surf—The Story of C.D.M." *Optima*, vol. 27, Johannesburg, 1978.

Part III

Arfe, Juan de, *Quilatador de la plata, oro, y piedras*. Valladolid, 1572.

Ball, Sidney H., *A Roman Book on Precious Stones*. Los Angeles, 1950.

Boot, Anselmus Boetius de, *Gemmarium et Lapidum Historia*. 1609. (*Le Parfait Joaillier*, Lyon, 1644.)

Bruton, Eric, *Diamonds*. Radnor, Pennsylvania, 1971.

Cellini, Benvenuto, *Due Trattati*, Florence, 1568.

Jeffries, David, *A Treatise on Diamonds and Pearls*. London, 1750.

Kaplan, Lazare, "Cutting of Gem Diamonds." *American Mineralogist*, no. 27, New York, 1942.

Mawe, John, *A Treatise on Diamonds and Precious Stones*. London, 1813.

Pagel-Theisen, Verena, *Guide d'évaluation du diamant* (adaptation by C. Tourneur of original German edition). Paris, 1978.

Smet, K. de, *Le Grand Diamant bleu ou "Wittelsbach,"* preface by J. Konkommer. Antwerp and Amsterdam, 1963.

Sutton, J. R., *Diamond: A Descriptive Treatise*. London, 1928.

Tillander, Herbert, *Six Centuries of Diamond Design*. London, 1965.

Tolkowsky, Marcel, *Diamond Design*. London, 1919.

Wade, Frank B., *Diamonds: A Study of the Factors That Affect Their Value*. New York, 1916.

Part IV

Bapst, Germain, *Histoire des joyaux de la Couronne de France*. Paris, 1889.

De Beers Consolidated Mines Ltd., *Man Makes His Own Diamonds*.

"Le Diamant dans l'industrie." *L'Usine Nouvelle*, Brussels, Spring 1969.

Evans, Joan, *A History of Jewellery, 1100–1870*, 2nd ed. London, 1970.

Frégnac, Claude, *Bijoux de la Renaissance à la Belle Époque*. Paris, 1967.

General Electric Company, *The Synthesis of Diamond: A Core History in Modern Science* (G.E. Press Conference). New York, 1970.

Gregorietti, Guido, *Le monde merveilleux des bijoux*. Paris, 1971.

Heiniger, E. and J., *Le grand livre des bijoux*. Paris, 1974.

Hughes, Graham, *The Art of Jewelry*. London.

———, *Modern Jewelry*. London, 1963.

Lanlier, Jean, and Pini, Marie-Anne, *Cinq siècles de joaillerie en Occident*. Fribourg, 1971.

Lenfant, Jacques, *Bijouterie—joaillerie*. Paris, 1979.

Musée du Louvre, *Dix siècles de joaillerie française* (catalogue d'exposition). Paris, 1962.

Pouget fils, *Traité des pierres précieuses et de la manière de les employer en parure*. Paris, 1762.

Smith, Norman R., *Industrial Applications of the Diamond*. London.

———, *Users' Guide to Industrial Diamonds*. London, 1974.

Streeter, Edwin W., *Diamonds*. London, 1895.

Vever, Henri, *La bijouterie française au XXᵉ siècle*. Paris, 1906–1908.

This book, typeset in 11-point Caledonia by
Precision Typographers, New Hyde Park, New
York, was printed in May, 1980, by Smeets Offset
B.V., Weert, the Netherlands.

The paper is a 100-pound, wood free, machine-
coated, matte, slightly glossy stock, supplied by
Cartiere Italiane Riunite S.P.A., Rome.

The lithography for all color illustrations was done
in the workshops of Rito A.G., Zurich.

The binding was done by Reliure Industrielle de
Barchon, Belgium.